More than a century on from the Balfour Declaration, more than 50 years since the fateful war of 1967, and a full decade into the inhuman siege of Gaza—painfully, absurdly, almost unbelievably, the Israel-Palestine conflict rolls on. Amidst a growing sense that the Palestinians' long struggle for self-determination has reached a crossroads, if not an impasse, this volume seeks to take stock, draw lessons from experience, and weigh paths forward.

Moment of Truth seeks to clarify what it would take to resolve the Israel-Palestine conflict, to assess the prospects of doing so, and to illuminate what is possible in Palestine. It assembles an unprecedented wealth of expertise—encompassing political leaders, preeminent scholars, and dedicated activists from Israel, Palestine, and abroad—in direct critical exchange on the issues at the heart of the world's most intractable conflict. Has Israel's settlement enterprise made a Palestinian state impossible? Can the Palestinian leadership end the occupation? Is Israel's rule in the Palestinian territories a form of apartheid? Could the US government force Israel to withdraw? In a series of compelling, enlightening, and at times no-holds-barred debates, leading authorities tackle these and other challenges, exposing myths, challenging preconceptions, and establishing between them a more sober and informed basis for political action.

Contributors: Musa Abuhashhash, As'ad Abukhalil, Mkhaimar Abusada, Gilbert Achcar, Ghaith al-Omari, Ghassan Andoni, Usama Antar, Nur Arafeh, Shaul Arieli, Arie Arnon, Tareq Baconi, Sam Bahour, Sari Bashi, Shlomo Ben-Ami, Suhad Bishara, Nathan J. Brown, Diana Buttu, Jan de Jong, John Dugard, Michael Dumper, Hagai El-Ad, Richard A. Falk, Norman G. Finkelstein, Neve Gordon, Ran Greenstein, Yoaz Hendel, Jamil Hilal, Khaled Hroub, Amal Jamal, Leila Khaled, Raja Khalidi, Rami G. Khouri, Lior Lehrs, Gideon Levy, Alon Liel, John J. Mearsheimer, Jessica Montell, Rami Nasrallah, Wendy Pearlman, Nicola Perugini, William B. Quandt, Mazin B. Qumsiyeh, Glen Rangwala, Glenn E. Robinson, Nadim Rouhana, Sara Roy, Bashir Saade, Robbie Sabel, Dahlia Scheindlin, Daniel Seidemann, Michael Sfard, Muhammad Shehada, Raja Shehadeh, Sammy Smooha, Mark Tessler, Nathan Thrall, Ahmed Yousef, Ido Zelkovitz.

MOMENT OF TRUTH

Tackling Israel-Palestine's Toughest Questions

EDITED BY JAMIE STERN-WEINER

OR Books
London • New York

First printing 2018

Cataloging-in-Publication data is available from the Library of Congress.
A catalog record for this book is available from the British Library.

Published for the book trade by OR Books in partnership with Counterpoint Press.

Distributed to the trade by Publishers Group West.

ISBN 978-1-944869-69-4 paperback
ISBN 978-1-944869-70-0 e-book

Typeset by Lapiz Digital Services, Chennai, India.

To my parents, to Offer, and to Kate.

TABLE OF CONTENTS

Part Two. Gaza

SECTION II: STRATEGY

SECTION III: INTERNATIONAL

ACKNOWLEDGMENTS

I am grateful for the assistance of Norman Finkelstein, Célestine Fünfgeld, Ofer Neiman, Michaela Collord, John Dugard, Eve Lacey, Mohammed Omer, Mouin Rabbani, Colin Robinson, Sara Roy, and Muhammad Shehada.

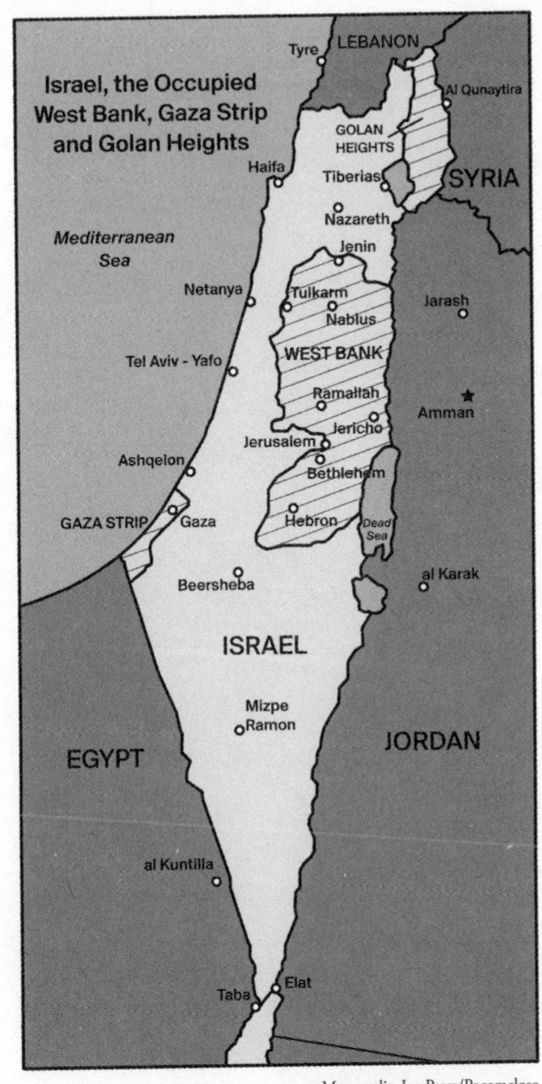

Map credit: Joe Perez/Pocomeloso

Israel and the Occupied Palestinian Territory (West Bank and Gaza Strip)

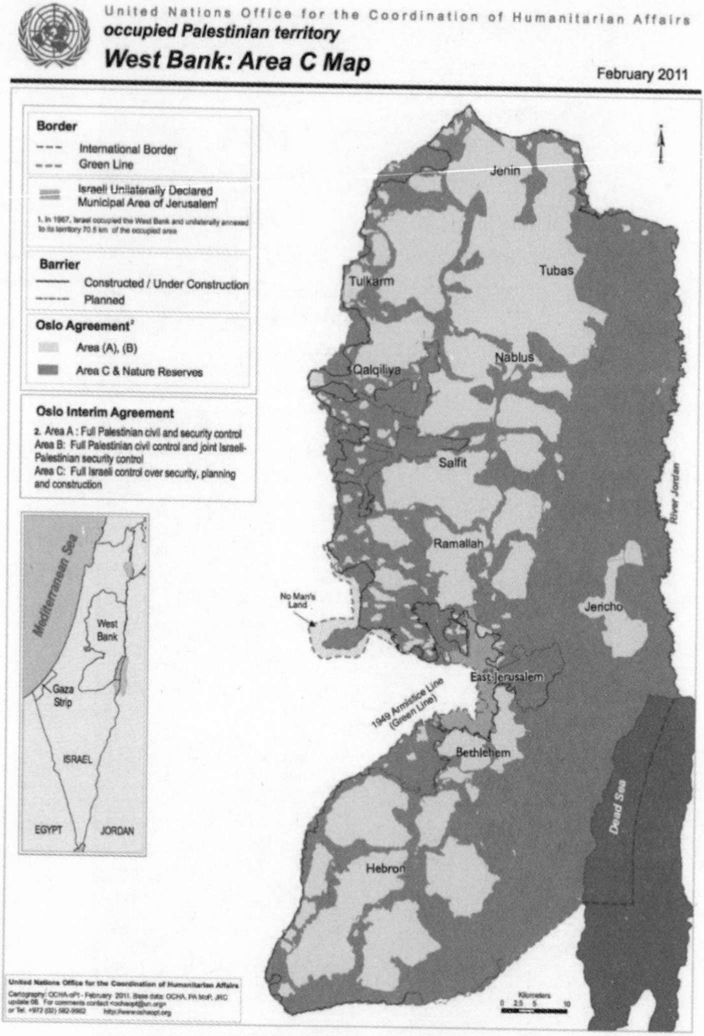

United Nations Office for the Coordination of Humanitarian Affairs

occupied Palestinian territory

West Bank: Area C Map

February 2011

Border

International Border
Green Line

Israeli Unilaterally Declared Municipal Area of Jerusalem[1]

1. In 1967, Israel occupied the West Bank and unilaterally annexed to its territory 70.5 km of the occupied area

Barrier

Constructed / Under Construction
Planned

Oslo Agreement[2]

Area (A), (B)
Area C & Nature Reserves

Oslo Interim Agreement

2. Area A : Full Palestinian civil and security control
Area B: Full Palestinian civil control and joint Israeli-Palestinian security control
Area C: Full Israeli control over security, planning and construction

Mediterranean Sea
West Bank
Gaza Strip
ISRAEL
EGYPT
JORDAN

Jenin
Tubas
Tulkarm
Nablus
Qalqiliya
Salfit
Ramallah
No Man's Land
Jericho
East Jerusalem
1949 Armistice Line (Green Line)
Bethlehem
Hebron
River Jordan
Dead Sea
Kilometers
0 2.5 5 10

United Nations Office for the Coordination of Humanitarian Affairs
Cartography: OCHA-oPt - February 2011. Base data: OCHA, PA MoP, JRC

Courtesy of United Nations OCHA oPt

The West Bank (2011)

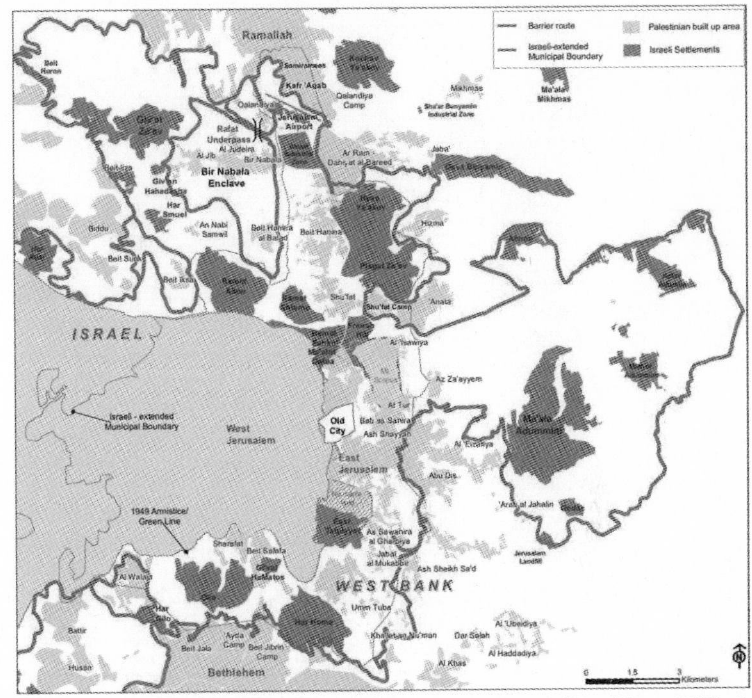

Courtesy of United Nations OCHA oPt

Greater Jerusalem (2007)

CHRONOLOGY

- **November 1917**: British Foreign Secretary Lord Balfour declares, "His Majesty's Government view with favour the establishment in Palestine of a national home for the Jewish people."
- **April 1920**: The San Remo Conference assigns the Mandate for Palestine to the United Kingdom. The text, which is adopted by the League of Nations in 1922, incorporates the wording of the Balfour Declaration.
- **1936–1939**: Arab Revolt in Palestine, which begins with one of the longest general strikes in history (April–October 1936), is crushed by the British authorities assisted by Zionist forces.
- **November 1947**: UN General Assembly adopts Resolution 181 (II), which recommends the partition of Palestine into an Arab and a Jewish State. Conflict breaks out in Palestine upon the resolution's passage.
- **14 May 1948**: Declaration of the Establishment of the State of Israel proclaimed by David Ben-Gurion, who becomes Israel's first prime minister.
- **15 May 1948–January 1949**: First Arab-Israeli War (the "War of Independence" or "*Nakba*"). During the hostilities, Israel expands its territory to encompass 78 percent of Mandatory Palestine, from which some 700–750,000 people—more than half the Palestinian Arab population—are driven into exile.
- **September 1948**: All-Palestine Government established by the Arab League to administer Egyptian-controlled Gaza. It is soon exiled to Cairo. Between 1949 and 1967, Gaza is under Egyptian control.

- **December 1948:** UN General Assembly adopts Resolution 194 (III) which, inter alia, resolves "that the [Palestinian] refugees wishing to return to their homes and live at peace with their neighbours should be permitted to do so at the earliest practical date."
- **February–July 1949**: Arab-Israeli armistice agreements establish demarcation boundaries. These become Israel's de facto borders until the 1967 War.
- **24 April 1950**: Jordan annexes the West Bank, including East Jerusalem. The annexation is recognized only by Pakistan and the United Kingdom.
- **29 October 1956**: Britain, France, and Israel invade Egypt (the "Suez Crisis" or "Tripartite Aggression"). Israel occupies the Gaza Strip and Sinai Peninsula. Under US pressure, Britain and France withdraw on 23 December. Israel withdraws in March 1957.
- **1958–1959**: Fatah, the Palestinian National Liberation Movement, established.
- **May 1964**: Palestine Liberation Organization (PLO) established.
- **January 1965**: Fatah launches armed struggle against Israel.
- **November 1966**: The regime of martial law that has been imposed on Israel's Arab citizens since 1948 is formally lifted.
- **5–10 June 1967**: The Six Day War pits Israel against Egypt, Jordan, and Syria. Israel achieves a resounding military victory. The West Bank, including East Jerusalem, and Gaza Strip, as well as the Syrian Golan Heights and Egyptian Sinai, come under Israeli military occupation.
- **27 June 1967**: Israel de facto annexes East Jerusalem.
- **22 November 1967**: UN Security Council adopts Resolution 242. This affirms the "inadmissibility of the acquisition of territory by war"; calls for a "just and lasting peace in the Middle East" based on "[w]ithdrawal of Israeli armed forces from territories occupied in the recent conflict"; and simultaneously calls for the "[t]ermination of all claims or states of belligerence and respect for and acknowledgement of the sovereignty, territorial integrity and political independence of every State in the area and their right to live in peace within secure and recognized boundaries free from threats of acts of force."

- **February 1969**: Yasser Arafat becomes chairman of the Executive Committee of the PLO.
- **September 1970**: PLO and Jordanian forces do battle in Jordan ("Black September"). The PLO is defeated and driven out to Lebanon.
- **October 1973**: The "Yom Kippur War" or "October War." Israel is surprised by an attack from Egypt and Syria; the fighting ends in military stalemate and a ceasefire.
- **October 1974**: Arab League recognizes the PLO as "the sole legitimate representative of the Palestinian people."
- **1975–1990**: Lebanese Civil War.
- **May 1977**: Elections in Israel won by the right-wing Likud, ending three decades of labor Zionist (Alignment, Mapai) rule. Menachem Begin becomes prime minister.
- **September 1978**: Israel and Egypt sign the Camp David Accords.
- **March 1979**: Israel-Egypt peace treaty signed at the White House in Washington, DC. The treaty provides, inter alia, for Israel's full civil and military withdrawal from the Sinai, mutual recognition, and normalization of relations.
- **June 1980**: European Community issues the Venice Declaration, which recognizes the "right to self-determination" of the "Palestinian people" and calls for "the PLO" to be "associated with . . . negotiations" to resolve the conflict.
- **August 1980**: UN Security Council adopts Resolution 478, which declares "all legislative and administrative measures and actions" by Israel to "alter the character and status" of Jerusalem "null and void."
- **December 1981**: Israel annexes the Golan Heights. UN Security Council Resolution 497 declares the annexation "null and void and without international legal effect," and demands that Israel "rescind forthwith its decision."
- **June 1982**: Israel invades Lebanon.
- **December 1987**: First Palestinian intifada. Palestinians in the West Bank and Gaza Strip enter into a mass civil revolt against Israel's occupation.
- **December 1987**: Hamas, the Islamic Resistance Movement, founded.

- **July 1988**: Jordan disengages administratively and legally from the West Bank (but maintains a guardianship role with respect to the Muslim holy sites in East Jerusalem).
- **November 1988**: Palestinian Declaration of Independence adopted by the Palestinian National Council (PNC). The PNC calls for negotiations to resolve the conflict on the basis of UN General Assembly Resolution 181 (1947) and UN Security Council Resolution 242 (1967).
- **December 1988**: Arafat publicly accepts US terms for talks, clearing the way for official US-PLO negotiations.
- **December 1988**: UN General Assembly adopts Resolution 43/176, which calls for an end to the conflict through Israel's withdrawal from the Palestinian and other Arab Occupied Territories, security and recognition of all States in the region, a solution to the Palestinian refugee question in conformity with UN resolutions, the dismantling of Israel's settlements in the Occupied Territories, and freedom of access to all holy places. The resolution is adopted by a vote of 138–2 (Israel and the United States), with two abstentions.
- **August 1990**: Iraq invades Kuwait. The PLO leadership is blamed for aligning with Iraq.
- **January–February 1991**: First Gulf War.
- **October 1991**: Madrid Conference on Middle East peace.
- **July 1992**: Yitzhak Rabin (Labor) elected prime minister of Israel.
- **September 1993**: PLO "recognizes the right of the State of Israel to exist in peace and security," while Israel "recognize[s] the PLO as the representative of the Palestinian people." The Israel-PLO Declaration of Principles on Interim Self-Government Arrangements (Oslo I Accord) is signed at the White House. This provides, inter alia, for the establishment of an interim Palestinian self-government pending a final status agreement to be reached within five years. As part of the Oslo peace process, the PLO leadership under Arafat is permitted to return from exile in Tunis to the Occupied Palestinian Territory.
- **May 1994**: Palestinian Authority established.
- **October 1994**: Israel-Jordan peace treaty.

- **September 1995**: Interim Agreement on the West Bank and the Gaza Strip (Oslo II Accord). Divides the West Bank into territories under full ("Area A") or partial ("Area B") Palestinian Authority control, amounting altogether to approximately 40 percent of the West Bank; and territories ("Area C") under full Israeli civil and military control, comprising approximately 60 percent of the West Bank.
- **November 1995**: Israeli Prime Minister Yitzhak Rabin assassinated by Yigal Amir, an Israeli religious nationalist opposed to the Oslo process.
- **January 1996**: First Palestinian elections. Yasser Arafat elected president of the Palestinian Authority.
- **May 1996**: Benjamin Netanyahu (Likud) elected prime minister of Israel. The vote takes place in the shadow of suicide bomb attacks by Hamas.
- **May 1999**: Ehud Barak (Labor) elected prime minister of Israel.
- **May 2000**: Israel withdraws from south Lebanon. The UN considers the withdrawal complete; Lebanon and Hezbollah do not.
- **July 2000**: Camp David Summit between Barak, Arafat, and US President Bill Clinton fails to reach an agreement to end the conflict.
- **September 2000–February 2005**: A visit by leading Israeli rightist Ariel Sharon to the Temple Mount sparks protests. Israel responds with heavy repression and the clashes escalate into what becomes known as the second intifada. Between September 2000 and February 2005, approximately 1,000 Israelis and 3,000 Palestinians are killed in the violence.
- **October 2000**: Palestinian citizens of Israel demonstrate in solidarity with Palestinians in the Occupied Palestinian Territory. In clashes that ensue, thirteen Arab civilians (including twelve citizens of Israel) are killed by Israeli police.
- **December 2000**: President Clinton presents guidelines for a permanent status agreement (the "Clinton Parameters"). Both Palestinian and Israeli leaderships accept the plan with reservations.
- **January 2001**: Taba Summit. Negotiations between Israel and the PLO continue until Ehud Barak withdraws to contest the election in Israel, which he loses.

- **February 2001**: Ariel Sharon (Likud) elected prime minister of Israel.
- **March 2002**: UN Security Council Resolution 1397 calls for "two States, Israel and Palestine," living "side by side within secure and recognized borders." The Arab League adopts the Saudi Initiative, which proposes normalization of relations between Israel and the Arab world in exchange for Israel's withdrawal from the Occupied Territories and a resolution of the refugee question.
- **June 2002**: US President George W. Bush's "Rose Garden Address" endorses the creation of an independent State of Palestine alongside the State of Israel and calls for "a new and different Palestinian leadership" (i.e., the removal of Arafat).
- **March 2003**: Mahmoud Abbas appointed first prime minister of the Palestinian Authority. His tenure lasts less than six months.
- **April 2003**: Quartet on the Middle East (comprising the EU, Russia, United Nations, and United States) presents "Road Map" for Middle East Peace.
- **December 2003**: Geneva Initiative, a non-official peace plan negotiated by prominent Palestinians and Israelis, launched.
- **July 2004**: International Court of Justice advisory opinion finds the route of Israel's West Bank Wall to be illegal under international law. The judges unanimously determine that the West Bank, including East Jerusalem, and Gaza constitute "Occupied Palestinian Territory" and that Israel's settlements are illegal.
- **November 2004**: Yasser Arafat dies.
- **January 2005**: Mahmoud Abbas elected president of the Palestinian Authority.
- **July 2005**: A coalition of Palestinian civil society groups issues a call for boycott, divestment, and sanctions (BDS) against Israel until it ends the occupation, recognizes the right of Palestinian citizens of Israel to equality, and respects the right of Palestinian refugees to return to their homes.
- **August–September 2005**: Israel unilaterally evacuates all settlements from Gaza, as well as four settlements in the West Bank. Israel retains control over Gaza's borders, waters, airspace, and population registry.

- **January 2006**: Hamas wins a majority of seats in the Palestinian legislative elections. The US and EU halt aid to the Palestinian Authority and refuse to engage diplomatically with the new government.
- **March 2006**: Ehud Olmert (Kadima) elected prime minister of Israel. Kadima is a centrist political party established in 2005 to support Ariel Sharon's unilateral disengagement from Gaza.
- **July–August 2006**: Second Lebanon War.
- **February 2007**: Fatah and Hamas form a government of national unity after months of internecine violence. The Quartet boycotts the government.
- **June 2007**: Hamas forces seize control of the Gaza Strip. Israel closes Gaza's border crossings. The Palestinian unity government is dissolved. Abbas unilaterally appoints the Western-backed Salam Fayyad prime minister.
- **September 2007**: Israel's Cabinet classifies Gaza a "hostile territory" and adopts a policy of restricting goods, fuel, electricity, and the movement of people to and from the territory. As of October 2017, the closure remains in force.
- **November 2007**: Annapolis Conference on Middle East peace, convened by the United States with broad international participation, initiates a negotiations process between Israel and the PLO. This fails to reach an agreement.
- **December 2008–January 2009**: Israel's "Operation Cast Lead" in Gaza. Thirteen Israelis and more than 1,400 Palestinians are killed.
- **February 2009**: Kadima wins the most seats in Israel's legislative elections, but is unable to form a governing coalition. Benjamin Netanyahu (Likud) becomes prime minister of Israel, a position he retains through subsequent elections in January 2013 and March 2015.
- **September 2009**: United Nations Fact-Finding Mission on the Gaza Conflict, chaired by Judge Richard Goldstone, issues a report ("the Goldstone Report") on the conduct of Israel and Palestinian armed groups during Operation Cast Lead. The report finds that Israel's operation was "a deliberately disproportionate attack designed to punish, humiliate and terrorize a civilian population." It is also critical of the conduct of Palestinian armed groups and of Israel's occupation policies more broadly.

- **May 2010**: A flotilla of activists seeking to break the Gaza blockade comes under attack by Israeli forces. Nine passengers aboard the flagship *Mavi Marmara* are killed; a tenth dies from his injuries in 2014.
- **November 2012**: Israel's "Operation Pillar of Defense" in Gaza. Six Israelis and more than 150 Palestinians are killed. UN General Assembly Resolution 67/19 upgrades Palestine to non-member observer State status in the United Nations.
- **July 2013–April 2014**: US Secretary of State John Kerry spearheads a diplomatic initiative to resolve the conflict. The talks collapse without an agreement.
- **July–August 2014**: Israel's "Operation Protective Edge" in Gaza. 73 Israelis and more than 2,100 Palestinians are killed.
- **December 2016**: UN Security Council Resolution 2334 endorses the two-state solution and reaffirms the illegality of Israel's settlements.

INTRODUCTION

A simple observation that ought to astonish more than it does: the Israel-Palestine conflict continues. 2017 marked the centenary of the Balfour Declaration, the United Kingdom's pledge of support for a "national home for the Jewish people" in Palestine, which might fairly be said to have inaugurated the national conflict there. It was the seventieth anniversary of the United Nations Partition Plan, which provided for a resolution of the conflict by means of dividing Mandatory Palestine into a Jewish and an Arab state. The proposed boundaries have since shifted in Israel's favor, as military victories have imprinted on law and politics, but the two-state solution remains the international consensus framework for a peace agreement. June 2017 completed a half-century of Israeli military rule over the West Bank, including East Jerusalem, and the Gaza Strip: an occupation that has persisted for nearly three-quarters of Israel's lifespan as a state, and which has dominated and constrained the lives of multiple generations of Palestinians. The high-water mark to date of the Palestinian struggle for national self-determination—the first intifada—erupted three decades ago in December 1987. The lessons and legacies of that heroic defeat form a red thread running through the debates and discussions that follow. Finally, and perhaps most pressingly, June 2017 marked ten years of the siege of Gaza, which, together with the periodic military assaults to which that territory and its people have been subjected, has shattered Gaza's society and all but extinguished its economy, along with a great many of its inhabitants.[1]

If this chronological survey does not give the reader pause, if the breath and heart remain steady as the eye slips from "centenary" to "half-century" to "decade," this is because the Israeli-Palestinian conflict has endured so long that it has acquired about it an air of timelessness, and normalized into background noise. Global economic crises come and go; devastating wars scar and reconfigure every quarter of the Earth; expansive empires disintegrate and the world's population of sovereign states more than triples; violence and inequality induce the most massive demographic movements in human history; a momentous opposition of superpowers emerges, ossifies, then abruptly collapses; ideologies mobilize tens of millions in sacrifice and struggle, and are then defeated or discredited; the living standards of billions are transformed beyond reckoning; humanity alights on alien worlds and extends its gaze to the very origins of the cosmos. . . and throughout it all, the conflict between Palestinians and Israelis, in a speck of land scarcely larger than West Virginia, rages on; a miserable constant in a world of flux, perpetuated by its own motion and engulfing generation after generation in gratuitous suffering.

All the historical landmarks surveyed above merit reflection. But not all are equally salient, and one's distribution of commemorative energy is not politically innocent. This volume's focus on the Israeli occupation that began in 1967 reflects its editor's belief that an end to the occupation would represent an important milestone in the Palestinians' quest for freedom, and, furthermore, that the occupation's demise is a prerequisite for more far-reaching, if still always and only partial, advances toward justice. It also reflects a political judgement that supplanting foreign military rule with self-determination and statehood in the Occupied Palestinian Territory is at present the most ambitious objective around which Palestinians and their supporters might effectively

---

[1] Sara Roy, *The Gaza Strip: The Political Economy of De-Development*, third edition (Washington, DC: Institute for Palestine Studies, 2016); Norman G. Finkelstein, *Gaza: An Inquest into Its Martyrdom* (Berkeley, CA: University of California Press, 2018).

organize. These assessments are increasingly controversial, at any rate among the conflict's participants and close observers, and the reader will find that many of the book's contributors reject them.[2]

The aura of permanence which surrounds the Israeli-Palestinian conflict carries with it the twin risks of complacency and despair. This volume was inspired by the conviction that the more appropriate response is sober reflection to guide political action. As Israel's occupation enters its sixth decade, and amidst a growing sense that the Palestinian struggle has reached a crossroads, if not an impasse, this collection takes stock, draws lessons from experience, and weighs paths forward. It seeks to clarify what it would take to resolve the Israel-Palestine conflict, to assess the prospects of doing so, and thus to illuminate what is and what is not possible in Palestine.

The book's structure, which brings together conflicting arguments in critical exchange, reflects the dispiriting truth that, notwithstanding decades of struggle and endeavor, by Palestinians first and foremost, the occupation is today more entrenched than ever, while the prospect of Palestinian self-determination has never been so remote. This is a record that should inspire intellectual humility as well as political urgency; a readiness to acknowledge that, on myriad questions bearing on the prospects for resolving the conflict, compelling arguments can be advanced from multiple sides.

There is, to my mind, an intrinsic pleasure to be had in witnessing good arguments collide—albeit one tempered in this case by the knowledge that the discussions which follow bear, even at their most seemingly technical or abstruse, on matters of immense and protracted suffering. Critical exchange—"the rough process of a struggle between combatants fighting

---

[2] Due to practical constraints, the book is not comprehensive, and important dilemmas go unaddressed in it. One in particular should be flagged: the implementation of the Palestinian refugees' internationally validated right of return. This lacuna does not indicate lack of concern: the plight of the refugees is an outrage and a tragedy. It is also a central component of the Palestinian struggle, which any resolution of the conflict will need to address. But, of all the issues at the core of the dispute, the refugee question is the one on which least concrete debate has unfolded, and there does not at this point appear to be much new to say about it.

under hostile banners"[3]—is also the most reliable path humanity has yet discovered to an accurate picture of the world. At a moment when few of us, Palestinians perhaps least of all, can afford the luxury of delusion: let the struggle commence.

[3] John Stuart Mill, "On Liberty," fourth edition, in John Stuart Mill, *On Liberty and Other Writings*, ed. Stefan Collini (Cambridge: Cambridge University Press, 1989 [1869]), p. 49.

SECTION I.

PALESTINE

PART ONE.

THE WEST BANK

CHAPTER ONE.

CAN THE CURRENT PALESTINIAN LEADERSHIP AND ITS INSTITUTIONS END THE OCCUPATION?

Nathan J. Brown

Palestinian society and politics are rich in institutions. But none of them are leading to statehood nor are they likely to do so. More significant but less noticed, few Palestinians expect statehood any time soon. Most have stopped orienting their political actions around the struggle for a state.

Nathan J. Brown is Professor of Political Science and International Affairs at George Washington University where he directs the Institute for Middle East Studies. He also serves as a Non-Resident Senior Fellow at the Carnegie Endowment for International Peace. His current work focuses on religion, law, and politics in the Arab world. Author of seven books, Brown's most recent work, *Arguing Islam after the Revival of Arab Politics*, was published by Oxford University Press in 2017. He is a past recipient of Fulbright, Guggenheim, Woodrow Wilson Center, and Carnegie fellowships.

As the dream of statehood recedes, Palestinian politics is metamorphosing from a political struggle over statehood into a generational contest for national liberation. For many decades, that nationalist struggle has been about statehood. There is, to be sure, continuing discussion among Palestinians about desired forms of statehood (one state, two-state, binational state, Islamic state). But all these possibilities seem distant and the outcome determined by long-term social and demographic trends more than concerted short-term political action. The center of attention has therefore shifted elsewhere. Palestinians still speak of resistance, rights, and struggle, but discussion about what is to be done is not as strongly connected to ultimate political ends as it was for earlier generations.

If the Palestinian national struggle is no longer so focused on a state, then what is its goal? What strategies will it pursue? Those are very good questions. They might take a generation to answer. But while the contours of the contest over national liberation are not yet clear, it is clear that Palestinian national institutions are no longer leading it.

Rich institutions, poor politics

In 1999 and 2000, on the eve of the second intifada,* I spent a year studying Palestinian institutions of many different kinds. It seemed to me at times that I was focusing on the most boring aspects of Palestinian politics—collecting the bylaws of the Palestinian Dentists Syndicate, asking journalists how their pensions were funded, visiting community centers where camp residents were taught marketable skills, and interviewing teacher training professionals on how they developed new pedagogical techniques. This led me off the beaten track of the "peace process," still at that point the subject of widespread interest and hope, and required me to engage as much in archeology as political science—at least in a metaphorical sense. I learned about the residue of Mandatory, Jordanian, Egyptian, Israeli, and Palestinian Authority (PA) regulations and

* *Editor's note:* See Glossary.

practices, each very much alive and united (uneasily and very incompletely) only by a consensus goal of Palestinian statehood.

The Palestinian consensus about statehood (at least in some form) was very broad. It had its roots back in the first decades of the twentieth century and had motivated the construction of a series of structures between the 1940s and the 1990s that were designed to represent Palestine as a political entity and spearhead the push to statehood: the declaration of statehood in 1948 and the formation of the All-Palestine Government, the formation of the Palestine Liberation Organization (PLO) in 1964, the declaration of independence of 1988, and the establishment of the PA in 1994. In the same period, various movements arose—known collectively today by Palestinians as "the factions"—to pursue national liberation. While the PLO and the PA sought to build state-like institutions, the factions emphasized what they termed "revolution." But all envisioned a State of Palestine as the ultimate outcome, even as they disagreed about what that state would look like.

The Oslo process* sharpened divisions as some of its advocates talked of moving from "*al-thawra ila al-dawla*" (revolution to state). They took great strides in building certain state-like institutions—a parliament, a constitution, ministries, a regulatory apparatus—that provided a framework for the rich institutional life that had developed over the decades. But others criticized those steps, arguing that they were premature and that the institutions being established were enabling authoritarianism and corruption rather than healthy state-building.

While the state-builders seemed to have the upper hand in the 1990s, the last seventeen years have been cruel to their project. The problems inherent in their efforts—authoritarianism and corruption—have not been corrected despite reform efforts; in some respects, they have grown worse. The national structures that were supposed to lead to revolution and then to statehood have decayed deeply under the powerful blows of uprising, division, occupation,

* *Editor's note:* See Glossary.

Israeli settlements, and international abandonment. The institutional rot at the national level may have reached the point of no return.

An empty cupboard of national political institutions

An inventory of Palestine's national political institutions shows the extent of the decay. The institutions themselves march on, but they have lost most of their vitality and all sense of strategic vision.

The PLO—the body founded in 1964 by the Arab League* but then taken over by Palestinian factions in 1969—led the fight for international recognition for many decades and successfully folded most Palestinian institutions, however loosely, under its umbrella. It remains the official interlocutor for "Palestine" in a diplomatic sense and has not lost its formal role as the sole legitimate representative of the Palestinian people. The Palestinian declaration of statehood and the international recognition offered by some states and multilateral organizations keep the PLO formally alive.

But it is a very hollow shell. Even at its most vital, the PLO never escaped domination by its constituent factions (and particularly Fatah). After the creation of the PA, it slowly shriveled, losing most of its presence in the diaspora and surviving today as a set of offices appended to the PA presidency. The Palestine National Council, the PLO's oversight body, has not met in eighteen years.

Reviving the PLO would require national consensus among a bitterly divided set of leaders—a very elusive prospect. Otherwise, it will continue to be seen (quite justifiably) as a device to serve the factional and short-term tactical purposes of the gerontocracy that formally heads the body. A true rebirth for the PLO would involve building genuine linkages with its constituent parts, making the body a real presence in the Palestinian diaspora, allowing it to become more than a tool of the dominant factions, and opening the organization up to new blood and new voices. None of these steps is likely to be taken any time soon, if ever.

---

* *Editor's note:* See Glossary.

The PA has a far more extensive and active institutional presence. It oversees schools, ministries, courts, and police in the occupied West Bank; the Gaza branch does the same under Hamas. The West Bank branch receives VAT revenues transferred by Israel, levies its own taxes, distributes international assistance, and pays salaries. The PA issues regulations and laws, and many of Palestine's rich set of institutions operate under its oversight. These activities are state-like in nature, and indeed, the PA was regarded by its leaders and by many Palestinians as building the practical attributes of statehood while the Oslo diplomatic process delivered its juridical substance.

No longer. The PA today has little raison d'être other than the lack of any attractive alternative. Its employees need their salaries, Israel desires the security coordination it enables in the West Bank, and Palestinians who live in areas under its oversight need the services and order it provides. Unlike the "Civil Administration"—the Israeli body operating under the Ministry of Defense that administered Palestinians under occupation from 1981 until the creation of the PA—the PA is headed by Palestinians. But its administrative presence is in some ways similar, while its popular legitimacy is scarcely more secure. To be sure, PA leaders are deeply frustrated with this frozen position, but they have no path to offer Palestinians out of the current impasse and few Palestinians regard the PA as anything more than a stale and slowly decaying administrative body. It is difficult to find anyone—even a high PA official—who does not view it as part of a debilitating holding pattern rather than a step toward statehood.

Finally, the factions are bereft of ideas and strategies. Most eschew the label of "party"—they present themselves as "movements" or "fronts," dedicated not to electioneering (even if most have competed in PA elections) but to leading the national struggle. Now they do neither. Elections are frozen by factional rivalry among other factors; rather than Palestinians being allowed to vote in order to select and give direction to their leaders, elections are blocked until their leaders agree on when and how to hold them. The two largest factions—Fatah and Hamas—are more focused on each other than on the national struggle. The division between the West Bank and Gaza—a product of this factional enmity—has exacerbated institutional decay and popular despair.

The paths the factions offer—for Fatah, diplomacy and resistance in various forms; for Hamas, steadfastness and resistance in various forms as well—have been deployed in various combinations but seem to lead nowhere. More ominously, perhaps, the strategic vision of each faction has evaporated without leaving a clear residue. It is difficult to find Palestinians who believe any faction has a viable program for reaching national goals of any sort.

To say that Palestinian national institutions are in crisis is therefore true, but does not go far enough. First, their declining viability is beginning to infect the rich array of Palestinian institutions in the broader society. To some extent, this is an older process. The first intifada was built on a strong network of grassroots organizations. The Oslo period, while ostensibly a stage of state-building, actually saw some institutional decay as well, as the PA took over functions that local communities had organized for themselves. The spirit of volunteerism that had animated the first intifada withered, while some of the most important non-governmental organizations (NGOs) turned into more professional organizations, sometimes depending on donor funding. The second intifada did not reverse these trends and produced no real grassroots movements; unlike the first intifada, most Palestinians experienced the second one as spectators.*

As national Palestinian institutions have suffered, squabbled, and lost purpose, so have many civil society organizations. Professional syndicates are divided by the geographical division and factional struggle; the worsening fiscal crisis of the PA undermines institutions and NGOs that work with its ministries; the declining ability of the PLO and PA to attract international financial support has orphaned some of those who came to depend on external funding; and the focus of governing Palestinian bodies on cementing their control and outmaneuvering their domestic rivals (in an often ruthless manner) has led to restrictions on free expression and association.

---

* *Editor's note:* For the intifadas, see Glossary.

Second, the PLO, PA, and factions have simply lost the ability to offer any program other than their own continuation. That may be barely sufficient for many in the older generation who have grown accustomed to them and see no alternative. But a new generation of Palestinians is reaching political maturity and views the existing national institutions as irrelevant relics.

An era ends but the new one is not yet born

Palestinian institutions perform necessary administrative functions and allow Palestinians to live their daily lives. But they are, nevertheless, deeply circumscribed by the occupation. And just as troubling, they cannot lead Palestinians in any meaningful sense. They make little policy, pursue no coherent strategy, expound no compelling moral vision, are subject to no oversight, and inspire no collective spirit. The generation that built these national institutions has already begun to leave the scene. It has tremendous accomplishments to its credit, but most of these are now profoundly threatened.

This situation is not unprecedented. At the close of the 1930s, after the failure of the uprising of 1936,* Palestinians were also bereft of strong national leadership. After several false starts (such as the formation of the All-Palestine Government in 1948), a generation arrived on the scene in the 1950s that operated, under extremely difficult circumstances, to build the national institutions that are now decaying so publicly.

Palestinians living today may likewise have to begin afresh. It is not clear how they can repeat the experience of the generation of the 1950s and 1960s, but it does seem that some younger Palestinians see this as their task. They appear to be proceeding by trial and error, with some pursuing freedom rides one year, others pushing for boycott, divestment, and sanctions (BDS)[§] the next. Even the wave of individual knife attacks of 2015 formed part of this flailing.

---

* *Editor's note:* See Chronology.

§ *Editor's note:* See Glossary.

In some ways, circumstances for the younger generation of Palestinians are more favorable than those under which their grandparents worked. National identity is still strong at a political level, the illegitimacy of the occupation is a matter of almost universal consensus among Palestinians and in international organizations, and the fabric of Palestinian society below the national political level—the boring institutions that drew my attention in the late 1990s—is still intact even if it is beginning to fray.

Palestinians as a people will not disappear. But they are only beginning to develop new tools to help them find a path forward.

RESPONSE:

BYPASSING THE INSTITUTIONS

Diana Buttu

In the aftermath of the first Palestinian intifada, the Palestinian struggle was redirected from liberation and decolonization to statehood and international recognition as goals in themselves. This approach may have yielded tangible achievements had Israel's insatiable appetite for Palestinian land been quelled or had the international community put a brake on Israel's relentless colonization. Instead, more than two decades of futile negotiations undermined existing Palestinian governmental and non-governmental institutions, while those degraded institutions in turn became obstacles to a genuine anti-colonial struggle. The miserable state of Palestinian national institutions today, as

---

Diana Buttu served as Legal Advisor to the Palestine Liberation Organization (2000–2004) and Advisor to Palestinian President Mahmoud Abbas (2004–2005). A Palestinian-Canadian lawyer, she has held fellowships at the Harvard Kennedy School of Government, Harvard Law School, and the Stanford Center for Conflict Resolution and Negotiation.

described in Nathan J. Brown's sobering and accurate account, is the logical and predictable outcome of this pursuit of folly.

During the years of the second Palestinian intifada, reform-minded Palestinians watched in horror as President Yasser Arafat played the "shuffle game" with Palestinian institutions: one day acting on behalf of the PLO and the next on behalf of the PA, rendering these structures meaningless and objects of ridicule and confusion. We witnessed the establishment under international pressure of the position of an "empowered" prime minister in order to dilute the authority of Arafat*—only to see those same powers removed, under pressure from those same international actors, from the democratically-elected Hamas prime minister three short years later. Subsequently, as the battle for democratic legitimacy continued (and continues), President Mahmoud Abbas and Prime Minister Salam Fayyad§ both abused Palestinian institutions to further their own illegitimate and often authoritarian rule. Fayyad spoke of and received international plaudits for "institution-building," even as the Palestinian Legislative Council (PLC) refused to confirm him prime minister as required by the Basic Law—the same Basic Law that had been amended to empower then-Prime Minister Abbas when the US and Israel had grown tired of Arafat.

Fayyad devoted his near six-year premiership to purportedly building Palestinian institutions. His blueprint for independence was set out in the planning document, "Palestine: Ending the Occupation, Establishing the

---

* *Editor's note:* The 2003 Roadmap to Peace, presented by the Middle East Quartet (the European Union, Russia, United Nations, and United States), called, inter alia, for the drafting of a "Palestinian constitution, based on strong parliamentary democracy and cabinet with empowered prime minister," and the "formal establishment of office of prime minister." The full text of the Roadmap is contained in UN Security Council, "Letter dated 7 May 2003 from the Secretary-General addressed to the President of the Security Council," S/2003/529 (7 May 2003).

§ *Editor's note:* Mahmoud Abbas was Palestinian prime minister between March and September 2003 and has been president of the PA since 2005. Salam Fayyad served as prime minister from 2007–2013.

State."[1] This amounted in practice to using donor money to build Palestinian infrastructure, such as government offices, while shunning the democratically-elected party and sidelining the democratic institution (i.e., the PLC) that is supposed to serve as Palestine's parliament before and after statehood. The international community pledged billions in support of Fayyad's plan, prioritizing "institution-building" at the expense of democratic accountability. As part of this policy, international donors would issue regular report cards on Palestinian "readiness" to live freely—as if a people's right to self-determination were conditional on passing international exams.

While Fayyad spoke of "institution-building" to cover his lack of legitimacy, Abbas has deliberately destroyed Palestinian institutions to entrench his authoritarian rule. In addition to serving as president for more than twelve years, though he was only elected to serve four, Abbas has blocked municipal, parliamentary, and PLO elections and staged controlled Fatah elections. He has ousted dissidents from the PLO and Fatah and appointed individuals to senior positions in violation of the rules of these institutions. To provide cover for his usurpations, he shifts between the PLO and the PA, first declaring that the PA supersedes the PLO, and then declaring the opposite. He has revived institutions such as the Palestine Central Council (which had been dormant for more than a decade) for the sole purpose of declaring his extended presidency legitimate, and then refused to hold elections for the (dying and dead) members of this same Council. That is, he looks to non-functioning institutions for worthless certificates of "legitimacy," while killing off those institutions that have genuine legitimacy to bestow. This leaves Palestinians with a series of administrative entities that barely qualify as institutions: the president rules by decree; the prime minister has never received confirmation; the parliament has not met in a decade and has not passed a single piece of legislation in eleven years; and the terms of the president, parliament, and municipal councilors expired years ago. The international community is well aware of

[1] Palestinian Authority, "Palestine: Ending the Occupation, Establishing the State—Program of the 13th Government" (Ramallah, 25 August 2009), reproduced in *Journal of Palestine Studies* 39.1 (Autumn 2009), pp. 173–78.

these pathologies, but continues to focus on "institutions" (for which, read "security") because this allows them to claim to be supporting Palestinian statehood even as they remain silent on Israel's colonization.

The young people of Palestine—most of the Palestinian population—are not as obsessed with institutions as their predecessors, because they have seen where this obsession leads and because generations of Palestinians have not had the luxury of pursuing internal political aspirations. The only route to advancement within the PLO and the Fatah-dominated PA is through nepotism and factional loyalty. Our broken institutions do not produce and are not open to new leaders; there is nobody under the age of forty in a leadership position in any of these bodies. Instead, official politics consists of the same (old, male) figures shuffled and promoted within them. As a result, younger Palestinians are directing their efforts toward modes of political action that bypass sclerotic official structures. This partly accounts for the growing popularity among younger Palestinians of the BDS Movement—as well as the reluctance of the PA and PLO to embrace it.

To be clear, institutions are important. The Anti-Apartheid Movement would likely not have spread as rapidly or as widely in the absence of the African National Congress. But, in the case of Palestine, a focus on "institution-building" and "statehood" has served only to further the goals of those seeking perpetual rule over Palestine, and not its liberation. Perhaps Abbas's passing[2] will usher in a new wave of thought, one which welcomes political pluralism and promotes diverse age, geographic, and gender representation in leadership positions. If not, this will demonstrate that existing Palestinian institutions are so rotted and paralyzed with inertia that reforming them from within is impossible.

In such a scenario, the project to revitalize and rebuild Palestinian institutions will, as Brown suggests, have to start over again from scratch. The new institutions will need to reflect a more youthful Palestinian demographic, the

[2] At the time of writing, we have no idea what the succession plan will be when Abbas dies—for, despite threats to the contrary, he will never resign.

fact that most Palestinians are now not affiliated to a political faction, and the reality that more Palestinians today live outside of Palestine than within. While such a program of institutional construction will be difficult, it is not impossible, as the achievements of the 1950s and 1960s demonstrate. For now, however, Palestinians are correctly prioritizing methods to challenge Israel's rule directly, rather than internal reform.

RESPONSE:

MUNICIPAL GOVERNMENT IN AN AGE OF NATIONAL COLLAPSE

Glenn E. Robinson

Nathan J. Brown is an astute observer of Palestinian political life, and he is right to argue that the defeat of the state project has led to severe institutional deterioration at the national level. The PLO, PA, and major political factions such as Fatah and Hamas mostly exist and function these days without energy or plausible vision. Even the once-vibrant institutions of Palestinian civil society have been diminished by the decay at the national level. It should be stated clearly that Palestinian national institutions that were paving the way for statehood are not dying a natural death, but have been effectively killed off by Israel's occupation. It will still take many years for the parties involved to acknowledge that Palestinian

---

Glenn E. Robinson is Associate Professor at the Naval Postgraduate School and Research Associate at the Center for Middle Eastern Studies, University of California, Berkeley. He is the author of *Building a Palestinian State: The Incomplete Revolution* (1997).

aspirations for statehood have been quelled, and before we know what the next chapter in Palestinian national liberation will look like.

In the face of national defeat, Palestinian political life has largely migrated to the local level, in part because this is where governance in matters of daily life mostly transpires. Municipalities in Palestine have a long history independent of the PLO and PA. Palestine's first municipality was Nablus, established in 1869 under Ottoman rule. The Ottoman Empire's *Municipalities Law* of 1877 ushered in a period of rapid formation of municipalities in Palestine; by the time the British Mandate was established there were twenty-two recognized Palestinian municipalities, covering most of the current major towns of the West Bank and Gaza (including Hebron, Ramallah, Jerusalem, Gaza, Jenin, Tulkarim, Bayt Jala, Bethlehem, and Khan Yunis, in addition to Nablus). Municipal expansion continued under British and Jordanian rule (in the West Bank) but virtually ceased under direct Israeli occupation. Since 1994, the PA has vastly expanded the number of municipalities and other local government units, to manage the significant demographic expansion since 1967 and as patronage structures by which Fatah could reward local supporters with minor offices.

Because all of Palestine's major municipalities long predate the PLO and PA, and have a legitimacy not tied to the ebbs and flows of the conflict with Israel, they are among the few sites of political and civil activity not tainted by the collapse of the Oslo "peace process." I conducted fieldwork at this local level during the heady days following the Oslo I Accord (1993) and in the current period of stagnation and defeat (most recently in 2014). While the collapse of the national movement was apparent in my interviews with senior PA officials, the continued energy at the local level was a welcome surprise. Mayors, council members, and local stakeholders still needed to get things done for their constituents despite the absence of optimism at the national level. Municipal governance and political activity have also birthed new Palestinian leaders with their own political ambitions, but they have typically been shut out of the leadership ranks of the PA. Municipal leaders are often tied to one faction or another (Fatah in the West Bank, Hamas in Gaza) but are rarely major decision-makers within those factions.

This is not to suggest that all is well at the local level. Municipalities face severe constraints and obstructions, including interference by the PA, a lack of legal clarity surrounding the 1997 local government law, and limited control over locally-generated tax revenues. Property taxes make up 40–50 percent of most municipal budgets in the West Bank, but are channeled first through the PA, which is often unresponsive in turning over those revenues to local governments. Most important, virtually all municipalities have "Area C" lands running through their borders, creating myriad inefficiencies and dysfunctions at Israel's hands. Routine planning has become a Herculean challenge.

Israel's overwhelming power in Palestinian territory—its "matrix of control"[1]—inevitably plays a role in any significant political outcome there. In this case, the relative success and energy of Palestinian municipalities is not due to Palestinian efforts alone, however heroic they may be. Relatively functional Palestinian local government is consistent with the right-wing Likud Party's vision of Palestinian autonomy in the West Bank under overarching Israeli control. There is a long history of tactical Israeli support for local Palestinian administration, from Menachem Begin's proposal for Palestinian autonomy under the Camp David Accords to the clumsily-constructed Village Leagues of the 1980s* and Ariel Sharon's never-announced but evident plan of stitching together about half the West Bank to form a contiguous Palestinian homeland—the sort of entity that Israeli Prime Minister Benjamin Netanyahu has embraced as a "state minus."[2] Killing off national Palestinian institutions and ambitions while permitting local Palestinian government to thrive (relatively speaking) is consistent with the objective of permanent Israeli control

---

* *Editor's note:* In 1982, Israel established a co-opted Palestinian municipal leadership in the West Bank as an alternative to the PLO. But the "Federation of Village Leagues" lacked credibility among Palestinians and was dissolved in 1984.

[1] Jeff Halper, "The 94 Percent Solution: A Matrix of Control," *Middle East Report* 216 (Fall 2000).

[2] "Netanyahu says Palestinians can have a 'state minus'," *Times of Israel* (22 January 2017).

over West Bank land without any accompanying political absorption of the Palestinian population.

Palestinians therefore face a conundrum: putting political and civil energy to work at the municipal level promises to improve the lives of ordinary Palestinians, but in so doing, it may also facilitate permanent Israeli control of Palestinian lands. Like the Bantustans in apartheid South Africa, autonomous Palestinian municipalities are no substitute for real sovereignty and will not bring peace or stability to the Holy Land. But in the aftermath of the crushing of Palestinian national institutions, municipal government is certain to loom large in Palestinian political life—as it has for many decades.

CHAPTER TWO.

IS ISRAEL'S ANNEXATION OF EAST JERUSALEM IRREVERSIBLE?

Daniel Seidemann vs. Yoaz Hendel

Daniel Seidemann

The essence of a two-state solution is an end to Israel's occupation of the West Bank, Gaza, and East Jerusalem in exchange for a recognized border, legitimacy, and security for Israel. All who have engaged in good-faith Israeli-Palestinian negotiations have concluded that the political division of Jerusalem, permitting the establishment of Palestine's capital in East Jerusalem

---

Daniel Seidemann is an Israeli attorney specializing in the geopolitics of Jerusalem. He is Founder of the Israeli NGO, Terrestrial Jerusalem.

Yoaz Hendel is Chair of the Institute for Zionist Strategies and former Director of Communications for Israeli Prime Minister Benjamin Netanyahu. He is a journalist and military historian, and has a PhD from Tel Aviv University.

with West Jerusalem recognized as Israel's capital, is the sine qua non of any permanent status agreement. Unfortunately, this requirement runs up against fifty years of Israeli policy, which has been explicitly dedicated to making the annexation of East Jerusalem irreversible.

In 1967, Israel annexed 6.5km^2 of land that was Jordanian East Jerusalem and around 0.5km^2 of adjacent land, including numerous villages. The resulting new municipal boundaries of Jerusalem comprised pre-1967 West Jerusalem and an expanded East Jerusalem. As regards East Jerusalem, these formal boundaries have remained unchanged since 1967.

In the ensuing years, Israel's policies in East Jerusalem have been directed toward two clear goals. First, to accelerate the development of the Israeli sector while restricting the development of the Palestinian sector, in order to establish and maintain a robust Israeli majority in the city. Second, to establish a critical mass of "facts on the ground" in order to render a division of the city prohibitively expensive.

To these ends, the Israeli government has expropriated more than 33 percent of the privately-owned land in East Jerusalem.[1] Today, there are approximately 212,000 Israeli settlers living in more than 55,000 residential units—some 210,000 in large settlement neighborhoods and the rest in settlement enclaves in and around the Old City.[2]

The distribution of these settlements and settlers, however, still allows for a division of the city. It has been broadly accepted by Israelis and Palestinians who have negotiated the two-state solution that a permanent status agreement will involve limited and agreed land swaps. Such swaps would permit Israel to incorporate certain large settlements into its sovereign territory while "compensating" the Palestinians with Israeli territory of equal size. Under the likely permanent status agreement, nearly 210,000 of the 212,000 Israeli Jews

[1] B'Tselem, *A Policy of Discrimination: Land Expropriation, Planning and Building in East Jerusalem* (May 1995), pp. 39–41.

[2] Jerusalem Institute for Israel Studies, *Jerusalem Statistical Yearbook 2017*, Chapters III and IX, and author's own research.

currently residing in East Jerusalem would not be relocated and their homes, now viewed by the world as illegal settlements, would be recognized as part of sovereign Israel. This would make it possible to delineate a viable border in Jerusalem and thereby "reverse" the annexation of East Jerusalem.

However, three caveats are in order. First, a solution will have to be found for the approximately 2,600 settlers living in and around the Old City.* While theoretically they could remain under Palestinian sovereignty, this would raise serious concerns about their potential to act as spoilers of a peace agreement. Moreover, the likely price for their staying would be a Palestinian demand for implementation of a "right of return" to properties in sovereign Israel. It is therefore highly likely that these settlers will need to be relocated in order to reach an agreement.

Second, binary border arrangements will not work in those few areas of greatest significance to both peoples and where the patterns of life of both peoples intersect—particularly the Old City and its visual basin. While it is inconceivable that Palestinians in and around the Old City would remain under Israeli rule, in all likelihood it will be necessary to establish a Special Regime (depriving either side of sovereignty) or special arrangements (dividing or sharing aspects of sovereignty) in order to address the issues that are unique to this area.

Third, while today one can accurately say that Israel's annexation is reversible and a viable border achievable, this will not be true much longer should current trends in settlement expansion continue. Specific settlement schemes, like Givat Hamatos and E1, as well as the cumulative impact of others threaten to so Balkanize the map of Jerusalem and its environs as to make the creation of a border virtually impossible in the absence of politically infeasible population transfers. (Givat Hamatos would result in the encirclement of the Palestinian village of Beit Safafa, making reversal of its annexation impossible; E1, located between East Jerusalem and the settlement of Ma'ale Adumim, would fragment any future Palestinian state and undermine its viability.) In the event this

* *Editor's note:* For the Old City, see Glossary.

scenario comes to pass, a negotiated resolution of the conflict will no longer be possible.

ꕤ

Yoaz Hendel

Jerusalem is just one aspect of the Israeli-Palestinian conflict. But its political and symbolic significance is such that, even if a magic wand were waved and mutually acceptable solutions on settlements, borders, and refugees conjured into existence, Jerusalem would still present a likely insurmountable obstacle to an agreement.

Consider, first, the facts on the ground. Jerusalem is effectively comprised of three distinct parts: the western city, where you can find Jews and Arabs—Jews who live there, and Arabs who commute from East Jerusalem to work; East Jerusalem, which comprises both Jewish and Arab neighborhoods, with significant "mixing" between the two populations; and five Palestinian neighborhoods located behind the Wall,* which form part of Jerusalem on paper only. One need only glance at a map, or climb Mount Scopus and look down, to see that the notion of separating Jerusalem into two cities bears no relation to the real world. The Arab and Jewish populations are not neatly segregated but, on the contrary, thoroughly intermixed. There is extensive infrastructure built by united Jerusalem's first mayor and his successors with the specific intention of precluding future division. Moreover, polls of Palestinians living in East Jerusalem indicate that most are far from enthusiastic about becoming citizens of a theoretical Palestinian state.

Now let's examine Israeli public opinion. Even if it were possible to draw a viable border inside the city, and even if it were possible to do so while protecting Jerusalem's security, the fact is, Jerusalem for Israelis is not just a rational or technical issue. "Zionism"§ derives from the Hebrew word "Zion," a name for Jerusalem. Despite its initially secular character, the Jewish national movement

---

* *Editor's note:* See Glossary.

§ *Editor's note:* See Glossary.

homed in on the Land of Israel because of its deep historical, cultural, and religious resonance with the Jewish people—a resonance centered on and symbolized by Jerusalem. It is true that few Israelis venture into Arab neighborhoods in the eastern city, while fewer still are aware of the daily challenges Jerusalem faces. For most Israelis, Jerusalem is a symbol more than a city—but it is a symbol to which they are deeply and near unanimously committed. An overwhelming majority of Israelis views the Old City—and Silwan, and most of the rest of East Jerusalem—as an integral part of their capital, and will not compromise on this.

One might argue that Israeli public opinion, particularly on issues framed in terms of national security, can be shaped by strong leadership. Israelis were strongly opposed to withdrawing from the Sinai until the government made the case for it and carried it out, at which point, most of the population quietly acquiesced in and retrospectively approved of it. The aspiration for peace still exists in Israel, even if few believe in its possibility, and in the right conditions a trusted leadership might persuade the Israeli people to support the peace process, disengagement from Gaza, or withdrawal from the Sinai. But the symbolic resonance and rational risks bound up with Jerusalem are on a qualitatively different level. If anyone could divide Jerusalem, it would have to be a leader from the right, like Menachem Begin with the Sinai and Ariel Sharon with Gaza.* But no leader from the right will compromise on Jerusalem. While it is conceivable that Prime Minister Benjamin Netanyahu, for example, would in certain circumstances be willing and able to evacuate parts of Judea and Samaria,[§] I see no plausible scenario in which a right-wing leader such as Netanyahu could give up Jerusalem and survive politically.

What, then, is Jerusalem's future? To answer this, we have to place it in a broader context. The possibility of a two-state solution to the Israeli-Palestinian conflict died many years ago. One can debate why. Contributory factors include Israel's construction of settlements in Area C, Jordan's opposition to

* *Editor's note:* For the 2005 "disengagement" from Gaza, see Chronology and Glossary.

§ *Editor's note:* See Glossary.

a Palestinian state on the Jordan Valley, and fundamental divisions among the Palestinians that have left them unable to form a government. However one distributes the blame, the fact of the two-state solution's demise remains. This is therefore, to some extent, a purely theoretical discussion.

In the absence of a negotiated solution, present trends are likely to continue. The land is increasingly divided into those areas with a strong Israeli demographic and infrastructural presence, including the settlement blocs,* East Jerusalem, and the Jordan Valley; and other areas, which lack sovereignty. In areas with a strong Israeli presence, there is no one inside or out of Israel who can change this. In areas which lack Israeli sovereignty, no one in Israel wants to change this. Over the past fifty years, a process has unfolded on the ground, not as the result of any calculated political action, of increasing separation between most Jews and most Palestinians. In the 1990s, Israel separated from some 40 percent of Judea and Samaria, which became the Palestinian Authority (PA). In 2005, we separated from two million Palestinians in the Gaza Strip and from north Samaria. In the same period, we constructed the Wall inside Jerusalem, effectively severing the city from five Palestinian neighborhoods numbering 100,000 residents or more.

In the coming years, Israeli governments will likely increase investment in the neighborhoods of East Jerusalem, reducing the disparities between them and the rest of the city. The five Palestinian neighborhoods behind the Wall will become less and less connected to a united Jerusalem, perhaps eventually transferring to the jurisdiction of the PA. Meanwhile, the settlement blocs and Israeli sovereignty in East Jerusalem will become increasingly accepted internationally. These de facto processes of convergence and normalization will continue—without paper, without agreement, and without peace.

ꕥ

* *Editor's note:* Large clusters of Israeli settlements, such as the Ma'ale Adumim and Gush Etzion blocs around East Jerusalem. See maps on pp. 93–96 and Glossary.

Daniel Seidemann

Since Yoaz Hendel and I differ on almost every point under discussion, let us begin with the one subject on which we agree. My colleague asserts that, "[i] n the absence of a negotiated solution, present trends are likely to continue." I concur wholeheartedly. However, while he sees settlement expansion and all that accompanies it as a de facto separation from the Palestinians, I see a Balkanization of geography and demography in a manner that not only perpetuates occupation but doubles down on it. He implies that this new reality will generate a reasonably stable equilibrium; I see a disequilibrium of such dimensions as to make periodic and recurring rounds of violence virtually inevitable. Most importantly, while Hendel embraces the emerging reality as optimal for Israel, I see that reality as posing the gravest threat to the sustainability of the Zionist enterprise in this generation.

I will now address our other points of contention, one by one.

Facts on the ground have made Jerusalem undividable. In fact, in all but the legal/formal sense, the border between Israelis and Palestinians already exists. It is a cognitive border, intuitively recognized by Israelis and Palestinians alike, which traces almost precisely where a future border would be located were Israeli and Palestinian leaderships to negotiate an agreement in good faith. This border is defined by the existing patterns of life in the city: where Israelis walk today will be Israel, and where Palestinians walk today will be Palestine. As Hendel concedes, most Israelis avoid East Jerusalem, while few Palestinians venture into the West. The rare exceptions to this—for example, Palestinians who reside in East Jerusalem but work in Israel, who would need to cross a border—do not undermine the feasibility of dividing the city. In permanent status Jerusalem, almost 210,000 of the approximately 212,000 Israeli Jews currently residing in East Jerusalem would cease to be settlers, but wouldn't even have to change the way they drive to work. Meanwhile, none of the 316,000 Palestinian residents of East Jerusalem would remain under Israeli sovereignty.

Shared infrastructure precludes division. Separation of infrastructure would in practice boil down to the logo that appears on the bill and the nationality of the technician making repairs. In this sense, the infrastructures of two major utilities are separate already: Israelis and Palestinians receive their electricity from different electric companies, the latter from the Palestinian-run Jerusalem District Electric Company (JDECO), while some 60,000 residents of Beit Hanina, Kfar Akeb, and their vicinity receive their water from the Ramallah system. To be sure, JDECO purchases 95 percent of the power in its grid from Israel, but this has not prevented JDECO from being perceived as one of the most important Palestinian national institutions still active in East Jerusalem. Experts who have examined this issue have concluded that, while it is possible to physically separate the infrastructures on a more fundamental level than the logo and workforce, this would be both costly and unnecessary.

Israeli public opinion will never allow for compromise in Jerusalem. When I began to deal with East Jerusalem, supporting the division of Jerusalem was considered tantamount to treason. A quarter-century later, two of Israel's last four prime ministers have agreed to just such a division. I find it baffling that, after the remarkable performances of the pollsters with Brexit, the 2016 Colombian peace agreement referendum, and the 2016 election of President Donald Trump, anyone could proclaim with confidence what Israelis will believe indefinitely into the future. The polling data are far more nuanced than Hendel suggests. Israelis tend to be of two or three minds about the political status of Jerusalem. Roughly speaking, when asked exclusively about the division of Jerusalem, Israelis tend to oppose it; however, when asked the same question in the context of support for or opposition to a comprehensive permanent status agreement, polls have found a significant majority in favor of dividing the city.[3] Offered an end of claims agreement by a duly empowered prime minister that would bring universal recognition of Israeli Jerusalem as our capital, I have reason to believe that a significant majority of Israelis would assent—but we will only know what Israelis believe when they are asked to support or reject the terms of a specific permanent status agreement.

There is no plausible scenario in which a right-wing leader could give up Jerusalem. I was unaware that Ehud Olmert and Tzipi Livni are graduates

---

[3] See, for example, Dahaf Institute, "Public Poll Findings: Peace with the Palestinians," *centerpeace.org* (December 2012).

of Hashomer Hatzair.* Both are and remain right-of-center—yet the former acknowledged the imperative of dividing Jerusalem while the latter held out the possibility of doing so.[4] Again, reality is more nuanced than my colleague suggests. Leaders from Israel's ideological right are indeed incapable of compromise on Jerusalem, not because of the empirical realities (which they largely ignore) but because a "united Jerusalem" is for them an article of faith. But any leader from the pragmatic right who is serious about negotiating in good faith invariably abandons that ideological bunker and recognizes the inevitability of dividing the city.

Palestinian residents of East Jerusalem prefer Israeli citizenship. The claim that in their heart-of-hearts East Jerusalemites want to be under Israeli rule is based on polling conducted on behalf of the Washington Institute for Near East Policy.[5] I have previously critiqued that polling and its methodology in a manner that I believe undermines the credibility of its findings.[6] For now, two brief points will suffice. In the last municipal elections, there were 157,000 eligible Palestinian voters in East Jerusalem, of whom 1,101 (0.7 percent) cast a ballot. Those who didn't sent a clear message: "we are not Israeli." Secondly, since July 2014 Israel has arrested almost 10 percent of Palestinian boys between the ages of twelve and eighteen in East Jerusalem in the course of clashes with the police.[7] Apparently East Jerusalem's eligible voters and adolescent boys are not familiar with the Washington Institute's

---

* *Editor's note:* Hashomer Hatzair is a Socialist-Zionist youth movement. Ehud Olmert was mayor of Jerusalem (1993–2003) and prime minister of Israel (2006–9); Tzipi Livni has held various ministerial positions, including foreign minister (2006–9). Both began their political careers on the Israeli right.

[4] Lahav Harkov, "'Abbas was Once a Terrorist, But He Isn't Now', Livni Tells JPost," *Jerusalem Post* (22 January 2015).

[5] David Pollock, "Poll Shows 40 Percent of Jerusalem Arabs Prefer Israel to a Palestinian State," *Washington Institute for Near East Policy* (2 November 2011).

[6] Daniel Seidemann, "The Perils of Polling in East Jerusalem," *Foreign Policy* (23 February 2012).

[7] Derived from police reports and author's own research.

research. As is the case with Israeli opinion, we will learn what East Jerusalem Palestinians believe only when they are asked to accept or reject a specific agreement, and not before.

Future Israeli governments will likely increase investment in East Jerusalem. I find this scenario highly unlikely. The fact that only a fraction of the relevant budgets—10–12 percent—is allocated to the Palestinian sector, which comprises 38 percent of the population, is rooted in an iron-clad law of democratic politics: politicians will never direct resources, funds, time, or entitlements to those who cannot or will not vote. Palestinians in East Jerusalem are not citizens and do not have the right to vote for the Knesset, while, as noted, they refuse to vote in municipal elections. This is not likely to change, and so one may anticipate the continuation of policies whereby resource allocation to the Palestinian resident is a small fraction of that allotted to the Israeli citizen.

Israeli sovereignty in East Jerusalem will become increasingly accepted internationally. It is unclear whether the US government will honor the pledge made by President Donald Trump to relocate the US Embassy to Jerusalem. Regardless, the international community has left nothing to doubt. In a statement issued less than a week before Trump's inauguration, the more than seventy countries participating in the January 2017 Paris Conference specifically called upon the parties to "refrain from unilateral steps that prejudge the outcome of negotiations on final status issues, including, inter alia, on Jerusalem."[8] More forthrightly, then-French Foreign Minister Jean-Marc Ayrault dubbed the proposed embassy move "a provocation."[9] I anticipate that the dissonance between Israel's position on Jerusalem and that of the rest of the world will only increase over time. While Israel celebrates the miraculous "reunification" of Jerusalem, the rest of the world marks fifty years of occupation in East Jerusalem—an occupation that even Israel's closest allies cannot support. The status of Jerusalem will in the end be determined neither by unilateral moves

---

[8] "Middle East Peace Conference Joint Declaration," *Diplomatie.gouv.fr* (15 January 2017).

[9] "France's Ayrault Says Trump Jerusalem Proposal Provocation," *Reuters* (15 January 2017).

nor by inertia, but through an agreement that will inevitably entail a political division of the city.

ꕤ

Yoaz Hendel

When we speak of dividing Jerusalem, we should remind ourselves of the boldness of this proposal. The State of Israel existed for only nineteen years without Judea, Samaria, and East Jerusalem. For the past fifty years, Israel has controlled these territories and built in them roads, houses, communities, infrastructure, and political and social institutions. In the case of East Jerusalem, it has pursued thorough economic integration of the area. If someone now proposes to radically alter this reality, he must give a persuasive and sober account of how it can be accomplished. Otherwise, it's just an imaginary scenario divorced from questions of practical policy.

I have argued that the facts on the ground in Jerusalem preclude its political and territorial division. By "facts on the ground" I don't just mean a few buildings. I am referring to the transformational changes that have taken place over a full half-century, the effect of which has been to erase, in practice, the existence of the Green Line inside Jerusalem.* I'm talking about the fact that the people who now live in Jerusalem, West and East, don't know any other reality. I'm talking about the Jewish neighborhoods in East Jerusalem—whole communities, which are today home to some 250,000 people. I'm talking about the Israeli institutions in East Jerusalem: not just the office of the Ministry of Justice and the headquarters of Israel's police, but universities, a college, schools, roads, a train station connected to West Jerusalem. . .

Of course, one might wave one's hands and say, "these things can easily be moved," just like President Trump's spokesperson can always point to "alternative facts." In my opinion, uprooting and relocating the extensive infrastructure

* *Editor's note:* The "Green Line" refers to the pre-June 1967 armistice boundary established in 1949, now recognized by the International Court of Justice as the legal border of the State of Israel.

Israel has constructed in East Jerusalem is not only not easy—it is impossible. Daniel Seidemann claims that only 2,600 Jewish residents of Palestinian neighborhoods would need to be relocated in a permanent status agreement. To be sure, in theoretical maps, you can do whatever you want. With a magic wand, one can even create one Jerusalem in Heaven and one on Earth. But on the ground, there is no real plan that can separate the major parts of the city.

Then there are the entrenched *political* facts. Let's start with the Palestinians. Palestinians in East Jerusalem are integrated into and depend upon Israel's economy for their livelihoods. Moreover, very inconveniently for supporters of a Palestinian state, most Palestinians in East Jerusalem see themselves as part of Israel. Revoking their Blue (Israeli) IDs and reclassifying them citizens of Palestine would not only be illegal under Israeli law, but would also spark serious conflict between the majority of Palestinians who want an independent state and many if not most Palestinian residents of East Jerusalem who prefer to live in a state that, whatever its flaws, is relatively modern, liberal, democratic, and prosperous.

Seidemann disputes the Washington Institute survey. Of course, these questions are matters of judgement and interpretation, not science. Perhaps it would be nice to have better evidence; the evidence we have is that poll, and it shows that Arabs in East Jerusalem have little desire to transfer to a theoretical Palestinian state. Personally, I find the result plausible. First, because Palestinians in East Jerusalem want jobs. And second, because if you approach someone in the street and ask whether he would prefer to live as part of the majority in a dictatorship or a minority in a democracy, I suspect most would choose the latter.

Seidemann is correct that many young Arabs in East Jerusalem engage in resistance to the authorities. There is strong incitement in Palestinian society, while the Government of Israel hasn't done nearly enough to promote "Israelization" among East Jerusalem Palestinians. It is a huge problem and Israel must take stronger action in the form of public investment and other integrative measures. Seidemann suspects this won't happen because Palestinians in East Jerusalem do not vote. I predict it will because it is in Israel's interest to stabilize its sovereignty over East Jerusalem and it is in Israeli politicians' electoral interests vis-à-vis Israeli Jews to demonstrate that they take a strong and united Jerusalem seriously. Either way, it does not follow from the fact that serious problems exist in East Jerusalem and with Israel's policies towards it that most East Jerusalem Palestinians wish to become Palestinian rather than Israeli citizens. On the contrary, whenever it is reported that an Israeli government might agree to cede Palestinian neighborhoods of Jerusalem beyond the Wall—Kfar Akeb, Qalandyah, Shuafat—one immediately sees Palestinians with Israeli residency permits* streaming to other neighborhoods in the city. Why? Because they don't want to lose those permits. They prefer to stay in Israeli Jerusalem.

Now let's turn again to Israeli public opinion. Most polls show that a majority of Israeli Jews are not only comfortable with the current status of East Jerusalem, but see themselves as a group which has a strong heritage in and connection to it. That is why, in election campaign after election campaign over the past five decades, candidates from all mainstream parties have accused their opponents of planning to give Jerusalem away (even though, in practice, such division was not in the cards). To persuade Israeli public opinion to relinquish East Jerusalem would require a great magician indeed. Seidemann disagrees with my claim that no right-wing Israeli leader would ever give up Jerusalem, citing, as examples to the contrary, Ehud Olmert and Tzipi Livni. But both Olmert and Livni offered to compromise with the Palestinians when they were on the left of Israeli politics, not the right.

Seidemann agrees with me that, in the absence of a negotiated settlement, current trends on the ground will continue. But whereas I think this will be manageable for Israel, he prophesies a downward spiral of destabilization and international isolation. The left in Israel has spent two decades brandishing these threats, but the facts do not bear them out.

---

* *Editor's note:* Palestinians living in East Jerusalem hold the status of permanent residents (not citizens) of Israel. This entitles them to live and work in Israel and East Jerusalem, receive state benefits, and vote in municipal (but not national) elections. Since 1967, more than 14,000 Palestinians in East Jerusalem have had their permanent residency status revoked by the state. See Glossary.

While international criticism of Israel's policies certainly exists, Israel is today more accepted in the international community than ever, and its substantive relationships are growing stronger year after year. Some historical perspective is useful here. Israel's ties with the Arab world, Africa, and even Europe were much weaker before the 1967 War than they are today. Until the 1990s, the Arab boycott deterred many major international companies from investing in Israel; by one estimate, this cost Israel as much as 10 percent of its potential exports and foreign investment each year.[10] Today there is a noisy discussion about the threat of boycott, divestment, and sanctions (BDS),* but the truth is, one can count the number of companies that boycott Israel on a single hand.

As for the threat of destabilization and violence, one has to concede that withdrawing from Palestinian territories and creating a border in Jerusalem is at least as likely to exacerbate instability as to reduce it. If one were to re-establish the Green Line tomorrow, there would be a significant chance that the next day Israel would find itself coping with unstable neighborhoods—and perhaps a fragile Palestinian state—flush with weapons and lacking strong control.

Israeli policy towards Jerusalem should be determined not by imagined threats but by Israel's own decisions about itself and its interests. The status quo in Jerusalem is bad for Israel and we need to take steps to improve it. Specifically, we should excise the five neighborhoods sitting behind the Wall in East Jerusalem from the city, promote integration of Jews and Arabs in East Jerusalem, and invest heavily in Arab neighborhoods to reduce the disparities with West Jerusalem. That being said, I cannot agree with Seidemann that Israel's survival depends upon an agreement with the Palestinians and upon splitting into two a city that has been united for fifty years. Seidemann may view himself an optimist. But if you put only one option on the table, and a utopian one at that, you will find yourself in the end with a set of very pessimistic conclusions.

---

* *Editor's note:* See Glossary.

[10] Estimate of the Federation of Israeli Chambers of Commerce, cited in Clyde Haberman, "Though Still in Effect, Arabs' Economic Boycott of Israel Weakens," *New York Times* (11 May 1993).

Given the impossibility of a negotiated peace, responsible actors seek to manage the conflict. This requires coming down from the clouds to argue about budgets; about neighborhoods; about promoting the city, East and West; and about civil rights for all the city's residents. People who are serious about improving life in Jerusalem should focus their efforts on concrete and achievable reforms such as these, rather than daydreaming out the window.

RESPONSE:

A SOLIPSISTIC DEBATE

Rami Nasrallah

After fifty years of occupation and doubtful "annexation," Israeli discourse is still characterized by a complete denial of Palestinian national and political rights. The Israeli argument about the future of occupied East Jerusalem is conducted between two poles of a Jewish-centric spectrum. Supporters of a two-state solution, like Daniel Seidemann, argue for division of Jerusalem as a means to safeguard the "Zionist" character of the State of Israel and ensure its legitimacy and security. The Oslo peace process* and the 2003 Geneva Initiative were based on the principle of *separation*, and this remains the dominant approach on the Israeli

---

Rami Nasrallah is Founder and Chairman of the International Peace and Cooperation Center in Jerusalem. He was General Director of the Jerusalem Affairs Department of the Prime Minister's Office, Palestinian Authority (2003–2006) and Director of the Special Projects Unit in the Orient House (1996–1998), where he formulated policy and position papers for future negotiations over Jerusalem. He was a Research Associate of the "Conflict in Cities" project at the University of Cambridge (2007–2012).

* *Editor's note:* See Glossary.

left and center. If leftists in different times and different places have been inspired by such ideals as "workers of the world, unite!" in Israel, the banner of the left reads, "us here, them there." Yoaz Hendel, at the other end of this narrow spectrum, presents annexation and selective integration as a more effective strategy for protecting Zionism. The fact that East Jerusalem has a Palestinian population of more than 316,000 does not trouble him, as it does proponents of separation, because he assumes that these Palestinians can be brought to acquiesce in their subjugation. Both Hendel and Seidemann accept the bulk of Israel's "facts on the ground" and consider them irreversible.

Hendel observes that Jerusalem is for Israelis a symbol more than a city. Indeed, most Israelis perceive the Old City as "theirs," even though it forms the urban and social core of East Jerusalem and notwithstanding that it was, until the construction of the Wall began in 2002, the metropolitan center of the entire West Bank and to a certain extent the Gaza Strip as well. Aside from the Jewish Quarter, Israeli symbolism in the Old City of Jerusalem is overwhelmingly expressed through its military and settler presence. The Wall amputates East Jerusalem from its direct environs, severing the city geographically and functionally from the rest of the West Bank.

Seidemann warns that permanent Israeli occupation of East Jerusalem represents "the gravest threat to the sustainability of the Zionist enterprise in this generation." Implicit here is the classic argument about the demographic threat posed by Palestinians to Israel's Jewish majority. Again, in the Israeli context such arguments are typical of the political left rather than the far-right. Against this, Hendel speaks of "civil rights" for Palestinians while at the same time calling for the expulsion by administrative fiat of the five Palestinian neighborhoods behind the Wall, an act that would reduce the Palestinian population of Jerusalem by at least a third.

It is misleading to argue, as Hendel does, that extensive infrastructure investment might so entwine Palestinians and Israelis in Jerusalem as to preclude a future division of the city. Major Israeli infrastructure developments in East Jerusalem—new housing, major roads, the Separation Wall—have been almost exclusively directed towards extending and entrenching Israel's territorial control and advancing the settlement project, and have exacerbated rather than eroded the divisions within the city. It has been estimated that more than a billion US dollars would be required to upgrade East Jerusalem's infrastructure to the levels of West Jerusalem. The chances of an Israeli government approving such a budget are slim, to say the least.

Since 1967, East Jerusalem has been characterized by physical fragmentation, environmental degradation, and social disintegration. Hendel urges reformers to focus on quality of life issues rather than grandiose political projects, but this distinction overlooks that discrimination and poverty in East Jerusalem are a product of its political condition. Planning authorities have deliberately restricted Palestinian spatial development in East Jerusalem, resulting in a vast housing shortage and severe deficiencies in public services and infrastructure. Whilst the Palestinian population of Jerusalem totals 316,000, the city's housing stock is estimated at less than 50,000 units. Between a quarter and one half of these are unlicensed; their inhabitants are consequently subjected to fines, home demolition, and even imprisonment by the Israeli authorities. Indeed, official data indicate there are more than 10,000 demolition orders outstanding.[1]

Many school-age children in East Jerusalem are not enrolled in any educational institution. According to the Palestinian Department of Education, approximately 9,000 children in East Jerusalem do not attend school. Among those enrolled, many fail to complete secondary school, with a dropout rate of 13 percent compared to 1 percent in West Jerusalem. There is a shortage of approximately 2,200 classrooms (including 400 preschool classes) in the school system. In 2012–13, of the more than 18,000 Palestinian children aged three to four living in Jerusalem, less than a third were enrolled in recognized schools, while only 6 percent attended official kindergartens.[2]

There is also a lack of recreational and cultural services for the youth of East Jerusalem. West Jerusalem has 1,000 public parks compared to only forty-five in East Jerusalem, thirty-four swimming pools compared to three in East

---

[1] Meir Margalit, *Demolishing Peace: House Demolitions in East Jerusalem, 2000–2010* (Jerusalem: International Peace and Cooperation Center, 2014), p. 34.

[2] Ir Amim and The Association for Civil Rights in Israel, *Annual Status Report: The Failing East Jerusalem Education System* (August 2013).

Jerusalem, twenty-six libraries compared to a mere two in East Jerusalem, and 531 sports facilities against only thirty-three in East Jerusalem.[3]

These enduring disparities are systematic and suggest that a process of Israelization, or forced integration, stands little chance of success. After withstanding fifty years of unrelenting pressure, Palestinian Jerusalemites will not now abandon their national aspirations—particularly given that the alternative on offer is one of institutionalized discrimination. Of course, for practical reasons, the priorities of Palestinians in East Jerusalem shift with the circumstances. Their concern is to maintain their presence in, and not be expelled either physically or administratively from, their city. Protecting their residency as individuals is naturally their top priority. But this does not make them Israelis, and the majority continue to reject Israeli citizenship.

Seidemann and Hendel present alternative Israeli solutions. Evidently, Palestinian rights and political aspirations are not a consideration for Israeli public opinion and policy. But they certainly are necessary considerations in any serious attempt to stabilize the city and reach a peace agreement. The "open city" model for Jerusalem's future, which would see the city united physically even as it is divided politically, was raised by neither Seidemann nor Hendel, and yet enjoys broad support among Palestinians. The open city model would enhance and strengthen the universal status of Jerusalem, enabling it to become a global religious, cultural, and economic center, while serving as a political capital for two states.

---

[3] B'Tselem, "Neglect of Infrastructure and Services in Palestinian Neighborhoods," *btselem.org* (1 January 2011).

RESPONSE:

INTERNATIONALIZING JERUSALEM

Michael Dumper

This is a fascinating discussion that draws out most of the main issues. These range from the role of Jerusalem in the construction of the national-political identities of both Israelis and Palestinians to the difficulty of separating out the infrastructure should there be a Palestinian capital in East Jerusalem. On the whole, I would give more credence to Daniel Seidemann's argument

Michael Dumper is Professor of Middle East Politics at the University of Exeter. His research focuses on refugees and Jerusalem as permanent status issues in the Middle East Peace Process, as well as archaeology, conservation, and politics in Jerusalem and other divided cities. He is the author of *Jerusalem Unbound: Geography, History, and the Future of the Holy City* (2014).

that, even after fifty years of occupation, the annexation[1] of the city is still reversible. Israeli sovereignty and control in East Jerusalem is eroded and undermined in myriad ways: by international law supported by key actors in the international community, by property ownership, by the semi-autonomous nature and extensive holdings of religious institutions in the city, by Palestinian demographic growth partly resulting from the unintended consequences of the separation barrier (the Wall), and by Palestinian cultural and civic resistance.[2]

Yoaz Hendel's argument is based largely upon an appeal that we should recognize and resign ourselves to the existing balance of power and current political trends, both of which tilt in Israel's favor. Policy-makers and analysts should certainly take these factors into account. Nevertheless, by focusing so narrowly on them, Hendel neglects to acknowledge the extent of Israel's failure to impose full sovereignty over East Jerusalem since 1967. In addition, and notwithstanding the incapacity of the PA to play an effective role there, his argument underplays the strength of Palestinian, Arab, and Islamic attachment to the city, which is able to marshal extensive and long-term financial and political reserves to offset Israeli encroachments.

The perspectives aired in the Seidemann-Hendel debate are important, but do not give the full picture. Palestinian nationalists approach negotiations over the future of the city from a broader historical context and a different starting point than that of Seidemann—1948, not 1967. Even an agreement based on the 1967 borders with territorial exchanges represents, for many Palestinians,

---

[1] The term "annexation" should not be accepted without qualification. In many crucial aspects, such as the imposition of citizenship, the incorporation of East Jerusalem into the Israeli state in 1967 did not meet all the legal criteria for the change of status to an annexed territory. The use of the term in its popular and conversational sense can risk confusing the debate and masking the colonial nature of many of Israel's policies there. (See this point developed in Ian S. Lustick, "Has Israel Annexed Jerusalem?" *Middle East Policy* 5.1 (1997), pp. 34–45, and "Reinventing Jerusalem," *Foreign Policy* 93 (1993–94), pp. 41–59.)

[2] Michael Dumper, *Jerusalem Unbound: Geography, History, and the Future of the Holy City* (New York, NY: Columbia University Press, 2014).

a concession on their part for which Israel is expected to make an equal concession in return. It is for this reason that the hopes of those who wish to see Palestinian participation in the elections for the Israeli Jerusalem municipality have foundered against the rock of Palestinian property in West Jerusalem. Palestinian municipal councilors would be subject to great pressure from their constituents to demand the return of Palestinian property in the neighborhoods of Beka'a, Talpiyyeh, and Katamon expropriated by Israel after 1948. This is an incendiary issue for Israelis across the political spectrum since it raises the question of Palestinian refugee property in general; restitution in West Jerusalem would risk setting a precedent that would open a Pandora's box of Palestinian claims inside and outside Jerusalem. As a consequence, Israelis will not accept a municipal arrangement that would permit Palestinian councilors to formally pursue this issue; at the same time, denying Palestinian councilors the right to do so would delegitimize their participation in the municipality. So, while the reversibility of the annexation in 1967 is certainly debatable, the resolution of that debate is not the end of the story.

Another way in which the debate needs to be extended relates to the complex nature of cities and the contradictions that are inherent when ethnonationalist ideologies determine the framework for sharing urban space and administration. The essential fact is that, since 1967, Israeli policies in East Jerusalem have been driven by Zionism. As in other cities that are or have been controlled by adherents of ethnically-based ideologies—Ulster Loyalists in Belfast, Maronites in Beirut, Serbian nationalists in several cities in former Yugoslavia—the privileging of the dominant community leads directly to the marginalization of the subordinate community. To some extent this takes place in all cities, but most have processes by which the needs of the subordinate community are recognized and addressed. In the case of Jerusalem, these processes are absent, and the subordinate Palestinian community is deprived on grounds of principle of resources and the means to secure its status and shape its future.

An inevitable result of this dynamic of exclusion is that the subordinate community will look elsewhere for representation, funds, and protection. It will forge political alliances which might in the end prove a formidable constraint on the dominant community's control. Herein lies the contradiction: the ideology that seeks exclusive control creates the very forces which will resist it. This internationalization of the conflict is exactly what is taking place in East Jerusalem, enabled by the presence of important holy sites in the city which serve to mobilize a wide spectrum of external players. While the external dimension is alluded to by both Seidemann and Hendel, they do not give it the importance it deserves. The fact that up to the time of writing, the greatest ally of the Israeli state, the United States, still has not recognized Jerusalem as the capital of Israel, while not one member of the international community has sited its embassy there, demonstrates the strength and endurance of international opposition to Israel's ideologically-driven attempt to incorporate East Jerusalem. So long as this international support for Palestinian rights in East Jerusalem is confined to speeches and paper resolutions, Hendel and Seidemann are doubtless right to prioritize the Israeli political sphere, and the horizon of political possibility will remain, as Hendel suggests, limited. But if Palestinians and sympathetic actors abroad are able to translate these international statements into meaningful action, happier alternatives for the city may yet be possible.

RESPONSE:

SHARING JERUSALEM

Lior Lehrs

The Hendel-Seidemann exchange focuses on whether it remains possible to physically divide Jerusalem. Hendel is correct that fifty years is a long time and that the city has changed significantly since 1967, while Seidemann is correct that, in many respects, Jerusalem still comprises two distinct cities. The challenge for both sides in future negotiations will be to recognize and address the new "facts on the ground" (for example, the years of social security and health insurance payments made by Palestinian residents into the Israeli system) while refusing to be prisoners of the past or to allow opponents of

---

Lior Lehrs is an Israel Institute Postdoctoral Fellow at the Taub Center for Israel Studies at New York University. He wrote his doctoral dissertation in the Department of International Relations at the Hebrew University of Jerusalem and served as a researcher at the Jerusalem Institute for Policy Research, where he focused on the topic of Jerusalem within Israeli-Palestinian peace negotiations.

an agreement to elevate challenges and difficulties into decisive obstacles to resolving the conflict.

Analysis of previous final status negotiations—during the Camp David (1999–2001) and Annapolis (2007–8) processes—reveals that, while Jerusalem was an object of significant disagreement, when there was genuine political will on both sides the gaps diminished and the parties were able to compromise and agree on creative solutions.[1] On the issue of the neighborhoods in East Jerusalem, both sides accepted the "Clinton formula": Jewish neighborhoods under Israeli sovereignty and Arab neighborhoods under Palestinian sovereignty; on the Old City/"Holy Basin," they discussed division of sovereignty or a special/international regime; on the Western Wall and Temple Mount/Al-Haram Al-Sharif,* it was agreed that the Western Wall would be under Israeli sovereignty, while for the Al-Haram Al-Sharif/Temple Mount, negotiators sought a creative solution that would allow Palestinian administration while addressing the disagreement about the question of sovereignty (various workarounds were suggested, such as the concept of "divine sovereignty"). It was also agreed that there would be two municipalities in Jerusalem, with a mechanism for coordination between them. In the course of these negotiations, the most intractable points of dispute concerned sovereignty over holy and historical sites (first and foremost the Temple Mount/Al-Haram Al-Sharif), not "facts on the ground" and infrastructure.

If Hendel seeks alternatives to physical separation, he will probably be interested in the proposal consistently put forward by the Palestinians since the 1980s: Jerusalem as an "open city." The late East Jerusalem leader Faisal Husseini was the first to raise this idea. It was also put forward by the Palestinians during final status negotiations, and it remains the official position of the Palestine Liberation Organization. Under this proposal, notwithstanding the political division of the city, Jerusalem would remain a single entity under an "umbrella authority," with freedom of movement across the city.[2] The concept is vague

* *Editor's note*: See Glossary.

[1] For further discussion, see Lior Lehrs, "Jerusalem on the Negotiating Table: Analyzing the Israeli-Palestinian Peace Talks on Jerusalem, 1993–2015," *Israel Studies* 21.3 (2016), pp. 179–205.

[2] See Faisal Husseini, "The Holy City Must Be Ruled Fairly," *Los Angeles Times* (9 July 2000).

and was rejected by Israeli negotiators because of the security implications, but it remains a useful option for discussion. Future negotiations should examine various models along the spectrum between power sharing and partition and between "open city" and "closed."[3]

On the question of public opinion, Hendel maintains that a peace agreement is not possible because the Israeli public will never agree to compromise on Jerusalem. I hope and believe that he is wrong. Peace Index public opinion surveys[4] conducted regularly since July 2000 consistently show that roughly 40 percent of Israelis support the "Clinton formula" on Jerusalem. Polls also show that the framing and wording of the question dramatically affect the results. For example, when the question refers specifically to withdrawal from neighborhoods "such as Sheikh Jarrah and Shuafat," support for withdrawal from Palestinian neighborhoods exceeds 60 percent.[5] Support also increases, as Seidemann notes, when compromise on Jerusalem is framed as part of a package deal constituting a permanent status agreement. The violence in Jerusalem during recent years has also impacted public opinion. An October 2015 poll, conducted in the wake of a violent escalation in Jerusalem, revealed that 50 percent of the public supports transferring Arab neighborhoods of East Jerusalem to the Palestinians, while in February 2016, a poll found that 58 percent of the public views Jerusalem as already divided.[6] The Old City is a different matter altogether, and it will be more challenging to secure public support for a compromise on this question, but it can be addressed through creative solutions already proposed by official and unofficial actors.[7]

---

[3] See, for example, SAYA, "The Border Regime for Jerusalem in Peace," *Sayarch.com* (n.d.).

[4] PeaceIndex.org.

[5] Chemi Shalev, "Israelis: Peace With Arab World More Important Than Recognition as Jewish State," *Ha'aretz* (13 March 2014).

[6] Daphna Liel, "50% of the Israelis: Transfer Arab Neighborhoods in East Jerusalem to the PA," *Channel 2 News* (27 October 2015) [Hebrew]; "The Peace Index: February 2016," *The Evens Program for Mediation and Conflict Resolution at Tel Aviv University and the Guttman Center for Public Opinion and Policy Research of the Israel Democracy Institute* (6 March 2016).

[7] See, for example, the "Jerusalem Old City Initiative," http://www1.uwindsor.ca/joci/.

Seidemann and Hendel also trade prophecies of Jerusalem's future, each making strong claims about what is and is not a plausible scenario. My work in conflict studies has taught me that one should be very careful when making predictions about intractable conflict situations. Certain scholars predicted that the Northern Ireland conflict could never be resolved even on the eve of the successful peace negotiations (1994–1998), while others prophesied peace and coexistence in Burundi a year before the civil war (1993). In the case of Jerusalem, one should be particularly cautious about predicting a stable status quo in a city that has experienced several rounds of terrible violence in just the past two decades.

Hendel predicts that the Israeli government will invest in East Jerusalem as an integrative and stabilizing measure. This would be a welcome policy in any future scenario but, given the experience of the past 50 years, one might justifiably wonder whether Hendel is not, to use his phrase, "daydreaming out the window." If investing in East Jerusalem were in the Israeli interest, why has it not happened? The small efforts in recent years were but a drop in the ocean of neglect, poverty (80 percent of families live below the poverty line), and despair. To judge by their actions, the electoral interest of Israeli politicians is to control the land in East Jerusalem but not to assist its residents, not to initiate building plans for them, not to foster a strong and independent economy, and not to promote social and cultural institutions.

Jerusalem lies at the heart of the Israeli-Palestinian conflict and was for many years—from the 1929 riots to the second intifada in September 2000—one of its most incendiary focal points. A reasonable and stable solution for the city is therefore indispensable for resolving the broader conflict. With this in mind, discussions about Jerusalem's future need to be reframed to ask how the city can be peacefully and productively *shared*. On what basis can Yerushalayim and Al-Quds exist side-by-side, while maintaining mechanisms for cooperation and coordination? The border regime is a crucial aspect of this discussion, but it is not the only one. It is vital, for example, that alongside the Yerushalayim municipality an elected and independent Al-Quds municipality is established to serve and represent Palestinian residents—rather than, as is the current practice, allocating this task to a Jewish adviser to the mayor.

An Israeli-Palestinian agreement on Jerusalem would not mean "turn[ing] the clock back half a century," as Hendel presents it. An agreement would entail moving forward, opening a new chapter in which the Palestinians of East Jerusalem would no longer be invisible and would, for the first time, have equal rights, a voice in the city's management, and control over their lives.

If peace negotiations are not on the near horizon, then there is an urgent need for immediate steps to prevent escalation, reduce tension, and pave the way for a future agreement in the city. These should include establishing the infrastructure for an Al-Quds municipality and leadership, preventing provocative pro-settlement activities by private Jewish organizations in Palestinian neighborhoods, preserving the status quo at the Temple Mount/Al-Haram Al-Sharif, and avoiding measures that promote Balkanization and make a future agreement impossible.

CHAPTER THREE.

HAVE THE SETTLEMENTS MADE A TWO-STATE SOLUTION IMPOSSIBLE? I: POLITICS

Shaul Arieli vs. Gideon Levy
Translated by Ofer Neiman

Shaul Arieli

The success of the Israeli settlement enterprise in the West Bank should be measured against the goal set at its launching: to create the physical and spatial conditions that would enable Israel to annex the entire territory

---

Shaul Arieli was the Commander of the Israel Defense Forces Northern Brigade of the Gaza Strip; Head of the Interim Agreement Administration in the governments of Yitzhak Rabin, Shimon Peres, and Benjamin Netanyahu; and Head of the Peace Administration in the government of Ehud Barak. Col. (ret.) Dr. Arieli has published five books about the Israeli-Palestinian conflict as well as four collections of articles. He teaches courses on the conflict at the Academic College of Tel Aviv-Yaffo, the Hebrew University of Jerusalem, and the IDC Herzliya.

Gideon Levy is a journalist for the Israeli newspaper *Ha'aretz*. His regular column, "Twilight Zone," has covered Israel's occupation since 1988. Between 1978 and 1982 he was an aide to Shimon Peres, then-leader of the Israeli Labor Party.

(Gush Emunim,* Likud) or a part of it (the Labor Party's Allon Plan) without damaging the Zionist vision of a democratic state with a Jewish majority.

The possibility of separation between the Jewish and Arab populations in the West Bank rests on the ability to divide the two communities at a reasonable national cost. Separating populations that inhabit a shared fabric of life (communities, roads, work) requires complex, difficult, and expensive—beyond a certain point, impossible—measures. Insofar as the populations conduct their daily affairs in a "two eggs," rather than an "omelet," relationship, separation becomes easier. Therefore, those desiring a separation in the West Bank must examine what kind of reality the Jewish communities have managed to create after fifty years of settlement. An "omelet" that cannot be disaggregated at reasonable cost? Or "two eggs" which can be divided along a clear line?

The spatial and demographic data of the Jewish communities in the West Bank show:

1. Palestinians constitute 83 percent of the West Bank population.
2. Palestinians also constitute a solid majority in each of the "security zones" delineated in the Allon Plan (1967–68) and the Sharon Plan (1977): in the Jordan Valley—88 percent; in Western Samaria—84 percent; in the "Jerusalem Envelope" area—63 percent; and in the Gav HaHar area—95 percent.
3. 109 of 126 Jewish communities belong to regional councils and are small in both size and population. Half comprise less than 200 families, and the other half less than 1,000 families.
4. Israelis make no use of two-thirds of the West Bank roads.

---

* *Editor's note:* Gush Emunim ("Bloc of the Faithful") was a right-wing national-religious movement dedicated to Jewish settlement in the Occupied Territories.

5. 60 percent of the Israeli workforce of the Judea and Samaria region works within the Green Line.*
6. Israelis cultivate less than 100,000 dunams in the West Bank, overwhelmingly in the Jordan Valley. With two exceptions, there are no significant Israeli industrial zones in the West Bank, and the workers in all of them are Palestinian.
7. Israeli control of the West Bank rests primarily on closed zone orders issued to Palestinians with respect to more than 50 percent of Area C,[§] as well as a stationary and mobile military presence.
8. In the Israeli settlement blocs, there is Israeli dominance in terms of demography and space (built-up area, roads).

One can conclude from these realities that Israel benefits from spatial and demographic dominance only in the main "blocs," which take up just 4–5 percent of the West Bank, while Palestinians benefit from spatial and demographic dominance in the rest of the territory. Territorial exchanges ("land swaps") on the order of magnitude of 3–4 percent, as proposed by Palestinian President Mahmoud Abbas to US special envoy George Mitchell in 2010,[1] would allow for Israel's annexation of the major settlement blocs (Ma'ale Adumim, Gush Etzion, Givat Zeev, Modi'in 'Ilit, Western Samaria, and the Jewish areas of East Jerusalem—but excluding Ariel) and make separation possible at a reasonable national cost.

හ෴

* *Editor's note:* "Judea and Samaria" is the official Israeli government designation for what is internationally termed the West Bank, excluding East Jerusalem. The "Green Line" refers to the pre-June 1967 armistice boundary established in 1949, now recognized by the International Court of Justice as the legal border of the State of Israel.

[§] *Editor's note:* The Oslo II Accord (1995) divided the West Bank into territories under Palestinian civil and military jurisdiction (Area A), Palestinian civil and Israeli military jurisdiction (Area B), and Israeli civil and military jurisdiction (Area C—approximately 60 percent of the West Bank). See Chronology and Glossary.

[1] Charles Levinson, "Palestinians Offer Wider Concessions on Land," *Wall Street Journal* (21 May 2010).

Gideon Levy

The two-state solution was and remains the most reasonable, just, and sensible historic compromise. Two peoples fighting for one piece of land: justice mandates partition. There is only one problem with this solution: it can no longer be implemented. The settlement enterprise, established to thwart forever the possibility of partition, has reached such an extent that it can without immodesty claim victory. The settlers have won. One needs to recognize this, however painful it may be. More than 600,000 settlers will not now or in the future be removed from their homes. Yet without such mass removal, there is no viable Palestinian state, and more important, there is no justice.

Justice is not merely an intrinsic good; it is a practical imperative. A solution which does not afford both sides a feeling of having reached a fair compromise cannot last. The establishment of a Palestinian state on a mere portion of the territories occupied by Israel would never give Palestinians that sense of justice and dignity which alone forms the psychological basis for a sustainable peace. Therefore, beyond being unjust, such a "solution" would also be impractical and pointless. It might yield another piece of paper, another Oslo Accord,* but a solution it would not be.

Numbers and statistics are important. But there are also collective symbols at stake. The Green Line is the minimum the Palestinians can with dignity accept, and there is no other way. Any encroachment on it—to leave a single settlement intact—would amount to rewarding those who have undermined international law and violated it so crudely, those convinced that the Palestinians have no rights in this land, and those who have done and are willing to do everything to deny them their rights. Given the moral, practical, and legal record of the settlement enterprise, and given the settlers' history of violence and abusive treatment of their neighbors, any house or outpost remaining intact in the West Bank would represent a daily insult, a gaping wound which would not heal.

---

* *Editor's note:* See Glossary.

In 1948, Palestinians lost 78 percent of their country forever. Their fight now is for the leftovers. They cannot compromise on these leftovers. They should not compromise on these leftovers. It is unjust to even try to demand this from them. The Occupied Territories are recognized by all states of the world as Palestinian, and there are no grounds to bite into them beyond that which was already taken seventy years ago. Israel's territorial greed must come to an end. If the settlements are a violation of international law, as they are, then they should be undone, to the last one. Crimes are crimes. There is no retroactive legitimation—not for murder, not for rape, and not for land grab. The settlements were born in sin, and only by undoing them can some sense of rectification of the historic injustice be granted. The Palestinians are entitled at least to that, after the decades of shocking ill-treatment they have endured.

Land swaps are the only solution for squaring the ideal of partition with the fact of the settlements—yet they are no solution at all. No Palestinian farmer would agree to exchange the land of his ancestors for the Halutza Sands (on the Gaza border). Their connection to the land and to their lands is deeper than any compromise put forward by experts who would find mathematical formulae of fictitious Justice.

If Israel wants to reach a just solution, which may even bring about peace, it needs to abandon its greediness, its experts' quibbling, and its arsenal of sophisticated algorithms. The pre-June 1967 borders, with no ifs and no buts, are the necessary minimum. Unfortunately, this solution cannot be seen on the horizon. And so now is the time to deal with what is possible, rather than with that which has been lost forever.

Shaul Arieli

Very few people believe it is possible to base the resolution of the Israeli-Palestinian conflict on justice, since each side believes its cause is the just one and that its claim to all of Eretz Yisrael* or Palestine has political, legal, historical, and moral validity. Few believe it is possible to truly forge a common narrative based on reconciliation, or on an honest and heartfelt recognition by each side of the other's right to self-determination in the land.

Instead, plausible visions of a resolution of the conflict are based on compromise and territorial partition, in which each side obtains only "half of what it desires," but is still able to preserve its national narrative and its territorial dreams. The Peel Commission concluded already in 1937 that a struggle between two national movements whose claims are valid and cannot be reconciled was solvable only by partition.[§] The justification for compromise by the two sides rests on what I call "the no-alternative realization." That is, one side or both realizes that they cannot attain or maintain their most important national interests without reaching a compromise with the other. For Israeli Jews, the overriding interest is to maintain a democratic state for the Jewish people; for the Palestinians, to establish an independent state.

The United Nations Special Commission that recommend partition in 1947 reiterated that the premise for partition was that Arab and Jewish national claims to Palestine were each valid and yet mutually irreconcilable. The resolution also stated that partition was the most practical of all the proposals put forward, and would make it possible to satisfy some of the demands and national aspirations of each side. The Zionist movement agreed to partition (even if only tactically) in 1937. The Palestinians agreed to it in 1988, as recalled by President Abbas: "The opportunity for the 1947 partition was lost, and before that the opportunity for partition by the Peel Commission had been lost. But we do not want to lose another opportunity. Therefore, we have accepted the

* *Editor's note:* Hebrew for the "Land of Israel."

§ *Editor's note:* The Peel Commission was appointed by the British government to investigate the "underlying causes" of the 1936 Arab Revolt. Its Report, published in July 1937, recommended the partition of Palestine into a Jewish state and an Arab area to be united with Transjordan.

position of 1948 and 1967, which includes no more than 22 percent of historical Palestine."[2]

A final status agreement between Israel and the Palestine Liberation Organization (PLO) must therefore be based on the common interpretation of UN Security Council Resolution 242, at the heart of which is the formula, *all the territories in exchange for peace*. That is, in the context of a peace settlement, a Palestinian state will be established on the entirety of the West Bank, East Jerusalem, and the Gaza Strip. However, the demographic reality in the West Bank together with Israel's difficulty in removing large numbers of settlers have given rise to the concept of land swaps—reciprocal exchanges of territory—which would permit both sides to be smart as well as just.

Land swaps on the order of 4 percent of the occupied territory, as previously offered to Israel by Abbas, would enable Israel to retain more than 80 percent of the settlers living beyond the Green Line in their homes and under Israeli sovereignty. This would eliminate the politically difficult requirement for Israel to remove some 600,000 Israelis to implement a peace agreement; instead, Israel would have to manage the evacuation and resettlement of fewer than 150,000. To be clear, the Israeli and Palestinian proposals for land swaps do not include the Halutza Sands (these were offered in the Beilin-Abu Mazen Agreement of 1995), but rather arable lands belonging to kibbutzim and moshavim in the Western Negev, Emek HaMa'ayanot in the Beit Shean Valley, and the Lakhish area, which the Palestinians have in past negotiations agreed amount to a fair exchange.

In this way, as part of a permanent status agreement based on the territorial parameters established in the Annapolis talks of 2007–8 (i.e., the pre-June 1967 lines as the basis, with agreed-upon 1:1 land swaps), the Palestinians will be able to establish their state on 22 percent of "historical Palestine" and even benefit from a corridor connecting the West Bank and Gaza Strip. The total area of the future State of Palestine would amount to 6,205km^2, as agreed between Abbas and Israeli Prime Minister Ehud Olmert.

---

[2] Interview, *Al-Arabiyeh* (23 April 2008).

That was Israel's position in 2008. Prime Minister Benjamin Netanyahu, who went back on this agreement, agreed in 2014 to the pre-June 1967 lines as the basis, but not to any specific ratio of land swaps. This hurdle will have to be cleared again, but it is not too high for any prime minister who wishes to resolve the conflict.

The settlement enterprise has not yet reached proportions that would physically torpedo the two-state solution. As explained, the geographic and spatial dominance of the settlements is restricted to the central "blocs." These, without Ariel and Qedumim, span just 4 percent of the territory and do not harm Palestinian contiguity or fabric of life. In the rest of the territory, there is clear Arab dominance.

Furthermore, the settlement enterprise is steadily declining, because Israeli Jews vote differently with their feet than with their ballots. Over the past two decades, the settlement project has become in effect the enterprise of a single social sector: the national-religious-messianic bloc. Israeli Central Bureau of Statistics (CBS) data chart a steady and dramatic decline in rates of settlement population growth, from 10.2 percent in 1995 to 4 percent in 2015. Around 70 percent of this comes from natural growth within the settlements. This ratio is the inverse of that which prevailed in 1995, when 70 percent of the growth came from Israeli migration east of the Green Line. Most of the natural growth takes place in the two ultra-Orthodox cities, Modi'in 'Ilit and Beitar 'Ilit, whose residents consider themselves "settlers by compulsion" (these cities were built to solve a housing crisis faced by the ultra-Orthodox sector in Israel). Both are located on the Green Line, and under every proposal, Israeli and Palestinian, will be annexed to the State of Israel.

Many of the secular settlements are stagnant. Ariel, the smallest Jewish city in the Territories, has not increased its population in twenty years. Population growth in Ma'ale Adumim is lower than the average annual growth in Israel. The same holds for the Jewish neighborhoods of East Jerusalem. Some of the secular settlements have witnessed an absolute decrease in the number of their residents. For example, only three of every four inhabitants of Ma'ale Ephraim who resided in the city in 2009 still reside there today. Aside from the two ultra-Orthodox cities, the only communities which are still growing, in low absolute numbers, are the national-religious settlements that profit from unprecedented benefits and subsidies. But these cannot have a significant impact on the demographic balance or on the spatial control of the West Bank. The socioeconomic index report recently published by the CBS demonstrates that, overall, the Jewish presence in the West Bank is becoming weaker. This is particularly evident in the isolated settlements (Kiryat Arba, for example, has become poorer over time, and is now placed by the CBS in the same socioeconomic category as the Arab and ultra-Orthodox communities in Israel), while those which are close to the Green Line, and which will be annexed to Israel, remain strong and wealthy.

In sum, the physical dimensions of the settlement enterprise do not threaten the feasibility of the two-state solution. Israel does not have to either withdraw to the Green Line or remove all Israeli residents of the West Bank to enable the establishment of a contiguous Palestinian state. The land swaps accepted by the Palestinian leadership would allow most Israeli settlers to remain in their homes under Israeli sovereignty, and compensate the Palestinians with similarly-sized land, without harming Palestinian contiguity or fabric of life. The trends on the ground over the past two decades have only strengthened this conclusion.

ꙮ

Gideon Levy

Shaul Arieli's response raises two key points. First, that a land swap is possible and acceptable to the Palestinian leadership, and that this would allow for the establishment of a Palestinian state without requiring Israel to evacuate a politically infeasible number of settlers. Second, that the remaining settlers would pose no physical obstacle to the establishment of a Palestinian state. I will address these points in turn.

I do not represent the Palestinians and have no idea what they would accept or reject. I am trying to see whether there is scope for an agreement that is not only practical, but also just. In this correspondence, I have argued that without a certain degree of justice, and without a genuine sense that justice has been done, no agreement will last. Arieli claims that a land swap proposal was accepted by the Palestinian leadership. He presumably means to say that the Palestinian leadership agreed to Israel's annexation of the largest settlement blocs, rather than insisting on a full Israeli withdrawal to the pre-June 1967 border. I have never heard a Palestinian leader declare he was willing to let Gush Etzion and Ma'ale Adumim remain. On the contrary: let Arieli provide one quote of a Palestinian statesman proclaiming, "Efrat forever!" Nor have I heard an Israeli statesman in any position of power pledge to dismantle Ariel or the Jordan Valley settlements. It is unclear what precise map Arieli is proposing. But Israel's definition of "settlement bloc" is notoriously elastic: every year the blocs get bigger. Ariel has already been incorporated into them. To many Israelis, perhaps most of them, the Jordan Valley has the same status, and perhaps the South Hebron Hills as well. On the area of Havat Gilad, which may be dismantled, it would be hard to build a state.

Even if the Palestinians are compensated with alternative lands, I do not foresee circumstances in which they will agree that between East Jerusalem, Bethlehem, and Hebron—their cities—tens of thousands of Jewish settlers could remain. But even if they do agree, and even if they are happy with the alternative land they receive in compensation, and even if this land is not the Halutza Sands, as claimed by Arieli, such an agreement will not last. You cannot have a "state" held together with bridges and underground tunnels. Such arrangements may be good for map rooms and lecture halls, but not for torn and bleeding reality, heavy with trauma, burdened by a century of fear and hatred which must somehow be released.

To build trust as well as belief in peace, Israel should present the Palestinians with another map. A map in which at least 22 percent of their land is completely liberated from the yoke of the occupier. A map in which the occupier does not continue to lurk above tunnels and slink below bridges, and in which villages and towns need not be "swapped" to permit Israel to retain its ill-gotten spoils. A map in which what remains of Palestinian territory stays Palestinian, in the fullest and most genuine sense. Nothing less than this will heal the wounds.

Arieli maintains that the settlements pose no physical obstacle to the establishment of a Palestinian state. Even if he proves this with maps and other data, he cannot ignore the formidable *political* obstacle the settlers now represent. Israeli society is hurtling at light-speed towards its religious, nationalist, messianic, violent, and racist extremes. The current government is the most extremist in Israel's history. The settlers have always been the strongest power lobby in Israeli politics, milking all governments since the 1970s and even terrorizing the Israeli military. They are only getting stronger. They have now established a political bloc—the most potent in the Knesset—that is able to veto the dismantling of any settlement and mandate continued settlement construction. See how the Government of Israel surrendered on its knees before the handful of Amona settlers—all of forty families—even when the government was equipped with a Supreme Court ruling that decreed their removal.*

No serious countervailing force exists. There is no parliamentary opposition nor active civil society on the question of the Palestinians. With the exception of a few small, brave, and determined groups, there is no opposition to the occupation in Israel. Worse: the occupation is not even on the agenda of Israeli society. In the past two election campaigns, hardly anyone mentioned the occupation; it was as if it did not exist. There is no plausible scenario in which this trend will be halted or reversed in the coming years. Israelis are too brainwashed, and life is too good.

---

* *Editor's note:* In February 2017, the Israeli government evacuated the illegal outpost of Amona in the West Bank. (For "outpost," see Glossary.) The evacuation had been ordered by the High Court of Justice in 2014, but its implementation was repeatedly delayed. The government and settlers eventually reached a deal in which evacuated families would be relocated within the West Bank and receive generous financial compensation.

Moreover, one cannot overlook the results of the 2016 US elections and trends in Europe, which, like Israel, is racing towards its nationalist and anti-Muslim right. These developments do not augur a change of course towards increased international pressure on Israel to dismantle settlements and accept two-states. On the contrary: under President Donald Trump, US rhetoric on the two-state solution has increasingly aligned with its long-standing opposition in practice. Meanwhile, the Palestinians have never been so divided and isolated. The Arab states have abandoned them, while Europe—absorbed in immigration problems, Islamophobia, and the Syrian crisis—has lost interest.

In this atmosphere, it is delirious to imagine that an Israeli statesman would want or be able to evacuate tens of thousands of settlers, the sufficient number according to Arieli, or hundreds of thousands, the number I am convinced one would have to remove.

ꟸ

Shaul Arieli

It is unfortunate that my friend Gideon Levy holds fast to arguments which I have already addressed. I would like to briefly recapitulate the essential points.

The State of Palestine will comprise 22 percent of Mandatory Palestine/ Eretz Yisrael, just as President Abbas proposed: "we have accepted the partition of 1948 and 1967, which includes no more than 22 percent of historical Palestine." That is, an independent state on an area of 6,205km^2, as agreed in Annapolis (2007–8), bordering on Israel, Jordan, and Egypt.

This would entail a land swap of up to 4 percent of occupied territory. This number is based on Abbas's position as conveyed to US special envoy Mitchell in 2010, as well as to Secretary of State John Kerry. Contrary to Levy's fears, a land swap of 4 percent need not create a state held together by bridges and tunnels; Palestinian and Israeli contiguity would be completely maintained.

The central blocs that would be swapped are Gush Etzion, Ma'ale Adumim, Givat Zeev, Modi'in 'Ilit, Western Samaria, and the Jewish neighborhoods of Jerusalem. Ariel is not included in these blocs, despite being part of the Palestinian proposal at Taba in 2001, since this would violate Palestinian contiguity. I am aware of the need for a stable border and of its importance to the reconciliation process. I recommend that Levy examine the proposals made by the Palestinian delegations to Taba and Annapolis. There he will find detailed exactly what the Palestinians proposed during the formal negotiations, even if no Palestinian leader has bothered to tell him this.

Therefore, one can clearly state that the two-state solution is physically feasible with respect to territory, Jerusalem, security, and borders.

Now to politics. I agree with Levy that the political feasibility of implementing this agreement is at this time very low. This is due primarily to Prime Minister Netanyahu's retreat from the negotiating parameters established in Annapolis and to the influence within his government of the nationalist-messianic (and, in some respects, fascistic) tendency in Israeli politics.

The deep divisions on the Palestinian side—Gaza-West Bank, Hamas-Fatah, Abbas-Dahlan*—constitute a further obstacle. There is no single Palestinian address vis-á-vis Israel and the international community. This casts doubts on the Palestinians' ability to reach an agreement, and even more so on their ability to implement and abide by one.

I agree, moreover, that Israeli public opinion is not favorable to reaching a two-state solution. This is due to the emergence within the Israeli public sphere of a discourse based on intimidation, incitement, lies, and an ethos of conflict. Without a drastic change in this discourse, no Israeli leader will be able to carry out the painful steps and concessions required for a solution based on compromise rather than Justice.

---

* *Editor's note:* Muhammad Dahlan was a senior Fatah and Palestinian government official until he was forced into exile and expelled from the party's ruling body in 2011.

The international community has played a decisive role in this conflict. It must now save both sides from themselves and muster all its strength to present both parties with a concrete framework for conducting negotiations on a final status agreement. I would like to emphasize by way of conclusion that a willingness from both parties to reach a final-status agreement must be based on the understanding that neither can subdue the other, but can at most force the continuation of a bloody and exhausting war of attrition. For each party, securing its basic interests—for Israel, a secure and democratic state with a Jewish majority; for Palestine, an independent state—requires adopting a compromise solution within a final-status agreement based on the well-known parameters:

- the pre-June 1967 lines as the territorial basis with land swaps on a 1:1 ratio;
- two capitals in Jerusalem;
- a demilitarized Palestinian state;
- a just and agreed solution to the Palestinian refugee question.

Such an agreement would stand a chance of leading both parties, at the end of a long process, to genuine reconciliation and an honest recognition of each side's right to a state in Eretz Yisrael/Palestine. It remains achievable, and it is better for everyone that it be implemented sooner rather than later.

Gideon Levy

I would love to endorse Shaul Arieli's plan. I wish it were possible. I believe it is no longer possible. If someone proves to me that it is still possible, I shall gladly admit to my mistake. Arieli, too, should agree that at some point his plan will no longer be feasible. Thus, our dispute is over timing; it does not concern key principles.

When the window of opportunity for a two-state solution closes—I believe it has already, while Arieli thinks not—those opposed to the status quo will have to consider the alternative. There is only one: a single state, the one which has existed in practice for more than fifty years. We should now begin the struggle over the nature of this already-existing regime.

Democracy or apartheid. I believe these are the only options remaining.

RESPONSE:

SAVING THE PARTIES FROM THEMSELVES

Shlomo Ben-Ami

Shaul Arieli should be commended for his meticulous research into the spatial contours of Israel's settlement expansion in Palestinian lands. His portrayal of the demographic decay of the settlement enterprise is truly eye-opening. The blocs of settlements in which more than 80 percent of the settlers are concentrated can still be swapped to allow for a 100 percent land restitution to the Palestinians. A benign separation between these two communities is still possible—but not for too long, he rightly warns.

Gideon Levy is not a possibilist. His is a moral perspective, heroically defended against the tremendous odds of an ethnocentric Israeli Zeitgeist. His

---

Shlomo Ben-Ami was Israel's Minister for Internal Security (1999–2000) and Foreign Minister (2000–2001). He is a historian of Spain and the Middle East and the author of *Scars of War, Wounds of Peace: The Israeli-Arab Tragedy* (2006).

peace plan, however, goes beyond what the Palestinians have already agreed to in practically every peace round of talks. Never did a Palestinian negotiator ask to receive back the territories entirely clean of settlements. They have always accepted the need to accommodate the changing demographic realities through a reasonable swap. This was the case in our Swedish talks with Abu Ala* in May 2000, and also in Taba, where we spoke of a 5 percent annexation while the Palestinians discussed between 2 and 4 percent. Nor did the Palestinians reject the proposal in the Clinton Peace Parameters (2000) to divide Jerusalem along ethnic lines, rather than on the borders stipulated by international law.

Peace agreements are not a simple implementation of international law. Peace requires defining a workable equilibrium between the fundamental requirements of the parties. Such a balance was embodied in Clinton's Parameters and in Ehud Olmert's 2008 peace proposals. Both were turned down by the Palestinian leadership not because they did not coincide with the requirements of international law but because the Palestinians wanted to tilt the equilibrium further to their side.

Levy is right to say that the settlements were born in sin. But while justice is an important component in peace agreements, this can never be an absolute and fundamentalist justice. Transitional justice is about reconciling moral and legal precepts with the political conditions surrounding the peace negotiations.

Sadly, this is an almost academic debate, conducted in the sterile zone of a resilient peace industry detached from increasingly desperate and disheartening political conditions. Both discussants eventually agree that this is the case. With peace plans and envoys coming and going, Israelis and Palestinians have finally come to share a common sentiment: both have become blasé about the prospects for a final settlement. The two-state solution is rapidly losing its appeal.

For the Israelis, a resolution of the conflict on these terms would entail a social and political earthquake of untold dimensions. It would mean a massive evacuation of settlers and a radical political realignment to deal with the threat of possible

---

* *Editor's note:* Ahmed Qurei, also known as Abu Ala, is a senior PLO and Fatah official who served as Palestinian prime minister between 2003 and 2006.

civil strife and perhaps even military disobedience. All this in order to return to a set of borders for which few Israelis feel nostalgia.

For the Palestinians, the chasm between the colossal tragedy of the *Nakba** and the poverty of the territorial solution, which would see a demilitarized Palestinian mini-state sandwiched between two hostile powers (Israel and Jordan), is bound to remain an open wound. Any resolution of the refugee problem that Israel might accept would be seen by the Palestinians as a betrayal of the constituent ethos of Palestinian nationalism. The State of Palestine would suffer from a serious deficit of legitimacy among the Palestinians themselves.

But the specter of a binational state, as it is now unfolding, is a greater nightmare. By blurring the borders between Israel and the Palestinian territories, Israel has created the conditions for a permanent state of civil war in which settlers, Palestinians, Israeli Jews, and Israeli Arabs—the latter seen by ever wider sectors of Israelis as a fifth column—find themselves trapped in a fatal embrace with no political exit in sight. The two-state solution represents the salvation of the Zionist project before it slides irreversibly into a South African situation that would not be susceptible to a South African solution.

For this reason, the Palestinian quest for self-determination is not the exclusive interest of the subjugated nation; the occupier's existence is also imperiled. Alas, the transformation of the Middle East strategic game, the changing agenda of global politics, a split Palestinian nation that has lost a common sense of purpose, and Israel's superior capacity for maneuver have diluted the salience of the Palestine question. A Palestinian state is today a more remote possibility than at any time since the start of the peace process twenty-five years ago.

Only a major cataclysm—peace breakthroughs in the Middle East have always followed conflagrations—or a robust international solution can save the parties from themselves. Why would the Iranian nuclear problem need a P5+1 framework and North Korea the so-called Six Party Talks but Palestine remain an American monopoly, in spite of Washington's proven incapacity to solve the problem single-handed?

---

* *Editor's note:* See Glossary.

RESPONSE:

THE SHRINKING TWO-STATE CONSTITUENCY

Dahlia Scheindlin

The political feasibility of the two-state solution depends in great measure on the interactive relationship between leaders and their publics. The bigger and more integrated into Israeli life the settlement enterprise becomes, the greater the electoral risk any Israeli leader takes in attempting to roll it back. This dynamic induces increasing numbers of politicians to focus on managing the conflict rather than working for its resolution. The Israeli public in turn infers from leaders' inaction that the country can tread water indefinitely—that peace is not truly necessary. This self-reinforcing interaction

---

Dahlia Scheindlin is a public opinion researcher and political advisor for electoral campaigns, governments, and civil society in Israel and more than a dozen other countries. She has expertise in public dynamics around conflict, negotiations, and post-conflict and transitional societies, and holds a PhD in Political Science from Tel Aviv University.

between risk-averse leaders and a complacent public is a powerful buttress for the status quo.

Notwithstanding outsiders' insistence on the two-state paradigm, it is increasingly difficult for people of the region to envision separation of Israelis and Palestinians. This is manifested in attitudes toward the principle of a two-state solution, opinions regarding the specific compromises on settlements that would be required in a two-state framework, and support for or opposition to the other key elements of that framework.

Support for the two-state solution

Among both Israelis and Palestinians, support for the principle of two-states has been declining since at least 2010 in small but steady increments. This context is key: lower support for the end goal means lower incentives to make the compromises required to get there.

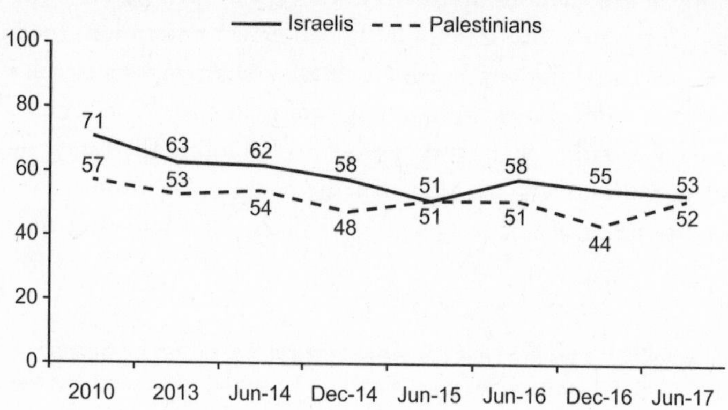

These findings call into question Shaul Arieli's assertion that, "For Israeli Jews, the overriding interest is to maintain a democratic state for the Jewish people; for the Palestinians, to establish an independent state." On the latter point, a December 2016 survey of Israelis and Palestinians found that just 44 percent of Palestinians now support the broad concept of a two-state solution, while a mere 42 percent support the detailed package of implementation.[1] A follow-up survey in June 2017 showed a rise in Palestinian support for the two-state solution concept to a bare majority, but as the graph above shows, the overall trend points downward, while support for the detailed package of implementation remained unchanged at just over 40 percent. These findings do not indicate an enthusiastic or stable majority for an independent state under the current circumstances.

Meanwhile, are Israeli Jews so committed to maintaining a democratic state? Support among Israeli Jews for a two-state solution has declined gradually but steadily over the past six years (see graph above). The December 2016 survey found that just 50 percent of Israeli Jews supported the two-state solution as a concept; in June 2017, support fell to 47 percent. Arab citizens of Israel generally show very high levels of support, which raises the total Israeli average to a majority.

Support in Israel for the detailed framework of implementation has also eroded. In June 2006, 55 percent of Israelis supported the Clinton-Geneva parameters;[2] in 2011, 53 percent of Israeli Jews and 58 percent of all Israelis supported a comprehensive two-state package on these terms.[3] In recent years,

---

[1] "The Palestinian-Israeli Pulse: A Joint Poll—Table of Findings," *Palestinian Center for Policy and Survey Research (PCPSR)* (December 2016). The Palestinian-Israeli Pulse survey was conducted by Khalil Shikaki for the Palestinian Center for Survey and Policy Research and Dahlia Scheindlin, together with the Tami Steinmetz Center for Peace Research, Tel Aviv University. Israeli sample: n=1207, margin of error +/-3 percent; Palestinian sample: n=1270, margin of error +/-3 percent.

[2] "Joint Palestinian-Israeli Public Opinion Poll—Poll #18: Strong Preference Among Palestinians and Israelis for a Comprehensive Settlement Over an Interim Political Track," *Harry S. Truman Research Institute for the Advancement of Peace and PCPSR* (25 December 2006), p. 16.

[3] "Joint Palestinian-Israeli Public Opinion Poll," *Harry S. Truman Research Institute for the Advancement of Peace and PCPSR* (December 2011), Question V11.

however, support has hovered just above or below the halfway mark, even after factoring in high Arab support. As of December 2016, only 41 percent of Israeli Jews supported the framework for two-state implementation, and the June 2017 follow-up survey registered further decline.[4]

This is not because Israelis are ignorant of what is happening. Surveys I conducted in 2016 and 2017 for the human rights groups B'Tselem and Gisha found surprising levels of awareness of the spread of settlements and the control exerted by Israel over Palestinian life.[5] Yet, other surveys of mine show that a final status accord is not at the top of Israeli priorities, but generally ranks fourth down the list. Combining knowledge with indifference, it is far from clear that withdrawal from the territories in order to secure Israeli democracy is perceived by many Israelis to be an overriding interest.

Attitudes towards settlements

Arieli argues that the two-state solution is still realistic because the settlement enterprise remains sufficiently contained geographically to enable a politically feasible withdrawal, while its demographic and socioeconomic growth have peaked, plateaued, and may be in decline. "Israeli Jews," Arieli observes, "vote differently with their feet than with their ballots."

Gideon Levy responds that we "cannot ignore the formidable political obstacle the settlers now represent. Israeli society is hurtling at light-speed towards its religious, nationalist, messianic, violent, and racist extremes." As evidence, he observes that the Israeli government is more extreme than ever, yet provokes no significant opposition. But Levy omits an essential point in support of his own argument: the settlers' political vision (if not quite their religion) has leaked into Israeli society within the Green Line.

---

[4] In June 2017, the Palestinian-Israeli Pulse joint survey found that just 32 percent of Israeli Jews support the full detailed package for implementing a two-state agreement. This was a marked decline from December 2016. Support among Arab-Israelis remained above 80 percent, bringing the level of support among all Israelis to 41 percent. See "Palestine-Israel Pulse," *PCPSR/Tami Steinmetz Center* (TAU, June 2017).

[5] Gisha, "10 Years into the Closure of Gaza: A New Public Opinion Poll Reveals," *gisha.org* (26 February 2017).

In the 2015 elections, the party that most closely represents settler ideology, Jewish Home, won 4.5 percent of the vote even in the Tel Aviv suburb of Givatayim. It received 7 percent in Dimona and in Beersheva and 11 percent in Raanana—all cities in the heart of Israel proper. These numbers are close to, or exceed, the national vote share for Jewish Home (6.87 percent). Meanwhile, the ruling Likud Party has come under the influence of settler leaders, settlers, or those identified with settler ideology in the party's Knesset faction, as well as pro-settler party members themselves.* Of course, Likud takes large portions of its support from cities and towns inside Israel; even in liberal Tel Aviv, over one-fifth voted in 2015 for either Likud or Jewish Home.[6]

In other words, Israelis don't *have* to "vote with their feet" by becoming settlers—a large number vote with ballots, because they trust the parties to protect the settlements on their behalf. This is the first key point about Israeli attitudes towards settlement evacuation: many vote for parties who they probably hope will never ask that question.

The second issue concerns what Israeli Jews think about settlement evacuation. When presented with the following item in a proposed peace agreement: "a Palestinian state in the West Bank, territorial swaps to annex settlement blocs, all the rest will be evacuated"—just 48 percent of Israeli Jews (together with more than 60 percent of Arabs) express support.[7]

Nearly three-quarters of the Israeli right opposes such an item in an agreement, while 89 percent of the left and some 60 percent of centrists support it.

---

* *Editor's note:* For the Jewish Home and Likud parties, see Glossary.

[6] Results of Israel's election by region, from the Israeli Central Election Committee website.

[7] The full question related to settlements included in the "package" people are asked to assess is as follows: "The Palestinian state will be established in the entirety of Judea Samaria and the Gaza strip territories, except for several large blocks of settlements which will be annexed to Israel and will not exceed 3% of the size of West Bank. Israel will evacuate all other settlements. The Palestinians will receive in return territory of similar size along the Gaza strip. Do you agree or disagree with this item?" Each item is asked separately and then respondents are asked whether they support or oppose the package as a whole. "Palestinian and Israeli Pulse," *PCPSR* (December 2016).

(About 40–45 percent of Israelis self-define as right-wing; the center and left together reach approximately the same portion, with one-fifth at most defining themselves as "left".) In sum, settlements rank among the most polarizing issues in Israel, essentially defining "left" and "right."

Political leaders tend to deal with controversy through evasion or manipulation. To forge ahead with risky policies and seek to shift public opinion in their favor takes a strength of leadership that no politician in Israel is currently demonstrating.

It's not just settlements

Polarization on settlements might also be read as an opportunity by a leader determined to advance compromise; after all, roughly half the population supports the approach of swaps, annexation, and evacuation.

But public attitudes towards other items in the two-state package present greater obstacles. There has never been a majority in Israel for the two-state division of Jerusalem. As of the June 2017 survey cited above, three-quarters of Jews opposed the item stating that Israel would have its capital in the West and Palestinians in East Jerusalem, while two-thirds of Arab-Israelis support this. Notably, 70 percent of Palestinians reject the same item.

Israeli opposition to compromise on the Palestinian refugees is even greater. The proposals mooted at Camp David and in the Geneva Initiative involve options for Palestinian refugees ranging from return to the future Palestinian state, remaining in a third country, immigrating to a third country, a small number returning to Israel at Israeli discretion, and compensation. This "package" approach to resolving Palestinian refugee claims is supported by just 20 percent of Jews; fully 80 percent reject it. Of the total Israeli population, two-thirds of Israelis reject the refugee item (just over half of Palestinians support it).

Notwithstanding widespread opposition to the likely two-state compromise on these items (Jerusalem, refugees), surveys have, at times, registered majority support among Israelis for the detailed two-state package, even when those items are included. This indicates a gestalt effect whereby the public accepts specific compromises it dislikes for the sake of a comprehensive agreement it favors. However, as noted earlier, the most recent two surveys have seen a decline in support for the full package to less than half of Israeli Jews.

Divided opinion, as exists on the question of settlements, presents politicians with a strategic dilemma. But a strong rejectionist majority, as prevails on two other core components of the two-state package, recommends a clearer course of action for all but the visionaries: inaction.

Conclusion and alternatives

Levy concludes that there are only two options remaining: democracy or apartheid. These are often held to correspond with two-states or one (respectively). But this conclusion overlooks emerging political frameworks that are increasingly being considered as options by both the left and the right.

Some on the left have proposed a confederation that would combine elements of both one- and two-state frameworks. Polling I conducted for *+972 Magazine* in late 2014 found that, after all the basic elements of a confederation approach were explained, 56 percent of Israeli respondents supported it.[8] On the right, the idea of annexation is rapidly gaining momentum. In January 2016, 45 percent of Jews expressed support for annexing all the Palestinian territories,[9] while in the December 2016 survey, support for annexation of certain areas without giving full rights to the Palestinians stood at an ominous 31 percent—nearly one-third—of Israeli Jews (Arabs were not asked).

As of today, the only plan the Israeli public appears to have fully embraced is complacency. In two separate surveys from 2010 and 2014, nearly two-thirds of Israeli Jews I asked chose a statement that this is not the time for a final status agreement, over an opposing position that Israel is at risk of becoming a binational state. Still, in 2016, the Peace Index found that only a third of

---

[8] Dahlia Scheindlin, "Are Israelis Ready for a Confederated Two-State Solution?" *+972 Magazine* (4 January 2015).

[9] "Peace Index," *Tel Aviv University and the Israel Democracy Institute* (January 2016). N=600. The question did not elaborate further and was asked only of Jews.

Jews believed that Israel can continue with the conflict indefinitely. Perhaps the direction is changing. Israeli politicians and the public may finally be moving—but if so, it appears they are inching away from, rather than closer to, a traditional two-state solution.

Ironically, despite the erosion in support, two-states is still favored by more Israelis and Palestinians than any other solution. If the top political leaders on both sides were to get behind such an agreement, historical precedent suggests that public opinion might be brought to accept it. During the Camp David negotiations in the summer of 2000, research I conducted with Ehud Barak's pollster Stanley Greenberg found incremental increases in support among Israelis for even the most sensitive compromises—especially when we added a clause that included the phrase "end of the conflict" and referenced an end to all further claims on either side.[10] We attributed this to respondents' belief that an agreement was truly within reach; this created a sense of momentum which encouraged more people to support a deal.

Two further precedents strengthen the point. Prior to the Oslo I Accord (1993), Israeli polling showed a bare minimum in support of establishing a Palestinian state. This crept up during the first intifada but still stood at under 30 percent in 1992.[11] Following the Oslo Accords, throughout the turbulent and traumatic years of the 1990s, support climbed steadily upwards, eventually reaching a majority that persisted even during the worst years of the second intifada.[12]

Finally, and further back, opinion surveys from the 1970s showed a large majority of Israelis opposing the return of the Sinai to Egypt. But following the signing of the Camp David peace treaty in 1979, support for withdrawal rose dramatically. Since the starting level of support for a two-state solution in general is significantly higher at present, it is fair to speculate that the Israeli

---

[10] Stanley Greenberg, *Dispatches from the War Room: In the Trenches with Five Extraordinary World Leaders* (New York, NY: Thomas Dunne Books/St. Martin's Press, 2009).

[11] Yehuda Ben Meir and Olena Bagno-Moldavsky, "Vox Populi: Trends in Israeli Public Opinion on National Security 2004–2009," *Institute for National Security Studies* (November 2010), p. 76.

[12] Ibid.

public might well get behind such an agreement should conducive circumstances arise.

It is not a fool-proof prediction. Peace deals in Cyprus (2004) and Colombia (2016) failed to pass popular referendums, confounding expectations that optimism would sweep public sentiment in favor of ending those protracted conflicts. But what can be said with certainty is that without courageous, visionary, or at the very least interest-driven leadership advancing an agreement, the world and the region will not know peace.

SETTLEMENTS II: TECHNICAL ASPECTS

RESPONSE TO SHAUL ARIELI: IT'S QUALITY, NOT JUST QUANTITY

Jan de Jong

It is increasingly argued that a two-state solution to the Israel-Palestine conflict is no longer feasible. The cause of death is said to be Israel's extensive settlement infrastructure in the West Bank and the more than 600,000 settlers who reside there. Shaul Arieli disputes this on the basis that a two-state solution would not require the evacuation of every settlement and settler. He argues, instead, that most of the settlers can remain in place and under Israeli sovereignty, while still permitting the establishment of a Palestinian state on territory free of Israeli settlements and encompassing the full area

---

Jan de Jong is a Strategic Development Planner who was a chief consultant of the Arab Jerusalem Rehabilitation Project (Passia, Jerusalem–2000), the PLO Negotiations Affairs Department (2000–2006), and the Office of the Quartet Representative in Jerusalem (2013). He was also a team leader commissioned to evaluate European land development programs in the Palestinian Territories (2012–2014).

designated for the exercise of Palestinian self-determination by the international community.[1]

Arieli's proposal

The key to understanding Arieli's position is to recognize the patterns he describes by which settlements are spread over the land in relation to population size and to distance from the pre-June 1967 boundary.

A glance at the map* shows that, indeed, some three-quarters of Israeli settlers reside relatively close to the Green Line. Arieli argues that by just slightly shifting this boundary eastward, those settler-residences can be "taken out" of Palestinian territory, while a similar adjustment elsewhere in the other direction would compensate the Palestinians with uninhabited land from Israel of equal size. A land swap of this sort would require exchanging no more than 4 percent of the Occupied Palestinian Territory (OPT).

This seemingly minute boundary modification would leave just a quarter of Israeli settlers (some 125,000) to be evacuated. This remains a formidable task. Most of these residences comprise tiny bedroom-communities, but they also include about a dozen township-settlements of which Ariel in the West Bank's center is the largest. Some of the smaller settlements, notably Kiryat Arba and Shilo, are considered Jewish religious-patrimonial sites and would likely fiercely resist evacuation. But such considerations need not fundamentally detract from Arieli's downsizing vision. Most settlers would be well accommodated, becoming part of Israel proper, while the Palestinians would at long last live in settler-free territory, in which their sovereign statehood could no longer be disputed or denied. So, eureka? Could this plan break the diplomatic deadlock, and form the basis for a permanent status agreement?

---

* *Editor's note:* This exchange should be read in consultation with the maps on pp. 93–96.

[1] That is, all of the West Bank, including Israeli-annexed East Jerusalem, and the Gaza Strip, in accordance with UN Security Council Resolution 242.

Arieli assures that "the Palestinians will be able to establish their state on 22 percent of 'historical Palestine'" and that "the 4 percent land exchanges do not harm Palestinian contiguity or fabric of life." The first assurance is quantitative and can be verified. An independent check of Arieli's projections through Geographic Information Systems (GIS) technology confirms that from a numerical and spatial point of view his numbers are correct.

The second assurance is qualitative and requires interpretation and judgment. Assessing it requires taking a critical look at those 4 percent land exchanges on both sides of the pre-June 1967 boundary. What are the characteristics of those lands, apart from their equality in size? Even a casual glance through the lens of Google Earth reveals dramatic differences.

Most of the lands to be ceded by the Palestinians are in the West Bank's urban core, stretching between Nablus and Hebron with Greater Arab Jerusalem as its metropolitan center. The latter, encompassing the whole Palestinian agglomeration between Ramallah and Bethlehem, is the crucial hub of West Bank residences, offices, utilities, and industrial and commercial estates, as well as of highways reaching out to provincial and international hinterlands.

Such areas are essential and indispensable for national economies, especially when they are transitioning from low productivity rural societies to higher value service-sector economies. They are how neighboring states like Jordan, Lebanon, and also Israel are securing their socioeconomic futures—without Amman, Beirut, and Tel Aviv, the viability of Jordan, Lebanon, and Israel would be in jeopardy. Equivalently, without an intact Arab Jerusalem metropolis, Palestinian national viability is severely, perhaps fatally, compromised.

Under Arieli's proposal, most of this indispensable metropolitan center is to be ceded to Israel in exchange for utterly peripheral lands scattered at the outer margins of the Palestinian territories.

Cities and commercial and industrial enterprises will not be built on those lands, because they would be too remote from the country's socioeconomic core. Such peripheries can at most make a limited local contribution to sectors like agriculture and forestry, which contribute only marginally to Palestine's gross national income.

In other words: although altogether equal in size, these lands are in every other respect radically unequal. What Palestine would cede to Israel is vital for its statehood; what it would acquire in return is irrelevant to that prospect.

It is essential to take a closer look at the areas of the West Bank demanded by Israel. Arieli's map* represents an evolution from the so-called Geneva Initiative (2003), perhaps the best-known plan to date to win a degree of tentative support from Israelis, Palestinians, and the international community.[2] This unusually broad support reflected Geneva's promise of a historic "land for peace" compromise with apparently minimal territorial implications.

The Geneva Map§ postulated land swaps of 2.2 percent of the Palestinian territories. In his proposal, Arieli has felt compelled to double this to 4 percent. In light of the remaining 96 percent, this may seem a negligible difference. But as we'll see, it dramatically exacerbates the adverse effects of the initial option, which the Palestinians already found problematic.

Arieli took the Geneva proposal's original base pattern as his point of departure. It shows the larger settlement suburbs in and around Jerusalem fragmenting, encircling, and constricting the urban fabric of Greater Arab Jerusalem from all directions. The settlement "finger" of Ramot-Givon closes in from the North-West, while Neve Yaakov-Pisgat Zeev and Ma'ale Adumim hem it in from the North and East.

In the South, a belt of settlement suburbs centered on Gilo and Har Homa connects to those of the Etzion bloc, suffocating the Palestinian city of Bethlehem. It is a pattern that can be visualized in the form of an outstretched

---

* *Editor's note:* See p. 94.

§ *Editor's note:* See p. 93.

[2] Arieli was himself a co-founder of the Geneva Initiative.

hand, with settlement-fingers squeezing, compressing, and deforming Arab Jerusalem underneath.

What remains of Arab Jerusalem between those fingers is the negative image of Israeli Jerusalem. It is a cluster of fragmented, ghettoized quarters, deprived of everything that is essential for city-survival: urban cohesion, growing space for residents, commercial and industrial areas, and adequate connections to city-hinterlands.

These deficiencies are not addressed in Arieli's proposal. The usual assumption is that the projected boundary alteration would induce a shift of Palestine's urban and metropolitan heart toward Ramallah, where space would be available. Likewise, a redirection of road trajectories around the settlement fingers would ensure Palestinian transportation contiguity.

These assumptions are highly contentious. The projected shifts would further marginalize and disintegrate the Palestinian urban fabric, not just in the center but also in the outer districts.

Ramallah has the capacity to serve as a provincial city. But it can never make up for the loss of the agglomeration of Greater Arab Jerusalem. Nor can any projected Palestinian road contiguity compensate for the connective capacity of Greater Arab Jerusalem as the West Bank's crucial hub and crossroads. Ramallah would have adequate road links only to the West Bank's North; it would leave the southern districts isolated.[3]

On an Excel spreadsheet, Arieli's numbers are promising. Transposed to a map, the plan is discomforting, even disturbing. It depicts the Palestinian urban heart of Greater Arab Jerusalem hollowed out as the West Bank's vital center. It cuts away essential foundations for viable Palestinian statehood, both spatially and socioeconomically. These spheres are closely interrelated. Without relieving Arab Jerusalem's fragmentation and encirclement by Israeli settlements, it cannot fulfil its metropolitan potential. Nor can

[3] Road links from Ramallah to southern regions would have to descend from higher/level ground far eastward over extremely difficult terrain (e.g., today's Wadi Nar). It would multiply distance by a factor of two or three and substantially increase transportation costs.

it regain its critical crossroads-capacity by which the Palestinian regions are connected. Arieli has hardly if ever been challenged on these issues. Discussion of Palestinian statehood tends to focus on territorial contiguity, but socioeconomic viability is a no less critical foundation.

While the latter aspect is absent from Arieli's proposal, he suggests that the former requirement—territorial contiguity—would be realized in the form of connected Palestinian territory on 96 percent of the West Bank. But without effective road links running through metropolitan Greater Arab Jerusalem, this contiguity would be illusory. Traveling from one part of the West Bank to another would often require huge detours to and from dead-end destinations, frequently over difficult terrain (for example around East Jerusalem). It would amount to restricted, sub-standard transportation contiguity only partly remediable by tunnels and bridges, of which the number is steadily growing.

Arieli's update of Geneva represents a drastic scale-jump in two vital respects. First, it adds considerable territorial "flesh" to the Jerusalem settlement-fingers described above, incorporating settlements like Bet Horon, Efrat, and Har Homa, and even the highly sensitive E1-expansion zone of Ma'ale Adumim. This comes at the expense of precious Palestinian urban growth space. Second, it extends the cross-border settlements east of Tel Aviv to include almost ten additional settlements, in the familiar settlement-finger pattern of Jerusalem.

Viewing these updated patterns through the prism of their aggregate effect reveals a crucial attribute. Around Jerusalem, the settlement-fingers proposed for annexation by Israel bisect the West Bank at its narrow waist east of the city. Palestinian contiguity fundamentally hangs on the single trunk route over the West Bank's hill spine. Squeezed from the West by Israel's land bridge to Jerusalem and from the East by steeply sloped terrain, only a narrow corridor is left to functionally connect the West Bank's North and South. It is precisely this narrow corridor that is blocked by the settlement blocs in and around Jerusalem.

In a similar fashion, the settlement-fingers east of Tel Aviv dramatically reduce Palestinian contiguity halfway between Ramallah and Nablus.

Together, these "finger"-systems form a two-pronged pincer which squeezes the Palestinian core district of Ramallah while effectively tearing the West Bank into three peripheral sections: one centered on the Northern city of Nablus, another around Ramallah in the middle, and a third around the city of Khalil (Hebron) in the South.

When Arieli asserts that this plan can be realized without harming Palestinian contiguity or fabric of life, he adds an important qualification. Implementation would be possible, he says, at a "reasonable national cost." By this he refers to costs for Israel (evacuating some 125,000 settlers); costs for Palestine are neither mentioned nor considered.

Arieli's proposal in context

Arieli defends his proposal in terms of one overriding benefit: the plan would achieve demographic separation of Palestinians from Israel behind fixed and recognized borders.

Indeed, Arieli's plan must be viewed within the perspective of the historical contest for land between Jewish settler state-building and the indigenous Palestinian population. This gave rise to a series of partition plans each of which reflected dramatic Palestinian and Arab defeats. The failed Palestinian uprising of 1936 eventually issued in the UN Partition Plan of 1947. This allocated less than half the country for Arab statehood, although Palestinians made up more than two-thirds of its population. The "*Nakba*" defeat of 1948–49 halved again the territory allotted for Arab sovereignty to just 22 percent of "historic" Palestine. The next defeat, in the June 1967 War, would have profound consequences. UN Resolution 242, issued several months after the war, upgraded the status of the 1949 ceasefire lines into a real border between two spheres of national sovereignty. This consecrated into international law the Arab territorial losses of 1948–49, while designating all areas conquered by Israel beyond the 1949 ceasefire lines "occupied" territories from which Israel was obliged to withdraw within the framework of a "land for peace" treaty.

Israel chose to ignore this formula and instead began colonizing the newly won territories. Initially it followed the guidelines of erstwhile military commander and cabinet minister Yigal Allon. Concerned to maintain Israel's character as a Jewish state, Allon recommended leaving the densely populated Palestinian areas for eventual transfer to Arab sovereignty. "Separation" became the key concept, and countless maps were drafted by Israeli institutions and officials over the next two decades showing how it might be achieved. None of these were acceptable in Palestine and in the Arab world, nor in the eyes of the radical Jewish settlers who began moving to the densely populated Palestinian interior in the late 1970s.

Paradoxically, the first Palestinian intifada (beginning December 1987) produced an outcome that was hailed, perhaps most of all by the international community, as a victory for reason and a step towards lasting peace: the Oslo Accords, signed in 1993 and 1995 by Israel and the PLO. But the Palestinian signature on these agreements represented an abandonment of the internationally recognized pre-June 1967 border separating two spheres of equal national sovereignty.

Under the Oslo framework, Palestinian sovereign statehood became subject to negotiated agreement on issues such as security, settlements, and Jerusalem, most of which were to be resolved by fixing an agreed, permanent status border. Determining the route of this border gave rise to a new series of option-maps, all of which bore the stamp of Oslo.

Probably the best known was that of the 2003 Geneva Initiative. It publicized the concept of "land swaps" as a seemingly convenient mechanism to achieve territorial and demographic separation at "reasonable national cost," requiring a minimal land exchange of just over 2 percent.

Today the Geneva Initiative is politically obsolete, if not in the principles it established then in the territorial dimensions it proposed. This is mainly the result of the so-called "Separation Barrier," whose construction began at roughly the same time the Geneva Initiative was presented.

Officially justified as a security measure, the Barrier carved out a trajectory east of the Green Line, incorporating an area largely free of Palestinian habitation—with the notable exception of Arab East Jerusalem. This area would absorb the settlements assigned to Israel in the Geneva Initiative, but generally in a much more ample fashion, incorporating also areas around them, as well as additional settlements not allocated to Israel under Geneva.

Along with "land swaps," the Oslo process also introduced the concept of "consensus" settlement blocs, referring to those clusters of settlements that Israel expects and demands to retain. Land swaps were the means to compensate the Palestinians for Israel's annexation of the blocs.

The extent of the settlement blocs has never been authoritatively defined. But the route of the Separation Barrier made their boundaries clear enough. Starting with the Geneva Initiative settlements, the Barrier protrudes eastwards toward the West Bank's center to encompass the Ariel and Adumim blocs. The meaning of the counter-category of compensatory land swaps was revealed to Palestinian President Mahmoud Abbas in 2008, when Israel's Prime Minister Ehud Olmert presented the combined configuration as a generous offer to the Palestinians. Olmert proposed that Israel annex more than 6 percent of the OPT (which the Palestinians assessed at more than 8 percent) in exchange for the equivalent of 5.5 percent.[4]

As per the Geneva Initiative, Olmert proposed exchanging core Palestinian territory for peripheral areas within the pre-June 1967 borders. However, whereas Arieli's option doubles Geneva's proposed land swap from 2.2 percent to 4 percent of the OPT, Olmert's proposal nearly quadrupled it. Relative to Arieli's plan, Olmert's proposal would have doubled the area

[4] There is uncertainty regarding the precise details of Olmert's map, since it has not been made public. Olmert did not permit Abbas to take a copy with him, and so Abbas made a sketch of the offer on a napkin. He reported that Olmert had offered a land swap in which Israel would annex 6.8 percent of the OPT in exchange for territory equivalent to 5.5 percent. Palestinian advisors assessed that this 6.8 percent in fact amounted to 8.7 percent. Subsequently, a figure of 6.5 percent was reported. For a projection of Olmert's offer based on the available details, see p. 95.

of troubled Palestinian contiguity and doubled the area of settlement blocs annexed by Israel. It would also have at most shared sovereign control of Jerusalem's "Holy Basin"* with the Palestinians.

Palestinians did not accept Olmert's offer out of hand but agreed to take it as a basis for further negotiations toward a more amenable compromise. Does Arieli's proposal represent such a compromise?

Arieli's key stipulation of a 4 percent territorial exchange puts it in between the Geneva Initiative's 2.2 percent and Olmert's offer of above 8 percent.

The Geneva Initiative was welcomed by the late Palestinian President Yasser Arafat as "a brave initiative that opens the door to peace,"[5] which was his way of saying that, in Palestinian eyes, it had potential for reaching a historic compromise. Arieli's upgrade, in almost doubling Geneva's land swap proposal to 4 percent, has jeopardized that prospect. Adding settlements like Efrat and Har Homa to the area required by Israel means crossing another Palestinian red line. There may have been evidence that the Palestinians were ready to cede the East Jerusalem settlements, but this willingness to compromise did not extend to disruptive settlements like Ma'ale Adumim or Efrat.

* *Editor's note:* That is, the Old City of Jerusalem and its environs. See Glossary.

[5] Arafat, quoted in "Geneva Initiative Gathers Momentum," *Daily Star* (3 December 2003).

Geneva Land Swap Option*

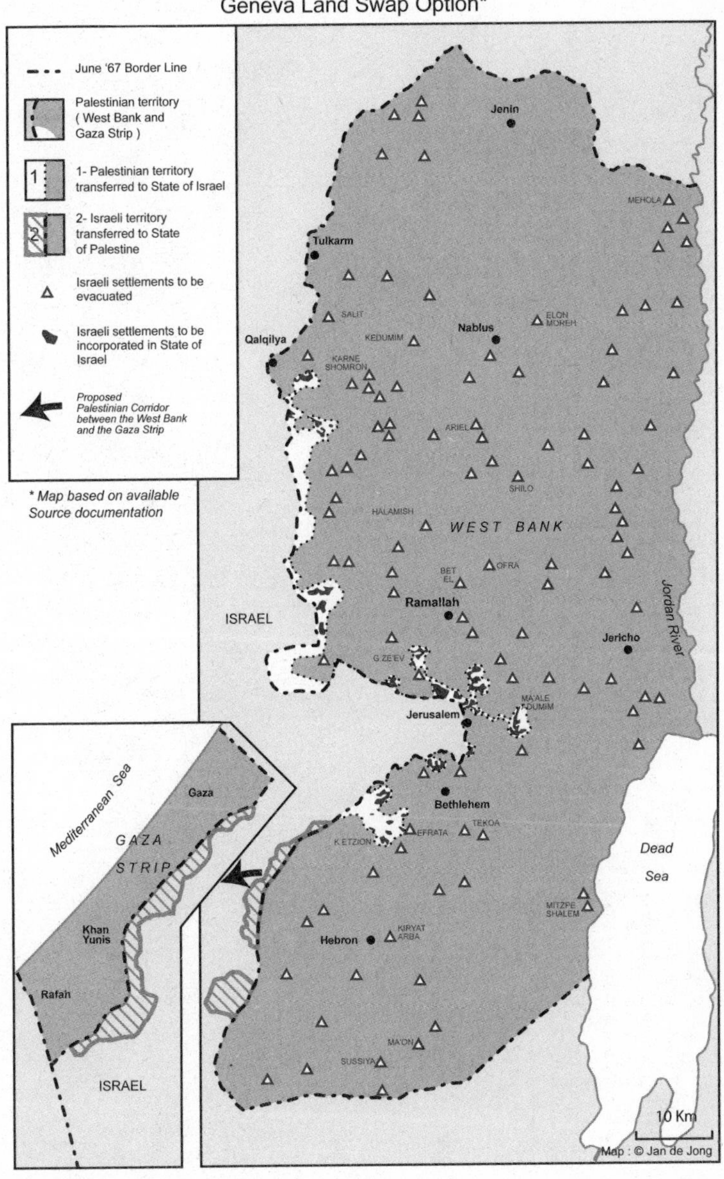
June '67 Border Line
Palestinian territory (West Bank and Gaza Strip)
1- Palestinian territory transferred to State of Israel
2- Israeli territory transferred to State of Palestine
Israeli settlements to be evacuated
Israeli settlements to be incorporated in State of Israel
Proposed Palestinian Corridor between the West Bank and the Gaza Strip
* Map based on available Source documentation
Jenin
MEHOLA
Tulkarm
SALIT
ELON MOREH
Nablus
KEDUMIM
Qalqilya
KARNE SHOMRON
ARIEL
SHILO
HALAMISH
WEST BANK
BET EL
OFRA
Ramallah
ISRAEL
Jericho
Jordan River
G.ZE'EV
MA'ALE ADUMIM
Jerusalem
Bethlehem
TEKOA
EFRATA
K.ETZION
Dead Sea
MITZPE SHALEM
KIRYAT ARBA
Hebron
MA'ON
SUSSIYA
10 Km
Map : © Jan de Jong
Mediterranean Sea
Gaza
GAZA STRIP
Khan Yunis
Rafah
ISRAEL

Arieli's Land Swap Option *

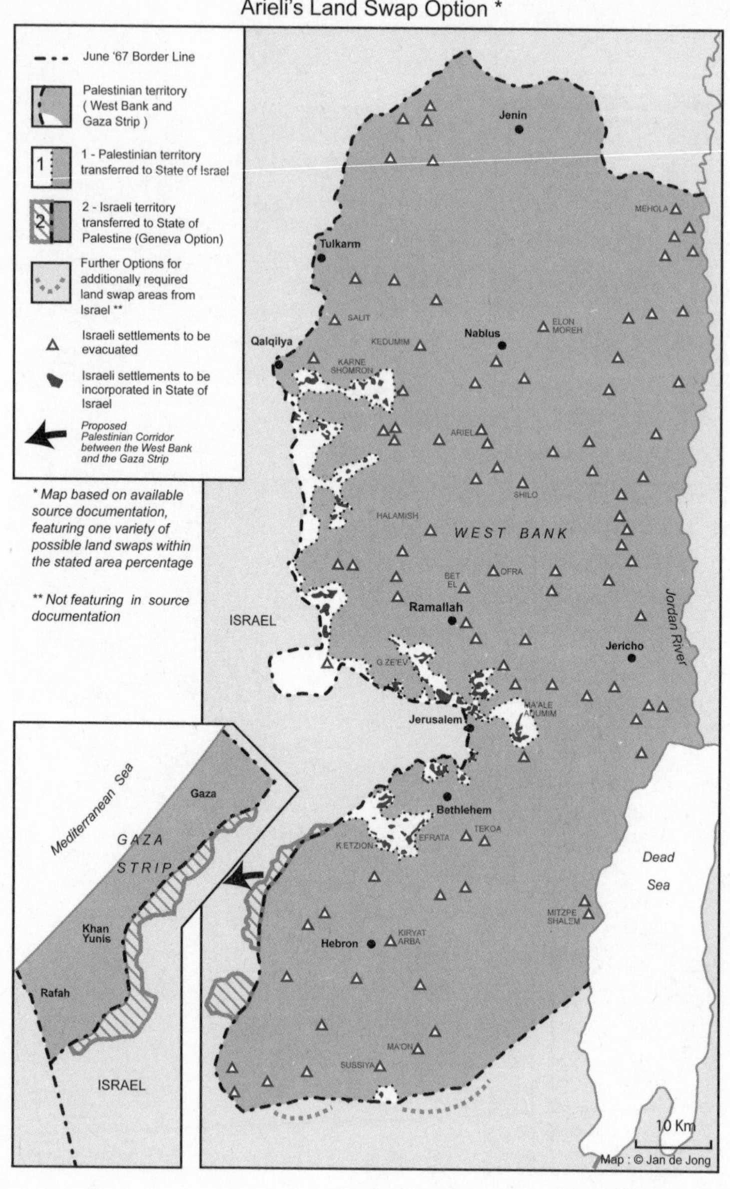

Projection of P.M. Olmert's Land Swap Option (2008)*

June '67 Border Line

Palestinian territory (West Bank and Gaza Strip)

1- Palestinian territory transferred to State of Israel

2- Israeli territory transferred to State of Palestine

Israeli settlements to be evacuated

Israeli settlements to be incorporated in State of Israel

Jerusalem's 'Holy Basin'

Proposed Palestinian Corridor between the West Bank and the Gaza Strip

** Map based on obtained area dimensions*

Jenin
MEHOLA
Tulkarm
SALIT
ELON MOREH
Nablus
KEDUMIM
Qalqilya
KARNE SHOMRON
ARIEL
SHILO
HALAMISH
WEST BANK
BET EL
OFRA
Ramallah
ISRAEL
Jericho
Jordan River
G.ZE'EV
MA'ALE ADUMIM
Jerusalem
Bethlehem
TEKOA
EFRATA
K.ETZION
Dead Sea
MITZPE SHALEM
Hebron
KIRYAT ARBA
MA'ON
SUSSIYA
Gaza
Mediterranean Sea
GAZA STRIP
Khan Yunis
Rafah
ISRAEL
10 Km
Map : © Jan de Jong

Projection of Post Oslo-Palestine according to INSS-Plan Recommendations*

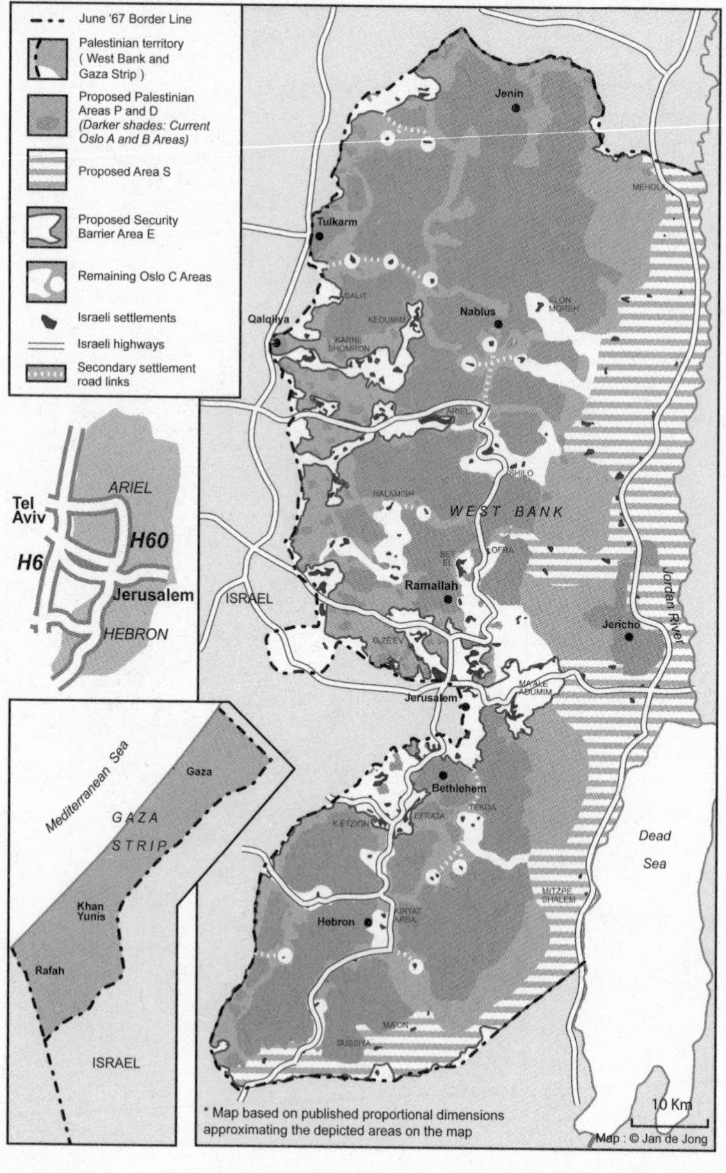

June '67 Border Line
Palestinian territory (West Bank and Gaza Strip)
Proposed Palestinian Areas P and D
(Darker shades: Current Oslo A and B Areas)
Proposed Area S
Proposed Security Barrier Area E
Remaining Oslo C Areas
Israeli settlements
Israeli highways
Secondary settlement road links
Jenin
MEHOLA
Tulkarm
Qalqilya
GALIT
KEDUMIM
Nablus
ELON MOREH
KARNE SHOMRON
ARIEL
SHILO
HALAMISH
WEST BANK
BET EL
OFRA
Ramallah
ISRAEL
Jericho
Jorden River
G.ZE'EV
MA'ALE ADUMIM
Jerusalem
Bethlehem
TEKOA
K.ETZION
EFRATA
Dead Sea
MITZPE SHALEM
Hebron
KIRYAT ARBA
MA'ON
SUSSIYA
Tel Aviv
ARIEL
H60
H6
Jerusalem
HEBRON
Mediterranean Sea
Gaza
GAZA STRIP
Khan Yunis
Rafah
ISRAEL
10 Km
* Map based on published proportional dimensions approximating the depicted areas on the map
Map : © Jan de Jong

Palestinian reservations and objections to all those plans, including Arieli's, were most clearly articulated in the sphere of compromised territorial and transportation contiguity. Israeli annexation of more than 2 percent of the West Bank would leave the Palestinians with only virtual contiguity, which would cement the fragmentation of the Palestinian territories and fatally undermine their socioeconomic viability.

Prospects for partition

Where does this leave prospects for Palestinian statehood on 22 percent of "historic" Palestine alongside a demographically separated State of Israel?

Today, land exchange maps such as the Geneva Initiative, Arieli's option, or the proposal of Ehud Olmert have been superseded by new maps emerging from the drawing boards of Israeli planning institutions. Two of these, whose dimensions have been released only descriptively, are highly instructive.*

In 2017, Israeli Transportation Minister Yisrael Katz presented an ambitious plan drawn up by the Ministry of Transportation to drastically upgrade the West Bank's vehicle and railroad infrastructure.[6] Its dimensions are indicative of how Israeli planners intend to divide up the West Bank's territorial spoils.

The plan calls for augmenting the West Bank's highway capacity with dedicated private and public transport lanes to unblock clogged intersections. This is intended to improve accessibility between Israel and the settlements and erode the distinction between Israel's metropolitan core and its rural periphery. Settlements once considered remote backwaters will become an integral part of the high-potential urban arc between Tel Aviv and Jerusalem.

---

* *Editor's note:* See map on p. 96.

6 Ofer Petersburg, "West Bank Roads to Receive NIS 5 Billion Upgrade," *ynetnews.com* (7 February 2017).

The Katz project essentially revives an older national road plan for the whole country. The principal difference is that, taking into account the country's binational reality, the plan prioritizes those West Bank areas Israel expects and demands to retain. The initial plan can be visualized as an extended grid with highways running from North to South and transversally from West to East. The Katz upgrade will prioritize the central section, aiming to extend Israel's metropolitan core eastward over the West Bank. Highway 60, the old Palestinian trunk road over the West Bank's hill spine, will parallel the coastal Highway 6 in Israel, while transversal highways from the West will link the two and establish a rectangular core-grid anchored at Tel Aviv, Ariel, Jerusalem, and Kiryat Arba (Hebron).

The Katz project is presented in strictly utilitarian terms as an effort to ameliorate congested infrastructure. But its details give indicative dimension to another plan that has been put forward to address Israel's geopolitical interests in the West Bank.

In January 2017, Israel's Institute for National Security Studies (INSS) published its yearly strategic survey, which featured a plan for responding to the stalled negotiations with the Palestinians.[7] Absent any progress toward a mutually agreed two state-solution, it recommends a "reorganization of the West Bank map, both conceptually and physically." It proposes to release about 40 percent of Oslo-designated Area C for Palestinian economic development (to be termed "Area D") and connect this to the current Palestinian Areas A and B (which, together, would be renamed "Area P"). Whereas Oslo established direct Israeli rule over 60 percent of the West Bank, the two areas P and D would reverse this ratio in Palestine's favor, bringing almost two-thirds of the West Bank under Palestinian self-rule.

[7] Assaf Orion and Udi Dekel, "Israel and the Palestinians: Conditioning and Capacity Building for Future Arrangements," in Anat Kurz and Shlomo Brom eds., *Strategic Survey for Israel 2016–2017* (Tel Aviv: Israel Institute for National Security Studies, 2016), pp. 161–74.

The remaining one-third would be split into three. Settlement construction would be concentrated in so-called "consensus"-blocs within the Barrier perimeter (termed "Area E," comprising 10 percent of the West Bank). The West Bank's eastern slopes and Jordan Valley would be reserved for securing Israel's eastern frontier (termed "Area S," comprising 20 percent).

This would leave 5 percent of the West Bank for settlement blocs east of the Barrier, in an area that would retain its current "Area C"-status as established under Oslo.

For Israel, this unilateral geopolitical reshuffle promises to legitimize the major settlement blocs. Re-division of the West Bank along these lines would reduce Area C, the whole of which is presently claimed by the "hawkish" side of Israel's political mainstream, to just a quarter of its current size. This responds to the urging of Israel's political "doves" to exclude all-out annexationist drives and preserve minimal prospects for residual Palestinian statehood. Otherwise, they fear, Israel might alienate itself prematurely and totally from the "land for peace" formula for a two-state solution, risking international sanction.

For Palestinians, the INSS proposal would aim to boost socioeconomic opportunities while curtailing settler aspirations to a level thought to be compatible with eventual Palestinian statehood on most of the West Bank.

What do the Katz and INSS plans mean for the internationally endorsed two-state solution, which would see the establishment of a Palestinian state on 22 percent of "historical" Palestine through the mechanism of land swaps?

Neither plan was presented to the public with accompanying maps. Both presentations stuck to a descriptive format, shying away from depicting uncomfortable dimensions. But the numerical precision of both plans enables a fairly accurate reconstruction of their territorial footprint, not least because essential features like the Separation Barrier and highway trajectories are well established landmarks.

The centerpiece of both plans is the above-introduced rectangular highway grid between coastal Highway 6 in Israel and Highway 60 on the West Bank, in between the settlements of Ariel and Kiryat Arba (Hebron). Without these two waystations, Israeli officials would still view their capital as dangling perilously at the tip of the narrow land bridge coming from the coast (the Latrun Highway). With highway access in all compass-directions, rather than merely to and from the West, Israeli Jerusalem would acquire strategic "depth" extending far in all directions.

All this works like the proverbial two-edged sword: what is gained by Israel is lost to Palestine. Where Israel solidifies and extends its grip on the country's metropolitan core, Palestine loses it. Where Israel cements its territorial cohesion across the country, the cohesion of Palestine is further dissolved. The same is true in the socioeconomic sphere. Where Israel creates room to invest billions in cross-border urbanization and infrastructure, Palestine loses all claim on these urgently needed potential windfalls.

Israel's land swap proposals can be made compatible with the requirement to leave 22 percent of the country for Palestinian statehood. Indeed, Olmert's offer to the Palestinians revealed that this is the least of Israel's worries. There is ample choice of peripheral lands to attach to the already marginalized Palestinian proto-state. These can be found mainly south and southwest of the West Bank, as well as east and southeast of the Gaza Strip. But "22 percent" does not ensure viability.

Conclusion

To conclude: Arieli's plan, while compatible with the political parameters of Palestinian statehood in 22 percent of the country, exacerbates the critical shortcomings of its Geneva predecessor. Apparently seeking a measure of accommodation with the "consensus" settlement blocs within the Separation Barrier, Arieli felt compelled to adapt his option to most of its ensuing territorial configuration.

In so doing, his option has fallen foul of resolute Palestinian as well as Israeli objections. In the eyes of Israel's political mainstream, it sacrifices too much of the country's primary geopolitical interests. In Palestinian eyes, even if it is compatible with political sovereignty over 22 percent of "historic" Palestine, it sacrifices all remaining prospect for indigenous, socioeconomically viable statehood.

ꙮ

Shaul Arieli

I will not repeat what I have already written in the exchange with Gideon Levy, but wish to elaborate on certain key points.

1. Unfortunately, de Jong ignores much of the history of the conflict and its development in the century since the Balfour Declaration. In particular, he ignores the Palestinians' consistent rejection, over decades, of the resolutions of the international community, as manifested in the Mandate Document of 1922 and in the Partition Plan of 1947. He also ignores the position of the PLO until 15 November 1988, which denied the State of Israel's right to exist and sought to destroy it. He criticizes UN Security Council Resolution 242 (22 November 1967), which serves as the basis of the political process between Israel and the Arab world, as confirmed in the second framework agreement of Camp David in 1978. This resolution, which the PLO accepted only in December 1988, stipulates that a Palestinian state would be established on 22 percent of historical Palestine. Thus, as I have previously noted, Palestinian President Mahmoud Abbas has stated: "The opportunity for the 1947 partition has been lost, and before that the opportunity for partition by the Peel Commission had been lost. But we do not wish to lose another opportunity. That is why we have accepted the 1948 and 1967 partition, which do not include more than 22 percent of historical Palestine."[8] Whoever wishes to find a solution to the conflict cannot just seek their own

[8] *Al-Arabiyeh* television interview (23 April 2008).

justice, but must search instead for a compromise based on the reality on the ground, international resolutions, and the two sides' political capabilities.

2. Arguing that my proposal for a 4 percent land swap is based only on one criterion, that of quantity, is ridiculous if not insulting. This proposal, which has several versions, is the fruit of a three-year academic research project based on the scholarly literature in the field of border determination.

   Charles Fawcett stresses that research and experience prove that a "good border" must have four properties, or approximate them as closely as possible:

   a) Its location and demarcation must be salient and clear so as not to arouse doubts with respect to its path or accidental crossings of it.
   b) The border must overlap, or be as near as possible to, the area of settlement of the peoples which constitute the population of any of the states it separates; that is, the political border should also be an ethnic border or approximate one.
   c) The border ought to impose no barrier within an area when there is mutual economic or other dependence between the inhabitants of its various parts, unless suitable substitutes for this dependency have been assured within each state.
   d) The border should not cross communities and their immediate areas of livelihood.

   Fawcett adds that a border which does not meet these properties during its demarcation may acquire them through agreed-upon and mutually coordinated measures that bring it closer to the quality of a "good border."[9] Douglas Gibler adds further considerations, arguing that

[9] Moshe Brawer, *Israel's Boundaries: Past, Present, and Future* (Tel Aviv: Yavneh, 1988) [Hebrew].

history, ethno-demographic characteristics, and additional factors may and should affect the delineation of a border.[10]

Martin Glassner suggests two additional criteria and qualifies them. Linguistic division might serve as a suitable criterion for border demarcation, but a map which describes the distribution of world languages reveals a complex picture and many states are multi-lingual. Furthermore, existing conflicts between language and nationhood cannot be entirely reconciled. Religious boundaries do not always overlap precisely with nationhood or language in terms of distribution across borders. However, in areas where religion has been a focus of conflict, it has also been the main basis for border demarcation.[11] Since in many cases one cannot draw a border, whether during its initial demarcation or subsequent correction, which possesses all the properties of a "good border," one must prioritize certain advantages over others.[12]

Every area suggested for land swap, on the Israeli side as well as on the Palestinian side, has been examined in view of all these criteria. Factors taken into consideration included land ownership; the number of agricultural farms; the number of affected permanent workers, temporary workers, people working in Israel, and people working in settlements; commercial relations between villages; family relations between villages; district services; water sources; health services; commercial centers; industrial zones; and transportation routes.

The research found a 4 percent land swap to be optimal in terms of the costs that would be incurred by three population groups affected

---

[10] Douglas M. Gibler, "Bordering on Peace: Democracy, Territorial Issues, and Conflict," *International Studies Quarterly* 51.3 (September 2007), pp. 509–32.

[11] Martin I. Glassner and Harm J. de Blij, *Systematic Political Geography*, third edition (New York, NY: J. Wiley, 1980).

[12] Brawer, *Israel's Boundaries*.

by the border: Palestinian villages in the West Bank, Israeli communities within the State of Israel that would be harmed as a result of the land swap, and Israelis residing in Jewish communities in the West Bank who would have to be evacuated to Israel as part of a final status agreement. Thus, contrary to what de Jong argues, the research upon which my proposal is based went out of its way to address anything he may have considered, and does not merely take into account the Israeli "national cost." It is no coincidence, to say the least, that Abbas has also spoken of a proposal involving a 3.8 percent land swap.

3. The Arab metropolis of Jerusalem is more contiguous and established than that of Jewish Jerusalem (i.e., West Jerusalem plus the Jewish neighborhoods in East Jerusalem). There is full contiguity and there are transportation solutions for both sides which do not harm the capacity of Arab Jerusalem to serve as an economic capital as well as a political one. This contiguity was planned by Israelis and Palestinians.
4. The proposed land swap would indeed grant Gaza significant additional territory at the expense of the West Bank. But isn't it a Palestinian interest to increase little Gaza (363km^2) at the expense of the West Bank (5,868km^2)? The lands transferred to Palestine as part of the land swap are agricultural lands, and at least half of these were demanded by the Palestinians during the Annapolis negotiations. In addition, some of these areas have symbolic significance as their transfer would enable Palestinians to re-establish several Arab villages destroyed in 1948.
5. It is true that Israel would have to confront the hard core of settlers as part of a final status agreement. But research shows that, contrary to the conventional wisdom among the Israeli public, it is feasible to dismantle these settlements and pull out of the West Bank in the context of a permanent status agreement. This feasibility is demonstrated in

Gilad Hirschberger's study,[13] which reveals that a very high percentage of Israeli residents of the West Bank express willingness to be evacuated as part of an agreement and to abide by the law even when they do not agree with it.

To summarize, the 4 percent land swap proposal is the "possible good." It would permit the establishment of a viable Palestinian state. The border regime and the future Palestinian state's relationship with Israel will be much more important than the factors focused on by de Jong in ensuring that such a peace is sustained. To these, one can add numerous additional variables—foreign investment, economic development, and so on—which we cannot address here.

I would like to remind de Jong that I was the one who conducted the territorial negotiations with the Palestinians' territorial advisor Samih El-Abed in the framework of the Geneva Initiative. This was a lengthy and complex process (two years), which continued the official negotiations that had come to an end in Taba (2001), where I had also negotiated the territorial issue with Dr. El-Abed. I therefore have an intimate acquaintance with Palestinian "red lines," as well as Israeli ones, on the issue of borders. I am also very familiar with the development of Palestinian and Israeli positions since the Oslo Accords and with the material and political considerations that have dictated

[13] Gilad Hirschberger and Tsachi Ein-Dor, "Defenders of a Lost Cause: Terror Management and Violent Resistance to the Disengagement Plan," *Personality and Social Psychology Bulletin* 32.6 (2006), pp. 761–69; Gilad Hirschberger and Tom Pyszczynski, "An Existential Perspective on Violent Solutions to Ethno-Political Conflict," in Mario Mikulincer and Phillip R. Shaver eds., *Human Aggression and Violence: Causes, Manifestations, and Consequences* (Washington, DC: American Psychological Association, 2011), pp. 297–314. Cf. Sivan Hirsch-Hoefler et al., "Radicalizing Religion? Religious Identity and Settlers' Behavior," *Studies in Conflict & Terrorism* 39.6 (2016), pp. 500–18; Sivan Hirsch-Hoefler and Cas Mudde, "Right-Wing Movements," in Della Porta Snow et al. eds., *The Wiley-Blackwell Encyclopedia of Social and Political Movements* (Chichester: Wiley-Blackwell, 2013), pp. 1116–24.

their positions in every official round of negotiations, as well as in the Geneva Initiative, which was informal and subject to numerous political constraints.[14]

Many Palestinians, including experts and officials, subscribe to similar versions of the 4 percent land swap scenario as part of unofficial negotiations which are taking place to this day. As I have stated, this is also the stated position of President Abbas. Therefore, the scenario I have proposed does not exceed the Palestinian "space of agreement." For example, I have refrained from suggesting the annexation of Ariel, despite the fact this was included in the Palestinians' proposal at Taba.

Finally, one should recall that the question of borders is but one of four issues at the core of the conflict. The flexibility each side can show while it negotiates on one issue in isolation is much less than the flexibility it can display when negotiating a package deal. The land exchange I propose, or a version of it, represents the best possible deal for all parties, given the full range of factors constraining them, and as part of a comprehensive final status agreement of all the issues in dispute.

ജ൫

Jan de Jong

Shaul Arieli's land swap proposal, like others before and after it, proposes to reduce the political cost to Israel of a two-state solution by adjusting the pre-June 1967 line separating Israel and Palestine. This adjustment would permit Israel to incorporate the majority of its core settlements, which would jut out like "fingers" into the territory of the future Palestinian state.

In assessing Arieli's option, I argued that those settlement indents would gravely damage the prospects for viable Palestinian statehood. Israel's

---

[14] One can read about this at length in the various books and studies I have published, most recently *A Border Between Us and You* (Tel Aviv: Books in the Attic, 2013) [Hebrew], as well as my PhD dissertation, "Political, Historical and Geographical Aspects of the Demarcation of a Political Border in Intra-state Conflicts—The Israeli-Palestinian case" (University of Haifa, 2016) [Hebrew].

annexation of the settlements around Jerusalem would deplete the capacity of Arab Jerusalem to realize its urgently needed metropolitan potential for the agglomeration between Ramallah and Bethlehem. The settlement-fingers would disrupt its urban cohesion, alienate badly needed growing space for residences and utilities, restrict area and transportation contiguity, and fragment the West Bank's crucial core.

These effects would be replicated in the northern West Bank by a similar settlement-finger configuration between the Palestinian cities of Qalqilya and Nablus. I argued that these settlement indents entail severe socioeconomic losses for Palestinians, not just locally and regionally but also on a national scale.

Arieli's contributions do not mention national costs for Palestine.[15] However, Arieli implies that any such costs can be compensated through land swaps. All Israeli land swap proposals rely upon the same formula: territorial losses are to be offset by territorial gains calculated in terms of a single attribute: the size of the territory concerned, expressed in square kilometers. I argued that this attribute does not fully capture the implications for national prosperity and viability of the proposed territorial exchanges. I reasoned that, "although altogether equal in size, these lands are in every other respect radically unequal. What Palestine would cede to Israel is vital for its statehood; what it would get in return is irrelevant to that prospect."

I will now address Arieli's substantive rejoinders in order.

1. My observation that international proposals for partitioning Palestine reflected Palestinian defeats was not, as Arieli interprets, a criticism of those proposals. Arieli deplores my failure to note the initial Palestinian rejection of international resolutions on the Israeli-Palestinian conflict. But he himself

[15] Arieli asserts that a 4 percent land swap is "optimal" in terms of costs incurred by "three population groups": "Palestinian villages in the West Bank," "Israeli communities within the State of Israel that would be harmed as a result of the land swap," and "Israelis residing in Jewish communities [i.e., settlements] in the West Bank." This leaves unmentioned the *national* costs to Palestine, that is, the implications of Arieli's option for the viability of a future State of Palestine.

is silent about Israel's ongoing repudiation of international law and political opinion, which rejects Israel's settlement and annexation of the Occupied Palestinian Territory.

2. Arieli takes offense at my description of his 4 percent land swap proposal as "based on only one criterion, that of quantity." He demurs that his proposal is "the fruit of a three year-academic research project based on scholarly literature in the field of border determination." In my view, the effort that goes into a proposal is irrelevant; what counts is the result. Arieli insists that the research on which his proposal is based "went out of its way to address" all relevant factors and "does not merely take into account the Israeli 'national cost'." If so, these deliberations remain hidden behind a bald assertion that a 4 percent land swap is "optimal."
3. Arieli claims that his option would leave the Arab metropolis of Jerusalem "more contiguous and established than that of Jewish Jerusalem." Terminology like "ridiculous" should be avoided in exchanges like these, but comparing a map of pre-1967 Arab Jerusalem with that of Arieli's proposal, and then describing the latter as more contiguous and established than Jewish Jerusalem, would raise many eyebrows, to say the least.
4. Arieli maintains that his proposed land swap would benefit the Gaza Strip. Additional land could indeed be put to local use here, but it would be of limited value. What Gaza needs above all is to be reconnected with its natural external markets, principally the West Bank, Egypt, and Jordan. This would unleash Gaza's potential as one of Palestine's gateways to the outside world and enable it to play its crucial role in ensuring Palestine's national viability.
5. Arieli describes a 4 percent land swap as the "possible good," and asserts that "[m]any Palestinians, including experts and officials, subscribe to . . . the 4 percent land swap scenario, as part of unofficial negotiations which are taking place to this day. . . . [T]he scenario I have proposed does not exceed the Palestinian 'space of agreement.'" This begs the question: if the Geneva option's 2.2 percent land swap was the "possible good" in 2003, and if the Palestinians' official offer in 2008 was an even lower 1.9 percent,

why does the "possible good" today require doubling the Israeli annexation to Arieli's 4 percent? It may be that elements within the Palestinian leadership have internalized the notion that most areas west of the Separation Barrier will be lost to Palestine, except for the Arab neighborhoods in East Jerusalem. In backchannel talks, away from the Palestinian public eye, certain officials may be amenable to an option like that proposed by Arieli. Eventually, such a plan might even be pushed through the Palestinian parliament, which is in ever increasing disarray. But the chances of such an offer being tabled by Israel are extremely slim, as Arieli notes, while Palestinian agreement would not demonstrate the option's compatibility with viable statehood. It might testify instead to the depth of Palestinian desperation.

The 15 percent scenario

What, then, remains of the much-heralded land swap formula as a bridge toward viable Palestinian statehood?

In my view, the INSS map* provides vital clues to that question. It projects one possible configuration of the Occupied Territories, based upon the INSS's plan for a "reorganization" of the West Bank. Like the preceding maps, the separation between the gray and white areas (the hatched areas as a special category) indicates the boundary between the Palestinian (gray) and the Israeli (white) population domains. It largely corresponds to the situation on the ground today. The INSS plan proposes a transfer of some of the West Bank territory that is now under direct Israeli civil and military rule (i.e., Oslo Area C) to the jurisdiction of the Palestinian Authority (i.e., Oslo Areas A and B). This would create a Palestinian entity encompassing approximately 65 percent of the West Bank. It would reduce the area under Israel's direct control to 35 percent of the West Bank. At a later stage, conditional on the reaching of satisfactory security coordination arrangements with the PA, the area under direct Israeli control could be further

* *Editor's note:* See p. 96.

reduced to 15 percent of the West Bank. This would be achieved by adding much of the Jordan Valley and Dead Sea slopes (the horizontally hatched area on the map) to what would effectively be a Palestinian proto-state.

It is beyond the scope of this contribution to assess the wider political implications of this 15 percent scenario. Prominent settler circles in Israel oppose it vehemently, pushing instead for a counter-move to annex Area C (the lighter gray and white areas on the INSS map). There is, however, a growing consensus that the 15 percent option would not be ill-received by key players in the international community, such as the Middle East "Quartet."*

The playing out of such a scenario could take many years, but it is already relevant to explore its potential as a basis for a two-state compromise.

Israel's annexation of the area west of the Security Barrier (Area E on the INSS map), which contains the so-called "consensus" settlement blocs, would require a land swap of 8–10 percent of the West Bank. The map depicting Olmert's 2008 option indicates how this might be achieved. Israeli settlers may also demand the incorporation of blocs beyond the Separation Barrier. Their primary concerns are the "Gav HaHar" (Hill Spine) settlements straddling Highway 60, such as those in the Shilo and Binyamin blocs, and possibly those in the Hebron bloc. The prospects for Israeli annexation of these blocs will depend, inter alia, on geo-spatial considerations: linkage prospects to the "consensus" Area E (i.e., west of the Separation Barrier) and the availability in Israel of suitable compensatory lands for transfer to Palestine.

Positioned along Highway 60 and already firmly attached to the "consensus" blocs of Ariel, Israeli Jerusalem, and Etzion, the Gav HaHar settlements face few difficulties in respect of the first factor.

What about the required land swaps? Incorporating the Gav HaHar settlements would necessitate an additional 5 percent territorial exchange, over and above the 8–10 percent required to compensate for the "consensus" blocs. A

* *Editor's note:* The Quartet comprises the European Union, Russia, United Nations, and United States. See Glossary.

close inspection of Israeli land reserves west and south of the Hebron District reveals that sufficient additional areas can be found not dissimilar from what was offered in Olmert's option.

Such an exchange of 15 percent probably represents the upper limit of land swap feasibility. It would enable Israel to incorporate approximately 90 percent of the settlers (including those in East Jerusalem) within augmented borders. It would also provide cover for Israeli unilateralism in predetermining the scope for residual Palestinian statehood. As long as a land swap-enabled two-state solution remains possible, even if in theory more than actuality, Israel can proceed at minimal diplomatic cost to expand its footprint of residences, utilities, and infrastructure in the West Bank, at least in the "consensus" settlement blocs. If at any point in the future the Palestinians are ready for a land swap deal, it may take the form depicted by the INSS map, with compensatory land swaps as indicated by Olmert's option (but slightly larger).

A fundamental flaw—or, depending on one's viewpoint, advantage—of the land swap formula as it has been pursued is that it can be rendered compatible with a wide range of options for establishing Palestinian statehood. The overriding interest guiding it has been to secure the core of Israel's settlement enterprise. I have argued that this comes squarely at the expense of sovereign and viable Palestinian statehood.

Shaul Arieli

De Jong's belief that my 4 percent land swap proposal is intended to reduce the political cost of the two-state solution for Israel underlies his mistaken approach to the potential for resolving this protracted conflict. This approach ignores the "new realities" referred to by US President George W. Bush in his letter to Israeli Prime Minister Ariel Sharon of 14 April 2004: "In light of new realities on the ground, including already existing major Israeli populations centers, it is unrealistic to expect that the outcome of final status negotiations will be a full and complete return to the armistice lines of 1949, and all previous efforts to negotiate a two-state solution have reached the same conclusion."

As I have already noted, a land swap on the order of 4 percent is acceptable to the Palestinians, as affirmed twice by Palestinian President Mahmoud Abbas.

My proposal seeks to draw a new borderline which reflects the "new realities" that have taken shape over the past 50 years. The proposal represents the optimal compromise based on the border's impact on three constituencies: the Israelis who are to be evacuated, the Palestinians who will lose part of their land, and the Israelis within the Green Line who would lose part of their land. The proposal also factors in the political, social, and consciousness-based constraints that prevent either party from attaining all that they might wish for.

De Jong argues that my proposed land swap would enable Israel to annex most of its "core settlements." It merits reemphasizing that the proposal would see Israel retain *fewer than one third* of the settlements in the West Bank—along with 80 percent of Israelis residing beyond the Green Line.

Turning to de Jong's response:

1. Israel has indeed violated international resolutions regarding the settlements, but the determination to bring the future borderline close to the 1967 lines at any cost seems to be a product of de Jong's desire to "punish" Israel for these violations. This is not the way to resolve a conflict.
2. It is not clear to me how de Jong can argue that the considerations for demarcating the border have remained hidden after I explicitly specified them. I shall elaborate in more detail here. I have already described the factors which determine a "good border" as adumbrated by Fawcett and other leading geographers. Two of Fawcett's criteria—that the border does not fragment an area that exhibits mutual dependence between its parts, and that the border does not harm the fabric of life—are especially pertinent to this discussion.

   To test the first of these, I examined the impact of the proposed border on Palestinian communities in the West Bank in terms of economic ties, family ties, and accessibility to the main city and to medical services.

   To test the second, I examined the proposal's impact on land owned and used by Palestinian villages, Palestinian workers (permanent and temporary) employed in the agricultural sector, and water resources.

My research also examined the implications of a proposed border for Israeli communities within Israel that would be harmed by the transfer of their lands to a future Palestinian state (this does not appear on the map). These were assessed in respect of factors such as the size of the area to be annexed, the impact on territorial contiguity, proximity to military training areas and bases, and the presence of vital infrastructure (e.g., main roads).

3. De Jong states that Palestinian contiguity in Jerusalem was much greater in 1967. This is of course correct, but we do not deal with the past. We deal with what can be done today, given that 70 percent of Israelis living beyond the Green Line (approximately 450,000 people) live in the Jerusalem area. My proposal that Israel annex the Jewish neighborhoods of East Jerusalem as well as the three "satellites"—Gush Etzion, Ma'ale Adumim and Givat Zeev (as also stipulated in the Geneva Initiative)—ensures Palestinian contiguity from North to South even more than it does the contiguity of Jewish Jerusalem from West to East.
4. De Jong argues that Gaza must first and foremost be connected to its natural external markets, principally the West Bank, Egypt, and Jordan. Have I proposed anything to the contrary? Under my proposal, Palestine would have a border with Egypt in Gaza and with Jordan in the West Bank; would determine its border regime with Jordan and Egypt independently; and, as in the Geneva Initiative and all previous rounds of negotiations between Israel and the PLO, would have a corridor established connecting Gaza and the West Bank under Palestinian control. This corridor is supposed to be at least 100 meters wide, and the Palestinians would be able to lay rail lines and water/gas pipes for their use.
5. De Jong questions the need to amend the "possible good" land swap offer put forward in Geneva. He ignores the fact that I oversaw the border negotiations in Geneva, and that I was aware of all the political considerations (which for obvious reasons I cannot specify) that, along with demographic and geographic concerns, dictated this line. Later, de Jong cites the Palestinian offer during the post-Annapolis negotiations in 2008. But a land swap of 1.9 percent represents the Palestinian proposal

only, not a proposal agreed upon by both parties; Olmert's offer in 2008 was 6.5 percent! Furthermore, did de Jong deliberately avoid mentioning the Palestinian proposal at Camp David in 2000, which amounted to a land swap of 2.4 percent?[16] Did he deliberately avoid mentioning the Palestinian proposal at Taba in 2001, which amounted to 3.1 percent?[17] And most importantly, what gives de Jong the right to dismiss President Abbas's declared willingness to swap land in the amount of 3.8 percent?

6. De Jong refers to the possibility of a 15 percent land swap. This possibility does not exist from Israel's perspective with respect to the parameters of a 1:1 land swap. Based on numerous studies I have conducted, the reasonable Israeli potential for land swap does not exceed 4 percent. Beyond that, tens of Israeli communities as well as vital national infrastructure would be gravely harmed. All of this is based on the assumption, which de Jong argues I had overlooked, that the Palestinians would not agree to accept desert land in the Arad Valley and in the Western Negev in exchange for land in the West Bank.

To summarize, such is the advantage granted to those who seek constantly to develop their tools and build new academic models for the demarcation of a more stable and more feasible border within the current political framework, rather than to those who cling to a line set a decade and a half ago without their participation or their being privy to the process of its demarcation.

[16] Based on unpublished information to which the author has had access.

[17] See also Miguel Moratinos, "Moratinos Non-Paper," published in Akiva Eldar, "The Peace That Nearly Was at Taba," *Ha'aretz* (14 February 2002).

PART TWO.

GAZA

CHAPTER FOUR.

CAN GAZA SURVIVE?

Sari Bashi

Three decades of Israeli-imposed closure have wreaked havoc on the Gaza Strip's infrastructure, natural resources, economy, and, most importantly, its people, who are denied the right to engage in dignified, productive work. Factory equipment and skills atrophy as raw materials are banned, markets are cut off, and power shortages make production too expensive. Universities are isolated from the cosmopolitan exchange that is their lifeblood. High-tech entrepreneurs are constrained by Israeli restrictions on 3G smartphone technology and the inability to meet clients face-to-face. Families are separated. Patients struggle to access adequate care.

The Palestinian factional split has exacerbated these ills, as Fatah and Hamas fight over who will pay for services in Gaza, and neither appears responsive to Gaza's needs.

Sari Bashi is co-Founder and former Executive Director (2005–2014) of the Israeli human rights organization Gisha—Legal Center for Freedom of Movement.

Understanding the de-development[1] of Gaza requires a close look at the evolution of Israel's movement and access policies and what they mean for the Occupied Territories. Undoing the de-development of Gaza requires changing the fundamental principle of those policies, namely, Israel's closure of borders and repudiation of responsibility for the people trapped inside. I will suggest that reversing course for Gaza also requires us to re-think the wisdom of interim Palestinian autonomy over local affairs, given the lack of Palestinian control over major aspects of life in both Gaza and the West Bank.

From integration to fragmentation

In the aftermath of the 1948 War, Gaza, ruled by Egypt, found itself briefly severed from the area of which it had historically been an integral part, as Jordan captured the West Bank and the State of Israel was established. The 1967 Israeli conquest re-integrated Gaza and its residents, most of whom were refugees from what became Israel, into historic Palestine or the Biblical Land of Israel, restoring freedom of movement and facilitating renewal of familial, social, and economic ties.

For the first two decades of the occupation, Israeli policy sought to integrate the economies of Gaza, the West Bank, and Israel.[2] Among the early orders that Israel's military governments issued were "general exit permits" authorizing Palestinians to travel freely between Gaza, Israel, and the West Bank, unless individually prohibited from doing so.[3] Palestinian workers were encouraged to find

---

[1] Sara Roy coined the term in *The Gaza Strip: The Political Economy of De-Development* (Washington, DC: Institute for Palestine Studies, 1995; third edition 2016).

[2] Roy, *De-Development*; Arie Arnon, "Israeli Policy towards the Occupied Territories: The Economic Dimension, 1967–2007," *The Middle East Journal* 61.4. (2007), p. 573; Shlomo Gazit, *The Carrot and the Stick: Israel's Policy in Judea and Samaria, 1967–68* (Washington, DC: B'nai B'rith Books, 1995 [1985]).

[3] General Exit Permit (No. 5) (Judea and Samaria), 1972; Corresponding Permit for the Gaza Strip.

jobs in Israel, providing cheap manual labor for Israeli employers and an influx of cash that raised the standard of living in Gaza and the West Bank.

Israeli policy toward the Occupied Territories served its own economic and strategic needs but included no real plan for Palestinian economic development beyond increased cash remittances. On the contrary, the Israeli military restricted Palestinian economic activity that was deemed competitive with Israeli businesses, Israeli investors were discouraged from partnering with Palestinian industries, and investment in Palestinian infrastructure and business initiatives was minimal.[4]

The outbreak of the first intifada or uprising in 1987 called into question the official Israeli hope that Palestinians would suspend their political aspirations in exchange for improvements in their standard of living.[5] The Israeli authorities responded to the violence by tightening limitations on Palestinian movement. Israel's 1949 armistice lines remained permeable in the outward direction, as Israeli civilians continued to settle the West Bank and Gaza. But the military increasingly prevented Palestinians from entering Israel and East Jerusalem and from crossing between Gaza and the West Bank. In 1991, against the backdrop of the first intifada and the Gulf War, Israel canceled the general exit permits, barring all Palestinians from traveling unless they obtained individual permits to do so.[6] Enforcement was gradual, as the criteria for receiving permits became stricter over time. In 1995, Israel built a fence around Gaza. The percentage of Gaza's workforce employed in Israel collapsed from a high of

---

[4] Arnon, "Israeli Policy towards the Occupied Territories," pp. 581–82; Gazit, *Ha-Makel ve-ha-Gezer*, pp. 220–21.

[5] See, for example, Oren Yiftachel, *Ethnocracy: Land and Identity Politics in Israel/Palestine* (Philadelphia, PA: University of Pennsylvania Press, 2006); Ahron Bregman, *Cursed Victory: A History of Israel and the Occupied Territories* (London: Allen Lane, 2014); Don Peretz, "Intifadeh: The Palestinian Uprising," *Foreign Affairs* 66.5 (Summer 1988).

[6] Order Regarding Suspension of the General Exit Permit (No.5) (Temporary Order) (Judea and Samaria), 1991 [West Bank]; Corresponding Order for the Gaza Strip.

45 percent in the 1980s to 6 percent in 1996.[7] Unemployment in Gaza soared to 30 percent.[8]

If the promise of the first two decades of the occupation was integration throughout what had been British Mandate Palestine, the promise of the Oslo Accords was separation from Israel but integration of Gaza and the West Bank, which were recognized as a single territorial unit.[9]

Yet the Oslo Accords in fact ushered in more fragmentation. Excepting a brief period between 1999 and 2000, during which a "safe passage" allowed transit for many between Gaza and the West Bank, Gaza became increasingly closed off. With the outbreak of the second intifada in 2000, Israel closed the safe passage as well as the airport in Gaza, and eventually destroyed the site where a seaport was to be built.

In 2005, Israel removed its civilian settlers and permanent ground troop presence from Gaza. Asserting that this terminated its responsibility to allow travel to and from the Strip,[10] Israel further tightened its restrictions on Palestinian movement. In March 2006, Israel stopped allowing workers from Gaza to reach their jobs in Israel. Citing security threats, Israel repeatedly closed Karni crossing—Gaza's commercial lifeline—during the height of Gaza's lucrative winter produce season, causing financial losses and

---

[7] Arnon, "Israeli Policy towards the Occupied Territories," p. 578.

[8] Ibid.

[9] "Declaration of Principles on Interim Self-Government Arrangements" (13 September 1993), Article IV.

[10] HCJ 11120/05, *Hamdan v. Southern Military Commander*, State's Response of 19 January 2006 [Hebrew]; HCJ 2990/06, *Mezan Center for Human Rights v. Southern Military Commander*, State's Submission of 11 July 2006 [Hebrew]; Gisha, *Disengaged Occupiers: The Legal Status of Gaza* (January 2007), pp. 23–24. The international community has not accepted this position, and the United Nations, the International Committee of the Red Cross, and most diplomatic interlocutors continue to consider Israel to owe duties to Gaza residents under the law of occupation. See Gisha, *Scale of Control: Israel's Continued Responsibility in the Gaza Strip* (November 2011), pp. 29–30; International Committee of the Red Cross, "International humanitarian law and the challenges of contemporary armed conflicts," 32IC/15/11 (October 2015), p. 12.

undermining the trust of Israeli and West Bank purchasers in suppliers from Gaza.[11] When Hamas took control of the Gaza Strip in June 2007, Israel closed the Karni truck crossing permanently, banning all outgoing goods and permitting only basic humanitarian goods to enter, in a publicly declared effort to cripple Gaza's economy.[12]

Between 2007 and 2010, Israeli policy toward Gaza was explicitly punitive. The Israeli authorities created mathematical formulae to determine how much food to allow into Gaza, based on a count of how many calories they determined that Palestinians in Gaza needed to consume.[13] Margarine in small packets was permitted into Gaza as a basic foodstuff. Margarine in large buckets was banned as an input for the food industry,[14] whose availability would enable factories to produce biscuits and employ workers—contrary to Israel's stated goal of "economic warfare" ("*lohama kalkalit*").[15] Gaza's GDP plummeted. By 2008, travel through the Erez crossing between Gaza and Israel averaged just over 2,000 exits of people per month, compared with more than half a million exits of Palestinians alone in September 2000, on the eve of the second intifada.[16]

---

[11] United Nations Office for the Coordination of Humanitarian Affairs for the Occupied Palestinian Territory (UNOCHA OPT), *The Gaza Strip: February Access Report, Closure at Karni Crossing* (8 March 2006).

[12] HCJ 9132/07, *Al-Bassiouni v. Prime Minister* (unpublished, 30 January 2008), State's Response of 2 November 2007, paras. 24–36 [Hebrew]. See also Gisha, *Legal Framework: Merchants and the Economy* (May 2010).

[13] Gisha, "Reader: Food Consumption in the Gaza Strip—Red Lines" (October 2012).

[14] Gisha, "Partial List of Items Prohibited/Permitted into the Gaza Strip," *gisha.org* (May 2010).

[15] HCJ 9132/07, *Al-Bassiouni v. Prime Minister*, State's Response of 2 November 2007 (unpublished, 30 January 2008), para. 29 [Hebrew].

[16] UNOCHA OPT, "Gaza Crossings Data," *data.ochaopt.org*.

The 2010 flotilla incident, in which Israeli commandos killed nine Turkish citizens[17] trying to reach Gaza by sea, brought an end to the explicitly punitive aspects of the policy. But the closure remains, now justified by reference to security threats and a claimed lack of obligation to permit more travel, given Israel's position that it no longer owes duties to Gaza residents under the law of occupation.[18] Beginning in June 2010, Israel eased restrictions on incoming goods to Gaza, although it restricts an ever-growing list of "dual use" goods, including some construction materials and some raw materials for industry, on the grounds that they might be used for military purposes. Some outgoing goods are now permitted, subject to quotas and burdensome logistical arrangements, while travel for people between Gaza, Israel, and the West Bank has been expanded. But, for the most part, Gaza remains closed.

Travel via Erez crossing averaged just over 13,000 exits per month in 2016, less than 3 percent of the level in September 2000.[19] Although Israel is the largest market for goods from Gaza, Gaza residents may only transfer limited quantities of eggplants, tomatoes, furniture, textiles, and scrap metal to Israeli buyers. The Rafah crossing with Egypt is closed most of the time, reflecting Hamas's sour relationship with the Egyptian regime. Israel refuses to permit the reopening of the airport or the construction of a seaport. The sweeping nature of the restrictions raises questions about Israel's stated security rationale.

The closure regime

Imagine taking the city of New York and cutting it off from the rest of the United States. Imagine expecting its water supply, electrical production capacity, industries, and institutions to function independently of the rest of the country. The airports and waterways would close. Universities located in New

[17] A tenth died from his injuries in 2014.

[18] Israeli Security Cabinet Decision (20 June 2010).

[19] UNOCHA OPT, "Gaza Crossings Data." For comparative data from 2010, see Gisha, "Exits of Palestinians to Israel and the West Bank via Erez Crossing," *gisha.org*.

York City would be available to New Yorkers only, and higher education in Long Island, Connecticut, or anywhere else outside the city would be off limits. Whatever water could be obtained from water sources in or under the city would be allocated to city residents; everything else would be purchased through commercial contracts, subject to funding, availability, and willingness to sell. The waste of New York's 8.5 million residents would be disposed of entirely within city limits. Broadway shows, restaurants, and Fifth Avenue clothing shops would be for residents only. Visiting a daughter in Westchester would be permitted in exceptional humanitarian circumstances only. Under such conditions, even a large, wealthy metropolis like New York would buckle and ultimately break.

Palestinians in Gaza, and to a lesser extent the West Bank, face that reality of closure.

Although the Palestinian education system was designed to serve all Palestinian students, Israel categorically refuses to allow students from Gaza to study at universities in the West Bank.[20]

Although 31 percent of Gaza residents have family in Israel and the West Bank, including East Jerusalem,[21] family visits are permitted for first degree relatives only in cases of death, grave illness, or weddings. The Israeli authorities ban family reunification inside Israel and the West Bank.[22]

Although prior to 2007, 85 percent of Gaza's outgoing goods were sold in Israel and the West Bank, quotas and restrictions limit transfer of outgoing goods from Gaza to those markets. In 2016, Gaza residents sold just 15 percent

---

[20] HCJ 11120/05, *Hamdan v. Southern Military Commander* (unpublished, 7 August 2007) [Hebrew]. See also Gisha, "Student Travel Between Gaza and the West Bank 101," *gisha.org* (September 2012).

[21] Gisha, "Survey Summary: Family Ties Between the Gaza Strip and the West Bank," *gisha.org* (September 2013).

[22] Citizenship and Entrance to Israel Law (temporary order), 2003-5763; Adalah, "Israel Extends Ban on Palestinian Family Reunification" (15 June 2016); Hamoked and Gisha, "New Procedure: Israel Bars Palestinians in Gaza from Moving to West Bank," *gisha.org* (June 2009).

of the pre-June 2007 levels of outgoing goods.[23] Access to the sea is limited by Israeli warships that keep fishing vessels within six nautical miles of the coast, while access to a third of Gaza's arable lands is limited by an Israeli-enforced "no-go" zone on the Gaza side of the border with Israel.[24] Gaza's unemployment rate is now 44 percent, and nearly 80 percent of Gaza residents are dependent on humanitarian assistance.[25]

Although Israel and the Palestine Liberation Organization (PLO) agreed in the Oslo Accords to treat Gaza and the West Bank as a single territorial unit, the Accords' provisions for water use separate the Palestinian water economy in two. The mountain aquifer, which runs under the West Bank and Israel, was designated for Israeli and West Bank use only, with Israel taking 80 percent of the water and Palestinians taking 20 percent.[26] The Gaza Strip was to rely on its coastal aquifer, which is inadequate for the needs of its 1.9 million residents, as well as small quantities purchased from Israel. Over-pumping has salinized the aquifer, rendering 90 percent of Gaza's water unfit for human consumption.[27] The UN warns that continued over-pumping will cause irreversible damage.[28]

Although Israel connected Gaza to its electricity grid in 1970,[29] at least since the Oslo period it has treated Gaza as responsible for its own electricity supply. Gaza receives less than half the electricity it needs, due to bombings of its power plant by the Israeli army, inadequate infrastructure, and funding disputes between the two Palestinian factions over the purchase of industrial diesel from Israel.[30] As

---

[23] Gisha, "Exit of Goods from Gaza via Kerem Shalom," *gisha.org*.

[24] UNOCHA OPT, "Access Restricted Areas (ARA) in the Gaza Strip," *ochaopt.org* (July 2013).

[25] World Bank, "Palestine's Economic Outlook–October 2017," worldbank.org (11 October 2017); World Bank, "West Bank and Gaza Overview 2016," *worldbank.org* (1 October 2016).

[26] B'Tselem, "Background: Water Crisis," *btselem.org* (updated 28 September 2016).

[27] United Nations Country Team in the OPT, *Gaza in 2020: A Liveable Place?* (August 2012).

[28] Ibid.

[29] Ariel Handel, "Chronology of the Occupation Regime, 1967–2007," *Theory and Criticism* 31 (2007), pp. 173–220 [Hebrew].

[30] Gisha, *Hand on the Switch: Who's Responsible for Gaza's Infrastructure Crisis*? (January 2016).

of early 2017, Gaza residents were receiving electricity for just three to eight hours per day.[31] Large factories and hospitals have back-up generators, but the power they supply is expensive and unreliable and the power fluctuations damage medical equipment and limit the procedures that hospitals can conduct.[32]

Gaza as a template

The Gaza Strip is the quintessential canary in the coal mine: the caged bird, susceptible to carbon monoxide poisoning, whose death warns miners to exit the mine immediately. The home of 1.3 million refugees from what is now Israel[33] and the epicenter of the first Palestinian uprising, Gaza is the symbol of Palestinian resistance to Israel's policies of displacement and dispossession. It is also a testing ground for Israel's responses to that resistance. Repeatedly, Israeli policies restricting Palestinian movement have been pioneered in Gaza and then gradually extended to the West Bank.

In 1989, Israel began requiring workers from Gaza to carry magnetic cards as a condition for entering Israel. In 1995, it extended that requirement to workers from the West Bank.[34]

In 1993, Israel prohibited Israeli citizens and residents from entering Gaza without a permit.[35] In 2000, it banned Israelis from entering West Bank cities without a permit.[36]

In 1995, Israel built a fence around the Gaza Strip, effectively hemming in its residents between the sea, the border with Israel, and the heavily patrolled

---

[31] B'Tselem, "Israel Cannot Shirk its Responsibility for Gaza's Electricity Crisis," *btselem.org* (16 January 2017).

[32] UNOCHA OPT, "The Humanitarian Impact of Gaza's Electricity and Fuel Crisis," *ochaopt.org* (July 2015).

[33] Palestinian Central Bureau of Statistics (PCBS), "Palestinians at the End of 2016," *pcbs.gov.ps* (December 2016). Gaza's total population numbers approximately 1.9 million.

[34] Handel, "Chronology."

[35] Ibid.

[36] Order Closing an Area (Prohibition on entering and remaining) (Israelis) (Area A) (5 October 2000).

border with Egypt. In 2002, Israel began building a separation barrier that severs large swaths of the West Bank from other parts of the West Bank and from Israel.

The Gaza Strip, together with the West Bank city of Jericho, were the first areas from which Israel withdrew in the context of the Oslo Accords in 1994. The 2005 "disengagement," after which Israel sealed Gaza's borders, included the dismantling of four settlements in the northern West Bank, widely seen as a pilot for the removal of additional isolated settlements in favor of reinforcing Israeli claims over the large settlement blocs.[37]

In 2007, citing the government's designation of Gaza as "hostile territory," Israeli banks severed ties to Palestinian banks in Gaza, refusing to transfer funds to accounts there.[38] In the years since, Israeli banks have repeatedly threatened to sever ties to Palestinian banks in the West Bank, too.[39]

These are just some of the indicators that the model Israel has employed for Gaza—withdrawing from the interior of areas where it has abandoned plans to settle its civilians, closing those areas off into an enclave, and disavowing responsibility for what happens inside—could be replicated in the West Bank. This would manifest as continued de facto annexation of Area C (the 60 percent of the West Bank containing Israeli settlements) and disavowal for what happens in the rest of the territory, where Palestinians are concentrated.

---

[37] The disengagement plan approved by the government noted, as part of its rationale for evacuating the four isolated West Bank settlements, that, "in the West Bank, there are areas which will be part of the State of Israel, including major Israeli population centers, cities, towns and villages, security areas and other places of special interest to Israel." Disengagement Plan of Prime Minister Ariel Sharon—Revised (28 May 2004).

[38] Letter from Leora Alkhanti and Ayelet Gabai of Bank Hapoalim to Eitan Diamond of Gisha (3 September 2015) [Hebrew].

[39] After receiving guarantees of immunity and indemnity from the Israeli government in 2017, the banks say they will continue to make transfers for now. Barak Ravid, "Amid Fears of PA Collapse, Israeli Banks Given Immunity for Deals With Palestinian Banks," *Ha'aretz* (22 January 2017).

Looking ahead

Palestinians in Gaza are resilient. They have maintained a strong social fabric and entrepreneurial spirit despite the burdens that Israeli and Palestinian leaders have cynically piled upon them. When Israel blocked the entrance of cash into Gaza in 2009, creating a shortage of the half-shekel coins used to pay the 1.5-shekel public taxi fare, drivers gave change in the form of sweets and packets of tissues. In 2008, when Israel blocked the transfer of petrol into Gaza beyond what it determined was necessary for "humanitarian" needs, Palestinians in Gaza converted cars, home appliances, and factory equipment to run on whatever source of energy they could find.

A friend recounted entering a public taxi in Gaza during that period of chronic fuel shortages. He turned to the driver, a quizzical expression on his face.

"Falafel," he said, sniffing the air. "Your taxi reeks of falafel."

"You don't know?" the driver responded.

The driver had converted the engine to run on recycled cooking oil from a falafel shop.

Gaza has endured much. But we should stop testing the resilience of its residents. Reversing the de-development of Gaza will require a fundamental shift in approach. Gaza, like the West Bank, cannot function as an enclave, any more than New York City could survive in isolation. The key to reversing course is recognizing the necessity of re-connecting Gaza not just to the West Bank but also to what is now Israel, and allocating to Gaza its fair share of resources from the power that controls its borders.

By actively pursuing Palestinian local administration in most of the West Bank and Gaza, in the absence of Palestinian control of borders, the international community, the Palestinian Authority (PA), and Hamas have—perhaps unwittingly—condoned and facilitated the twin tenets of Israel's occupation policy: separation and repudiation of responsibility for civilian life in the territory Israel occupies. The Oslo interim framework formally exempted Israel from funding the needs of the civilian population it continues to control. Its provisions requiring the PA to pay for healthcare, education, sewage treatment, and other public services have been extended and endorsed by all parties, including the PA's Western and Arab donors. Hamas, although self-branded a resistance organization, also assumed responsibility for administering daily life in Gaza, despite its lack of control over critical government functions like the ability to regulate who and what enters and leaves.

We owe it to Palestinians—and Israelis—to acknowledge that the framework of Palestinian responsibility without Palestinian control is not working. It is feeding and reinforcing its mirror image: Israeli control without Israeli responsibility.

I suggest that activists and policymakers reorder our approach to Gaza and reframe our demands of the Israeli government. Yes, we should continue to oppose the occupation as an inherent suspension of the right to self-determination. But so long as the Israeli government exercises control over Palestinians, it should be accountable for meeting their needs and respecting and promoting their rights, as the law of occupation requires.

We should question the framework of Palestinian local autonomy, in which the Palestinian authorities are financially responsible for meeting the needs of Palestinians even though they don't control their borders or most of the interior of the West Bank. Indeed, the PA's very ability to operate is predicated on consent from Israel, rendering it acutely vulnerable to Israeli pressure. Should the PA be expected to purchase Gaza's water and electricity from Israel? Or, given the unsustainable shortages and the fact that the so-called Israeli water supply draws on a shared Israeli-Palestinian water source, should Israel supply it at the same levels allocated to its own residents, charging consumers for use, subject to subsidies for those unable to pay? Why do we accept a differential right to health for Israelis and Palestinians, conditioning Palestinian access to Israeli hospitals on the willingness and ability of the PA to pay for it? Should we continue to affirm and reify the Green Line, the 1949 armistice line between Israel and the Palestinian territory? It is porous in one direction only—for Israeli civilians to move outward to settle land. Could we not demand reciprocity, affirming the right of Palestinians to travel into Israel as well, where they might take advantage of educational and economic opportunities, reunite with family members, and use Ben Gurion Airport to travel abroad?

Staking these claims requires neither that we give up on Palestinian autonomy or self-determination, nor that we abandon the demand for Israel to dismantle settlements and terminate its control over Palestinians. But in the context of an indefinite military occupation and "interim arrangements" that persist two decades past their stated expiration date, we should pay close attention to what is happening to human beings—to an entire society—in the so-called interim. Indeed, requiring Israel to bear the cost of the occupation would also provide Israel with a financial incentive to end it.

Of course, there is a tension between fighting for Palestinian independence and demanding Israeli accountability to civilians living under occupation. We do not want a return to the oxymoron of "enlightened occupation." But I suggest that the balance we are striking now, rooted in the hopes of the 1990s, is anachronistic. So-called Palestinian autonomy over local affairs exempts Israel from responsibility for the devastating consequences of its movement and access policies. Palestinian authorities could continue to participate in local governance, but where resources are inadequate, Israel as the occupying power has an obligation to fill the gap. This would be not unlike a federal system in which local authorities provide services, but the central government retains responsibility for providing a floor of protection and may be required to supplement local budgets to ensure adequate service provision.

The closure of Gaza is stifling the beautiful potential of its 1.9 million residents, 54 percent of whom are children and teenagers.[40] Perhaps this generation of young people will succeed, where we have so far failed, and end the occupation. In the meantime, we adults should dedicate ourselves to reopening their closed horizons.

---

[40] PCBS, "Palestinians at the End of 2016."

CHAPTER FIVE.

CAN ARMED STRUGGLE END THE SIEGE OF GAZA?

As'ad Abukhalil vs. Mkhaimar Abusada

As'ad Abukhalil

Zionists have historically argued that force is the only language the Arabs understand.[1] This maxim has guided Israel's occupations of Arab territory. But

---

As'ad Abukhalil is Professor of Political Science at California State University, Stanislaus. He writes a weekly column in *Al-Akhbar* and is the author of, among other books, *Historical Dictionary of Lebanon* (1998) and *The Battle for Saudi Arabia* (2004).

Mkhaimar Abusada is Associate Professor of Political Science at Al-Azhar University in Gaza.

[1] Leading Zionist intellectual Ahad Ha'am observed of the Zionist pioneers that, "the only language that the Arabs understand is that of force. . . . [They] behave towards the Arabs with hostility and cruelty, trespass unjustly upon their boundaries, beat them shamefully without reason and even brag about it, and nobody stands to check this contemptible and dangerous

history has proven the reverse: the more violence Israel has inflicted on the Palestinians, the more determined the Palestinians have become in rejecting Israeli occupation and subjugation. Who, after all, could have imagined that, a full century after the proclamation of the Balfour Declaration, the Palestinians would remain steadfast in refusing to accept the consequences of the violent takeover of their homeland?

The Palestinian people have resorted to a variety of methods to resist the encroachment of Zionism on their lands. They have tried strikes, protests, petitions, silent vigils, demonstrations, and violent outbursts, especially in response to violent and political Zionist provocations. Arab and Western leaders have consistently advised Palestinians to foreswear or postpone resort to violence, so that those outside leaders might achieve the goals of the Palestinians on their behalf. In 1936, when Palestinians were in the midst of a great revolt in defense of their homeland, pro-British Arab potentates pressured the Palestinians to put down their arms and allow for peaceful negotiations between Arab and Western powers to take place.[2] But the Arab and Western leaders lied to the Palestinians and betrayed their promises to them. Tragically, the Palestinian leadership complied with the wishes of the Arab potentates. This would become a pattern.

Notwithstanding the failure of the Arab states to prevent the displacement and dispossession of the Palestinians from their homeland in 1948 and the collaboration of certain Arab regimes with the Zionist project, the Palestinians continued for many years to entrust the cause of the liberation of Palestine to Arab leaders. During the 1950s, rather than arming and forming resistance militias, Palestinians relied on assurances from

---

tendency." Cited in Nur Masalha, *Expulsion of the Palestinians: The Concept of "Transfer" in Zionist Political Thought, 1992–1948* (Washington, DC: Institute for Palestine Studies, 1992), p. 7.

[2] See Ghassan Kanafani, *The 1936–1939 Revolt in Palestine* (New York, NY: Committee for a Democratic Palestine, 1972).

the Jordanian monarchy, the Ba'athist regimes, Egyptian President Gamal Abdel Nasser, and the rest of Arab leaderships that Arab governments would take care of Israel and its occupation. Before the 1960s, the Palestinian struggle was waged primarily through peaceful means; this nonviolence did not prevent thousands of Palestinians being shot by Israeli border police as they entered their homeland to check on their farms and homes.[3] It was only after the catastrophic defeat of the Arab armies in the 1967 War that the Palestinians resolved on armed struggle to liberate Palestine by their own hands.

For many decades, Israel was accustomed to killing Arabs and destroying their homes without worrying about Palestinian or Arab retaliation. It was use of arms by Arab forces that caused this calculus to change. Before the 1980s, Israel invaded Lebanon at will and regularly attacked sites throughout the country. But with the rise of the Hezbollah military force, and especially after the humiliation of Israel in the July 2006 War, Israel became fearful of the consequences of invading. For the same reason, it is now too afraid to invade Gaza. Today, Gaza is a small portion of what remains of Palestine. It is under Israeli military occupation as well as a brutal economic siege. In recent years, the resistance groups in Gaza have fended off successive attacks, assaults, and wars by Israel, which controls Gaza's air, land, and sea. During the massacres of 2008–9, 2012, and 2014, Israel inflicted massive destruction on Gaza. But the armed resistance groups also exacted a cost in return—particularly during the conflict of summer 2014, when Palestinian militants killed 62 Israeli soldiers.[4] The result is that, just as in south Lebanon, Israel has become deterred. No Arab state army has been able to impose such deterrence on Israel.

---

[3] Benny Morris, *Righteous Victims: A History of the Zionist-Arab Conflict, 1881–2001* (New York, NY: Vintage, 2001), p. 274.

[4] B'Tselem, "50 Days: More than 500 Children: Facts and Figures on Fatalities in Gaza, Summer 2014," *btselem.org* (19 September 2016).

An armed resistance movement forced Israel out of Lebanon. This achievement exacted an enormous cost on the fighters and civilians of Lebanon because Zionists never care to distinguish between civilian and military targets. Worse, Israel purposefully attacks civilians because it adheres to the military doctrine that the terrorization of civilians will put pressure on the resisters.[5] Without an armed force in Gaza, Israel would still be there, engaging in the same brutal and savage repression that it employs in the West Bank. Furthermore, without an armed resistance movement in Gaza, Israel would prop up a collaborationist regime there like the one in Ramallah.*

The practice of armed struggle by the Palestinians—just as by non-Arabs worldwide—has been marred by mistakes, setbacks, and even violations that harmed the liberation movement. Hamas has made more mistakes and committed more violations than members of the Palestine Liberation Organization (PLO), which have generally been careful to distinguish between military and civilian targets.[6] But for the Palestinians to put down their arms and to disband resistance groups would be to invite Israel to extend and entrench its occupation of Gaza and the rest of Palestine. The lesson of July 2006 was clear and compelling: Israel behaves differently when humiliated on the battlefield, no matter how much terrorism it inflicts on the occupied.

---

* *Editor's note:* Ramallah, in the West Bank, is the seat of the Palestinian Authority.

[5] See, for instance, the "Dahiya doctrine," applied in Lebanon in 2006 and Gaza in 2008–9. (UN Human Rights Council, *Report of the United Nations Fact-Finding Mission on the Gaza Conflict* (25 September 2009), para. 62)

[6] Even the leading Popular Front for the Liberation of Palestine militant Wadi` Haddad was most careful in his instructions to avoid harming civilians, contrary to the bloodthirsty reputation concocted by Israeli propaganda. See Bassam Abu Al-Sharif, *Wadi` Haddad: Tha'ir Am Irhabi* (Beirut: Riyad al-Rayyis lil-Kutub wa-al-Nashr, 2014) [Arabic]. To be sure, even these groups committed mistakes—like every liberation movement, including the French Resistance, which punished collaborators ruthlessly (sometimes killing even their relatives) and publicly humiliated and even killed women who had fraternized with Nazi soldiers.

The history of Gaza in the decade since the redeployment of Israeli occupation forces* shows that the preservation of arms by the resistance groups, while not accomplishing full liberation from Israeli aggression and sieges, does reduce Israel's appetite for occupation and more aggression. The Israeli redeployment did not in any way relieve the plight of the Palestinian population, but the presence of armed resistance groups prevented Israel from even contemplating the option of returning to Gaza in full force. Remember that Israel engaged in tactical advances and retreats of its occupation forces in south Lebanon for decades. The stiff resistance mounted by the groups in Gaza has increased the deterrent capabilities of the people of Gaza, who have nothing else to rely on.

For decades, the Palestinians have been lectured and hectored to put down their arms and to rely instead on diplomacy. The Oslo process[§] was the culmination of putting faith in a diplomatic "peace process" managed and choreographed by a superpower that guarantees the expansion and bolstering of Israeli occupation. The Palestinian population has become quite hostile to the fruits of Oslo, which saw the number of Israeli settlers in the Occupied Territories nearly double and PLO Chairman Yasser Arafat pay the price for believing the proclaimed intentions of his American and Israeli interlocutors. Today, as Western powers talk incessantly about the "peace process," Gaza is all but forgotten. The Palestinians therefore have no choice but to continue to pursue the armed struggle along rational and strategic lines.

After Hamas won Palestinian legislative elections in 2006, the American-Israeli alliance weakened the capacity of the Palestinian people for armed struggle by dividing Gaza from the West Bank. Hamas moved to take control in Gaza in June 2007 after a failed attempt by the US and Israel to violently reverse the results of the elections in collaboration with elements of the Palestinian Authority (PA).[7] Fatah veteran Muhammad Dahlan was chosen to strike at Hamas in Gaza,

---

* *Editor's note:* See Glossary ("Disengagement").

§ *Editor's note:* See Glossary.

7 David Rose, "The Gaza Bombshell," *Vanity Fair* (April 2008).

but Hamas moved first and foiled the plot. The coup was prevented by force of arms, not diplomacy.

To be sure, Hamas and other armed groups in Gaza don't possess the ability to lift the siege or to reverse Israeli control. The disparity of military strength is too great. But without the deterrence and leverage provided by arms, Israel would have set up in Gaza an arrangement like that in the West Bank, where a PA force (quite similar to the South Lebanon Army during the Israeli occupation of south Lebanon) smothers any resistance to occupation. Furthermore, the preservation of arms in Gaza constrains Israel's ability to commit war crimes and conduct arrests, as it habitually does in the West Bank.

In sum, the Palestinians in Gaza don't have many options. They are besieged by Israel and by all Arab regimes. But their ability to maneuver in a turbulent region would diminish were they to surrender their arms unilaterally, even as Israel continued to possess the most advanced weapons and the US remained committed to ensuring Israel's "qualitative military edge."* Hezbollah's experience in south Lebanon demonstrates that deterring Israel does not require conventional military capabilities. And the potential of armed struggle in Gaza would be greatly enhanced once the artificial political division between the West Bank and Gaza is removed. It was the occupation which imposed that division to weaken the resolve of the resistance.

ᘓᘐ

---

* *Editor's note:* Successive US administrations have affirmed their commitment to ensuring Israel's qualitative military edge (QME) vis-à-vis its regional rivals and adversaries. Congressional legislation has defined QME as the "ability to counter and defeat any credible conventional military threat from any individual state or possible coalition of states or from non-state actors, while sustaining minimal damage and casualties, through the use of superior military means, possessed in sufficient quantity." Naval Vessel Transfer Act of 2008, Public Law 110-429 [H.R. 7177], 122 Stat. 4842 (approved 15 October 2008), Sec. 201(d). See further Jeremy M. Sharp, "U.S. Foreign Aid to Israel," *Congressional Research Service* (22 December 2016).

Mkhaimar Abusada

As'ad Abukhalil's claim that armed struggle in the Gaza Strip has established a degree of deterrence vis-á-vis Israel is correct, but it does not follow that armed struggle can break the siege or end the occupation, while the limited achievements of armed resistance must be set against its devastating costs.

It is true that Israel is now afraid to enter Gaza's population centers with ground forces for fear of the combatant casualties it would inevitably suffer. Nor is Israel keen to reoccupy Gaza. But the deterrence is, to say the least, mutual. In the last three rounds of conflict, Israel wiped out much of Gaza's infrastructure and obliterated what remained of its economy. Hamas has no desire to hand Israel a pretext for another assault—in which, Israel's Defense Minister Avigdor Lieberman has promised, Israel "will completely destroy them."[8] The net result is that the status quo persists. The status quo is just fine for Israel, whereas it spells doom for Gaza.

Abukhalil argues that armed struggle has prevented Israel from establishing a collaborationist regime in Gaza. This is correct, but only to a point. Since Hamas took over the Gaza Strip in June 2007, it has deployed an iron fist against collaborators and significantly reduced their number. Moreover, as Abukhalil points out, it was force of arms that prevented the extension of Palestinian Authority rule to Gaza. However, Hamas has as a result developed a stake in the status quo, and it uses its military muscle to maintain it. Just like the PA, Hamas represses its opponents in Gaza, especially those that threaten to destabilize the situation through resistance. Hamas has arrested hundreds of radical jihadi Salafists* as well as leftists accused of launching rockets against Israel to destabilize the ceasefire brokered by Egypt in August 2014.

---

* *Editor's note:* See Glossary.

[8] Lieberman, quoted in Bethan McKernan, "Israeli Defence Minister: Next War with Hamas Will Be the Last Because 'We Will Completely Destroy Them'," *Independent* (24 October 2016).

Armed struggle may have induced Israel to redeploy its settlers and military forces to the borders of Gaza in 2005 and thereby spared Gazans from daily abusive interactions with them. However, this is cold comfort when the alternative is that Gazans are being suffocated by the siege and periodically massacred. After Israel redeployed from Gaza, it closed all but two border crossings and waged three destructive wars, killing thousands of people and flattening whole areas. In each of these conflicts, Hamas set as its objective the lifting of the siege. The result was the systematic—perhaps fatal—destruction of the underpinnings of collective life in Gaza. And yet the siege remained in place. If this constitutes a success for armed struggle, defeat does not bear contemplating. To be sure, Israel embarked on those massacres, and for political rather than military reasons. Nevertheless, Hamas's commitment to violent resistance provided Israel with a pretext and helped legitimize the Israeli massacres internationally.

To repeat: after multiple attempts, and notwithstanding immense sacrifice and suffering, armed struggle has failed to end or even ease the siege.

Perhaps recourse to arms does, as Abukhalil says, afford Palestinians a degree of leverage with Israel. But it does not give them enough leverage to end the siege, and still less to end the occupation. Abukhalil cites the precedent of Hezbollah in southern Lebanon. But the analogy fails, for the simple reason that Hamas is no Hezbollah. In terms of military potency, there is no comparison. Meanwhile, Hamas's commitment to and occasional use of violence divides and weakens international opposition to Israeli massacres and the siege, which together are so catastrophic that the territory has become borderline unviable.[9]

Abukhalil assumes that the alternative to armed struggle is to wait passively for external salvation. But there is a third option: mass nonviolent resistance. This has the potential to deter Israel, and even to force it on the defensive, without legitimizing a violent Israeli response. The first intifada—the mass nonviolent civil uprising that erupted in December

---

[9] United Nations Country Team in the OPT, *Gaza in 2020: A Liveable Place?* (August 2012).

1987—was far more successful than armed struggle at recruiting international support and sympathy for the Palestinians. Internationally, the Boycott, Divestment, and Sanctions (BDS) Movement* is succeeding in delegitimizing Israel and international companies and institutions that do business with Israeli settlements in the Occupied Territories. Israel's standing is at an all-time low. Perhaps the only comfort Israel can take from the countless surveys documenting its unpopularity in the West is that, in certain important constituencies, Palestinians are even less popular. However unfairly, previous resort and continued commitment to armed struggle is partly responsible for that.

Successive rounds of conflict against the backdrop of the ongoing economic siege have destroyed the resilience of the Palestinians in Gaza. Surveys indicate that more than 40 percent of the Gaza population is ready to leave, especially Palestinian youth, who are suffering unemployment rates of above 60 percent.[10] The basic fabric of life in Gaza has been ripped apart, visible, for example, in rising social problems and drug addiction. The bottom line is: what is the purpose of armed struggle in Gaza if there are no longer people who wish to live in Gaza? What is more important: armed struggle or the welfare and dignity of human beings? The Palestinians have endured enormous suffering since 1948. Many Palestinians in Gaza consider the past ten years under Hamas and its commitment to armed struggle as their second *Nakba*.[§] Only this time, they can't even flee.

---

* *Editor's note:* See Glossary.

§ *Editor's note:* See Glossary.

10 "Public Opinion Poll No (65), *Palestinian Center for Policy and Survey Research (PCPSR)* (19 September 2017), p. 8; "Public Opinion Poll No (64)," PCPSR (5 July 2017), p. 4; World Bank, "Palestine's Economic Outlook–October 2017," *worldbank.org* (11 October 2017).

As'ad Abukhalil

Armed struggle cannot break the siege and end the occupation overnight; that is for sure. Armed struggle in Vietnam and Algeria also did not end foreign occupation overnight. The benefits and fruits of armed struggle are incremental and cumulative, as they—over a period of time—change the political culture of the occupying country and the political culture of the occupied.

Abusada refers to "the devastating costs of armed struggle." There have indeed been costs, but these must be put into perspective. In the period after 1948, the Palestinians—under pressure from Arab governments—refrained from the practice of armed struggle. The devastating costs of that period's occupation were even greater. Israel would hit the Palestinians wherever they resided, and Palestinians would submit and do nothing because they lacked arms and because the host Arab governments prevented the Palestinians from fighting back. I am not recommending armed struggle for the sake of it, or to implement revolutionary theories. Rather, armed struggle has become a necessity against an enemy that launched its program through mass violence, perpetuated and expanded its occupation through mass violence, and continues to terrorize the Palestinians through mass violence.

Abusada describes how Israel has destroyed the Gaza economy and "wiped out" much of its infrastructure. No one is denying the brutality and savagery of the Israeli project. But Abusada seems to be implying that the only choice for the Palestinians is to submit and surrender in the hope that Israel will one day suffer remorse and offer the Palestinians some land in repentance. Would Abusada have recommended that the Algerian people (who suffered three *million* casualties, caused directly or indirectly by French occupation, already by 1872[11]) or the Vietnamese people submit to the dictates of their occupiers because their enemies were brutal in their punishment of the civilian population? Resistance to occupation always comes at a price, and the occupied—all the occupied, universally—are aware that liberation is costly.

---

[11] See "Terror and Religion: Brittany and Algeria" in Edmund Burke III, *France and the Sociology of Islam* (forthcoming).

The Palestinian people have sacrificed for more than a century their lives and material well-being in the hope of attaining liberation. Abusada worries that the status quo "spells doom for Gaza," but what is the implication of this for armed struggle? That if the Palestinians were to surrender their arms, Israel would immediately offer benefits and concessions to the Palestinians? The author seems to have far more faith in the Israeli occupiers than the Palestinian people. When in the long history of the Arab-Israeli conflict did the Israelis make concessions out of good will, without direct pressure from the practice of armed struggle by Arabs?

I agree with Abusada that Hamas's rule in Gaza is far from exemplary and that it is repressive. But the collaborationist regime in Ramallah is much worse. The latter regime is not only far more repressive but exists for the sheer benefit of the occupiers and is staffed at the senior levels with collaborators in the name of "security cooperation." Importantly, Hamas rule in Gaza is not the only governing model that armed struggle can bring about; the Palestinian people in Gaza should organize to bring about a better regime, but certainly not the model of Ramallah, which Abusada seems to want to emulate all over Palestine.

I am not sure what Abusada means when he catalogues Israeli war crimes and then says that Israeli massacres were "for political rather than military reasons." Does he wittingly or unwittingly provide pretext and justifications for Israeli war crimes? And what about the period when the Palestinians were unarmed in the 1950s and early 1960s: did the Israeli occupiers ever refrain in those years from committing massacres against Arabs? The Zionists brought mass violence and war crimes with them from the early twentieth century, as soon as Zionist settlements in occupied Palestine began to spread. Is Abusada suggesting that if the Palestinians in Gaza were to surrender their arms (as they have done in the West Bank with the assistance of the collaborationist regime) then the Israeli state would convert to pacifism?

I am not suggesting that armed struggle, or the possession and preservation of arms in Gaza, will end the siege immediately. But it does bring about a more even balance of deterrence—quite an achievement given the great imbalance in military power between a state armed with nuclear weapons and a near defenseless population. The history of armed struggle by liberation movements suggests that its success is not measured in days or in weeks but through a gradual process of attrition over many years. Abusada disputes the applicability of these lessons from history on the grounds that "Hamas is no Hezbollah." I am not sure I know what that means. The Palestinian people can produce movements and organizations superior to Hamas, and it has done so in the past—just as the Lebanese people formed a resistance movement when none existed in 1982, under the brutal Israeli occupation of Lebanon. But the resistance in south Lebanon was a protracted process which saw countless setbacks, sacrifices, and localized gains before ultimate victory was achieved in 2000.

Abusada seems to realize that there are no serious alternatives to armed struggle, but presents "mass nonviolent resistance" almost as an afterthought. How would that work? When it was tried in the 1980s it did not move the occupiers, while the Western world—the sponsors of Israeli occupation and war crimes—did nothing to help the Palestinians. Also in the 1980s, a Palestinian-American established a center in Jerusalem to promote nonviolence; the office was quickly closed down and its leader—Mubarak Awad—was expelled from his land. Apparently Abusada thinks that armed struggle does not deter Israel but that unarmed Palestinians, presumably with pots and pans, can force Israel out. The author talks about the first intifada as a success, but how does he measure that? He says that "the standing of Israel" suffered, but where, when, and to what effect? The US continued to endorse and arm and finance the Israeli occupation; the EU, despite some perfunctory statements, also continued to follow the American lead on Middle East policy. The author relishes the decline of Israel's popularity in the West, but this has not in any way affected Western policies toward the Palestinians, which remain at the mercy of the US lead.

Here is the major flaw of Abusada: he seems to want the Palestinians to pursue options that are not necessarily in the interest of the cause of liberation in order to impress Westerners. But Western governments (and Western populations to a large degree) have been the biggest and most stubborn benefactors of Israel. And while public opinion in Western countries (outside of the US) has shifted to the advantage of the Palestinians, this happened due to armed struggle, which more than anything else in the 1960s and 1970s introduced and publicized the Palestinian cause in the West. And what does Abusada do when the interests of the Palestinians clash with the standards and sensibilities of the West?

As for the polls the author cites suggesting that many Palestinians in Gaza wish to leave, I am not sure how reliable they are. Many polls are funded by enemies of the Palestinian people and often produce results that are of interest to Western governments and Israel. The resilience and perseverance of the Palestinian people is never in doubt, and arms have only solidified that resilience and perseverance. As much as Israel pushes the Palestinians to leave, Palestinians have proven that their attachment to the land is unshakeable.

౨ృ

Mkhaimar Abusada

I have not disputed the legality or legitimacy of armed struggle against occupying and imperial powers. The question at issue is tactical: in what conditions can armed struggle be effective? There is no doubt that armed resistance worked in Algeria and Vietnam. It is unlikely to yield the same results in Gaza, for two reasons. First, Palestinians do not by themselves possess sufficient military might to force Israel to end the siege, still less to end the occupation. Second, Palestinians must therefore rely to some extent on auxiliary international support, and international opinion on the legitimacy of armed struggle has completely changed since the heyday of anti-colonialism in the 1960s and 1970s.

Abukhalil's comparison between Palestinian armed struggle in the twenty-first century and the use of armed struggle in Algeria and Vietnam is misleading. Algerian armed resistance was supported by President Nasser of Egypt and other countries, while the Vietnamese armed struggle was supported by China and the Soviet Union. Palestinian military action against Israel receives no equivalent regional support, while the international order is today characterized by the hegemony of Israel's closest ally, the United States. In addition, global public opinion is today much less sympathetic to violence in the service of national liberation. As anti-colonial movements succeeded and became the ruling parties of often fractious and unstable states, international support for the legitimacy of armed force by non-state actors declined. In the West, meanwhile, public opinion during the "war on terror" declared by the George W. Bush administration came to view Palestinian armed resistance through the lens of terrorism. The armed actions of the second intifada, particularly those directed against Israeli civilians, aroused international condemnation and helped legitimize Israel's repression.

Abukhalil claims that "the benefits and fruits of armed struggle are incremental and cumulative" in that, over time, they "change the political culture of the occupying country." But not all change is positive. Unlike the French and Americans who protested in the streets calling on their respective governments to withdraw from occupied land, Israeli public opinion swung to the far-right during the years of the second intifada. While Palestinian violence was not the only cause of this, attacks against civilians contributed to the collapse of the Israeli peace camp and the triumph of the right.

Abukhalil inadvertently gets to the heart of the problem when he says that armed struggle in Gaza "bring[s] about a more even balance of deterrence . . . between a state armed with nuclear weapons and a near defenseless population." That is the point. Palestinian armed resistance may establish a degree of deterrence vis-á-vis Israel. But is it plausible that a "near defenseless population" can militarily coerce one of the world's leading military powers—one supported by many allies, including the global military superpower—to end the siege of Gaza, let alone to abandon its rule everywhere in historic Palestine (as per Hamas and Islamic Jihad's declared objectives)? If not, isn't it time, or well past time, to examine alternative strategies?

It is not the case that I advise Palestinians to "submit and surrender and just hope that Israel will one day" withdraw of its own accord. The Palestinian struggle against Israel has never been limited to the use of arms, and I suggested that in the conditions which prevail today mass nonviolent resistance has real potential. But even as Abukhalil overestimates the potential of armed resistance, he underestimates the power of nonviolent struggle, which played a major role in ending the British occupation of India and apartheid segregation in South Africa, as well as the inspiring victories of the civil rights movement in the United States.

Abukhalil states that nonviolent resistance was tried in the 1980s but failed to move Israel and its Western sponsors. Let me remind him that the first Palestinian intifada led to the signing of the Oslo Accords, which in turn brought about Israel's redeployment from more than two-thirds of the Gaza Strip in July 1994 and populated areas of the West Bank in 1995, the complete opening of the Rafah border crossing between Gaza and Egypt, the opening of the Gaza international airport between 1998 and 2001, and preparations for a seaport to enable Gaza to trade with other countries. This period also saw thousands of Palestinian laborers working inside Israel, able to bring bread to their families. Today, Gazans are sunk in poverty and unemployment—the only "fruits" two decades of armed struggle have delivered.

Consider, more recently, the achievement of the 2010 Gaza Freedom Flotilla. A small number of international peace activists sailed to Gaza determined to break the illegal blockade and were met by extreme violence and brutality from the Israeli military. The international furor caused by Israel's killing of nine of the nonviolent activists* put Israel under enormous pressure and obliged it to ease the siege. Internationally publicized nonviolent resistance, even on a small scale, forced a change in Israeli policy. By contrast, three rounds of armed conflict have only reinforced the siege while devastating Gaza and bringing agony to its people. Note that it was *because* the activists were nonviolent that their massacre generated an outcry. Israel sought to portray the activists on board the flotilla's flagship vessel, the *Mavi Marmara*, as violent terrorists; it was because these slanders failed to convince that Israel was subjected to irresistible international pressure. There are lessons here.

June 2017 saw the tenth anniversary of the illegal Israeli siege. It also marked two years since the UN Human Rights Council called on Israel to lift

* *Editor's note:* A tenth died from his injuries in 2014.

the Gaza blockade "immediately and unconditionally."[12] Imagine that these grim anniversaries had seen one million Gazans, of all ages, political beliefs, and sectors of society, march nonviolently on the border crossings, while Palestine solidarity activists around the world engaged in sit-ins, occupations, marches, and hunger strikes demanding an immediate and unconditional end to the siege. Would this not have generated enormous pressure on Israel to end its collective punishment? If Israel began to fire on the unarmed demonstrators in Gaza, wouldn't the outcry have been deafening? This is how to end the siege. By contrast, the strategy of launching Qassam rockets merely provokes Israeli retaliation while helping to legitimize the destruction this causes.

Abukhalil also fails to sufficiently acknowledge the dramatic changes in "Western" opinion and policies toward the Palestinians. These were illustrated in the overwhelming Western support for upgrading Palestine to a non-member observer state at the UN General Assembly in November 2012 and, most recently, in the adoption of UN Security Council Resolution 2334 (December 2016) by unanimous vote with a US abstention. This resolution condemned Israeli settlement expansion in the West Bank, which it characterized as illegal and illegitimate. Many European countries have also introduced labels on Israeli products warning consumers that they were produced in illegal settlements. This international consensus against the settlements and in favor of Palestinian statehood is an achievement of decades of Palestinian struggle—more specifically, of the mass nonviolent resistance of the first intifada. International consensus is, of course, insufficient to change the reality on the ground. But it does limit Israel's freedom of action and, should another mass Palestinian uprising develop, could serve as a useful weapon.

The world is changing around us and the Palestinians should make creative and strategic use of every tool available to shorten the days of siege and occupation. Meanwhile, they should refrain from violent acts which merely play into the hands of the Israeli right while alienating international support for their cause.

---

[12] UN Human Rights Council, *Report of the Detailed Findings of the Independent Commission of Inquiry Established Pursuant to Human Rights Council Resolution S-21/1* (June 2015), para. 681(d).

RESPONSE:

POLITICAL UNITY IS THE PRECONDITION FOR EFFECTIVE STRATEGY

Wendy Pearlman

As'ad Abukhalil and Mkhaimar Abusada offer a provocative debate on the question of whether armed struggle can end the siege of Gaza. Beyond their divergent answers to the question guiding the exchange, the two disagree about history (was the first intifada successful?); analogies (is the experience of Hezbollah in Lebanon a useful model for Palestinians?); the role of international opinion (should Palestinians endeavor to win sympathies in the West?);

Wendy Pearlman is the Martin and Patricia Koldyke Outstanding Teaching Associate Professor of Political Science at Northwestern University. She is the author of *Occupied Voices: Stories of Everyday Life from the Second Intifada* (2003), *Violence, Nonviolence, and the Palestinian National Movement* (2011), and, most recently, *We Crossed a Bridge and It Trembled: Voices from Syria* (2017).

and, most critically, the spectrum of viable strategies (do effective alternatives to armed resistance exist?).

Each scholar presents an impassioned case for his assessment of these and related questions, as well as a thoughtful rebuttal of the other's specific arguments. Rather than judge who won the debate, I will dedicate this commentary to identifying the participants' unexpected points of convergence. If common ground can exist between these markedly opposing viewpoints, it is surely worth recognizing and exploring. Such shared understandings might serve as a launching pad for development of a strategic vision capable of bringing together rival poles of the Palestinian national movement. And few would disagree that what Palestinian politics needs most today is unity and strategic vision.

First, neither Abukhalil nor Abusada calls for Palestinians to put down their arms entirely or to disband armed groups. Both analysts affirm the legitimacy of armed struggle against occupying and imperial powers. Both agree that possession of arms, and their occasional defensive employment, has contributed to Palestinian deterrence; that is, they agree that Israel hesitates to invade Gaza more than it would if Palestinians there did not have weapons. In this sense, Abusada concurs with Abukhalil's argument that armed struggle has given Palestinians a degree of "leverage" with Israel which it would not otherwise enjoy.

Second, both recognize that fundamental asymmetry of power is the context in which Palestinians make strategic decisions vis-à-vis Israel. Abusada argues that Gazans are "suffocated by the siege and periodically massacred," while Israel is "one of the world's leading military powers . . . supported by many allies, including the global military superpower." Abukhalil does not dispute this asymmetry, conceding the "great imbalance in military power between a state armed with nuclear weapons and a near defenseless population." Though the authors draw different conclusions about the possibilities for armed resistance inherent in this power imbalance, it is important that both recognize the enormous constraint that it imposes on Palestinians.

Third, both authors concur that resistance can be a slow and cumulative process, and that it might take time for the utility of any tactic to become apparent. Abukhalil writes, "[t]he history of armed struggle by liberation movements suggests that its success is not measured in days or in weeks, but through a gradual process of attrition over many years." Abusada adopts a similarly long-term perspective when he invokes the example of the struggles against the British occupation of India, apartheid in South Africa, and racial discrimination in the United States, and likewise when he argues that the political fruits of the first intifada were harvested in the 1990s or later.

Fourth, the essays converge in recognizing that the deficiencies of Palestinian governments in both the Gaza Strip and the West Bank impede and complicate Palestinian strategy at this juncture. Abukhalil denounces the "collaborationist regime in Ramallah" which exists "for the sheer benefit of the occupiers." Abusada adds that Hamas also "represses its opponents" and has developed a "stake in the status quo," despite the suffering it causes civilians.

The authors are right to highlight the importance of the destructive domestic political landscape and the territorial and political schisms that it has generated. The long record of nonviolent and violent protest over eighty years of Palestinian history demonstrates that the pursuit of either strategy is crucially shaped by the movement's own degree of internal political unity or division.[1] Self-determination movements must be internally cohesive to carry out large-scale nonviolent protest because such protest requires the coordination and collective restraint that only unified movements with authoritative leaderships can provide. When the Palestinian movement used mass unarmed protest, as in the 1936 general strike and the uprising of 1987, internal cohesion was crucial in making it possible. In those episodes, a legitimate leadership and grassroots institutional network helped people across social classes and regions to participate in demonstrations, boycotts, and acts of noncooperation and disengagement from the state apparatus that they opposed. While Palestinians did not use nonviolent protest to the complete exclusion of violence, a structure

---

[1] Wendy Pearlman, *Violence, Nonviolence, and the Palestinian National Movement* (Cambridge: Cambridge University Press, 2011).

of coordination and cooperation enabled them to channel much of the will to rebel into unarmed activities and sustain them on a broad scale.

By contrast, when a movement is fragmented its structural divisions generate incentives and opportunities that increase the likelihood not only that it will use violence, but also that violence will not be guided by the kind of political logic and strategic discipline that best enables it to realize its goals. In the Palestinian case, various forms of competition within and between rival factions drove escalation in an armed revolt in the late 1930s, guerilla warfare in the 1960s, transnational attacks on civilians in the 1970s, and the militarized uprising that began in the year 2000. Throughout the history of the national movement, weak authority structures invited the formation of militant splinter groups and obstructed leaders' efforts to reach ceasefires or diplomatic agreements. Cracks in the self-determination struggle invited external actors to intervene and induce or coerce Palestinian parties to act in ways that furthered their interests, often by taking up arms. Fragmentation thus goaded violence, often in ways that served particularistic rather than national aims. Moreover, it left the movement without the institutional capacity to carry out mass nonviolent protest, even when support for such a strategy existed.

Neither Abukhalil nor Abusada directly interrogates how domestic political fragmentation bears upon the Palestinian national movement's capacity to carry out unarmed or armed struggle in general, or how to do so successfully in particular. Nonetheless, this query is consistent with their argumentation, and is worth considering in tandem with their analyses. In this sense, I believe that Abusada articulates the fundamental question when he asks, "in what conditions can armed struggle be effective?" Far from contesting the appropriateness of this query, Abukhalil can be read as offering an answer to it when he endorses "armed struggle along rational and strategic lines." The question with which we are thus left is: do the conditions exist today for armed struggle—or, for that matter, mass nonviolent struggle—to be used on rational and strategic lines? If not, Palestinians' main imperative is not to contest the general usefulness of either armed or unarmed approaches, but rather to deliberate what can be done to bring about the political structures necessary for any approach to be employed rationally, strategically, and ultimately effectively.

RESPONSE:

WHAT GAZA NEEDS IS HOPE AND LIFE

Usama Antar

The legitimacy of armed and nonviolent resistance to occupation is indisputable. Neither law nor morality obliges the people of Gaza to acquiesce in their slow death and resign themselves to the dying of the light of their free nation. The question before us, and which urgently confronts the people of Gaza as they teeter on the brink, concerns not the legitimacy of armed struggle, but its efficacy in the conditions which currently prevail.

Israel's strategy has relied on the political ineptness of the Palestinian leaderships and has succeeded in dramatically lowering Palestinian ambitions. Israel has been able to transform the Palestinian struggle from a quest to end the occupation and establish an independent Palestinian state to a series of disputes about how the occupation is administered. The PA in Ramallah now

---

Usama Antar received his PhD in Political Science & Economic Policy in Germany in 2004. He has worked as a university lecturer in Gaza and served in several Gaza-based international organizations.

sets its sights on freezing settlement expansion; Hamas in Gaza on lifting the siege. In light of the balance of power and the infinite weakness of the PA, which has consented to and even embraced the role of Israel's policeman in the Occupied Territories, the current leadership of the PA will not succeed in halting settlement construction nor in establishing a viable, contiguous, and sovereign Palestinian state. As for Hamas, which de facto rules the Gaza Strip: can its armed resistance approach liberate the land or even just end the siege? On these points, I share the skepticism of Abusada.

Abukhalil is correct that armed resistance has established a measure of deterrence vis-à-vis Israel. But I disagree that it brought about Israel's 2005 disengagement from Gaza. A more important factor was Israel's realization that it could not engineer a Jewish demographic majority in Gaza, where a paltry 7,000 Jewish settlers were living amidst nearly two million Palestinians. The settlements in Gaza had neither the political-ideological resonance nor the strategic significance of those in the West Bank, while Israel's investment of considerable diplomatic, military, and financial resources on behalf of so few settlers made no strategic sense. The disengagement was intended to rationalize the occupation and facilitate settlement in the West Bank. Armed resistance in Gaza may have forced the issue, but it was pushing at an open door.

When Israel left Gaza, it was predicted by some observers—correctly, as it turned out—that Hamas's military wing would seize control of the Strip. A Hamas-controlled Gaza is not a problem for Israel. Hamas, because of its commitment to and history of armed struggle, is easy for Israel to market abroad as a terrorist organization; indeed, the US and EU have classified it as such since 2001 and 2003 respectively. This made it easy for Israel to deal with the Gaza Strip as a hostile entity and to impose the blockade on it in September 2007—two months after Hamas had taken over Gaza militarily and expelled the security forces of the PA.

Abukhalil notes that armed resistance proved effective in resisting and repelling European colonial occupations in Africa, Asia, and Latin America. But these successes depended on popular support for and participation in the armed struggle, along with trust in its leaders. Those victories also depended significantly, often decisively, on regional and international support. In Gaza today, all these conditions are absent.

Popular support. Few in Gaza believe that armed struggle will yield anything other than further rounds of conflict, for which there is no appetite. Readers living abroad must try to imagine: the besieged population of Gaza has endured three wars in the past ten years, during which thousands were killed, thousands more injured, hundreds of thousands displaced, vast swaths of infrastructure destroyed, and the economy all but extinguished. The devastation still scars the landscape; the horrors still wrack the mind. The popular will and support required for the successful prosecution of armed resistance is not there.

Leadership. The division between Gaza and the West Bank, between Fatah and Hamas, is acknowledged by everyone to be fatal for Palestinian welfare and the national struggle. Yet it has persisted for years and appears no closer to resolution. The rational conclusion is, Palestinian welfare and the national struggle are not priorities for the two factions. Meanwhile, the record of the authorities in waging armed resistance does not inspire confidence: after three rounds of conflict, many lives and buildings have vanished, but the siege remains.

Regional and international support. The Arab world is undergoing a catastrophe. Syria and Iraq are no longer coherent political entities, Egypt is struggling with political instability, and the Gulf states are improving ties with Israel in common opposition to Iran. Further afield, the US administration appears determined to enable the worst tendencies in Israel, to which Europe, preoccupied with more pressing matters, will offer little resistance.

Forcing an Israeli withdrawal is also likely to require greater pressure than was necessary to end European colonial occupations. Those earlier occupations involved territories that were geographically separate and distant from the colonizer, and which were not considered "core" components of the colonizer's territory. The colonial state could always, when the cost of occupation became too high, pack up and return home. But Israel considers Palestine its rightful homeland. It took Palestinians a long time to appreciate this. Prior to the 1967 War, and even for some time after it, Palestinians and the Arab states operated within the classical anti-colonial framework: they would reject the Zionist project absolutely, and, after a struggle, the colonial settlers would return from whence they came. When the understanding sunk in that Israelis born in the Hebrew state are deeply committed to and ready to sacrifice for their country, it led to a transformation of the Palestinian political approach in the form of acceptance of a two-state solution.

In these conditions, armed resistance in Gaza cannot fundamentally transform the situation in Gaza or in Palestine. It lacks foundation in domestic public opinion and the protective shield of regional and international support. If it were embarked upon in these conditions, the inevitable Israeli retaliation would not be restrained by international pressure, while the people in Gaza would be in no position to endure the consequent sufferings with resilience. Hamas appears to realize this, which is why its support for armed struggle has for some time been merely rhetorical.

What, then, is the alternative? Abukhalil rightly dismisses reliance on external salvation, particularly at the hands of the Arab regimes. The only option for Palestinians is the one outlined by Abusada: a return to the mass nonviolent resistance of the first intifada, which was one of the few moments in the history of the Palestinian struggle when Palestinians were able to move beyond defensive reactions to Israeli decisions and regional changes, take the initiative, and transform the regional and international equations.[1] Experience has shown that Israel is dismayed by popular uprisings because only an intifada can expose it as a repressive occupying power and move the people of the world to act.

The state of strategic thinking in the West Bank and Gaza Strip is strangely inverted. Where there must be resistance in the West Bank, we find construction; and where there should be reconstruction in Gaza, we find the slogan of resistance. People in Gaza no longer care about the political horizon. They simply want to recover a measure of economic and social dignity. This requires ending the blockade, raising the standard of living, encouraging investment, reducing unemployment, reconnecting psychologically and materially with the outside world, and establishing a culture of tolerance and common life with our neighbors. What Gaza needs now is not more armed struggle, but a moment of respite, a glimmer of hope and life.

---

[1] Another such moment was the decision by the Palestinian leadership-in-exile to declare a Palestinian state on 15 November 1988.

RESPONSE:

LESSONS FROM HEZBOLLAH

Bashir Saade

Both participants in this debate agree that military resistance by Hamas will not by itself end the siege of Gaza. But whereas As'ad Abukhalil thinks use of armed force will continue to be necessary to force Israel to rethink its policies, Mkhaimar Abusada argues that it will merely exacerbate the humanitarian disaster in Gaza while legitimizing Israel's repression in the sphere of international public opinion. It is worth noting that Abusada does not demonstrate the viability of his proposed alternative to armed struggle, namely, nonviolent resistance.[1] Still, the challenges he poses to the strategic case for armed struggle are serious and worthy of consideration. One way to address

---

Bashir Saade is Lecturer in Religion & Politics at the University of Stirling. He is the author of *Hizbullah and the Politics of Remembrance: Writing the Lebanese Nation* (Cambridge: Cambridge University Press, 2016).

[1] The nonviolent BDS Movement is laudable and worthy of support. However, except for raising awareness and putting some pressure on Israel to refine its public relations pitch, it has yet to

them is to examine Hezbollah's record of armed resistance to Israel's occupation of Lebanon, which culminated in Israel's withdrawal from most of south Lebanon in 2000 and in the Second Lebanon War of July 2006.

A key point of contention between Abukhalil and Abusada concerns the extent to which Hezbollah's use of armed force can serve as a model for Gaza. For Abukhalil, Hezbollah's experience demonstrates the effectiveness of armed resistance in deterring Israel. For Abusada, the differences in the military capacity of and international support for Hamas and Hezbollah, respectively, are sufficient to render the analogy misleading. Hamas indeed operates in a significantly more difficult environment than Hezbollah. However, what emerges from analysis of Hezbollah's experience as the crucial variable determining the success of armed resistance—regional support—remains in flux in the case of Gaza today.

The importance of regional support

Shortly after Israel's invasion of Lebanon in 1982, a resistance movement against the Israeli occupation began to coalesce. The pervasive fear at the time was that Israel's occupation could become a permanent compromise. Israel wanted to establish a buffer zone in the south to fend off Palestinian resistance, while the sovereignty of the Lebanese state over its territories had broken down under the weight of internecine conflict. In the vacuum, there was a risk that Israel's occupation would be normalized. In particular, the ill-fated 17 May Agreement (1983)* might have formalized the status quo and delegated to Israel the authority to police southern Lebanon with only a vague commitment to withdraw at some undetermined point in the future. Only the Syrian regime of Hafez al-Assad prevented that agreement from being implemented.

---

produce any tangible political achievements. Israel's continued construction of settlements is a case in point.

* *Editor's note:* The 17 May Agreement (1983) between the governments of Israel and Lebanon provided for Israel's partial and conditional military withdrawal from Lebanon—or, as critics saw it, for continued Israeli military presence in southern Lebanon. It was not implemented.

Hezbollah resulted from the convergence of several socially and ideologically distinct strands of resistance enthusiasts around the organizing of military operations against Israel. They were united by the conviction that a quietist attitude towards Israel's occupation would lead to normalization or "*tahwid*."[2] This position stemmed from a scrupulous analysis of previous experiences of resistance against Israel. The PLO was at this point on the wane. Examining its trajectory, Hezbollah militants concluded that the PLO's decline had resulted from, first, its entanglement in the various Lebanese civil wars, and second, its progressive isolation from major regional patrons. Hezbollah media in the 1980s and the 1990s—especially after the 1993 Oslo I Accord between Israel and the PLO—were strongly critical of PLO Chairman Yasser Arafat's decision to pursue negotiations with Israel independently of the Arab states. For Hezbollah, the main lesson from the PLO's sorry fate, which culminated in Arafat's virtual imprisonment in Ramallah and the Palestinian Authority's recruitment as a quasi-police force for Israel, was the folly of unilateralism.

The crucial strategic lesson to be drawn from Hezbollah's experience in Lebanon is therefore one which Hezbollah itself drew from the experience of the PLO, namely, that effective resistance requires regional support. Hezbollah's achievements reflected not just its military capabilities but also complex political maneuverings both within Lebanon and vis-à-vis regional actors such as Syria and Iran. For example, while Hezbollah clashed with the Syrian regime several times in the 1980s and 1990s, it wound up accommodating with the Syrian president because of its conviction that a regional security axis was essential for the success of its militant efforts.[3] Bolstered throughout

---

[2] *Tahwid* literally translates as "Judaize," reflecting the concern that Israel would seize land and then claim title to it on the basis of Jewish scripture. The term was commonly used in the early 1980s by Hezbollah media outlets such as *Al Ahd*.

[3] By contrast, the personal enmity between Arafat and Hafez al-Assad was well known. See, for example, Patrick Seale, *Asad of Syria: The Struggle for the Middle East* (Berkeley and Los Angeles, CA: University of California Press, 1995 [1988]), pp. 125–26.

the 1990s by the Pax Syriana—which provided a safe conduit for weapons, a relatively calm border, and close working relations with the Lebanese state security system—Hezbollah was able to organize an effective military struggle that yielded significant victories.

Different operating environments

The multitude of Israeli concessions and policy retreats that Hezbollah was able to extract over the 1990s and 2000s reinforced its belief in armed struggle as the correct strategy. Hezbollah managed to successively alter the military balance from 1996 onwards,[4] as it established itself as a force to be reckoned with. This led to Israel's decision in May 2000 to withdraw. Hezbollah was also able, over time, to secure an exchange of prisoners. Even individuals whose release was deemed taboo in the eyes of Israeli authorities were eventually freed. Supporters of Hezbollah's movement became convinced that Israel had been put in a position of reacting to Hezbollah's moves, rather than the reverse.

As well as forcing Israeli concessions, the efficacy of armed resistance by Hezbollah is also measured in terms of deterrence. The absence of major conflict on the Lebanese-Israeli front since 2006, notwithstanding the turmoil and chaos that has engulfed the region and in which Hezbollah has been deeply embroiled, is the most convincing proof of the deterrence established by Hezbollah's military performance in the 1990s and during the 2006 War. However, Abusada is correct to highlight a crucial difference between Lebanon and Gaza in this respect. It may be that, as Abukhalil argues and Abusada concedes, Hamas is able to establish a degree of military deterrence vis-à-vis Israel, much as Hezbollah has done on the northern front. But mutual deterrence is much less acceptable for Hamas than it is for Hezbollah, because Gaza,

[4] In 1996, Israel launched "Operation Grapes of Wrath." This caused humanitarian carnage but achieved no significant military gains. Israel launched similar attacks every year after that, as Hezbollah continued to inflict damage on its occupational infrastructure (kidnapping soldiers, attacking outposts, etc.).

unlike Lebanon, is under siege. Whereas Lebanon has benefited from the post-2006 quiet, notwithstanding the periodic media hysteria about an impending Hezbollah-Israel war, for Gaza, such a "quiet" is not sustainable while the blockade persists.

Historically, the principal difference between Hamas and Hezbollah has been the relatively favorable climate in which the latter has operated. First, Hezbollah benefited from the clout of the Lebanese state, not just through a sizable parliamentary presence—a feature it shares with Hamas—but because of a tight security/intelligence arrangement with a Lebanese and Syrian elite and close cooperation with the Lebanese army, even as it faced sizeable local opposition.[5] Second, Hezbollah had access to areas outside of Israeli control: it first trained its militants in the Bekaa, for instance, a region that was largely out of reach of Israel's military apparatus. By contrast, Hamas is confined to territories under Israeli occupation and, in the West Bank, subject to the security control of the Palestinian Authority. Third, while Hezbollah, like all resistance movements, had to face the problem of collaboration, Hamas is confronted with a Palestinian leadership (i.e., the PA) that is engaged in overt and systematic security cooperation with Israel. Fourth, Hezbollah was able to keep open a pathway to Syria, which enabled it to translate regional alliances into large-scale and reliable material assistance. Hamas, contrariwise, is physically isolated from potential allies and surrounded by hostile forces. Hamas has not yet lost all regional support, although its alliances were strained by the crisis in Syria,[6] but the practical benefits accruing from that support are limited by the blockade.

---

[5] This arrangement was severely tested after the Syrian withdrawal from Lebanon in 2005. That withdrawal may help to explain Hezbollah's strategies and decisions in the years since, as it has struggled to re-establish a stable security situation for its military organization.

[6] While Syrian President Bashar al-Assad cut ties with Hamas, Hamas is reported to have resumed relations with Iran. See "Assad: Syria Has 'No Relation At All' with Hamas," *Ma'an News* (19 April 2015).

Lessons

Hezbollah's experience supports Abukhalil's contention that armed struggle is the only effective tool at the disposal of any actor confronting Israel. However, it also suggests that the effective deployment of armed force will ultimately depend upon a broader regional alignment and the ability of the Palestinian resistance to cultivate and exploit this. Abusada's warning that Hamas's militant posture will be counterproductive if it leads to the organization's isolation internationally is therefore justified, albeit—so long as Hamas's commitment to armed struggle does not jeopardize support from regional patrons—premature.

Abusada argues that the international support which prevailed in the 1960s and 1970s for armed struggle against colonial rule has since disappeared. I am skeptical that there was ever significant international support for such initiatives. Moreover, if we remove the "anti-colonial" label, regional and international powers continue to back the use of armed force by an array of state and non-state actors, for a variety of political reasons. Ultimately, the power-struggles being waged today across the Middle East—the US-Iran rapprochement, the internationalized civil war in Syria (where "international support" has created complex relationships and alliances), the evolving foreign policies of the Gulf states—will determine Hamas's future bargaining power. The Palestinian cause is a factor in all these dynamics and the strategic options available to the different Palestinian factions going forward will reflect developments in the regional balance of forces as the various crises play out. If militant actors in Gaza end up bereft of regional support, then Abusada's case against armed struggle in Gaza will be vindicated. For now, it must remain an open question.

Finally, in the debate about whether armed struggle can contribute to peace in Palestine, one dimension that is often overlooked concerns the *quality* of the peace attained—i.e., the degree of *justice* that such a peace would embody. As appealing as the slogan sounds, successful nonviolent struggle has been a historical exception rather than the rule. It can work only in very particular circumstances. It was effective in India because the British

Empire had, by that point, a serious deficit of legitimacy both internationally and among certain sectors of British society, creating a moral climate that Gandhi understood and exploited. By contrast, Israel's existence as a state enjoys broad international legitimacy. Even if nonviolent resistance had the potential to end the occupation and dismantle the settlements, therefore, it would not be able to secure a resolution of the conflict on terms which reflect the full spectrum of Palestinian demands, including the implementation of the Palestinian refugees' right of return* and an end to discrimination against Palestinian citizens of Israel.§ The only possible route to such a peace is armed struggle, which might force Israel to reconsider, albeit gradually and incrementally, its ambitions.

---

* *Editor's note:* See Glossary.

§ *Editor's note:* See Glossary.

RESPONSE:

WHY HAMAS SUPPORTS ARMED STRUGGLE

Ahmed Yousef

Hamas as a liberation movement with an Islamic hue firmly believes in armed struggle as a legitimate right granted by international law for peoples under occupation, and while not considering it to be a sufficient strategy, it remains an essential one. Hamas observed the failure of the peace process for more than two decades, with endless futile negotiations between Israel and the Palestinian Authority, and concluded that the only way to make the Israeli government withdraw from the West Bank and Jerusalem is to continue its armed struggle. Israel's withdrawal from the Gaza Strip came as a result of fierce armed resistance; the same would result in the West Bank if Israel was exposed to strong resistance there and its occupation was similarly made too costly.

Ahmed Yousef is Senior Political Adviser to former Palestinian Prime Minister Ismail Haniyeh. He was previously Deputy Minister of Foreign Affairs.

After Hamas won the election in January 2006, its elected government wrote a letter to the Middle East Quartet* committee urging: Engage, Do Not Isolate Our People. It identified its position as follows:

> Firstly, the new Palestinian government was neither elected on a platform of war, nor was it interested in exacerbating the violence. On the contrary, most Palestinians preferred a negotiated settlement with Israel—although many are doubtful that the Israeli government desires such a settlement. The Palestinian government was indeed elected to reinforce this popular demand, and intends to achieve it for the good of our people as well as the good of the entire region. The peace we wish for, however, is a peace with justice, dignity, and partnership, not coercion, imposition, and intimidation.
>
> Secondly, we also wish to clarify our position regarding violence. Naturally, we don't revere or condone violence. The Palestinian people have struggled long and hard to bring an end to it. If by violence they mean self-defense, we insist that international law gives the uncompromising right for an occupied nation to resist its occupier, especially a very violent one whose history of wantonly targeting civilians is well known.[1]

Abukhalil's argument that military power is required to achieve deterrence and stop Israel from continuing its aggression against the people of Gaza is valid, but at the same time we shouldn't ignore the diplomatic work undertaken by Hamas internationally and over many years, reaching out to the whole world in order to gain solidarity and support and to expose Israel as a rogue state that violates international law by committing war crimes and crimes against humanity. It is justified self-defense, not a propensity for violence, which inevitably

* *Editor's note:* That is, the European Union, Russia, United Nations, and United States. See Glossary.

[1] This is a direct quote from the letter, which has not previously been published. It was sent in November 2006 via a United Nations interlocutor in New York. Hamas received a verbal answer from the same interlocutor.

places Hamas in continuing conflict with an Israeli juggernaut determined to extend—not reduce—its illegal occupation. While the power of deterrence may may not be sufficient to achieve the liberation of Palestine or end the siege of Gaza, it undoubtedly prevents Israel from assuming total control of the West Bank and Jerusalem and from reoccupying Gaza.

The lack of military parity does make it difficult for Hamas to defeat Israel by itself. Thus, another Hamas strategy is to maintain as one of its diplomatic activities the commitment to the liberation of Palestine as a central issue for the Muslim *ummah*.* It solicits support from Arab and Islamic nations to put pressure on Israel to withdraw from Occupied Territories—an occupation which Israel continues to extend through illegal settlements and other ongoing illegitimate forms of control such as the Wall,§ which was condemned by the International Court of Justice.

Mkhaimar Abusada is wrong to describe the Hamas objective in 2014 as being to lift the siege. This confuses the primary Hamas objective—to defend Gaza from an Israeli invasion and threatened reoccupation—with what was only one of several points of negotiation for a ceasefire deal. It also ignores the considerable diplomatic efforts made by Hamas before, during, and after the 2014 Israeli offensive.

Abusada claims that Hamas persecutes its opponents in the Gaza Strip, especially the Salafist jihadists and leftists, because they fire rockets on Israel in violation of the ceasefire agreement signed in 2014. In fact, Hamas and the resistance factions consider these rockets to be ineffective. They could also lead to a war that the Palestinians do not want, and which the Israelis might use as a pretext to destroy the Gaza Strip. So, yes, Hamas security forces fulfilled their duty to protect national security and arrested some members of the Salafist extremists—not to persecute them, but because of what they consider a violation of the ceasefire agreement on the one hand, and of the national consensus of the resistance factions on the other hand.

---

* *Editor's note:* The Muslim 'nation' or world.

§ *Editor's note:* See Glossary.

It should be noted that Hamas is held accountable by Israel, usually militarily, for every rocket fired from Gaza regardless of who fired it, and that Hamas has the very real obligation to maintain Gaza's peace and national security. As such, Hamas cannot stand by while rockets are fired from within its territory, but must act to prevent breaches of the peace in the interests of the entire population, not just small portions of it.

Abusada's claim that the Hamas commitment to armed struggle gives Israel ammunition to justify its massacres globally misses the very important points made above, and risks endorsing the Israeli narrative. It must be emphasized: Palestinians have the right under international law to resist occupation by whatever means necessary, including armed struggle.

Abusada's view is also an injustice to the Hamas movement because it posits that Hamas objects to nonviolent resistance. This is clearly not true. For example, Hamas did not object to Abbas negotiating with the Israeli side when they were partners in the government. However, Hamas is now convinced of the fruitlessness of negotiations following continued exploitation of the process by the Israeli side, with its ever-expanding settlements, Judaization of Jerusalem, and refusal to negotiate on these issues.

As stated, the Hamas movement is not, as Abusada suggests, merely pro-violence. Hamas considers armed resistance one extremely important and legitimate strategy among several—including nonviolence (such as BDS) and diplomacy—and it will not cede the right to utilize *any* of them. Hamas is for any solution that will restore to the Palestinians their rights and contribute to the establishment of their free and independent state.

Setting aside the fallacious argument that the legitimate use of armed struggle in 2014 did not end the siege (it was not designed to), we move on to Abusada's claim that the armed struggle has failed to liberate Palestine. Even a brief glance at history reveals that liberation struggles are not only never won by diplomacy alone, but that they take decades (and sometimes centuries) to succeed, as we saw in Algeria, Vietnam, South Africa, Latin America, and Afghanistan. Settler colonialism has never gone quietly or quickly; Abusada's apparent desire for instant gratification in this respect flies in the face of historical experience, and is based on mistaken assumptions regarding the equation of the conflict with Israel. As he confused the Hamas objective in 2014 with just one aspect of the ceasefire agreement, so he is confusing the length of the liberation struggle with its success. That armed struggle has not yet liberated Palestine in no way implies it never will.

Finally, Abusada's description of the years of Hamas rule as a second *Nakba* for the Palestinians lacks accuracy and credibility. Yes, there are many who are suffering, but they are suffering because of the Israeli siege and because of the Israeli occupation. The national division is a terrible mistake that certainly contributes to their suffering, but the division is not the principal cause, and nor is it solely the responsibility of Hamas.

If these claims of Abusada were true, then why does Hamas enjoy overwhelming popular support in the West Bank and the Gaza Strip?

The goal of the siege is to force the resistance to give up its weapons and to hand over our land and holy places to the Israelis. This is rejected by the vast majority of Palestinians. We firmly believe that armed resistance—and all other means of struggle—are necessary both to end the siege of Gaza and to liberate Palestine.

Palestine—historically speaking—is the cradle of all Abrahamic faiths: Judaism, Christianity, and Islam. From its gates the long march to enlightenment began, and we look forward to the day that the olive branch replaces the gun. This day will only arrive when Palestinians, too, can enjoy their rights with dignity and justice in their homeland.

ꕥ

Mkhaimar Abusada

I agree with Ahmed Yousef that the Palestinians have the right under international law to resist the Israeli occupation. The issue at hand is whether armed struggle can end the siege of Gaza and liberate Palestine from Israeli occupation, given the prevailing internal, regional, and international conditions.

Yousef defends Hamas's authoritarianism: "Hamas security forces fulfilled their duty to protect national security and arrested some members of the Salafist extremists—not to persecute them." But in a 2012 interview with the

Washington Post, discussing the Hamas regime's quashing of dissent and arrests of perceived political opponents, Yousef admitted that Hamas "became like a police state" and "became scared of any rally or demonstration."[2]

Yousef explains that Hamas considers rockets from the Salafists to be ineffective and dangerous because they could precipitate a destructive war with Israel. This is precisely my position with respect to Hamas rockets. Does Yousef maintain that the efficacy of rockets depends on whether they were fired by a Salafist or a member of Hamas? Yousef also says that Hamas "must act to prevent breaches of the peace," but which peace he is talking about? For God's sake, Gaza has been under Israeli siege for ten years, during which time it has endured three full-scale aggressions by Israel.

Regarding Palestinian-Israeli negotiations, Yousef argues: "Hamas did not object to Abbas negotiating with the Israeli side when they were partners in the government." But what about when they were not partners with Abbas in government? Hamas vowed to derail the Oslo peace process from its inception, and put this rejection into practice with suicide bombings in the 1990s. In addition, many senior Hamas leaders have accused Abbas of treason on allegations that he conceded the right of return of Palestinian refugees and made considerable concessions on Jerusalem. Hamas has waged incitement through its media outlets against negotiations between Abbas and the Israelis.

Yousef denies that armed struggle legitimizes Israel's violence and occupation internationally on the basis that Hamas also pursues diplomacy. Which diplomacy he is referring to? Hamas has refused direct talks with Israel on the grounds that Israel is an illegitimate entity, unless Yousef is aware of secret negotiations between Hamas and Israel. It is true that Hamas has made diplomatic efforts, but this work is hampered by Hamas's primary commitment to armed struggle, an albatross that makes it easier for Israel and the US to reject Hamas's diplomatic overtures while still portraying Hamas, and not themselves, as the rejectionists.

---

[2] Yousef, quoted in Karen Brulliard, "In Gaza, Hamas rule has not turned out as many expected," *Washington Post* (18 April 2012).

Yousef says that Hamas's objective in previous rounds of conflicts with Israel was not to lift the siege. If true, then, why wasn't it? Is ending the siege not a priority? But in fact, it surely *was* the objective. Before Cast Lead in 2008–9, for example, Hamas offered to extend the truce brokered by Egypt six months earlier, provided that its terms were implemented—namely, that the crossings be opened. During the conflict, Hamas conditioned a resumption of the ceasefire on a commitment by Israel to end the siege. To be clear: it was Israel which started that conflict. Still, it seems evident that Hamas's objective prior to and during it was to ease or end the siege.

Yousef claims that Hamas supports nonviolent resistance, but this is just lip service. Senior Hamas official Mahmoud al-Zahar has dismissed the call for popular resistance in Gaza as irrelevant since Gaza is no longer under occupation.[3] Yousef himself states that, "Israel's withdrawal from the Gaza Strip came as a result of fierce armed resistance, and the same would result in the West Bank if Israel was exposed to strong resistance there." Hamas is clearly convinced that armed struggle is the only way to end Israel's occupation of the West Bank, as they did in Gaza in 2005.

Hamas has utilized armed struggle for more than a quarter-century, long before the siege of Gaza was in effect. The Israeli occupation has not disappeared in this period; in fact, the number of Israeli settlers has more than tripled since Hamas's inception in 1987.* I think it is time for Hamas to genuinely consider other strategies. For example, why did it not stage a mass nonviolent march and hunger strike on the tenth anniversary of the siege, coordinated with international solidarity movements around the world? Doesn't Yousef think actions

---

* *Editor's note:* The UN Office for the Coordination of Humanitarian Affairs (OCHA) puts the settler population in 1987 at 169,200. B'Tselem estimates the number of Israeli settlers at the end of 2015 at 588,000. See UN OCHA, *The Humanitarian Impact on Palestinians of Israeli Settlements and Other Infrastructure in the West Bank* (July 2007), p. 20; B'Tselem, "Statistics on Settlements and Settler Population," *btselem.org* (updated 11 May 2017).

[3] Zahar was quoted as saying: "Against whom could we demonstrate in the Gaza Strip? When Gaza was occupied, that model was applicable." Hillel C. Neuer, "Hamas Says Gaza 'Not Occupied'; UN Disagrees," *Jerusalem Post* (4 January 2013).

like this have more potential to arouse international opinion and force Israel on the defensive than "ineffective" rockets?

Finally, Yousef asserts that Hamas enjoys "overwhelming popular support in the West Bank and the Gaza Strip." From where arises this confidence, when no municipal, legislative, presidential, or even student union elections have been held in the Gaza Strip since 2006? How could Hamas enjoy overwhelming support in Gaza while 70 percent of Gazans live beneath the poverty line and unemployment has reached 44 percent? How could Hamas enjoy overwhelming support when Gaza's border crossings are snapped shut and the residents struggle to procure such luxuries as electricity and potable water? No doubt, primary responsibility for these outrages lies with Israel's occupation and siege. However, the Palestinians in Gaza hold Hamas responsible as well. Palestinians say, not unreasonably: if you propose to govern us, you must find solutions to our problems and sufferings.

Ahmed Yousef

It is reassuring that Abusada agrees that armed struggle against occupation and imperialism is legitimate in international law. However, I must take issue with his implied insistence on the primacy of what he terms "prevailing internal, regional, and international conditions" in shaping Hamas strategy.

Hamas strategy is determined by solid principles, not pandering to the vagaries of public opinion, whether national, regional, or international. The Hamas constant—the liberation of Palestine, where under the wing of Islam followers of all religions can coexist in security and safety—is neither negotiable nor dependent on the whims of others.

To forgo legitimate and necessary armed struggle in order to appease external forces is in my view a very short-sighted approach. Historically speaking, multifaceted strategies which include both belligerent and nonviolent approaches have been essential to the success of various liberation struggles, such as those of the Irish Republican Army (IRA) and the experience in South Africa. Furthermore, "prevailing conditions" are not static—they change, as does the nature of the struggle. US policy regarding sanctions on South Africa reversed in just one decade, for example.

It was not public opinion that formed the demands of the IRA or the African National Congress (ANC). Rather, IRA and ANC conceptions of social and political justice led public opinion to change—and with it, the national, regional, and international conditions necessary to realize those demands.

The *Washington Post* statement attributed to me was a misquote. All societies have organs responsible for maintaining public order—this does not define them as authoritarian. The Hamas reluctance referred to was to permit large rallies and demonstrations that could be misused to create chaos in an already-polarized society. Many rallies and demonstrations by supporters and dissenters alike have been given permits and continue to take place.

Who fires the rockets is not important; the rockets' technical and strategic effectiveness is. Hamas rockets are more technically advanced and fired at military targets in response to Israeli aggression or incursions. Salafist rockets are unsophisticated, and although rarely causing damage are recklessly fired without obvious cause or target, outside of the collective resistance strategy.

"Breaches of the peace" is a term describing civil order. This order is most definitely threatened by Salafist rockets, which inevitably result in Israeli military retaliation on civil society. Simply put, the "peace" referred to is the ability of Palestinians in Gaza to go about their daily activities unassailed by airstrikes resulting from *random* rocket-fire.

It must be stressed that Hamas was not alone in its opposition to the Oslo peace process; its opposition was shared by most of the Palestinian people and by other factions. As partners in government, Hamas had an opportunity to influence Abbas and restrict his giving of more concessions to the Israelis. As time wore on, it became clear that the negotiations were fruitless, deceptive, and achieving nothing, much less the liberation of a Palestine growing smaller by the day through settlement construction that accelerated in almost exact proportion to the intensity of negotiations. Hamas would be abdicating its responsibilities to its constituents to maintain a media silence while Palestine disappeared in the "piece" process: conceding a piece here, a piece there, until there is nothing left to fight for.

Abusada conceded the legitimacy of armed struggle against occupation. Israeli violence has no such legitimacy—that an occupying power cannot claim self-defense is enshrined in a 2004 International Court of Justice advisory opinion which also held that self-defense under Article 51 of the United Nations Charter is inapplicable to measures taken by an occupying power within occupied territory.[4] Nothing, including Hamas or its actions, legitimizes Israeli violence and occupation. It is simply illegal, and no amount of diplomacy can change that fundamental fact.

Hamas has carefully observed the negotiations and diplomatic relations between the Israeli and the Palestinian authorities for twenty years and concluded that direct talks between the parties have achieved—to use the words of Ahmed Qorea, chief Palestinian negotiator in Oslo—"a big zero." It is not a matter of legitimacy, which the PLO has already given Israel, but rather of negotiating in good faith—something the Israeli side has shown it is incapable of, as demonstrated by its failures to honor past agreements, e.g., the Oslo Accords, the Shalit prisoner swap agreement,* and its almost daily breaches of the 2014 ceasefire agreement. As such, direct negotiations in any form between Hamas and the Israelis are considered pointless unless and until good faith is established by Israel honoring in full all previous agreements.

Abusada's persistent inability to distinguish between the primary Hamas objective in confronting an Israeli aggression (defending its people and territory) and its multiple objectives in moving towards the cessation of hostilities (ending the fighting and laying the foundations for future peaceful co-existence) again undermine his argument. The objective of ending the siege—along with other terms of the ceasefire such as a Gaza port, extended

---

* *Editor's note:* In 2011, Israel and Hamas reached an agreement according to which Israel would release 1,027 prisoners in exchange for the release by Hamas of the captured Israeli soldier Gilad Shalit.

[4] International Court of Justice, *Legal Consequences of the Construction of a Wall in the Occupied Palestinian Territory* (advisory opinion of 9 July 2004), para. 139.

buffer zones, etc.—existed prior to the most recent offensive as well as during and after it. They are, and will be, constants until the siege is lifted and the occupation ended. But they were not the primary goal in the face of the Israeli aggression.

As stated in the previous response, Hamas considers armed struggle to have had demonstrated success and to be *one of several* legitimate strategies to achieve the liberation of Palestine. It thus declines to forgo *any* legitimate means to achieve self-determination.

Abusada justifies his call for a change of Hamas strategy by pointing to the increase in settlements since the founding of Hamas. It is equally true to say that the number of settlers has tripled since the inception of the Palestinian Authority in 1994. Why then is Abusada not calling for a change of strategy from the PA? Why must it be Hamas that stages a mass nonviolent march and hunger strike, and not the PA? The PA is the internationally recognized representative of the Palestinian people—surely *its* involvement "has more potential to stir international public opinion and force Israel on the defensive than 'ineffective' rockets." Or perhaps this is an admission that Hamas is much better at this than the PA…

After all, Abusada must surely concede that most of the change in international public opinion in the West has happened as a result of Hamas's calls to people of conscience around the world to stand with the people of Gaza and Palestine. The number of humanitarian convoys and flotillas heading for Gaza to break the siege is testament to the success of these efforts.

Popularity is not measured by poverty and unemployment rates but by elections. Who cancels and postpones the various elections—Hamas? No. Why do 70 percent of Gazans live below the poverty line and 44 percent have no jobs? Because of Hamas? No—as Abusada himself says, because of the Israeli siege, because of Israeli import restrictions that stifle the economy; because of Israeli-enforced buffer zones that prevent farmers and fishermen from providing food for the populace; because of Palestinian banks closing the accounts of charities that once kept many of these people above the poverty line and employed.

Who collects the money from the international community and the taxes to be used for the benefit of the Palestinian people, including those in Gaza? The Hamdallah government.*

Abusada's conclusion is absolutely correct—"If you propose to govern us, *you* must find solutions to our problems and sufferings."

---

* *Editor's note:* That is, the PA. Rami Hamdallah was appointed Palestinian prime minister in June 2014.

CHAPTER SIX.

CAN HAMAS BE PART OF THE SOLUTION?

Nathan Thrall vs. Ghaith al-Omari

Nathan Thrall

In the coming exchange, I will argue in defense of the proposition that Hamas can be part of the solution to the Israeli-Palestinian conflict. But before doing

---

Nathan Thrall is the author of *The Only Language They Understand: Forcing Compromise in Israel and Palestine* (2017). He is a regular contributor to *The New York Review of Books* and the *London Review of Books* and is Senior Analyst for Israel/Palestine at the International Crisis Group.

Ghaith al-Omari, a Senior Fellow at The Washington Institute for Near East Policy with extensive experience in the Palestinian-Israeli peace process, is a former Executive Director of the American Task Force on Palestine. He has also served in various positions within the Palestinian Authority, including Advisor to former Prime Minister Mahmoud Abbas and Advisor to the negotiating team during the 1999–2001 permanent status talks.

so, the terms of the debate should be clarified. The first point to be made is that, whatever one's view of the most likely Israeli-Palestinian settlement or lack thereof, the opposing view in this dialogue—that Hamas cannot be part of the solution—is untenable. Only someone purporting to possess prophetic powers could claim to know in advance that Hamas or any other party cannot be part of the solution. Narrowly interpreted, my task here is to defend a mere possibility, and, unless one is claiming foreknowledge, it must be conceded that it is at least possible that Hamas could be part of "the solution." We could then declare this debate finished. A broader interpretation, which I will expand upon later, is that it is not only possible but highly probable that, if there is a solution, Hamas, one of the two largest factions in Palestinian politics and the one with the most capable armed wing, will be a part of it. Indeed, it is hard to imagine a lasting solution that does not entail Hamas's acquiescence.

Next, what do we mean by "the solution"? This term, unless defined, could be used as another means of smuggling in the claim that Hamas cannot be a part of it. Israeli Prime Minister Benjamin Netanyahu states that "the solution" will entail recognition of Israel as the national homeland of the Jewish people. If one agrees with Netanyahu, prescriptively, that this should be a part of the solution, or if one instead agrees, descriptively, that any solution will entail such recognition, then one could claim that Hamas will not offer such recognition and therefore Hamas will not or cannot be part of the solution. (Likewise, based on the stated positions of every other Palestinian faction, one could assert on this basis that they also cannot be part of the solution.) But this claim, too, stands on shaky ground, for it assumes that "the solution" will demand of all Israeli and Palestinian political parties that they themselves make the ideological, narrative, and other concessions that will be required of the two governments. The Tkuma Party in Israel, now part of Jewish Home, is unlikely to accept Palestinian statehood, Israeli withdrawal from Hebron, or Palestinian sovereignty over the Noble Sanctuary/Temple Mount.* But if a peace treaty were to include such provisions, would the Jewish Home Party be obligated to formally accept these concessions in order to concretize an

* *Editor's note:* See Glossary.

agreement? Or would it be permitted to continue to oppose elements of the agreement, so long as the government representing Israel had accepted it?

To take another example, this time from the Palestinian side: in the past Israel and the international community have demanded ideological concessions of the Palestine Liberation Organization (PLO)—including recognition of Israel and renunciation of armed struggle—not of its individual constituent factions. Thus Fatah, for example, has never renounced armed resistance, and to this day there are those claiming membership in Fatah who conduct armed attacks, including from Gaza during the past several conflicts with Israel. Does that mean that Fatah cannot be part of the solution? Likewise, the Likud Party has never accepted a Palestinian state. Will it be required to do so as part of a two-state solution, and does its refusal to do so thus far constitute support for the claim that Likud, one of the largest parties in Israel, cannot be part of the solution? Or do those who state that Hamas cannot be part of the solution intend to apply different standards to each side, demanding that in Israel only the government accept an agreement, while in Palestine, all political parties must do so?

What if Hamas and Likud both refuse to change their platforms to accommodate a two-state settlement, but both also permit individual members of the party to serve in a government that recognizes the other state? Would that, in some narrow interpretation, constitute affirmation of the claim that neither Hamas nor Likud can be part of the solution? Do those holding this view claim to know in advance that Hamas or Likud or Jewish Home will not take such a position or even change their platforms or charters?*

What if Hamas were to refuse to accept an agreement but kept to its longstanding vow to abide by the results of any referendum of the Palestinian people? If such a referendum were to pass and as a result Hamas agreed to not violently oppose the peace treaty and perhaps even to run in elections for the Palestinian government that recognizes it, would that constitute Hamas being part of the solution? What if there is no referendum but Hamas and Likud both abide by a peace treaty, opposing it only in words?

---

* *Editor's note:* For Hamas, Fatah, Likud, and Jewish Home, see Glossary.

And what of a long-term truce between two states—in other words, an armistice agreement, as prevailed between Israel and Jordan for over forty years? This is a solution that is favored by many in Hamas and also by some on the Israeli right. Hamas has repeatedly stated that it is willing to accept an armistice lasting decades in exchange for the establishment of a Palestinian state on the pre-1967 lines, the evacuation of all settlements, and the release of all Palestinians prisoners from Israeli jails. However unlikely such an outcome may seem, would it not constitute a solution, and is that not something that Hamas is likely to accept?

Leaving these interpretive questions aside, what, practically, would it mean for there to be a solution of which Hamas is not a part? Would it mean a "solution" that excludes Gaza—that is, a Palestinian state in the West Bank alone (where membership in Hamas is presumably criminalized)? In which of these senses does my colleague contend that Hamas cannot be a part of the solution?

ꕥ

Ghaith al-Omari

It is worth noting at the outset that any discussion about resolving the Palestinian-Israeli conflict at the present time is theoretical given the extremely low likelihood of such a solution in the foreseeable future.

That said, the international consensus has for many years defined the solution to the Palestinian-Israeli conflict as follows: a negotiated, conflict-ending agreement that brings finality to all claims and creates a State of Palestine alongside the State of Israel, coexisting in peace, security, and mutual recognition. By its choice of objectives and its methods, Hamas as it stands today cannot be part of reaching a negotiated two-state solution and should not be engaged as part of the solution.

Hamas is, legally and empirically, a terrorist organization. It not only supports, incites, and celebrates terrorism—it directly practices terrorism. Indeed, terrorism, under the guise of resistance, is one of the two pillars used by Hamas to differentiate itself from the PLO and to build domestic legitimacy and secure regional patronage. In Hamas's parlance, "armed resistance" is the only path to Palestinian liberation while diplomacy is a form of treason and a religious transgression. Hamas's commitment to terrorism is not only rhetorical but also organizational. Hamas's military apparatus, the Qassam Brigades, has emerged as the strongest wing within the organization.

The second pillar of Hamas's self-definition is its rejection of the two-state solution and categorical refusal to recognize Israel. Certain Hamas leaders occasionally make vague statements, usually to Western media, that could be interpreted with some linguistic gymnastics as an indication that Hamas might be willing to accept a two-state solution at some point. Yet such statements never make it into Hamas's Arabic literature or its messaging to members and local and regional supporters. Instead, its domestic messaging focuses exclusively on destroying Israel as a patriotic and religious duty.

Hamas has chosen to define itself in opposition to the internationally accepted framework for resolving the Palestinian-Israeli conflict. Without changing either the terms of this framework or the nature of Hamas, the latter cannot be part of an internationally endorsed solution, nor does it seem interested in playing such a role. This is not only an ideological position on the part of Hamas but also one designed to yield political benefits for the organization while discrediting the PLO. Hamas's doctrinal radicalism has won it the support of various constituencies among the Palestinians and beyond, including those despairing of the prospects for a diplomatic solution as well as those who did not believe in one to begin with. It has also gained Hamas significant regional support, from Iran, which continues to provide assistance to the Qassam Brigades, and from countries such as Qatar and Turkey, which support it as part of the wider Muslim Brotherhood regional camp.

This handful of countries aside, the international community's refusal to engage with Hamas has undermined the movement's legitimacy. While legitimacy is ultimately a domestic matter, any movement that aspires to lead the Palestinian people needs to demonstrate that it can navigate the international arena and garner broad international support. This desire for international acceptance explains why Hamas media play up any interactions the organization has with Western parliamentarians, journalist, or activists. Such interactions, however, have thus far been too insignificant and unofficial to have an impact on Hamas's image.

Official engagement by Western governments would change that. It would validate Hamas's argument that it can become mainstreamed without compromising on its agenda or methods. Such a message would be devastating to the foundation of the international consensus around resolving the Palestinian-Israeli conflict: diplomacy as a path to a two-state solution. It would also have more far-reaching implications, allowing any non-state actor to argue that it can ignore the international consensus, engage in terrorism, and still—if it holds fast for long enough—win international acceptance. At a time when the Middle East is beset with pernicious non-state actors, such a message would only add to regional instability and undermine those who have committed to playing by international rules.

Assuming that the international consensus framework for resolving the conflict remains the same, Hamas can become part of the solution in one of only three scenarios. It can change its program to accept the two-state solution and renounce terrorism in word and deed. This scenario is unlikely given the political costs involved and Hamas's internal dynamics. Alternatively, Hamas's ability to spoil a deal may be degraded to such a degree that it becomes an insignificant irritant, akin to certain marginal PLO factions. But this is also unlikely given Hamas's secure control over the Gaza Strip. Lastly, Hamas may agree to abide by and accept the legitimacy of a solution adopted by the PLO. But for this to be convincing, Hamas will have to be willing to disarm, which is currently not an option given the Qassam Brigades' dominant position within the organization.

In present conditions, therefore, Hamas is part of the problem and not the solution. This does not mean that Israel and international actors should not seek to reach security understandings, through third-party mediators, to avoid a new war in Gaza. Nor does it mean that the international community should not explore ways to alleviate the humanitarian situation in Gaza. What it means is that Hamas should not be allowed to enjoy the benefits of international recognition while maintaining positions and practices that run counter to the internationally agreed terms for resolving the conflict. Premature and unprincipled engagement would have negative implications for the peace process and for the wider regional objective of fighting terror and promoting respect for international norms.

ꙮ

Nathan Thrall

In support of his contention that Hamas cannot be part of the solution to the conflict, Ghaith al-Omari has made two types of claims: *descriptive* ones regarding the unlikelihood or impossibility of Hamas being part of the solution, and *normative* ones concerning the undesirability of governmental engagement with Hamas.

I will first address the descriptive assertions. Let me state at the outset that senior figures in Hamas, like senior figures in Fatah and the Likud and a number of other Palestinian and Israeli political parties, have made wildly inconsistent pronouncements on any number of subjects, including the desirability of establishing a Palestinian state in the West Bank and Gaza. Although the present debate would become quite tedious if the two sides were to supply a series of quotes supporting each position, I think it important to correct several inaccuracies.

First, it is not true that for Hamas "diplomacy is a form of treason and a religious transgression." Of course, Hamas has relentlessly criticized PLO leaders for the manner in which they have negotiated with Israel, for the concessions they have allowed Israel to pocket, for the repeated failure of the talks, and for the seeming inability of the PLO to seriously pursue any other strategic option. But these criticisms, which are hardly exceptional among Palestinians, are quite different from stating that negotiations in principle are prohibited, religiously or otherwise. In fact, Hamas has often repeated—in English and in Arabic, in private and in public—that diplomacy is entirely permissible, and it has cited *sunnah* and *hadith* to demonstrate to its constituents that there is no religious transgression in negotiating with enemies and unbelievers. Hamas has indirectly negotiated ceasefires and prisoner exchanges with Israel; its municipal officials have worked directly with the Israeli Civil Administration;* its employees in

* *Editor's note:* See Glossary.

Gaza have cooperated and coordinated with counterparts in Israeli ministries; and when it signed a reconciliation agreement with the PLO in May 2011, its leader, Khaled Meshaal, delivering a televised address in Arabic, gave the PLO explicit approval to continue negotiations with Israel: "We have given peace, from Madrid to now, twenty years. I say: We are ready to agree as Palestinians, in the arms of the Arabs and with their support, to give an additional chance for agreement on how to manage it." In 2014, in an interview in Arabic to a Hamas-affiliated TV station, the deputy head of the movement, Mousa Abu Marzouk, stated that Hamas could negotiate directly with Israel: "From the point of view of Islamic law, nothing prevents negotiations with the occupation. Just as you negotiate with it using weapons, you can negotiate using words."

Second, it is not true that proclamations Hamas makes in English regarding a two-state solution "never make it into Hamas' Arabic literature or its messaging to members and local and regional supporters." While it is true that Hamas never says in Arabic that it would recognize Israel, this is a highly misleading charge, since Hamas never says this in English either. Broadly speaking, Hamas's position, frequently repeated in both languages, is that, as a party, it advocates the liberation of all of Palestine, from the river to the sea, and it believes armed resistance is not only a legitimate tool but the most effective one. At the same time, Hamas recognizes that a large number of Palestinians do not share this view, and it has repeatedly stated that it won't impose its will on the Palestinian people. If a majority of Palestinians accept a negotiated solution to the conflict, including the establishment of two-states on the pre-1967 borders, Hamas says it will abide by that decision. Furthermore, Hamas explicitly affirms that it will accept a Palestinian state on the pre-1967 lines, and it has been saying this loudly and clearly since the 1990s. What it says it will not do, however, is recognize Israel. When asked whether it would accept a two-state solution, its answer is consistent: it would accept a Palestinian state on the pre-1967 lines; it will not recognize Israel; and, as such, Hamas itself will not use the phrase "two-state solution," though the rest of the world can use whatever term it likes.

This was also the position of the PLO for many years, when it refused to accept UN Security Council Resolution 242—which called for "respect for and acknowledgment of the sovereignty, territorial integrity and political independence of every State in the area"—while confirming that it would agree to a Palestinian state in the West Bank and Gaza. I would not claim that Hamas, like the PLO before it, will eventually abandon its refusal to recognize Israel. No one can know whether that will happen, and certainly there is little evidence to suggest that it will. What I am asserting is that a negotiated two-state settlement is possible without making such a demand of Hamas, just as an agreement is possible without demanding mutual recognition from Fatah, the PFLP, Jewish Home, and the Likud, none of which has been asked to recognize the other state that would be established in a future peace. Hamas has said that it would abide by the results of a Palestinian referendum on a negotiated settlement. For those who want to see the establishment of two states, that ought to be good enough. For those who don't, insisting on Hamas's recognition of Israel is a useful tactic of obstruction.

This brings us to a point on which al-Omari and I agree: Hamas is currently too powerful—too able, in al-Omari's words, to "spoil a deal"—for there to be a lasting two-state settlement without its acquiescence. This means that, unless Hamas's capabilities are seriously downgraded or its positions significantly altered, the only realistic way to reach a negotiated settlement is for Hamas to abide by an agreement obtained by the PLO. Al-Omari writes that for this to work Hamas would have to disarm, but he rules out such a possibility on the grounds that the armed wing of Hamas is currently dominant within the organization. Needless to say, the fact that the armed wing is strong is not proof that it would refuse to integrate into the security forces of a future Palestinian state. In fact, senior leaders of the organization have said, publicly and in Arabic, that if there were an end to occupation there would no longer be a need for the weapons of the factions resisting that occupation. Al-Omari is entitled to doubt Hamas's sincerity on this point, but he cannot claim that the position of the movement is to refuse to submit to the authority of a Palestinian state established in a democratically endorsed agreement that Hamas has said it would honor. Before such an agreement is reached, however, Hamas is indeed unlikely to disarm, for reasons recently spelled out by former Mossad head Efraim Halevy: "Imagine that Hamas does disperse its military units and they lay down their arms. What will Israel do if it doesn't kill them? What incentive will we have to negotiate with them if they are no longer a threat to us? . . . There is no such thing as a society that is in a state of combat with another country accepting demilitarization in return for something that is untenable."

Finally, al-Omari makes several prescriptive arguments urging the international community not to engage with Hamas, since doing so would bolster Hamas's legitimacy at the expense of the PLO, undermine the prospects for peace, and encourage terrorism throughout the world by opening the door to Western engagement with other non-state groups that have practiced terrorism (the latter argument ignores the long history of Western engagement with such groups as the IRA, the ETA, Hezbollah, and the Taliban). Although the question of whether to continue boycotting Hamas is not the subject of this exchange, I will say that, so far as the peace process is concerned, talk of engaging Hamas is premature: once the countless rounds of negotiations between Israel and the relatively pliant PLO come anywhere close to successfully concluding, it might begin to make sense to ask about the positions of less malleable parties. Until then, there is no point in discussing Hamas's hypothetical acceptance of an agreement that has little current prospect of materializing.

Yet if and when a negotiated settlement does seem to be within reach, and if one plans for the peace to include Gaza and have some prospect of lasting, there will be no alternative but to engage with Hamas on the solution, including on how the movement can be convinced at the very least not to undermine it.

ᢀ

Ghaith al-Omari

I previously defined a "solution" as "a negotiated, *conflict-ending* agreement that brings *finality to all claims* and creates a State of Palestine alongside the State of Israel." Some Hamas leaders have occasionally expressed willingness to engage in diplomacy, but never towards that end. The maximum that Hamas has signaled it is prepared to accept is a long-term ceasefire—or *hudna*—which falls short of this objective. The very citation of *hadith* and *sunnah*, such as the

Hudaybiyyah treaty, is designed to show that negotiations and agreements do not constitute an acceptance of a conflict-ending agreement or a recognition of Israel. The kind of diplomacy that Hamas is willing to accept is one that brings a temporary lull to the conflict, not one that ends it.

It is possible to argue that Hamas leaders understand that Israel is here to stay, and are sending signals that they are willing to live with it without formal recognition. This is exactly what the PLO tried to do in the mid-1970s. Hamas today, just like the PLO in the seventies and eighties, wants the benefits of international diplomacy without paying the price with its constituencies of formally revising its positions to conform with international norms and principles. Indeed, the precedent of the PLO is instructive. Until the PLO was willing to make overt, formal changes to its positions on a two-state solution and on terrorism, it was not considered a part of the solution. This conditionality was imposed not because the international community did not understand that the PLO in that period spoke for the Palestinians, but because only the PLO's acceptance of UN Security Council Resolution 242 and renunciation of terrorism could have made possible a process leading to mutual recognition between it and Israel and the establishment of the two-state solution as a consensus formula for peace.

Nathan Thrall points to a number of Palestinian and Israeli parties that have not accepted the two-state consensus but which could still be part of a solution. This is a misleading analogy. While the Likud, Jewish Home, and Fatah do not formally adopt the two-state solution as parties, they have abided by their respective nations' commitments and more importantly have not used terrorism to pursue their goals. Hamas, on the other hand, has repeatedly deployed its terrorist apparatus to scuttle Palestinian-Israeli negotiations and to advance its domestic objectives.

Indeed, Hamas's desire to maintain its armed spoiler capacity while simultaneously enjoying a seat at the diplomatic table goes to the heart of the problem. Citing Hezbollah as precedent of Western engagement with terrorist groups is hardly reassuring. Since its establishment, Hezbollah had vowed never to turn its arms against its Lebanese compatriots but to direct them exclusively against the Israeli occupation of southern Lebanon. Yet when Israel withdrew from southern Lebanon in 2000, Hezbollah did not disarm, and in 2008, in the midst of a political crisis, Hezbollah militias turned their guns against their Lebanese compatriots when they took control of Beirut and imposed their conditions. With this precedent in mind, and recalling also Hamas's violent takeover of Gaza in June 2007, Hamas leaders' highly conditional vows to disarm upon the establishment of a Palestinian state do not convince.

It is not inconceivable that Hamas will pursue the path of the PLO and become part of the solution. This would be a positive development. But it is clear that Hamas will not do this of its own volition. The ultimate prize of international acceptance should remain available to Hamas, but the conditions for receiving this prize should be clearly spelled out, as they were by the Middle East Quartet in 2006.* Thrall is right to observe that Hamas is unlikely to accept the Quartet conditions any time soon. But until it does, any international retreat from those conditions would only serve to convince Hamas that it can have its cake and eat it too, hardening its positions.

While I maintain that Hamas, as it stands today, cannot contribute to the ultimate resolution of the Palestinian-Israeli conflict, and should on that account be isolated, this does not mean that the situation in Gaza should remain as it is. Understandings regarding a long-term ceasefire in Gaza are possible. These understandings can be arranged by Arab and other international parties that have preexisting channels with Hamas, so that Hamas does not get the political benefit of gaining additional international interlocutors. Even without such understandings, efforts need to be intensified to address the humanitarian situation in Gaza, both as a matter of principle and as a pragmatic step to reduce the possibility of future armed hostilities with Israel.

---

* *Editor's note:* After Hamas won the 2006 Palestinian legislative elections, the Middle East Quartet (comprising the European Union, Russia, the United Nations, and the United States) conditioned economic assistance to any Palestinian government on adherence by it to three "principles": "nonviolence, recognition of Israel, and acceptance of previous agreements and obligations." ("Quartet Statement," 30 January 2016)

RESPONSE:

THE PLO AS CAUTIONARY TALE

Khaled Hroub

After Hamas's victory in the 2006 Palestinian Legislative Council elections, Israel imposed three conditions that the movement had to meet to be acknowledged as a "political partner": it was required to recognize Israel's right to exist, renounce "terrorism," and adhere to previous agreements between Israel and the PLO. Under American pressure, these conditions were endorsed by the Middle East Quartet (composed of the EU, Russia, UN, and US). In return, Hamas was promised a seat at the diplomatic table.

This was an unimaginative sequel to the late 1980s, when US and Israeli engagement with the PLO was conditioned on the PLO recognizing Israel's right to exist and renouncing violence. In neither case were the international

---

Khaled Hroub is Professor in Residence of the Faculty of Liberal Arts at Northwestern University in Qatar. He is also a Senior Research Fellow at the Center of Islamic Studies at the University of Cambridge, where he was Director of the Cambridge Arab Media Project. Between 2000 and 2007, he hosted a weekly review of books on Al Jazeera. His own works include *Hamas: Political Thought and Practice* (2000) and *Hamas: A Beginner's Guide* (2006, 2010).

conditions applied consistently. The PLO and Hamas were required to recognize Israel's right to exist, while Israel was required merely to recognize these organizations as diplomatic interlocutors (i.e., Israel was not required to recognize the right of the Palestinian people to self-determination and a sovereign state). And while both Palestinian organizations were required to renounce the use of violence against Israel, Israel was granted a free hand to use violence against the Palestinians.

When the PLO recognized Israel, Israel and the US kept their end of the bargain and began to talk with it. Indeed, they have talked endlessly since the early 1990s. But from these talks, the Palestinian people and their national aspirations gained almost nothing. The "solution" stipulated in the exchange between Nathan Thrall and Ghaith al-Omari never materialized despite the major and historic compromise that the PLO had made in the Oslo Accords: recognizing Israel's right to exist on more than 77 percent of Mandatory Palestine.* After almost a quarter-century of meaningless "talks" with the PLO, Hamas is now presented with the same ultimatum and the same deal.

In the long years of the "talks" between the PLO and Israel, the issues at the core of the conflict—East Jerusalem, the settlements, the right to return of the Palestinian refugees, borders and security arrangements, natural resources—remained almost untouched, blocking any real progress toward a final status agreement. In approaching these issues, Israel's strategy was to push to the fore its self-defined "security concerns" as if these were equivalent in status to the internationally ratified rights of the Palestinian people, and galvanize local, regional, and international actors behind them. Israel's fear was not that these "security concerns" would go unaddressed but that the PLO would persuasively answer them, thereby undermining the plausibility of Israel's pretext for diplomatic rejectionism.

When the PLO acquiesced in international pressure and formally recognized Israel as a state, Israel was forced, reluctantly, to engage in talks with it. But in the course of those talks, it invented a new condition for a diplomatic

* *Editor's note:* See Glossary.

agreement. PLO recognition of Israel was no longer sufficient; now, the PLO had to recognize Israel *as a Jewish state*. This was a wholly novel requirement, one which had no basis in international law or in Israel's peace treaties with Jordan and Egypt and which served to extend the list of conditions on the Palestinians and reduce the prospects for a solution. Today, Israel's coupling of its "security concerns" with recognition of its "Jewishness" has become difficult to undo. While repeatedly shifting the diplomatic goalposts in this fashion, Israel proceeded as usual on the ground, constructing illegal settlement units and other infrastructure that further complicated any future resolution of the major issues specified by the Oslo Accords.

Whereas strict conditions were imposed on international engagement with Hamas and the PLO, Israeli political parties and leaders are free to run on platforms that explicitly repudiate what al-Omari describes as the "consensus" terms of a resolution, without international consequence. For example, Naftali Bennett, Israel's Minister of Education and head of the right-wing Jewish Home Party, pledges with impunity "to do everything in my power to prevent giving away even one inch of Israeli soil [*sic*] to the Arabs" and boasts without fear of repercussion that, "I've killed lots of Arabs in my life—and there's no problem with that."[1] The extremism, racism, support for ethnic cleansing, and disparagement of any future diplomatic solution reflected in these statements surpasses anything found in the discourse of Hamas's leaders.

It is an open question whether, if good-faith negotiations between Israel and the Palestinian leadership were to reach agreement on a solution to the conflict that addressed the core issues while respecting internationally recognized Palestinian rights, Hamas could be part of making that solution work. It is an open question because Israel has never engaged in good-faith negotiations with the Palestinians. My own assessment is, Hamas would find it extremely difficult to remain on the margins were the majority of the Palestinians and Arabs to accept a proposed deal. Even if Hamas opposed the terms of such

[1] Naftali Bennett, Tweet by @Naftali_Bennett (25 February 2015), http://tinyurl.com/legtzxd; "Naftali Bennett: 'I've Killed Lots Of Arabs In My Life And There's No Problem With That'," *The World Post* (29 July 2013).

an agreement, the movement has the political tools and practices—see, for instance, Hamas's repeated offers to Israel of a *hudna*, or long-term truce, and its declared willingness to accept the outcome of a Palestinian referendum on any proposed agreement—to allow it to reconcile ideology with political pragmatism.[2]

The possibility of Hamas being part of a solution increases or decreases depending on the nature of the solution itself. Moreover, Hamas's participation in such a solution might be either active or passive. If the proposed solution was relatively close to Palestinian demands, Hamas's participation could be active, and it would be no surprise to find Hamas seeking to participate in shaping and negotiating the outcome (perhaps under a national umbrella or by forming an affiliated political party). If the solution was less attractive to Hamas but still enjoyed critical mass support among the Palestinians, Hamas would likely opt for a stance of "passive" participation/opposition (similar to its position on the 1994 Gaza-Jericho Agreement, to which it declared its "peaceful" opposition).

This must remain a matter for speculation so long as the reality remains one in which Israel is committed to rejectionism and continued colonization. Given the sorry experience of the PLO and in light of Israeli policies designed to erode any remaining possibility of a two-state solution, it is breathtaking that al-Omari or anyone else should endorse the Quartet's "three conditions" that Hamas must abide by to be considered as partner to a (non-existing) solution and hold up the experience of the PLO as a model to be emulated. (While we're at it, shouldn't Hamas also agree to Israel's recently-added fourth condition of recognizing the Jewishness of Israel?) Palestinian and Arab commentaries frequently criticize the PLO for more than two decades of failed "peace talks," cautioning Hamas against pursuing a similar track of yielding to Israeli "conditions" unilaterally. The record amply bears out these warnings.

---

[2] For discussion of Hamas's approaches to "peace proposals," see Khaled Hroub, *Hamas: Political Thought and Practice* (Washington DC: Institute for Palestine Studies, 2000).

RESPONSE:

HAMAS WITHOUT *JIHAD* IS NOT HAMAS

Ido Zelkovitz

The complexity of the Israeli-Palestinian dispute stems not only from the struggles arising between the two national movements as they attempt to realize their aspirations and justify their own existence, but also from the internal conflicts produced by their respective social and political structures. The debate between Nathan Thrall and Ghaith al-Omari on whether Hamas might be part of the solution to the conflict, or will always be an obstacle to such a solution, evidences this complexity.

The first point which needs to be taken into account, as al-Omari emphasizes, is that, despite the growing strength of the right-wing of Israeli politics, the Likud coalition government, many of whose members would not welcome a two-state solution, is still committed to the political

---

Ido Zelkovitz is Head of Middle East Studies at the Max Stern Yezreel Valley College, Israel. He is a Research Fellow at the Ezri Center for Iran and Persian Gulf Studies at the University of Haifa and a Policy Fellow at Mitvim, the Israeli Institute for Regional Foreign Policies.

framework of the agreements signed by its predecessors. This is an important point to understand. Israel is a democratic state that is committed to international law. As such, its elected government cannot cancel the agreements entered into by its predecessors, even when they are inconsistent with its own ideology.

The Palestinian political system is quite different. One of the major obstacles to finding a formula that would enable a resolution of the conflict is the continued political rift between Fatah and Hamas. This division is grounded not only in a struggle for resources, power, and influence, but also in fundamental disagreements over the basic character of a future Palestinian state.

The fact that there is no tradition of democracy in the Palestinian Authority (PA) exacerbates and entrenches this factional rift.

Whereas every elected government of Israel is committed to continuity, in the Palestinian polity one finds a paradoxical situation. Hamas was elected through a democratic process to rule a body—the PA—that was established as a result of the mutual recognition agreement signed between the PLO and Israel, yet Hamas does not recognize the right of the State of Israel to exist.

This has created an intractable dilemma. As both Thrall and al-Omari point out, Hamas is an important political actor that must be included in any serious attempt to arrive at a political solution or even to manage the conflict. It wields sufficient veto power to undermine the capacity of the PA to make credible agreements. But it itself also lacks diplomatic credibility, since it repudiates previous agreements between the PLO and Israel.

Hamas is a terrorist organization with a codified doctrine. It is true that when Hamas found itself charged with performing governmental duties in the Gaza Strip, it was compelled to adapt to its new responsibilities. Even so, I consider that the canonical texts of the organization do serve as binding on it. On the core issues of the Israeli-Palestinian conflict, these texts offer no room for compromise. Hamas's 1988 Charter states, "The Islamic Resistance Movement believes that the land of Palestine is an Islamic *Waqf* [endowment] to all Muslim generations until the day of resurrection. It is not right to give up it or any part of it."[1] The more pragmatic stances which Thrall cites as possible stepping-stones to a formula enabling Hamas to take part in shaping a regional agreement are merely tactical maneuvers reflecting Hamas's assessment of what is currently achievable given Israel's military strength. It may be possible to reach temporary understandings on such a basis, but it is not a stable foundation for a long-term resolution of the conflict.

In May 2017, Hamas published a document which purported to reflect evolutions and developments in the movement's principles since 1988.[2] Contrary to much wishful thinking from international observers, this text was not intended to replace or nullify Hamas's founding charter. In the words of Mahmoud al-Zahar, a prominent Hamas leader, "the pledge Hamas made before God was to liberate all of Palestine . . . The charter is the core of (Hamas's) position and the mechanism of this position is the document."[3] Rather, the text is a tool intended to enable Hamas's leadership to maneuver more adroitly between three fields: Palestinian politics, where Hamas struggles to maintain the upper-hand over Fatah; inter-Arab politics, where Hamas seeks to maintain and accrue legitimacy at the expense of the PLO; and the international community, in whose eyes Hamas wishes to appear more moderate. It would be a mistake to confuse tactical expediency in response to a crisis situation for a genuine shift in strategic vision.

Furthermore, we should bear in mind that the harsh humanitarian situation in the Gaza Strip, together with the ideological challenges posed by the Salafist organizations to Hamas's doctrine of resistance, do not afford Hamas the luxury of abandoning its advocacy and practice of violent *jihad*. Indeed, *jihad* is one of Hamas's fundamental precepts: Hamas without *jihad* would

[1] Hamas, "The Covenant of the Islamic Resistance Movement," (18 August 1988), Article 11. Translation from Shaul Mishal and Avraham Sela, *The Palestinian Hamas: Vision, Violence, and Coexistence* (New York, NY: Columbia University Press, 2006 [2000]), p. 181.

[2] Hamas, "A Document of General Principles and Policies," *hamas.ps* (1 May 2017).

[3] Nidal al-Mughrabi, "Leading Hamas Official Says No Softened Stance toward Israel," *Reuters* (10 May 2017).

not be Hamas. Hamas's slogan is, "Allah is its target, the Prophet is its model, the Koran its constitution: *Jihad* is its path and death for the sake of Allah is the loftiest of its wishes."[4] The movement's leadership, which promoted the jihadi mythos, is aware of its importance both to Hamas's public image and to its activists, and cannot abandon it. Partly for this reason, even were a unity government between Fatah and Hamas achieved, it does not seem likely that it would succeed in integrating Hamas's military wing, the Izz al-Din al-Qassam Brigades, into a Palestinian Army.

For these reasons, al-Omari is correct that it is difficult to envisage Hamas traversing the route travelled by the PLO from the 1970s, from rejection to recognition of Israel. Hamas has scope for a degree of tactical flexibility, but it cannot renounce its core commitments to armed struggle and "liberation" of the entirety of historical Palestine. These are too fundamental to its identity, and the imperatives of ideological and factional competition are too constraining.

In short, any solution to the conflict will have to involve Hamas, while, in present and foreseeable conditions, there is no prospect of Hamas's positions shifting to the point where it could be a party to such a solution. The upshot is, no solution will be possible until the internal Palestinian conflict is resolved and Hamas either transforms itself or is no longer a powerful political actor.

[4] Hamas Covenant, Article 8. For Hamas's definition of *jihad*, see Article 15.

RESPONSE:

AGAINST ANTI-HAMAS DOGMATISM

Tareq Baconi

The debate between Nathan Thrall and Ghaith al-Omari is one between pragmatism and ideology. Whereas Thrall offers a close examination of Hamas's readiness to participate or acquiesce in a political resolution of the conflict, al-Omari articulates an ideological opposition to any engagement with the movement. He urges that Hamas "not be allowed to enjoy the benefits of international recognition while maintaining positions and practices that run counter to the internationally agreed terms for resolving the conflict." In support of this position, al-Omari points to the successful international effort to pressure the PLO into renouncing its military struggle before the doors of the international community were opened to Palestinian representatives in the 1980s. That is indeed a useful parallel to consider and one to which

---

Tareq Baconi is the author of *Hamas Contained: The Rise and Pacification of Palestinian Resistance* (2018). He is a Visiting Scholar at Columbia University's Middle East Institute.

Hamas publications often refer.[1] Unfortunately, al-Omari fails to pursue the precedent to its logical conclusion. Has the PLO's ideological softening brought about a "solution"? Close to three decades after the PLO was first granted international legitimacy, what does it have to show for the ideological concessions it made?

Ideological commitment to marginalizing Hamas is the product of its depiction as merely a terrorist organization. This oversimplification leads scholars and analysts to spurious conclusions and politicians to harmful policies. For instance, al-Omari asserts that Hamas's "domestic messaging focuses exclusively on destroying Israel as a patriotic and religious duty" and that "the international community's refusal to engage Hamas has undermined the movement's legitimacy." Both these claims are patently false.

Hamas's domestic messaging is devoted to destroying Israel. Having read thousands of Hamas's Arabic publications produced from 1987 onwards, I can attest with full conviction that to portray Hamas as a movement dedicated to Israel's destruction is to misrepresent its political ideology. As Thrall points out, Hamas has communicated to its constituents a complex vision for a political resolution. Hamas's leaders have given a plethora of interviews affirming their commitment to a Palestinian state on the pre-June 1967 borders, with Jerusalem as its capital and without recognition of Israel. But perhaps more convincing than interviews (which are widely available in Hamas's Arabic publications and therefore public to its constituents) has been Hamas's demonstrated readiness to enshrine these principles on the political level.

After Hamas's election victory in 2006, its commitment to an independent Palestinian state was repeated often by its politicians and agreed upon in writing in inter-factional talks. Following discussions between Prime Minister Ismail Haniyeh, then Hamas's leader in the Gaza Strip, and

[1] Hamas's publications frequently refer to the PLO's "capitulation" as a decision that was made "solely for admission into the White House." See, e.g., Maha abdel Hadi, Ibrahim al-Said, Ahmad al-Hajj al-Khalil, Nizar al-Falouji, and Abdel Sattar Qassem, "The PA in Ten Years: Fall of Illusions," *Filastin al-Muslima* (7 July 2004), pp. 34–35 [Arabic].

President Mahmoud Abbas to form a unity government in 2006, Hamas's government declared its commitment to "establish an independent and sovereign Palestinian state on all the land which was occupied in 1967 . . . We are supported in this by our nation's historic right to the lands of our fathers and forefathers, by UN conventions and by the body of international law . . . [We continue to uphold] the right of the Palestinian people to maintain resistance . . . in all forms. Resistance will be focused on land occupied in 1967. [This is alongside] political efforts, negotiations, and diplomatic initiatives."[2]

Not only did Hamas explicitly recognize the 1967 border, it also nodded towards the body of relevant international law (which inter alia recognizes Israel within its pre-June 1967 borders) and noted that negotiations and diplomatic initiatives have a role to play in resolving the conflict. Yet Hamas's refusal to explicitly recognize Israel meant that agreements of this type were rejected by members of the international community, which reacted to overtures from Hamas by piling on yet more pressure. In the face of this reaction, Khaled Meshaal, the then-head of Hamas's political bureau, responded, "We cannot say more than the official Arab and Palestinian position, which is to call for a Palestinian state on the land occupied in 1967. The problem is not with us. It is not with Hamas, as in the past it was also not with the official Palestinian and Arab positions. The problem has always been with Israel."[3]

Hamas's acquiescence in the 1967 borders was reiterated several times in subsequent unity agreements with the Palestinian Authority, to no avail. With such agreements, Hamas moved closer to the two-state model than several political parties within Israel. As Thrall also points out, Hamas has repeatedly offered to abide by the outcomes of public referenda carried out by the

[2] "Doc. 205: Modified National Dialogue Statement, June 28, 2006," in Mohsen M. Saleh and Wael Sa'ad, eds. *Mukhtarat min al-Watha'iq al-Filastiniyyah li Sanat 2006* (Beirut: Al-Zaytouna Center, 2006), pp. 514–17 [Arabic].

[3] "Doc. 188: Interview with Meshal, June 13, 2006," *al-Watha'iq al-Filastiniyyah*, p. 479 [Arabic].

Palestinians. It has also agreed on multiple occasions to designate the PLO the official representative of the Palestinian people in talks with Israel. Since 2007, Hamas itself has been in indirect negotiations with Israel.

So much for Hamas's rhetoric and political practice. What about its military conduct? Hamas has consistently managed to control its military wing in order to pursue political outcomes with both the PLO/PA and with Israel. Through successive ceasefires during the second intifada, it limited its resistance activities to the West Bank and the Gaza Strip and offered to differentiate between Israel proper and its occupation and to avoid targeting Israeli civilians in return for reciprocal guarantees from Israel. For example, in June 2001, as the intifada was rapidly militarizing, Hamas responded to Prime Minister Ariel Sharon's threats of escalation with a leaflet stating, "we give the Zionist street an opportunity to have its word, to demand from its government to stop terrorism, murder, assassinations . . . and to withdraw from our land. In return, we will stop all martyrdom and armed operations in the occupied land of 1948."[4] Hamas's offers to restrict its resistance activities to the Occupied Territories were accompanied by explanations that its goal was to end Israel's military control of these lands. These gestures were consistently brushed aside. For the past decade, acting as the ruling government of the Gaza Strip, Hamas has also become quite effective in restraining rocket fire into Israel to maintain stability.

Both in discourse and in practice, then, Hamas has managed its military wing and offered credible long-term ceasefires in return for the creation of a Palestinian state. But given that Hamas refuses to offer recognition of Israel, does this position qualify as an end of claims? Even the creation of a Palestinian state, al-Omari avers, would not end Hamas's desire to "liberate" the rest of historic Palestine by destroying Israel as a Jewish state.

Hamas does indeed reiterate its commitment to the indivisibility of the Historic Land of Palestine. But what is the real significance of this? Would a two-state solution mark the end of revisionist Zionism's "Greater Land of Israel"

---

[4] "Joint Release by al-Qassam and al-Aqsa," *Al-Nahar* (5 June 2001), Institute for Palestine Studies archive, Beirut [Arabic].

ideology? Would the Likud Party revise its ideological platform to refrain from territorial claims to the West Bank as the biblical land of Judea and Samaria, belonging exclusively to the Jewish people? Would Naftali Bennet's Jewish Home Party renounce its commitment to the Knesset Regulation Law, which permits the Israeli government to expropriate land from individual Palestinians against their will?

Ideological commitments and extremist views in both Palestinian and Israeli societies will not disappear overnight, even following a peace agreement. But if there is a political framework within which these parties are forced to operate, then their ability to pursue maximalist ends will necessarily erode. In the event that a Palestinian state is established, and Israel's illegal occupation of Palestinian lands is dismantled, the likelihood that Palestinians would continue to support Hamas's use of violent resistance is slim. This is not merely conjecture. Support for suicide bombing drops whenever Palestinians are hopeful that negotiations can bring justice.[5]

There is little that Hamas has not offered in the way of pragmatic compromises that would not entirely undermine its standing amongst its constituents, up to and including joining a unity government that recognized Israel (without changing the ideology of the movement itself). Instead of encouraging Hamas pragmatism, members of the international community have insisted on complete

---

[5] In the late 1990s, before the expiration of the final deadline of the Oslo Accords, even with Benjamin Netanyahu's election and receding Palestinian confidence in the negotiations, opinion polls indicated that Palestinian support for suicide bombing was very low. In November 1998, 75 percent opposed suicide bombing; in 1999, support for suicide bombing was under 20 percent and for Hamas below 12 percent. (Mia Bloom, *Dying to Kill: The Allure of Suicide Terror* (New York, NY: Columbia University Press, 2005), p. 25) As faith in peace negotiations plummets, polls show rising support for suicide bombing. (Mia Bloom, "Palestinian Suicide Bombing: Public Support, Market Share, and Outbidding," *Political Science Quarterly* 119.1 (2004), pp. 65–69) In 2001, as Hamas reactivated its suicide bombing campaign, Hamas publications quoted a Birzeit University poll which stated that support for the peace process had dropped to 17 percent while support for suicide bombing had increased to 53 percent. Hamas used this poll to justify its resumption of these operations. ("Al-Aqsa Intifada Proceeds," *Filastin al-Muslima* (17 March 2001), pp. 14–15 [Arabic])

ideological capitulation (i.e., explicit recognition of Israel) as a pre-requisite for engagement. Having witnessed the sorry fate of the PLO, what is Hamas's incentive to follow suit?

The international community's refusal to engage Hamas has undermined the movement's legitimacy. Hamas's popularity rating within the Gaza Strip has indeed fallen, largely as a result of the movement's authoritarian tendencies. In protests over electricity cuts in January 2017, demonstrators expressed anger with the movement. Opposition is growing to Hamas's governance and its commitment to armed struggle given the misery that has been inflicted on civilians in the course of Israel's blockade and numerous assaults on the Strip.* But those sentiments directed towards Hamas as both movement and government co-exist alongside widespread support for "resistance" to Israel's occupation, including in Gaza.[6] Hamas has a core legitimacy among broad Palestinian constituencies because of its refusal to acquiesce in or be subservient to Israel's occupation. Hamas also enjoys significant support in the West Bank.[7] Meanwhile, the PLO, which by al-Omari's assessment has international legitimacy, is suffering perhaps its greatest crisis of legitimacy to date amongst Palestinians. Discontent with both Hamas and the PLO does not reflect a renunciation of these movements' ideologies, but frustration at their inability to end Israel's occupation.

The reason for Hamas's enduring popular legitimacy is that the drivers which animate Hamas's ideology are not limited to the movement itself. The

---

* *Editor's note:* See Chronology and Glossary ("Siege of Gaza").

[6] Many Gazans I interviewed in summer 2015, a year after Operation Protective Edge, were resentful at Hamas for dragging them into another war, but all nevertheless expressed conviction in the sanctity of resistance and the Palestinian right to armed struggle in the face of Israeli atrocities.

[7] "Special Gaza War Poll," *Palestinian Center for Policy and Survey Research* (2 September 2014).

refugees' right of return,* ending Israeli settlement, and the right to self-determination form the essence of the Palestinian struggle. If Hamas is pushed to abandon these political commitments, the principles themselves will not dissolve. Rather, support for them will seamlessly transfer to the next institutional or ideological vehicle willing to articulate the Palestinian struggle for historic rights.

Rather than address the numerous internationally sanctioned grievances that fuel Palestinian support for Hamas, the international community has isolated the movement because of its resort to illegitimate forms of armed struggle to pursue them. Many observers assume that isolating Hamas because of its actions rather than addressing its political motivations is a more just approach. But history tells a different story.

Since its establishment in 1948, Israel has sought to obfuscate the *political* drivers animating Palestinian nationalism. This was as true of the PLO's *fedayeen*§ as it is of Hamas's *jihad.* Dealing with the Palestinians first and foremost as a security and humanitarian challenge depoliticizes and dehumanizes their struggle. Viewing Hamas solely as a terrorist organization whitewashes the collective punishment of Palestinians in Gaza and allows Israeli politicians to present their war crimes in Gaza as "self-defense." Suggesting that Hamas cannot be part of the solution because of its terrorism legitimizes Israel's rejectionism and violations of international law. This language is what enables Israel to manage, rather than resolve, the conflict. Those interested in a peaceful resolution ought to bring greater pragmatism and moral consistency to bear in addressing the complexities on the ground.

---

* *Editor's note:* See Glossary.

§ *Editor's note:* Palestinian guerillas.

CHAPTER SEVEN.

FLOATING IN AN INCH OF WATER: A LETTER FROM GAZA

Sara Roy

It was my last day in Gaza after a week of intensive interviews and fieldwork in the fall of 2016. I was exhausted, aching to leave and aching to stay. Gaza felt more like a ghetto than it ever had, sealed at every passage, fraying at every edge. I was in a UN bus with several UNRWA employees leaving for the Erez checkpoint at Gaza's border with Israel. We were driving along Omar el Mukhtar Street, one of the main commercial streets in Gaza City. The bus

---

Sara Roy is Senior Research Scholar at the Center for Middle Eastern Studies at Harvard University. Her most recent book is an expanded third edition of *The Gaza Strip: The Political Economy of De-development* (2016; previous editions 1995, 2001). A shortened version of this chapter appeared in Sara Roy, "If Israel Were Smart," *London Review of Books* 39.12 (15 June 2017). Republished with permission. The story of the old man and the little boy was first published in Sara Roy, "Hunger," *Middle East Research and Information Project (MERIP)* (9 June 2017).

stopped at a red light at a very busy intersection. I was staring out the window and noticed below me, in the lane next to ours, an old man in a car. He held some pita bread in his hand and was attempting to make a sandwich with some other kind of food that I could not make out.

Suddenly the old man looked up from his sandwich and motioned to a young boy of no more than eleven or twelve years who was standing on the sidewalk peddling packs of cigarettes he held in a big wooden tray. The tray hung like a millstone around the boy's neck, the weight too much for such a small child to bear. The young boy approached the old man and a brief exchange ensued. I assumed the old man was going to buy a pack of cigarettes but instead the child handed him two individual cigarettes, which, it seemed, was all he could afford. The old man paid the boy and then, in a gesture that surprised the youngster, threw half of his pita sandwich into the boy's tray. As the boy scurried away, I stared at the old man, thinking about his small but generous act of kindness. As our bus began to move, I looked up and saw the boy at the corner of the intersection voraciously eating his half of the sandwich. He ate with a hunger that stunned me.

Gaza has always been easy to understand and impossible to understand, painfully transparent and frustratingly opaque, full of contradictions—all of them true. This time was no different, except perhaps in one critical respect: translation seemed much more arduous. Words commonly used to describe (and reduce) Gaza, such as "impoverished," "violent" and "resilient" (the last a word I have come to dislike)—while always lacking and deficient, now felt hollow and irrelevant, even specious. This time, my encounter with Gaza demanded much more—something I felt the moment I entered the territory.

My previous visit to Gaza had been in May 2014, just before Israel's brutal assault (known as Operation Protective Edge) that began a few weeks after I left. The changes I saw in the near two-and-a-half-year period between visits were dramatic. The most stunning weren't physical, as I had expected, but societal. Two things struck me: the truly damaging and frightening impact of Gaza's decade long separation and isolation from the rest of the world, and the sense that an increasing number of people simply cannot take much more and are reaching the limit of what they can endure.

So much has been written about Gaza—her economic decline and political dysfunction and the unending predictions of another imminent war. "Why even talk about Gaza?" a friend asked rhetorically. But that, of course, is not the right question because the answer is obvious. The far more relevant and difficult question—especially now—is: "*How* is one to talk about Gaza?" What follows is my attempt at an answer.

"We are people who can float in an inch of water"

Gaza is in a state of humanitarian shock, due primarily to Israel's intensified closure or blockade, now in its eleventh year, and disgracefully supported by the US, the EU, and Egypt. The blockade has created severe hardship. It has ruined Gaza's economy, largely by ending the normal trade relations upon which Gaza's tiny economy depends. The impact has been devastating. Gaza, historically a place of trade and commerce, has relatively little production left, largely reduced to one common denominator, consumption. Although an easing of Israeli restrictions throughout 2016 and early 2017 led to a relatively moderate increase in largely agricultural exports to the West Bank and Israel—long Gaza's principal markets—the level of exports is minimal and not nearly sufficient to catalyze Gaza's weakened productive sectors, which have all but collapsed under Israel's continuing blockade and three destructive assaults in six years.

Gaza's debility, deliberately and consciously planned and successfully executed, has left almost half the labor force without any means to earn a living. Unemployment—especially youth unemployment—is *the* defining feature of life. Overall, unemployment now hovers around 42 percent (it has been higher), while for young people (fifteen to twenty-nine years) it stands at 60 percent. Everyone is consumed by finding a job or some means of earning money. "Salaries control people's minds," said one colleague.

In fact, one of the greatest sources of political tension between the Hamas government in Gaza and the Palestinian Authority (PA) in Ramallah (West Bank) concerns the continued refusal of President Abbas to pay the salaries of people working in the Hamas government. I was consistently told that if Abbas wanted to win the support of Gaza's people all he would have to do is pay the salaries of government employees (loyalty is given to the employer). Abbas has been unwilling to do so, claiming in part that such salaries would be funneled to Hamas's military wing, and he therefore bears a great deal of responsibility for Gaza's suffering.

Abbas's refusal is all the more galling because he has been paying full salaries—ranging from an average of $500–$1,000 monthly, a huge sum in Gaza today—to at least 55,000 civil servants in Gaza who worked for the PA before Hamas took control of the territory. These people are being paid *not* to work for the Hamas government (although they support around 250,000 people) because of the intense hostility between the PA and Hamas authorities. This costs the PA $45 million every month, monies that are largely financed by Saudi Arabia, the EU, and the US.[1] Paying people not to work has institutionalized yet another distortion within Gaza's deeply impaired economy.

However, in April 2017 Abbas cut these salaries by 30 percent overall, meaning that there is $20 million less in circulation in Gaza every month. On an individual level, some people report cuts ranging from 42 to 70 percent, according to a colleague, Brian Barber, working in Gaza. He writes, "Abbas's salary cuts have come like an earthquake, leaving frightening anxiety over how [people] can manage and a sense of deeply insulting betrayal."[2] In July 2017, Abbas deepened Gaza's crisis still further by dismissing 6,145 employees working in health, education, and other public sectors. This measure, like the salary cuts that preceded it, was intended to exert pressure on Hamas to relinquish control of the Strip.

---

[1] Shlomi Eldar, "Will Abbas Stop Paying Gaza Employees' Salaries?" *Al-Monitor* (9 March 2017). According to reports in February 2017, donor governments are reevaluating their contributions to these salaries and to the PA overall, with potentially ominous consequences. See Adnan Abu Amer, "What EU Shift in Financial Support Means for Gaza," *Al-Monitor* (20 February 2017).

[2] Email exchange with the author (31 May 2017). See also Ahmad Melhem, "PA Faces Backlash after Slashing Gaza Salaries," *Al-Monitor* (20 April 2017); Jack Khoury, "PA Workers in Gaza Take to Streets to Protest 30-percent Cut in Salaries," *Ha'aretz* (9 April 2017).

Personal need is everywhere. But what is new in my long experience in Gaza is the sense of desperation, which can be felt in the different ways people behave and respond and the boundaries they are willing to cross that once were inviolate. Such behavior is not hidden but in full view, an emerging feature of daily life. In one painful example, a well-appointed woman, her face fully covered by a *niqab*, came to the Marna House Hotel where I was staying, to beg. When politely asked to leave by the hotel staff, she aggressively refused and insisted on staying, raising her voice in anger and obliging the hotel staff to forcefully escort her off the property. She clearly was not asking to stay and beg but demanding to do so. I had never seen this before in Gaza.

In another instance, also at the Marna House, I was sitting with a colleague in the hotel restaurant when a boy, a teenager with acne on his face, came to our table quietly pleading for money for his family. By the time I reached for my wallet, the waitstaff had approached and gently ushered him out of the restaurant. He did not resist. (He was so gentle and fragile in contrast to the woman in the *niqab*.) This young boy was well dressed and educated and I kept thinking he should have been home studying for an exam or out with his friends by the sea. Instead he was begging and humiliated, asked to leave the hotel and never return.

Perhaps the most alarming indicator of people's desperation is the growth of prostitution in Gaza's traditional and conservative society. Although prostitution has always been present to varying (but very limited) degrees in Gaza, it was always considered immoral and shameful, carrying immense social consequences for the woman and her family. This appears to be changing as individual and family resources dissolve. A colleague who is a well-known and highly respected professional in Gaza told me that women, many of them well dressed, have come to his office soliciting him and "not for a lot of money." (He also told me that because of the rise of prostitution, it has become harder for girls to get married because "no one knows who is pure." Families plead with him to provide a "safe and decent space" for their daughters by employing them in his office.)

Another friend told me how, while sitting in a restaurant, he witnessed a young woman trying to solicit a man with her parents present at a nearby table.

When I asked him how he explained such incomprehensible behavior, he said, "People living in a normal environment behave in normal ways; people living in an abnormal environment do not."

And Gaza's environment is abnormal by many measures. "People have no money," said a close friend. "They roll tobacco because they cannot afford a pack of cigarettes. Others do not have one shekel to give their teenage children so they wander aimlessly in the streets." At least 1.3 million out of 1.9 million people, or 70 percent of the total population (other estimates are higher), receive international humanitarian assistance, the bulk of which is food (sugar, rice, oil, and milk), without which the majority could not meet their basic needs. (Not that long ago, Gaza together with the West Bank was considered a lower middle-income economy.) By August 2016, 11,850 families or approximately 65,000 people remained internally displaced (from 500,000 at the height of the 2014 hostilities), of whom 7,500 families or about 41,000 people were in urgent need of temporary shelter and cash assistance.[3]

Gaza's abnormal environment is now characterized by other painful dynamics. I have written elsewhere about rising suicide rates in Gaza from hanging, immolation, jumping from heights, drug overdose, ingestion of pesticides, and firearms.[4] Gaza's divorce rate, historically low at 2 percent, now approaches 40 percent according to the UN and local health-care professionals. "There are 2,000 domestic disputes a month in Shati camp," said one UNRWA official, "and the police cannot cope. The courts alone receive hundreds of complaints every month. The Hamas government cannot deal with the number of problems." One must also remember that almost three-quarters (72.5 percent) of

---

[3] United Nations Office for the Coordination of Humanitarian Affairs (UNOCHA OPT), "The Gaza Strip: The Humanitarian Impact of the Blockade," *ochaopt.org* (November 2016); UNOCHA OPT, "Gaza: Two Years after the 2014 Hostilities," *ochaopt.org* (August 2016).

[4] Sara Roy, "Introduction to the Third Edition: De-development Completed: Making Gaza Unviable," *The Gaza Strip: The Political Economy of De-development*, third edition (Washington, DC: Institute for Palestine Studies, 2016).

Gaza's approximately two million people is twenty-nine years old and younger and remains confined to Gaza, prohibited from leaving the territory; most never have.[5]

Amid such disempowerment, young people have increasingly turned toward militancy as a livelihood, joining different militant and extremist organizations simply to secure a paying job. I was repeatedly told that growing support for extremist factions in Gaza does not emanate from political or ideological belief as these factions might claim, but from the need to feed their families. Joining an ISIS-affiliated group is now an income earning activity for many, perhaps most of its recruits. (This is likely one reason why Hamas is desperate to secure enough funds to keep paying the salaries of its military wing, the al-Qassam Brigades, which is reportedly seeing an increase in its ranks as well). It seems that young unemployed men in Gaza increasingly face two options—possible *life* if they join a military faction, or possible *death* if they do not.

One colleague, himself a religious Muslim, argued, "If the Israelis were smart, they would open two or three industrial zones, do a security check and find the most wanted among us and employ them. Al-Qassam would evaporate very quickly and everyone would be more secure. There is a difference between what is said in the mosques and what people would settle for. I tell you the mosques would be empty." I repeatedly heard about former al-Qassam fighters who left the organization when they obtained new homes in one of Gaza's housing projects, not wanting to risk the security of their home as a possible Israeli target.

In a similar vein, a local businessman told me: "what we need is Israeli factories and Palestinian hands. One sack of cement employs thirty-five people in Gaza; with one worker in Israel you have seven people in Gaza praying for Israel's security. Imagine a 'Made in Gaza' brand. We could market regionally and it would sell like hotcakes. Gaza would benefit and so would Israel. All we want are open borders for export."

---

[5] Palestinian Central Bureau of Statistics, "Indicators—Population," *pcbs.gov.ps* (n.d.).

Gazans are entrepreneurial and resourceful and want desperately to work and provide for their children as they once did. Instead they are forced into demeaning dependency on humanitarian aid, which is given by the very same countries that contribute to their incapacity. This is criminal and obscene; it is also outrageously stupid.

To be rich in Gaza

Amid Gaza's misery and impoverishment lies a striking contrast, an inconsistency as it were: Gaza's privileged. This sector is tiny—the number I kept hearing was 50,000—but highly visible. For some, their wealth derives from the now almost defunct tunnel trade, which once kept Gaza's economy functioning, even thriving, albeit artificially, under Israel's damaging closure. The existence of this miniscule sector of affluence is sometimes used to argue that conditions in Gaza are much better than portrayed.

The privileged, historically vital to local production, are consumers of goods since relatively little is produced in Gaza right now. They fill Gaza's hotels, shopping malls, and restaurants that have grown in response to their demand. I call it the "Gaza Bubble"; others have called it "a welcome sign of normalcy."[6] One human rights worker told me that the fastest growing business in Gaza City today is restaurants because they are one of the few profitable activities left in Gaza.

The pervasive consumerism that characterizes the prosperous in Gaza is certainly not specific to Gaza, and nor is the great disparity in class and scale. Of course, people should not be denied the right to consume whatever they want. Yet like the vast majority of Gazans, the affluent are also confined and beleaguered, enraged and demeaned by their inability to live freely or with any semblance of predictability. One of Gaza's richest and most successful businessmen spent an evening with me pouring out his frustration and describing in painstaking detail the restrictions imposed on his business by Israel, which

---

[6] Fares Akram, "Gazans Excited over Territory's New Indoor Mall," *Associated Press* (22 February 2017).

used to be an essential market. "The Israelis are destroying my business, my ability to work, and why? They squeeze, squeeze, squeeze, and towards what end? Where will this bring all of us?"

Others were present at this evening gathering—all of them members of Gaza's social and economic elite—and no one could see a way out. The evening alternated between exasperation and silence . . . always ending in irresolution. Yet my friends' disgrace, and fundamentally that is what it is, does not derive from any sense of defeat but from the knowledge that no amount of reason, law or morality has had or will have any impact on their situation. To the contrary, appeals based on fairness, principle or rationality have only brought them more destruction.

The moneyed may live well but they cannot buy their freedom. This is what binds them to the rest of Gaza; yet, despite their shared fate, many seem to avoid any common ground with those outside their class, something, again, not peculiar to Gaza. But while the difference between privilege and poverty is very visible in Gaza, it is also very proximate. Sometimes the distance between the two can literally be measured in yards. One evening, a Swedish friend who I happened to run into invited me to dinner at one of Gaza's best restaurants. The place was packed with families and tables of well-dressed teenagers playing with their iPads and iPhones. How many of them, if any, had ever been inside al-Shati refugee camp, literally a short walk from the restaurant? I know that some, perhaps most, never have.

Those who are considered privileged in Gaza are not necessarily people with a great deal of money. They are people with a source of income—until April 2017, those salaried employees paid not to work by the PA, people working for UNRWA, international NGOs, local public and private sector institutions, and those (not many) who are successfully self-employed, usually merchants. There are those who do what they can to help others, but amid the despair that now permeates Gaza, charity is no longer a simple, unencumbered act of giving. It is burdened with a set of expectations and demands that can never be satisfied. A dear friend from a prominent Gaza family described his dilemma: "After paying my taxes to Hamas, new fees springing up all the time, household expenses, food and helping friends, I am depleting my personal funds. Soon I will have to sell some assets just to pay my bills. Yes, I am much better off than most people here and I do what I can to help others but where does it stop? The tragedy of this situation is that friends look at you as a source of money. And friendships end when you can no longer provide that money. Think of what it takes to make people behave in this way. No one seems to be considering the pressure it takes to change one's core values. This is what we have been reduced to. This was never Gaza."

The question never truly considered let alone answered by Israel (beyond the propaganda) is, why is Gaza being punished in so heartless a manner? What does Israel truly hope to gain by its cruelty, and where is this awful, senseless policy headed? If one thinks about it crudely, Israel has exhausted all of the ways it can pressure people in Gaza. When Gazans worked in Israel, Israel had leverage; it would seal the borders and extract whatever concessions it sought.[7] Now, Israel can no longer do that in much the same way because people have adapted. They suffer but they have adapted. They even find happiness at times. All Israel can really do is menace Gaza as it long has, a policy that emanates not from any logic or examination but, as former Israeli Prime Minister Ehud Barak once explained, from "inertia." Inexplicably—or not—Israel's "security cabinet has not held a single meeting on Israeli policy concerning Gaza for at least the last four years."[8] At what point does menacing stop working as a form of coercion or as a way to achieve capitulation (to what)? What more does Israel hope to gain with its next attack on Gaza, when people there already speak about the wiping out of entire families as a normal topic of conversation?

---

[7] As of December 2016, Israel stated its "willingness to grant hundreds of work permits to laborers from the Gaza Strip." See Moath Al-Amoudi, "How Serious is Israel About Allowing Return of Gaza Workers?" *Al-Monitor* (2 December 2016).

[8] Noam Rabinovich, "Groundhog Day in Gaza," *Ha'aretz* (7 March 2017); Ben Caspit, "Israel Has No Gaza Policy," *Al-Monitor* (1 March 2017).

The end of politics and ideology

Survival, I learned, is also Hamas's obsession. Financial resources have contracted significantly over the last few years (although this may change with improving Iranian relations), with government employees long being paid only 40 percent of their salary (slight increases were announced in February 2017) and other public sector demands consistently unmet. The Hamas government has tried to compensate for the shortfall by "gouging people for money," said one analyst, imposing a range of revenue-generating measures—new taxes, fees, penalties, and price increases—that feel extortive. I was told the price of cigarettes has tripled from 8 NIS to 25 NIS, quarterly property taxes have doubled, a new "cleanliness tax" is now charged for street cleaning and sanitation services, and car licenses must be renewed every six months at a cost of 600 NIS—an impossible sum for most Gazans. Failure to pay can result in the confiscation of the license followed by the car. Some maintained that tunnel smuggling has been renewed (albeit at nowhere near historical levels) to generate additional tax revenue for Hamas, something I did not have the time to examine. Another well-placed source claimed: "50–60 percent of Hamas would give up Jerusalem for a Rafah [border] opening."

One trusted source argued that since most people in Gaza do not have money to pay any of these taxes and penalties, Hamas officials target those who can pay and have a sliding scale for those of somewhat lesser means. Apparently the government is successful in collecting revenue. Said this same individual, "the pressure they [the Hamas government] are under, like all of us, is considerable but they will not break. Instead they have become more vicious. Hamas was not like this before. Extreme self-preservation is taking them far away from politics." I heard constant references to Hamas as an organization or movement rather than as a government or authority that is representative and purposeful. Nor is the PA immune from popular disdain and alienation. Some of the most poisonous criticism was reserved for Ramallah.

Hamas, one analyst pointed out, "can't exert any more control over the population than they already have. They have total control." Much like Israel, there is not much more Hamas can do to strengthen its control of Gaza. Hence, Hamas's priorities, say my sources, are now shifting from the consolidation of control—itself a diminished priority from one that earlier emphasized political ideology as the basis of Islamist rule—to "pure survival mode." This is perhaps best expressed, my colleagues say, in the unrelieved tunnel construction believed to be making its way underneath Gaza City's streets and neighborhoods. These tunnels are rumored to be 150 meters (492 feet) deep, part of a larger, murky infrastructure that would, in times of conflict, ferry the Hamas leadership underground to relative safety.

I cannot comment on the tunnel system in Gaza City other than to say that some of the people I know and trust in Gaza believe it to be a reality. Assuming they are correct, a conclusion naturally follows that is quite horrifying: in order to destroy the tunnels (if, in fact, that is possible), Israel—with Hamas's de facto consent—would have to destroy entire neighborhoods. It also follows that the Hamas leadership hopes Israel would not go to such an extreme, but it appears willing to take that risk.

The tunnel system may be understood as a powerful expression of Gaza's post-political reality, where political engagement and good governance have declined in favor of something more coarse. If in fact Hamas's power now derives less from ideological belief and political vision than from coercion and retrenchment, then what accounts for this dramatic shift in strategy, especially given Hamas's political pragmatism and past attempts at diplomatic engagement?

I was given several reasons. In the crushing aftermath of the 2014 war, the Hamas leadership was gravely disappointed with the painfully slow pace of change and the continued refusal of the international community to work with them—something my respondents say the Islamist leadership was willing to do. Another critical factor influencing Hamas's thinking was the continued and at times intensified blockade of Gaza by Israel, the West, Egypt, and even Jordan. How, following the devastation inflicted, could this be justified? Adding further to the mix was the repeated failure of reconciliation efforts irrespective of who was to blame (and the weakening connection between reconciliation and peace), and last, of course, was the Hamas government's eroding finances.

Hamas's shifting focus has another dimension: the potentially larger role of its military wing in political decision-making and governance (particularly given the consistent failure of the political leadership to achieve any meaningful change). This arguably was made clear with the election in early 2017 of Yahya Sinwar to head the political wing of Hamas in the Gaza Strip. Sinwar, who sat in Israeli jails for over twenty years, was a founding member of the al-Qassam Brigades. Although it remains to be seen what Sinwar's election will bring to Gaza and to Israel,[9] one thing is clear: "Gaza is simmering."[10]

Questioning Hamas . . . and God

There is also in Gaza a struggle to create a normal society. There always has been. Some people, no doubt more than I realize, have not abandoned possibility and creative resistance; they see scarcity as a catalyst for change and their work assumes a variety of forms. One uses religion to reexamine social behavior and *critique* it. This is altogether new in Gaza and it is quite stunning.

Although the trend among some in Gaza is to turn to religion as a refuge, there has emerged a counter-trend that also seeks refuge of another sort. This is how it was explained to me (admittedly, I did not have the time to examine this claim deeply): The misconduct and fraudulence now associated with Hamas and the inability to challenge it in any meaningful and effective manner have given rise to a social commentary on, and even critique of, Hamas's conduct that uses religion as its analytical instrument. This critique is not about conditions of life in Gaza but about the use of religion by Hamas as a coercive tool and justification for abusive behavior. By linking political behavior

---

[9] Ben Caspit, "Why Some in Israel are Wary of Hamas's New Gaza Boss," *Al-Monitor* (15 February 2017).

[10] Analyst to the author. According to Ben Caspit, Israeli officials share this belief: "The state comptroller's report points to many other warnings coming from Dangot and the office of the COGAT [Coordinator of Government Activities in the Territories] and Maj. Gen. Yoav Mordechai, who replaced Dangot in January 2014. Both of them said that the situation in Gaza was like a bubbling pressure cooker about to explode. The bottom line is clear: If nothing is done, it will end in an explosion." (Caspit, "Israel Has No Gaza Policy") See also Dov Lieber, "Open Up Gaza or it Will Explode, Hamas Threatens Israel," *Times of Israel* (13 March 2017).

to religion and using religion to judge the defects in that behavior, people are "putting power on the defensive" in an altogether unprecedented way, at least in Gaza. This critique is taking place entirely on social media—Facebook, Twitter, WhatsApp—beyond the control of Hamas, which is apparently very frustrated by its inability to control or extinguish the increasingly harsh commentary. According to my sources, this social media phenomenon reaches tens of thousands of followers.

For example, I heard about the story of a cow and the brutal, unconscionable way the animal was slaughtered. The cow's cruel treatment apparently became an internet sensation, viewed by thousands. While some people justified the slaughter in the name of Islam, others railed against it, asking, "Is this Islam? Why are we behaving like this?" A vibrant exchange apparently followed. The critique, my respondents argued, is all the more astonishing because it is not confined to a religious critique of Hamas alone but increasingly, and carefully, includes the idea of Islam and god as well. The emerging questioning of religion and god—an incendiary act by any measure in the Middle East—represents a "potential earthquake in the Islamic world," said one friend, "and it continues to grow." Given the enormous risks associated with even engaging in such a discourse, to do so is a courageous act and one, in my view, that speaks powerfully to the nonexistence of other viable and acceptable options. It certainly bears watching.

Gaza is also home to other forms of creative rethinking and rebuilding: there is a burgeoning of cultural production—art, theater, photography, music—and volunteerism among the young is apparently growing. A range of initiatives has emerged that attempt, in their own way, to address Gaza's predicament. Without a guiding (and functioning) central authority, these efforts are, by nature, self-contained and confined; still, they remain vibrant and persistent. They include the renewal of small-scale agriculture, human rights monitoring, mental health rehabilitation, environmental repair, and technological innovation. The last was strongly emphasized. Gaza has a highly talented, "tech-savvy" population; if ever there were peace, an American investor stated, "Gaza's internet sector would become another

India." The number of internet users in Gaza is reportedly equal to that of Tel Aviv, and a limited number are already subcontracting for companies in India, Bangladesh, and Israel.

The constraining factor in Gaza has never been insufficient talent.

Aspiring to the mundane: Some concluding reflections

Perhaps the most striking feature of life in Gaza is attenuation—a narrowing of space and the certainty of that space as a place to live, and a narrowing of desire, expectation, and vision. Given the immense difficulties of everyday life, the particular and the mundane—having enough food, clothing, electricity[11]—have been elevated to an aspiration. Concerns have been pared, as have yearnings. They have become inward looking and confined, focused, understandably, on self and family. When a friend of mine asked some of his students "What is your wish?" they answered, "a new pair of trousers," "a new shirt," and "ice cream from the shop on Omar al-Mukhtar street."

The craving is not for a homeland and the fear is not its absence. The craving is for a livelihood (no matter how meager), clean water, and sanctuary, and the fear is that they are unattainable. Within such incarceration, there is simply no place for dreams. Why dream when opportunities do not exist and cannot be created? Why plan when there is little if any possibility of realizing those plans? Why even resist when it is unclear who should be resisted, who will benefit, and what it will achieve?

"We have no leaders with a national vision and no central authority," said an economist friend. "We need a common agenda but in Gaza today that does not exist. We are a fragmented, carved up entity with a variety of internal and external actors each pursuing their own agenda and using Gaza as a way to promote it." I heard a common lament: we are losing our ability to think

[11] The steady reduction in electricity in Gaza reached crisis levels in June 2017, leaving Gazans with only three to four hours of electricity per day. See, for example, United Nations, "Humanitarian Impact of the Gaza Electricity Crisis," *reliefweb.int* (May 2017); Gisha, "Gisha in an Urgent Letter to Minister of Defense Avigdor Lieberman: Reducing Israel's Electricity Supply to Gaza is a Red Line that Must Not Be Crossed," *gisha.org (*11 June 2017); Edo Konrad, "Humanitarian Crisis Looms as Israel Cuts Gaza's Electricity," *+972 Mag* (19 June 2017).

speculatively and analytically, and the capacity "to accurately judge our predicament and how to address it."

How then does one even begin to think about the greater good, of moving forward as a society—a feature that was so defining during the first intifada, which too many young people in Gaza know little, if anything, about. In fact, I was struck by how little the young (but well educated) adults I met knew of the first intifada and the Oslo years, and how acutely embedded they were in the present day. Detached from their future, they are also disconnected from their very recent past, and the many important—and now lost—lessons contained within it.

My friend, the respected professional I mentioned earlier, made a powerful observation: "People are afraid to enter the world or they enter it defensively with weapons. Our openness to the world is narrowing and more and more people are afraid of leaving Gaza because they do not know how to cope with the world outside, like a prisoner released from prison after years of confinement. People must be taught to think more broadly. Otherwise we are lost."

Israel's "incomprehensible intentions" [12]*: A final thought*

"What do the Israelis want?" This question was repeatedly asked with each questioner looking at me searchingly, sometimes imploringly, for an answer, for some insight they clearly felt they did not have.

Stated a colleague in his early fifties, "If the Israelis were [thinking], everyone could benefit. All they must do is give us a window to live a normal life and all these extremist groups would disappear. Hamas would disappear. The community must deal with . . . these groups, not IDF [i.e., Israeli military] tanks and planes. Our generation wants to make peace and it is foolish for Israel to refuse. The next generation may not be as willing as we are. Is that what Israel truly wants?"

---

[12] Frances Fitzgerald, *Fire in the Lake: The Vietnamese and the Americans in Vietnam* (Boston: Little Brown & Company, 1972), p. 5.

During the first six months of 2016, the Ministry of Interior reported that 24,138 babies were born in the Gaza Strip, averaging 132 babies born per day.[13] During the month of August 2016 alone, 4,961 babies were born in Gaza,[14] or 160 babies per day, more than six babies every hour and one baby every nine minutes. The distance between Gaza City and Tel Aviv is forty-four miles.

"What will Israel do when there are five million Palestinians living in Gaza?"

---

[13] "Ministry of Interior: 24,138 Babies Born in Gaza during the Last 6 Months," *The Palestine Chronicle* (12 March 2017).

[14] Data provided by a Gaza-based journalist.

SECTION II:

STRATEGY

CHAPTER EIGHT.

LESSONS FROM THE INTIFADAS

Ghassan Andoni

Palestinian resistance to Israel's colonial occupation is best described not as a continuum model, with gradual movements up and down, but rather a series of outbursts localized in geographical location, time, and methods.

Looking closely at the first, second, and 2015–16 knifing intifadas,* one can conclude that such outbursts follow and reflect generational change and cultural transformation.

The first intifada erupted as a result of the deadlock reached by the Palestine Liberation Organization (PLO) after Israel's 1982 invasion of Lebanon. Yet it

---

Ghassan Andoni is Professor of Physics at Birzeit University. He is co-Founder of the International Solidarity Movement (ISM) and Founder of the International Middle East Media Center (IMEMC).

* *Editor's note:* For the 2015–16 knifing intifada, see p. 247*. For the first and second intifadas, see Chronology and Glossary.

also reflected a dramatic change in the long-standing traditions and norms of resistance established by the diaspora resistance.

Diaspora resistance sought liberation of and return to a lost Paradise—"Palestine"—through armed struggle and guerrilla war. By contrast, the first intifada was primarily a movement of nonviolent civil disobedience. It aimed to end Israel's occupation and establish an independent Palestinian state. The generation that led this movement was liberal, educated, secular, and—most importantly—hopeful.

Following the establishment of the Palestinian Authority (PA) and as a result of the collapse of diplomatic negotiations in 2000, a new generation, formed by a new cultural background, took charge of the second intifada. It cut all ties with the first one, which it viewed as a failure.

Radically opposed to the spirit behind the first intifada, the second intifada was launched by a furious generation, whose hopes of independence had been raised and then dashed by the diplomatic process. This crop of activists and leaders resorted to extreme violence to continue the fight. They reflected the cultural changes that had taken place in Palestinian society during the 1990s. As the first intifada lost its popular dimension, it was followed by the establishment of the PA and the rise of political Islam. Palestinian society became increasingly conservative, religious, and—most importantly—desperate.

It also took a new generation and radical cultural developments to create the conditions for the 2015–16 knifing intifada, which is in many ways disconnected from the previous one.

This generation grew up under the PA in small, crowded areas, totally controlled and besieged on all sides by Israeli soldiers and settlements. A prisoner-like mentality characterized much of their behavior and acts. They were without any prospect of a fulfilling future. Desperation and hopelessness hardened into a determination to fight, even though lack of resources effectively limited them to suicidal means.

The common dynamics of the three intifadas can be summarized as follows:

1. All introduced tactical innovations that initially took the enemy by surprise;
2. The generations that took the lead in each were possessed of a high level of patience and ability to endure losses, which allowed each to extend the uprising geographically and over time;
3. All were informed by a high level of knowledge of what hurts the enemy most;
4. All three failed to achieve their end goals;
5. All three lacked a solid political leadership.

Evidently a lack of weapons, money, and allies in the face of an enemy endowed with huge resources and unlimited support from the world's superpower was the dominant factor in the intifadas' inability to achieve victory.

But even when they did not achieve their ultimate goals, each of the intifadas managed to accrue important gains.

The first intifada corrected the world's false image of the conflict, making clear who is the underdog and who the oppressor. It raised awareness of the brutal realities of Israel's military rule, banishing forever notions of a "benign" or "enlightened" occupation. It was also the crucial factor in forcing Israel, against its will, to engage in negotiations with the PLO.

The second intifada proved, especially to Israelis, that containing the enemy inside you is much more harmful than separating from him. The idea of separation gained ground in the Israeli political arena. This trajectory has since been partially reversed by the cultural changes that took place in Israeli society due to the prolonged conflict, but even now, Israel's right-wing prime minister talks of separation, albeit an apartheid version of it.

The 2015–16 knifing intifada challenged the concept of a unified Jerusalem, which was one of the focal points of the car-ramming and knife attacks. It also put paid to the false image of coexistence in Hebron, the other epicenter of the attacks.

While the first intifada sent a message mostly to the international community, the second and third were addressed to Israeli society directly.

Why, even with no substantial goals achieved, do Palestinians still endure such hardships? The answer is straightforward: they have no other option but surrender.

In my opinion, none of us can predict or plan what the next outburst will look like and which means it will use. It is totally in the hands of the new generation, who will, and must, seize the initiative.

Leila Khaled

Notwithstanding the painful costs involved—the death, the destruction, the risk of disappointment—the Palestinian people have repeatedly risen in revolt against Israeli rule. The odds have been stacked against them. So what explains their resolve?

The Israeli occupiers thought their power could suppress the Palestinian people and silence them forever. They continue to use their military and security forces to crush even the idea of resistance among the Palestinians under occupation.

Since 1948, the Israeli occupiers have put more than one million Palestinians in jail,[1] using all means of torture in an attempt to break the will of the Palestinians and their struggle for freedom and justice. In July 2017, there were more than 6,000 Palestinian prisoners in Israeli jails, including women,

---

Leila Khaled is a member of the Palestinian National Council and the politburo of the Popular Front for the Liberation of Palestine (PFLP). In 1969 she became the first woman to hijack an aircraft, following which she became a global icon of Palestinian and anti-colonial struggle.

[1] Commission of Detainees and Ex-Detainees Affairs and Palestinian Prisoners Club and Palestinian Central Bureau of Statistics, "Press Release on the Occasion of Palestinian Prisoners' Day," *pcbs.gov.ps* (15 April 2017).

elderly people, and children.[2] At the same time, the Israeli government has confiscated Palestinian land to construct settlements, destroyed houses, uprooted olive trees, built the apartheid wall,* and established hundreds of checkpoints all over the Occupied Territories.

These measures and procedures made life a hell for the people.

The people living under Israel's occupation cannot accept it, and cannot bear its atrocities. Occupation is the reason for the intifadas.

First intifada, 1987–1993

On 9 December 1987, the first intifada broke out in the Gaza Strip and West Bank after the killing of Palestinian workers who were returning to their homes after work. People stormed the streets in huge demonstrations in cities, towns, and villages throughout the Occupied Territories. This intifada lasted for six years. A Unified National Leadership was established to coordinate and sustain the uprising. It comprised representatives of all Palestinian resistance organizations as well as independent activists. The intifada leadership announced a daily program for people to follow. There were days for demonstrations, days for strikes, days for sit-ins, and so on. The main goals of the intifada were Freedom and Independence.

The Israeli army ruthlessly confronted the intifada, yet people continued their non-violent resistance regardless of the Israeli soldiers' brutal measures. Hundreds of martyrs were killed in the streets; thousands were wounded and left with permanent disabilities.

People from all different classes joined this intifada because they were incensed by the horrors of occupation. Women, children, elderly, youth—all joined the struggle. With stones and bare hands, they faced down Israeli soldiers armed with all kinds of weapons.

---

* *Editor's note:* See Glossary ("Wall").

[2] Addameer, "Statistics," *addameer.org*.

Lessons of the first intifada:

First Lesson: The Palestinian people refused to co-exist with the Israeli occupation.

Second Lesson: The Palestinians demonstrated and enacted their unity as a people for their cause of Freedom and Independence, despite being physically dispersed within and outside of Palestine. Palestinians living in the part of Palestine occupied in 1948 participated in this intifada in their own way. Palestinian refugees all over the world supported the intifada.

Third Lesson: This intifada won sympathy and support from people across the world, especially the progressive forces that organized committees and institutions to support the Palestinian liberation struggle against the Israeli occupation. These committees are still functioning today.

Fourth Lesson: This intifada exposed Israel's ugly face to the international community. Images of Israeli soldiers brutally beating unarmed demonstrators destroyed the myth of a "benign occupation." People all over the world began to change their attitude towards Israel. They realized that it was an undemocratic state which tried to deceive the world by pretending to be the only democracy in the Arab region.

Fifth Lesson: The intifada elicited increased political and material support for the Palestinians from the Arab regimes and peoples.

Sixth Lesson: This intifada prevented Israel from using its full military arsenal and eroded the morale of its soldiers, which showed that the will of the people in their conflict with the occupiers is more powerful than weapons.

Seventh Lesson: The role of women in the intifada was significant. Women were on the frontlines of the demonstrations facing down Israeli soldiers. Women initiated self-sufficiency projects via home gardens and food production, to reduce dependence on Israel. They organized alternative education for children whose schools were closed by the occupation authorities.

They broke old traditions that had excluded them from public life. Their role in the intifada was recognized by political parties and Palestinian society at large.

Eighth Lesson: Freedom is a human value. In spite of the atrocities inflicted by the Israeli occupation, people realized that freedom could be obtained by making the battle against the occupation continuous. To gain freedom is to gain one's humanity and dignity. This lesson endures deep in the minds of the people who revolted.

Second intifada, 2000–2005

The second intifada erupted after the Oslo Accords had permitted the PLO leadership to return from exile and establish an administrative authority in the West Bank and Gaza Strip. This intifada was a response to Israeli violations of the Oslo Accords, ignited by Israeli Prime Minister Ariel Sharon's deliberately incendiary visit to the Aqsa Mosque.* People realized that the Oslo Accords and the diplomatic process were not leading to freedom. They felt deceived by the path their leadership had pursued. Arms were used in this intifada. The balance of forces between the Palestinians and the Israelis was uneven. Added to this, the Palestinian Authority continued its security cooperation with the Israelis to the detriment of the popular resistance. In spite of the fact that the Israeli army had re-deployed from areas of the Occupied Territories, it attacked the people and leadership brutally and reoccupied the West Bank.

Lessons of the second intifada:

First Lesson: The masses did not participate in this intifada as they had in the first one. This deprived the intifada of its popular strength, although the masses supported it.

Second Lesson: The lack of a unified leadership was the weakest point of this intifada, which ended with compromises: the evacuation and

---

* *Editor's note:* See Glossary ("Temple Mount/Al-Haram Al-Sharif").

deportation of fighters from the Nativity Church and the delivery of the PFLP's Secretary-General Ahmed Sa'adat to the Israelis along with four other PFLP activists.

Third Lesson: Any intifada should be based on a deep understanding of the possibilities afforded by the situation: the means of struggle, the readiness of the masses to participate and endure. the unity of the forces, the enemy's response, and the objectives to be achieved.

Third intifada, 2015–2016

The knife intifada broke out in 2015, when hope for a political solution to the conflict was at an all-time low. Israeli land confiscation, settlement building, and house demolitions were accelerating; Jerusalem's demography was being continually altered in the occupier's interests; Gaza was enduring the tenth year of a brutal siege; the factional divide between Fatah and Hamas* seemed impossible to bridge; and the PA continued to cooperate with the Israelis in policing the occupation.

Amidst mounting despair, and in spite of the PA's opposition, hundreds of Palestinians took resistance upon themselves. This intifada was characterized by knife attacks on Israelis by individuals and small groups acting alone, many of whom were summarily executed in the process of, or shortly after, carrying out the attack.

Lessons of the third intifada:

First Lesson: People create their own ways of resistance, reaffirming that there is no possibility of co-existence with the occupation.

Second Lesson: Without a unified leadership, the third intifada marked a new chapter in resistance but failed to achieve any goals.

* *Editor's note:* The two largest Palestinian factions. See Glossary.

Third Lesson: It is necessary to change the Palestinian leadership in order for popular resistance to be successful in the future. The strategy of negotiations as a substitute for mobilizing people has proven bankrupt a hundred times over, yet still the leadership clings to it. It must be replaced through democratic and peaceful means, by ending the division between Fatah and Hamas and rebuilding the PLO on a democratic basis such that all components of the movement are represented. This revived PLO could then develop a new strategy based on a common program. A priority would surely be to end all cooperative relations with the occupation regime, including security coordination.

Fourth Lesson: Israeli policies and measures against the Palestinians and their land will continue to create new intifadas. It will be the task of a revived Palestinian movement to channel them in productive directions.

Musa Abuhashhash

This past year marked the fiftieth anniversary of the occupation of the Palestinian territories by the Israeli army. Did many Palestinians notice? Did they remember the milestones of occupation and resistance—the first intifada, which erupted three decades ago and changed the course of the conflict, or the second intifada which followed? How many Palestinians still think of ending the occupation, or have an appetite for another uprising?

These and similar questions are frequently raised, but remain without serious answers from either the Palestinian people or their leaders. Even so, thinking about them can tell us much about the present situation and the prospects for the Palestinian struggle.

The recent history of Palestinian resistance can be divided into the periods before and after the 1993 Oslo Accord and the establishment in 1994 of the Palestinian Authority.

The transition of the West Bank and Gaza Strip from Jordanian and Egyptian rule to Israeli military occupation transformed the lives of Palestinians living there. From the beginning of the occupation in 1967 to the outbreak of the first intifada two decades later, Palestinians under Israeli

---

Musa Abuhashhash is Hebron Field Researcher for B'Tselem, The Israeli Information Center for Human Rights in the Occupied Territories. He grew up in Fawwar refugee camp. This contribution is written in a personal capacity and does not necessarily represent the view of B'Tselem.

rule were integrated into the Israeli economy. This employed hundreds of thousands of Palestinian workers whose wages enabled them to start new families and adapt to the new standard of living. Compared to the situation that prevails today, this period was relatively benign. In these years, Palestinian political life was vibrant and active; almost *every* Palestinian found his place in one of the myriad factions and parties.

As a result, when the first intifada broke out in December 1987, Palestinians were organized and ready to participate. While the uprising began spontaneously, Palestinian institutions quickly sprang into action. In no time, the revolt was well organized and run by the Unified Leadership, which led the daily events and distributed daily leaflets which guided the protests and strikes. The eruption of the intifada surprised not only Israel and the international community but also the PLO leadership exiled in Tunis. While it was not involved in organizing the uprising on the ground, the PLO leadership sought to exploit it as much as possible, especially after the November 1988 Palestinian National Council meeting in Algiers, where PLO Chairman Yasser Arafat announced the PLO's acceptance of an independent state on West Bank and Gaza.

The intifada was at this point still going strong, with a broad swath of Palestinians from all social sectors involved in protests in the towns, villages, and camps. They found themselves in an unprecedented situation which threw up completely new challenges; still, none doubted that their sacrifices would succeed in ending the occupation and securing their right to self-determination. The Israeli government also found itself confronting a new and uncomfortable situation. As its repression generated international outrage, Israel's isolation grew and its leaders realized that the continuation of the intifada would bring heavy international pressure on it to reach an agreement with the Palestinians. The moral questions posed by the intifada also created political divisions inside Israel over the future of the occupation. The Labor Party led by Yitzhak Rabin understood the predicament of the PLO leadership, and seized the opportunity to contrive an escape from Israel's own dilemma.

Arafat sought to exploit the political momentum generated by the intifada to reach a diplomatic agreement, at a time when the PLO was losing support from the Arab world. The PLO therefore started to interfere in the intifada by sending money to individuals and organizations in the Occupied Territories. This money changed the course of the intifada—indeed, for many observers, it killed it. The money corrupted the intifada and the people, while distorting the real principles that were its genesis. Sacrifices and activities now had to be paid for in order to continue. The intifada began to lose energy, as fewer and fewer people participated. The intifada was not defeated by Israeli violence, but by Arafat's interference and his overly-hasty desire to secure an agreement.

For all its limitations, the uprising had a dramatic impact on Palestinian and international opinion. It presented, in a way that was impossible to dismiss and difficult to oppose, the demand for the occupation to end. This, after twenty years during which most Palestinians almost forgot they were under occupation. Even as popular participation declined, there was still hope that the intifada would yield a positive diplomatic agreement through the Madrid Conference (1991). But this was undermined by secret negotiations between Israel and the PLO, which issued in an agreement that was worse than Palestinians could have ever expected. If Arafat had been less desperate to move from Tunis to Gaza, or if the Unified Leadership of the intifada had been represented in the negotiations, the first intifada could have brought a solution which could in turn have led to a Palestinian state. In the event, for most Palestinians, the Oslo Accords have proven a catastrophe and the cruelest of rewards for their great sacrifices during the splendid intifada.

Today, Palestinians mark the anniversaries of the first intifada half-heartedly at best. This reveals much about the psychological transformation brought about by the establishment of the PA. Everything changed: the values, the constitution of Palestinian society, and the nature of resistance to the occupation.

As the hopes kindled by Oslo went unfulfilled, growing Palestinian anger and despair manifested in the second intifada, which broke out in October 2000. From almost the very start, it was different from the first uprising. It was heavily militarized, and the Israeli army used even greater violence to repress it. The second intifada also saw Hamas and other Palestinian groups launch suicide attacks inside Israel. Such levels of violence were incompatible with popular participation and, apart from the first weeks of the uprising, most people observed the struggle from the sidelines. The outcome of the second intifada was catastrophic for many Palestinians. Israel constructed the Separation Wall and increased its restrictions on Palestinian movement, which sharply reduced Palestinian employment inside Israel. Then came three devastating wars and the complete siege of Gaza.

Palestinians still have every reason to start an intifada. The occupation is much worse now than it was in the 1980s. Every Palestinian has suffered from its continuation and from the outcomes of Oslo. And it remains the case that an uprising similar to the first intifada is the only way to bring the occupation to an end. But very little can be done at this point to develop a mass movement. Palestinians are tired. Activists have no sway over the masses, many of whose life-needs are dependent on Israeli work permits. Many activists believe that the PA is now the major obstacle to resistance; every activist and most Palestinians know that the PA will not permit a real uprising. But PA repression alone could not stop the masses from starting an intifada. The more fundamental obstacle is the change in values that took place over recent decades.

Lt. Gen. Keith Dayton once spoke approvingly of the "new Palestinians." He was referring to the PA security forces the US had trained to police the occupation and combat Hamas. Three decades on from the first intifada, and fifty years since the beginning of the occupation, one can say that many Palestinians living now can be classified as "new." The first intifada erupted when Palestinians were filled with hope for freedom and self-determination. Today, they could scarcely be less confident about the future and less involved in struggle and resistance. They no longer trust their political leaders. They are characterized by despair and apathy; when they do participate in resistance, it takes an individualistic form. Former and potential political leaders are now with NGOs, whose activities have nothing to do with resistance and whose privileges changed their priorities and busied them with their lifestyles. Most left their political parties.

The dream of a third intifada has become unrealistic, no matter how much objective factors demand one.

Calls by the national leadership and political factions to develop popular nonviolent resistance are no more than hollow slogans that cannot work in the present circumstances. Developing a genuine mass movement is incompatible with PA-Israel security cooperation and the split between Fatah and Hamas. Nor can it work without Arab state support for the Palestinian cause.

Experience alone cannot help. Palestinians are well-versed in resistance, and they have passed this experience on to many other peoples. Ironically, it is they who have failed to learn from this experience—especially from the first intifada, their finest hour, whose three-decade anniversary will likely pass all but forgotten.

I have been documenting human rights violations for almost two decades. When I started, I believed that the accumulation of evidence would lead to change. Unfortunately, it did not. On the contrary, the state of human rights is worse than ever under an increasingly professionalized occupation. I gradually came to believe that human rights, especially when it comes to Israel's occupation, is a big lie. I continue to document abuses only for the sake of the victims and for the record: to prove the ugliness of the occupation, and the hypocrisy of the world.

I have lost hope for change in my lifetime. And I am scared that worse is coming. Palestinians, including my family and I, feel stuck. There is no hope, no trust. We are waiting for the unknown.

CHAPTER NINE.

IS A THIRD INTIFADA POSSIBLE?

Jamil Hilal

The real wonder is, why hasn't a third popular uprising in the West Bank and Gaza erupted already? The objective conditions for revolt certainly exist, as Palestinians continue to be subjected to intense repression, discrimination, and humiliation in the service of the systematic violation of their internationally validated collective rights. Beginning in October 2015, young Palestinian men and women carried out brave acts of individual resistance, which powerfully expressed the depth and endurance of Palestinian opposition to Israel's occupation.* This collective resolve also manifested at the funerals of the young

---

Jamil Hilal is an independent sociologist affiliated to Birzeit University and a Senior Research Fellow at Muwatin—The Palestinian Institute for the Study of Democracy and the Institute of Palestine Studies. He is based in Ramallah and has authored many books and articles. He has been a member of the Palestinian National Council since 1983.

* *Editor's note:* Over a period of several months beginning October 2015, individual Palestinians conducted spontaneous, mostly "lone wolf" attacks on Israeli civilians and soldiers. By the end of

men and women felled by Israeli bullets, at popular demonstrations demanding the handover of their bodies, and in demands to re-open streets blockaded following individual attacks as a form of collective punishment. But those of us who saw in these acts of fearlessness and defiance the tidings of a popular movement were disappointed.

An effective uprising requires the active support and participation of the mass of the people, organized under a legitimate and unified leadership. These conditions were present in the early years of the first intifada, when people from all sectors of Palestinian society engaged in resistance, coordinated by a network of deep-rooted civil society institutions and a unified grassroots political leadership (the Unified National Leadership of the Uprising, UNLU). It was less true of the second intifada, during which the two principal political parties (Fatah and Hamas) adopted increasingly elitist tactics which marginalized popular participation. In subsequent years, the international, regional, and Palestinian political environments have been radically transformed. Assessing the prospects for a third intifada requires understanding the impact of these changes. I will focus on developments in the Palestinian political and social fields.

Political fragmentation. The Palestinian political field that was constructed and led by the Palestine Liberation Organization (PLO) was marginalized in 1994 by the newly established Palestinian Authority (PA). It was replaced by a multiplicity of local political fields: Palestinians with Israeli passports, Palestinians in the West Bank, Palestinians in the Gaza Strip, Palestinians in Jordan, Palestinians in the Gulf, and the Palestinian diaspora. In the absence of an overarching organizational superstructure, each local field came to be run by

March 2016, there had been 211 stabbings, eighty-three shootings, and forty-two car-ramming attacks, killing thirty Israelis and two US citizens. In the same period, more than 200 Palestinians were killed, many in what human rights organizations found to be extrajudicial executions. See Peter Beaumont, "Israel-Palestine Outlook Bleak as Wave of Violence Passes Six-Month Mark," *Guardian* (31 March 2016); B'Tselem, "Unjustified Use of Lethal Force and Execution of Palestinians who Stabbed or were Suspected of Attempted Stabbings," *btselem.org* (16 December 2015).

its own political forces and dynamics. Attempts to reconstruct the old organizational superstructure (i.e., the PLO) or to construct a functional replacement have failed. What remains is a strong attachment to the Palestinian historical narrative, sustained and updated by a vibrant Palestinian cultural field, which remained intact despite the political fragmentation.

Neoliberalization. International financial institutions and the PA's major donors oversaw the implementation of neoliberal economic policies in the West Bank and Gaza Strip. The PA was established at the height of the neoliberal period, and was from early on scrutinized and supervised by the World Bank and International Monetary Fund. Adherence to "free market" principles was enshrined in the Palestinian Basic Law (2002),[1] while an emerging private sector, dominated by expatriates, was given great leeway to shape the territories under PA administration. In the 2000s, the private sector's role was further enhanced as banks began to lend mortgages to those with steady salaries (both in the public sector and private sectors). This, together with the fact that the major political factions were transformed into inaccessible ruling bureaucracies (Fatah in the West Bank, Hamas in Gaza), encouraged the prioritizing of individual interests over the collective good, hastening a process of individualization that reversed the ethos which dominated the 1960s, 1970s, and 1980s.[2]

Co-option. The Oslo Accords established an interim governing authority in the West Bank and Gaza Strip. Overnight, tens of thousands of individuals who had seen themselves as freedom fighters in a national liberation movement became employees of PA bureaucracies operating under colonial occupation and confinement. This transformation was replicated by Hamas in 2007 as it established governing structures in the Gaza Strip. Fatah became the administrative authority in the West Bank and Hamas the authority in Gaza, both of which areas remained firmly under Israeli colonial rule. Elites in both parties thereby

---

[1] Article 21.

[2] An elaboration on this process can be found in Jamil Hilal, "Rethinking Palestine: Settler Colonialism, Neo-liberalism and Individualism in the West Bank and Gaza Strip," *Contemporary Arab Affairs* 8.3 (2015), pp. 351–62.

developed a stake in the status quo and progressively abandoned their efforts to overthrow it.

The PA also effectively co-opted or neutralized significant swaths of Palestinian society. The establishment of the PA stimulated the development of a relatively large middle class (defined by possession of high education and professional skills), which made up about 30 percent of the labor force by the middle of the first decade of this century. These professionals populated the PA's bureaucracies; managed the newly established financial and service sectors (communications, insurance, banks, etc.); filled out a ballooning NGO sector centered in Ramallah; and ran an increasing number of schools, colleges, and universities. The new middle class was divided politically (between liberal nationalists, Islamists, and various strands of leftist), by source of income (public sector, modern private sector, NGO sector, self-employed), by education (Palestinian universities, Arab universities, East European universities, Western universities), and by territory (West Bank, East Jerusalem, Gaza Strip). It was also increasingly tied down by office work and bank loans taken out to finance consumption and housing costs. The new middle class was therefore difficult to mobilize in large numbers. The majority of the commercial class, meanwhile, tended to be well-connected to PA elites, and was inclined to keep relations smooth with the Israeli authorities for the sake of business.

Elite delegitimization. An economy heavily dependent on external transfers, operating in a globalized neoliberal order, and dominated by a repressive colonial regime will inevitably be characterized by high rates of unemployment and impoverishment, cohabiting with a small, wealthy elite.[3] Palestinians in urban centers have witnessed the spectacle of an elite indulging without shame in conspicuous consumption and display. The result is that the national question became increasingly eclipsed by social concerns over unemployment, sharpening inequalities, and privation. In 2016, the West Bank saw large-scale strikes and demonstrations

---

[3] West Bank-Gaza Strip unemployment stood at 29 percent in the second quarter of 2017 (20.5 percent in West Bank, 44 percent in Gaza). See Palestinian Central Bureau of Statistics (PCBS), *Press Report on the Labour Force Survey Results (April–June, 2017) Round* (7 August 2017), p. 5.

against a social security law proposed by the PA which discriminated against workers with low wages and insecure jobs. Similar protests were directed against the Hamas government in Gaza. The fact that no such popular action was organized against Israeli atrocities and repression reflected, at least in part, the perception that the ruling Palestinian factions would thwart such actions. Indeed, some observers read in the actions of youths against Israeli soldiers a double meaning: not just a rejection of Israel's colonial presence, but a protest against the feebleness of the existing Palestinian political class in the West Bank and Gaza Strip.

Repression. The largest portion of the annual budget in the West Bank and Gaza Strip is consumed by the security sector.[4] Security forces in both areas have been used to suppress unwanted popular unrest. It is almost impossible in these conditions for a popular uprising across the 1967-occupied territories to erupt and be sustained without the support of both Fatah and Hamas. Israel's delegation of responsibility for policing the occupation to Palestinian security forces also reduced the opportunity for street politics directed against the Israeli military and colonial settlers, as Israeli soldiers redeployed to the peripheries of West Bank towns and villages and to the borders of the Gaza Strip. (East Jerusalem and Hebron are exceptions, since Israeli troops and settlers remain physically present.)

Disorganization. The Palestinian working class comprises more than half the labor force, but is scattered among tens of thousands of very small establishments (89 percent employing less than five employees).[5] Most workers are not unionized, and therefore cannot play the role of trade unions in Tunisia and Egypt or of workers in the first intifada, who were organized and mobilized by political groups. Furthermore, some 15 percent of the labor force in the West Bank is employed in Israel's labor market, making these workers vulnerable to Israeli pressure and

[4] It is estimated that the security sector absorbs fully a quarter of the PA budget. Sabrien Amrov and Alaa Tartir, "After Gaza, What Price Palestine's Security Sector?" *Al-Shabaka* (8 October 2014).

[5] PCBS, *Establishment Census, Main Findings* (April 2013).

victimization.[6] The social sector most ripe for political organization is the unemployed, a high percentage of which comprises graduates and women. This sector could lead an intifada, because it is angered by the PA and Hamas governments and has little to lose from an uprising against Israel's occupation. In principle, leftist factions are best equipped to mobilize and organize this constituency, because they have not been corrupted by participation in self-administration under Israeli rule. However, the Palestinian left is fragmented and has lost its role and status following the marginalization of the PLO institutions, in which leftist groups once had a recognized and acknowledged standing.

Given these conditions, it is difficult to envisage the emergence of a sustained popular uprising. Israel's continued repression and frustration of Palestinian rights keep hatred of the occupation aflame. This is powerfully reflected in the Palestinian cultural field, which has flourished over the past decade in literature, film, poetry, painting, song, and theater. But the fragmentation, illegitimacy, co-option, and inertia of the Palestinian national movement remains a decisive obstacle to mass political mobilization. More and more Palestinians are recognizing and expressing the urgent need to construct effective, representative, and democratic institutions, to lead a revitalized Palestinian liberation struggle. This is a necessary condition for Palestinians to escape their present fate.

ဢ

[6] PCBS, *Labour Force Survey (April–June 2017)*, p. 5.

Mazin B. Qumsiyeh

Decades of Zionist colonialism transformed the Palestinian people from among the most economically and educationally advanced in Western Asia to among its most dependent and desperate. Seven million of us are refugees or displaced people. Many thousands have been killed. This begs the question: how can a people in such a position resist and overcome? My book on the subject, published in 2010, focused on the victories and accomplishments of Palestinian resistance, and projected a very optimistic note. Subsequent developments—the destruction and disarray in the Arab world; the disastrous impotence and complicity of the United Nations in Syria, Yemen, and elsewhere; the ascendance of belligerent populism around the world, including the United States—have cast a heavy shadow on this optimism. But Palestinians under occupation do not have the luxury of despair.

Resistance to colonialism never develops in a linear fashion. Any struggle experiences peaks and troughs, and suffers regressions even as it advances. In South Africa under apartheid, there were perhaps fourteen or fifteen uprisings before the system collapsed. Many Palestinians and international observers focus on the short-term symptoms of this conflict and feel despondent. Others look at

---

Mazin B. Qumsiyeh is Professor and Director of the Palestine Museum of Natural History and Palestine Institute for Biodiversity and Sustainability. He is the author of *Sharing the Land of Canaan: Human Rights and the Israeli/Palestine Struggle* (2004) and *Popular Resistance in Palestine: A History of Hope and Empowerment* (2010).

the same situation and perceive that it is near boiling point. In my view, one has to take a longer perspective.

The Palestinian struggle is today at a low-point. The Oslo process set in motion in 1993 has given Israel much, including international recognition, regional economic integration, a subservient Palestinian Authority which acts as a sub-contractor to the occupation, and, most importantly, time and diplomatic space to dramatically expand its colonial presence in the Occupied Territories. Even now, a full quarter-century after the "peace process" began, and notwithstanding its manifest and acknowledged bankruptcy, international powers use diplomacy as a pretext to avoid action. The European states condemn Israel's occupation in words while enabling it in practice. As for the United States, President Barack Obama dropped 26,000 bombs in 2016 on seven different countries,[1] and Palestinians do not expect better from President Donald Trump. Nor do Arab leaders inspire hope: Palestinian President Mahmoud Abbas believes in talking for the sake of talking, while the King of Saudi Arabia is preoccupied with bombing hospitals and schools in Yemen.

In other words, the conditions for revolution are in place:

1. The Palestinian factional leaderships are disconnected from the people's needs and thoughts, enjoy little popular legitimacy, and attract great and growing popular resentment.
2. Most people have given up on political structures and international diplomacy—Palestinians today realize that the so-called "peace process" is an industry of empty talk and serious profit for elites.
3. The colonizer-occupier is so confident it has the natives under control that it has become complacent and reckless, killing unarmed demonstrators and demolishing homes as collective punishment. Gratuitous provocations can accelerate the onset of uprisings.

[1] Micah Zenko, "How Many Bombs Did the United States Drop in 2016?" *Council on Foreign Relations* (5 January 2017).

4. The international community does not attach importance or urgency to Palestinian suffering, and, driven by its own interests, has become complicit in the crime.

These conditions were present before every one of the uprisings in Palestine.

For example, in 1936 the Palestinian political scene was, as it is today, divided into multiple competing factions (most of which did not long survive and have since been forgotten). In the years leading up to the 1936 Revolt, the British authorities and the Zionist movement felt secure in their control, having suppressed the 1929 uprising and integrated many Palestinian elites into subordinate positions in the Mandatory administration. (The 1929 uprising itself came in a context of widespread collaboration by Palestinian institutions—including the Palestinian police—with the Mandatory authorities.) By 1936, the White Paper of 1930* was already fading into memory, and the period 1920 to 1936 had seen a near doubling of the colonial settler Jewish population. The British government and underground Jewish terror organizations like the Haganah and Irgun were straining to transform the multi-cultural and multi-religious Palestine into Eretz Yisrael,§ as the prelude to a Jewish state. Analogous conditions prevailed before the outbreaks of the first and second intifadas in 1987 and 2000, respectively, and we see them again today.

Lack of trust in Palestinian authorities, a divided and complicit leadership, an ever-more arrogant and flagrantly repressive occupation, and increasing Palestinian isolation—these conditions are always cited by skeptics as factors preventing an uprising, but history shows that they in fact they precipitate one.

It is normal to experience lulls between uprisings. This partly reflects the generational character of waves of resistance. Palestinians have gone through fourteen uprisings in 130 years—a rate of about one a decade. The next one

* *Editor's note:* The 1930 Passfield White Paper was the result of a British inquiry ordered in the wake of the 1929 revolt. It recommended restricting Jewish immigration into Palestine.

§ *Editor's note:* Hebrew for the "Land of Israel."

is overdue. Let us hope it will be the last. Palestine is the world's sole remaining unresolved case of colonialism, and it will most likely be settled in the same manner as it has been in more than 140 other countries: by sharing the land and agreeing to coexist. Until this freedom and equality is achieved, Palestinians will continue to resist.

ꙮ

Muhammad Shehada

Gaza has been wrecked by sophisticated artillery and prolonged siege.* It is no longer suitable for collective life. The refugees and children crammed into desert limbo, who have endured so much, and for so long, are trying to hold themselves together—and failing. But with the whole region drowning in blood and the Palestinian people missing from their own struggle, Gaza's torment attracts little attention. Gaza has never been so desperate, or so alone.

One might imagine three paths out of this existential peril. Unfortunately, two are fantastical while the third is not being pursued.

Armed struggle

Muqawama, or armed struggle: it's the word that keeps on giving, for Israel and Hamas alike. For Hamas, *muqawama* is a crucial source of legitimation and the primary means by which it distinguishes itself rhetorically from the Palestinian Authority. Criticism of *muqawama* is denounced by Hamas as opposition to the Palestinian struggle as such—and dissent from Hamas is presented as

Muhammad Shehada is a writer and civil society activist from the Gaza Strip. He is a student of Development Studies at Lund University, Sweden, and was a Field Researcher and Public Relations Officer for the Gaza office of the Euro-Med Monitor for Human Rights.

* *Editor's note:* See Chronology and Glossary ("Siege of Gaza").

criticism of *muqawama*. For Israel, Hamas's commitment to armed resistance has been invaluable in justifying its blockade of and massacres in Gaza, as well as its occupation of the West Bank ("We withdrew from Gaza and got rockets—now you want us to leave the West Bank?").

In truth, the notion of Palestinian armed resistance never had much substance. These days, it is confined almost entirely to obsolete slogans. After three major confrontations, Israel and Hamas have reached a quid pro quo whereby Hamas deploys "field control" forces authorized to shoot-to-kill whoever attempts to launch a projectile at Israel, in return for which Hamas leaders are permitted to emerge from their hiding holes and walk fearlessly down the street. That is, Hamas polices the Israeli siege while Israel no longer targets senior Hamas officials for assassination. Former Prime Minister Ismail Haniyeh has begun a daily routine of running around the city pretending to try to lose weight. Hamas's Gaza chief, Yahya al-Sinwar, just bought a nice house in al-Sheikh Radwan neighborhood. Qassam Brigade* commanders can be seen every other day barbecuing on the beach.

Haniyeh's new exercise regimen does not inspire everyone. Disaffection has developed in the Hamas rank and file, particularly among the youth, who unlike their leaders gain nothing from the status quo. Some defect to jihadist groups and fire primitive rockets at Israel to provoke a response. The Israeli response always targets Hamas facilities to remind Hamas of its duties. To dampen dissent and preserve self-respect, Hamas leaders shout apocalyptic slogans, recordings of which are then used by the Israeli propaganda machine to prove the necessity and justice of the strangulation policy. Another win-win. Hamas supplements these verbal pyrotechnics with periodic military processions to remind the masses of its might. As for Israel—if its leaders are intimidated by the sight of desperate people parading ineffectually to somebody else's tune, then between Hamas and the PA, the liberation of Palestine cannot be far away.

---

* *Editor's note:* The Qassam Brigades is the military arm of Hamas.

Factional reconciliation

Hamas leaders constantly fantasize about seizing control of the West Bank.

In March 2014, a reconciliation agreement was signed between Hamas and the PA in al-Shati Camp, according to which the PA would no longer persecute Hamas activists in the West Bank (and vice versa in Gaza). Immediately, Hamas leaders began to publicly advocate that the battlefield be moved to the West Bank, so that resistance might continue while sparing Gaza further confrontations with Israel. This manifested in the kidnapping and killing of three Israeli teenagers in Gush Etzion, an operation planned by Hamas leader Saleh al-Arouri (without informing Hamas's political office) that led, in the end, to Israel's summer 2014 massacre in Gaza. This massacre destroyed the Gaza Strip and the reconciliation agreement with it.

Undeterred, senior Hamas leaders like Mahmoud al-Zahar never stop proclaiming the need to "move the *muqawama* to the West Bank," which—Zahar promises—"would liberate Palestine in 24 hours."[1] Hamas's demands for factional reconciliation are an end to the persecution of Hamas members by PA intelligence, which would permit *muqawama* be moved to the West Bank, and that the PA pay for Hamas's expenses in Gaza. Unsurprisingly, PA President Mahmoud Abbas does not accept the presence of military brigades that are out of his control, nor is he willing to fund a government in Gaza over which he has no authority. Reconciliation has therefore reached a dead end, and the debilitating factional divide looks set to persist and deepen.

Popular resistance

The authorities in Gaza are too incompetent to inspire a collective will to sacrifice, but just competent enough to thwart any effort to organize outside approved channels. To be sure, Hamas claims to believe in people power, and its 2017 Charter recognizes a role, albeit supplementary and subordinate, for

[1] "Zahar Calls for Transferring the Resistance's Capabilities and Tools to the West Bank)," *Quds Press* (2 November 2016) [Arabic].

civil society in "resistance."[2] But in practice, Hamas's faith in the masses is confined to its own staged demonstrations. These performances generate no attention and inspire no solidarity, because nobody believes they are real.

In 2017, Hamas elections brought to power members of the Qassam Brigades as well as former prisoners who were released by Israel in 2011 after spending decades in solitary confinement. The former have spent their entire lives on the run in a state of paranoid isolation; the latter believe they are living the good life—Gaza is as big as the universe in their eyes compared to Israeli prison cells. Yahya al-Sinwar reportedly told a June 2017 meeting of Hamas officials from northern Gaza, "Hamas has never seen better days than the present time." Hamas's suppression of popular feedback mechanisms exacerbates its leaders' already dangerous detachment from reality.

Caught between the Israeli army and Hamas, the people of Gaza have sunk into apathy and depression. Life is suffocating and stagnant. There is no movement, no dynamism, no future; just a dead present, extending indefinitely in all directions. With any improvement liable to be obliterated in the next Israeli assault, the very idea of "progress" has been eroded. Some people believe that their martyrdom might do more use than their existence, but most have become indifferent. And why not? They have tried on more than one occasion to organize and demonstrate for change, but were obstructed by the Hamas authorities, which detect in any independent initiative the hidden hand of the PA or Israel.[3] If the PA leadership hardly inspires a will to sacrifice, Hamas rule

---

[2] Hamas, "A Document of General Principles and Policies" (1 May 2017), para. 33.

[3] On 15 March 2011, a demonstration against the factional split was broken up by Hamas police force. On 29 April 2015, a protest against the Gaza blockade was disrupted by Hamas groups. In May 2016, a handful of unemployed graduated students protested in Jundi Square, calling upon the PA to take responsibility for their situation. The group started with one hunger striker, "Sa'id Lolo," and grew to about fifteen hunger strikers. By the tenth day, when Lolo's health deteriorated, Prime Minister Rami Hamdallah pledged to assist them with a temporary employment program, but the protest continued. At this point, Hamas authorities detained two of the protestors and confiscated their belongings. See Nidal al-Mughrabi, "Palestinian Unity Rally in Gaza Ends in Violence," *Reuters* (15 March 2011); Asmaa al-Ghoul, "Gaza's Youth Protestors

has also left many of its former supporters disillusioned. Its practices of torture and detention are sometimes cloned from Israeli intelligence.

The youth of Gaza, highly educated with no prospects, feel excluded and superfluous. Many believe Gaza is beyond salvation. The "every man for himself" mentality that developed over three decades of demoralization, defeat, and corruption offers people only two ways to survive: exodus to the diaspora[4] (many fantasies have developed about these promised lands, with some believing that even the air smells differently on the other side) or competition in Gaza for jobs in foreign-funded NGOs. These NGOs use young volunteers to attract Western donations for pointless projects, promising that they will acquire skills and recommendations that will help them get a paid NGO job or a scholarship outside of Gaza. In most cases, these hopes are disappointed. I have many friends who studied civil engineering and who have now been volunteering in youth societies and English clubs[5] for years on end.

As the quality of life in Gaza plunges, suicidal tendencies increase. Sometimes this desire for escape at any cost takes collective form: in 2015, young Gazans hastened to protest at the borders or jump the fence into Israel, many hoping to get shot and be relieved of their agony. This routine took place every Friday in the poor villages around Khan Younis and the refugee camps of Burij, Maghazi, and Nusirat; every week saw a casualty. (Israel was initially fearful that these protests would gather momentum, forcing the army into embarrassing confrontations with nonviolent youths; but with no support from Hamas and no publicity abroad the demonstrations fizzled out.) Drugs

---

Remain Divided," *Al-Monitor* (8 May 2015); "Gaza Police Detain 2 Hunger-Striking Palestinians Protesting High Unemployment," *Ma'an News* (16 May 2016).

[4] Alice Su, "If Gaza's Borders were Opened, '100,000 Young People Would Leave'," *Al Jazeera America* (6 May 2015).

[5] People meet in "English clubs" to discuss novels and movies, produce and share their own work, participate in video conferences with Anglophone activists, etc., in English. Participants hope to improve their language skills and hence their competitiveness for scholarships and (non-existent) jobs.

offer a more individualized route out. Addiction began with the tens of thousands of bored PA employees in Gaza who have been out of work since June 2007, paid by Ramallah to stay home, and is now spreading to young people as well.

Thus proceeds the irreversible social destruction of the Gaza Strip. International powers value their relationship with Israel over the well-being of Gazan refugees, while Palestinian political parties have become invested in the status quo. As for the people of Gaza: lacking optimism and trust, it will at this point require a major upheaval for them to move, such as the death of Abbas or the collapse of the international aid system. Their incredible resilience and adaptability has become, in some ways, their biggest disadvantage.

CHAPTER TEN.

CAN THERE BE A RESOLUTION OF THE CONFLICT IF PALESTINIAN CITIZENS OF ISRAEL ARE NOT INVOLVED?

Amal Jamal

Most literature on the Israeli-Palestinian conflict approaches it from the perspective of the two-state solution. However, Israel has constructed an undemocratic one-state reality spanning the entirety of Mandatory Palestine.* This confronts Israel and the Palestinians under its control with a quite different set of challenges and choices. The most fundamental of these for Israeli Jews is

---

Amal Jamal is Professor of Political Science at the School of Political Science, Government, and International Affairs at Tel Aviv University. He was Chair of the Political Science Department (2006–2009) and is co-Editor-in-Chief of the political science journal *The Public Sphere*. His books include *Arab Civil Society in Israel* (2017), *The Nakba in Israel's National Memory* (2015), and *Arab Minority Nationalism in Israel: The Politics of Indigeneity* (2011).

* *Editor's note:* See Glossary.

whether the one-state reality Israel has established is to be democratic or apartheid. At present it is not democratic, since millions of Palestinians have lived under Israeli military rule for five decades without civil or national rights. The expansion of Jewish settlements, the growing influence of the settler movement on the major right-wing political bloc that dominates Israeli politics, and the Jewish majority's complete distrust of Palestinians and their leadership all indicate an intention by Israeli Jews to assert total control over all Palestinians living west of the Jordan River. These dynamics deepen the internal Jewish struggle as to the meaning of Jewish self-determination, whether within the Green Line* or beyond it. They also underline the observation made by Edward Said in the late 1970s that no matter where Palestinians live, and regardless of their legal or administrative status—citizens or not, they are targeted by Israel as enemies of Jewish sovereignty.

Imposed fragmentation

Israel's approach to its conflict with the Palestinians has become hegemonic principally because it has fragmented the Palestinian people into multiple discrete sectors, each of which is forced to conduct negotiations and struggle in isolation from the others. The establishment of the Jewish state on 78 percent of Mandatory Palestine dispersed Palestinians throughout the region as refugees, where many still remain. Today, Palestinians in the West Bank and Gaza Strip must accept harsh Israeli conditions—amounting to acquiescence in a demilitarized and non-contiguous mini-state—if they are to achieve national sovereignty, while Palestinians living inside Israel must acquiesce in their status as second-class citizens in the state of the Jewish people if they are to retain access to what has become Jewish land. Israel's strategy to impose its will has been to block the development of any common Palestinian struggle while expressing disingenuous intent to reach a peaceful solution to the conflict,

* *Editor's note:* The "Green Line" refers to the pre-June 1967 armistice boundary established in 1949, now recognized by the International Court of Justice as the legal border of the State of Israel.

thereby preventing Palestinians from amassing political, diplomatic, or military power to counter the asymmetry between the two sides.

Palestinians, for their part, have resisted this imposed fragmentation. The Palestine Liberation Organization (PLO) struggled mightily to gain recognition as the sole legitimate representative of all Palestinians. In so doing, it was forced to compromise its comprehensive and inclusive disposition towards Palestinians and lower its political ambitions. This shift began in 1974, when the PLO, which had previously called for full liberation and independence for the entirety of Mandatory Palestine, began to assert sovereignty on areas occupied by Israel in 1967. This implied that Palestinians must accept the political reality established on the ground in 1948, leaving those who remained inside the Jewish state to fend for themselves. The Oslo I Accord (1993), which became the reference point for subsequent efforts to negotiate a peaceful settlement of the conflict, carved the post-1948 reality into the legal and diplomatic consciousness of the international community and, by extension, that of Palestinian diplomatic institutions. But Israel's policies towards the territories occupied in 1967 led to growing recognition among Palestinians that any sovereignty they might acquire in those territories would be emptied of substantive content. These policies are myriad and include, most notably, the ceaseless expansion of Jewish-Israeli settlements in the West Bank; the rise of extreme nationalist political forces in Israel, which seek to violently reconfigure the demographic and topographic realities on the ground; the isolation and siege of Gaza; and proposals to reduce the number of Palestinians inside Israel through territorial exchanges with a future State of Palestine, including "the Triangle," an area of Israel in which more than 300,000 Palestinians have been living as second-class citizens since 1949.

The increasingly entrenched one-state reality makes Palestinian citizens of Israel a more salient constituency in the Israeli-Palestinian conflict as a whole. The last two decades, especially, have seen growing recognition by Palestinians that their community in Israel has become a strong political player that could significantly influence future Israeli-Palestinian relations. This recognition is warranted, given these Palestinians' Israeli citizenship and thus their status (albeit limited) as an in-group member. Palestinian citizens of Israel live in better economic and social conditions than their brethren under occupation. They possess greater freedoms and can participate in the political game through elections, as well as choose their representatives to the Israeli Knesset (parliament). Nevertheless, they feel targeted by the dominant Jewish nationalistic majority, with the encouragement and incitement of leading ministers and officials. Aggressive nationalistic legislation, offensive administrative regulations, and blunt economic discrimination validate the common sentiment among Palestinian citizens of Israel that the Israeli state and the Jewish majority within it seek not merely to guarantee exclusive Jewish hegemony over state resources, but to subordinate all Palestinians—citizens or not—to Jewish hegemony. This presents Israel's Palestinian citizens with several options. They can surrender, which is unlikely; resort to violence, which is not effective; seek to protect the limited privileges afforded to them by the status quo; or pursue diplomatic means to delegitimize Israel and increase international pressure on the state to withdraw from Palestinian areas occupied in 1967.

Electoral participation

Palestinians living under occupation have shown, and to a great extent still show, much understanding as to the special conditions in which Palestinians inside Israel live. Most have not expected Palestinian citizens of Israel to join a violent struggle against the occupation. Nonetheless, Palestinian-Israelis are expected to lobby for Palestinian aspirations for statehood inside the Israeli political system, and for that to happen they must fully integrate into it. These expectations have thus far not materialized, since the rising nationalistic trends in Jewish-Israeli society have blocked Palestinians' attempts to engage with them politically. This structural rebuff has led, in turn, to calls from Palestinians to boycott Knesset elections, reducing their electoral impact still further.

Palestinian citizens of Israel have participated in Israeli elections since 1951. The failure of this participation to yield effective, positive changes in their prospects, together with the rise of an oppositional ideological consciousness among nationalist and religious sectors, has led to a continuous and steady decline in Palestinian electoral participation. Whereas over 80 percent of Palestinian citizens participated in the elections before the 1980s, and delegated an increasing number of Arab members of parliament to the Knesset, the decades since have witnessed a growing election boycott as Palestinians have sought alternatives to the formal political system. Electoral participation by Palestinian citizens declined from 79.3 percent in 1996 to 63.5 percent in 2015, while more than 80 percent of Palestinian citizens boycotted the special election in 2001.* The 2001 boycott meant that Labor's Ehud Barak was replaced as prime minister by the right-wing leader Ariel Sharon.

TABLE 1. PARTICIPATION IN ELECTIONS BY PALESTINIAN CITIZENS OF ISRAEL, 1996–2015.

Year	Participation (%)
1996	79.3
1999	75
2003	62
2006	56.3
2009	53.6
2013	57.3
2015	63.5

This reduced participation is an expression of growing Palestinian disillusionment in the capacity of Israel's political system to represent them. The long-term fall in Palestinian participation was slightly affected by the establishment of the Joint Arab List, which united all the Arab parties ahead of the 2015 election (see Table 1). The reversal of the decline in participation between 2009 and 2015 is an important development, but one that is likely to persist only if the Joint List manages to demonstrate political efficacy or if future

* *Editor's note:* Israel held a prime ministerial election in February 2001 after Ehud Barak resigned as Prime Minister in December 2000.

elections take place in the wake of a major clash between the State of Israel and Palestinians in Gaza, as occurred in the 2013 and 2015 elections. The Gaza conflicts of 2012 and 2014 inflamed national sentiments among Israel's Palestinian citizens, which translated into higher turnout for Arab parties as an act of protest.

Many Palestinian leaders in Israel call on members of their community to utilize every available institutional opportunity to advance their interests. Notwithstanding its limitations, the Knesset does provide some resources to Arab parties—resources which might be used to enable Palestinian society to articulate its needs and desires in a sanctioned Israeli forum. Others reject such participation on the grounds that it legitimizes the Israeli system and enables Israel to assert its "democratic" character without affording Palestinians any real influence over Israel's discriminatory policies. If the Joint Arab List does not manage to significantly affect Israeli policy—and this is the most likely scenario, given its dwindling legitimacy in the eyes of most Jewish parties and the unwillingness of the latter to integrate it into their decision-making processes—the influence of the latter camp will grow and the percentage of Palestinian citizens participating in Israeli elections will decrease further. If this happens, an increasing number of Palestinian citizens will seek alternative means to express their dissent and protest their subordination.

Ideological differences, tactical consensus

One might generalize that Palestinian citizens of Israel prefer to avoid totalizing, "either/or" diagnoses of existing Palestinian reality and strategies for improving it. Palestinians in Israel are demonstrating much political maturity in avoiding the traps set by the Jewish far-right, which views them as enemies and seeks to push them into a direct clash with the state. They tend to pursue a "selective" strategy, remaining committed to their Palestinian nationality while simultaneously struggling for the full individual and collective rights of citizenship. This approach represents the most effective utilization of the opportunities available to them. Through this selective engagement, the Palestinian minority in Israel seeks to overcome the "double marginality" imposed on it by Israelis and occupied Palestinians alike, and to utilize its "double consciousness"—identifying as both Israeli and Palestinian—to promote the best possible reality for all parties, including itself. In other words, the Palestinian community in Israel does not aspire to be a "bridge" for peace, as if it were the United Nations rather than one of the victims of Zionism.* Instead, it seeks to use what influence it has to end the suffering of millions of fellow Palestinians living under brutal occupation.

The double consciousness of Palestinians in Israel reflects the rise of the Arab middle class, which is both nationally conscious and has accrued great economic wealth in recent years. Growing prosperity—despite the fact that around 50 percent of the Palestinian community in Israel still lives under the poverty line—has raised this group's expectations and demands, but also its fears that existing gains might be lost. This class resents Jewish discrimination but elects to participate in the Israeli economy in an effort to raise Palestinians' standard of living. It seeks to integrate with the Jewish-Israeli population and expects to be given a chance, not only on the economic but also on the political level. This same class anticipates that the state and the Jewish majority will permit it to translate its growing economic power into political influence, without having to entirely submit to perpetual Jewish hegemony. It believes it can achieve this delicate balance without disengaging from the Palestinian national question, especially in the form of opposition to Israeli policies in the Occupied Territories.

Having said that, and notwithstanding the many commonalities among Palestinians in Israel, this group is nonetheless split over future visions and strategies. Broadly speaking, three different approaches have gained support in the community, all of them driven and articulated primarily by the rising Palestinian middle classes.

---

* *Editor's note:* See Glossary ("Zionism").

The first camp strives to reconcile its Palestinian-ness with its Israeli-ness. It supports the two-state solution, opposes Israel's formal definition as a Jewish state, and struggles against discriminatory policies. This camp enjoys the support of at least one-third of the Palestinian community in Israel, manifested politically in the Hadash Party as well as a small number of voters for Zionist parties.

The second camp more firmly situates Palestinian citizens of Israel within the broader Palestinian reality, beginning with the centrality of Palestinian national identity and the search for just solutions to the Palestinian problem in all its aspects. It rejects the Jewish character of the Israeli state and supports the struggle of Palestinians under occupation not just for national independence but for comprehensive liberation, utilizing all means legitimated by international law, including boycotts. Many members of this group envisage a democratic, one-state future for Israel/Palestine. This camp attracts the support of more than 20 percent of the community and finds institutional home in the Balad Party and the Abna'a Al-Balad (Sons of the Village) Movement.

Finally, there is the Islamic camp. It is ambiguous about its ultimate political aspirations and is sub-divided into two groups. The first argues that Muslims in Israel should exploit all available opportunities to promote the well-being of Muslim citizens, including representation in official Israeli institutions. The second is more dogmatic and less open to engagement with Israeli institutions. It views the conflict in religious terms and asserts that only religious beliefs, values, and practices offer hope for resolving it. This group is affiliated with the more conservative and dogmatic elements of the Muslim Brotherhood, and seeks first and foremost to transform the values and behavior of the Muslim community in Israel. It supports the movement for boycott, divestment, and sanctions (BDS)* against Israel, without announcing this position explicitly. These two groups together attract the support of more than 50 percent of the Palestinian community in Israel.

---

* *Editor's note:* See Glossary.

Since all camps share the belief that Israel's Jewish majority is radicalizing, they agree that it should not be given any excuses to use force against the Palestinian community. This results in a broad tactical consensus overlaying the political and ideological differences. Most opt for those tactics that are least vulnerable to persecution, such as establishing civil society organizations to resist governmental policies and protect the safety of their members by legal means and international advocacy.

So long as Israel does not precipitate a major crisis, whether in the Occupied Territories or inside Israel, the Palestinian minority will maintain its current approach, combining civic resistance to state discrimination (for instance, countering the Judaization policies of Arab areas by building beyond state-permitted housing zones and buying houses in Jewish towns) with efforts to build community-state relations to improve understanding and empathy and attract increased state resources. This approach is complemented by efforts to strengthen social, economic, and cultural ties with Palestinians in the West Bank and the diaspora, as well as with the wider Arab world. This "bonding and bridging" strategy seeks to maximize the resources available to Palestinians in Israel to endure and challenge the state's policies of Israelization, subjugation, and economic and cultural neglect.

Balancing in this way between Israeli and Palestinian societies reflects a quality rooted in the double consciousness of the Palestinian community in Israel, and its ability to transform this duality from a weakness into a major source of strength.

Suhad Bishara

The idea that Palestinian citizens of Israel are suitably placed to act as a possible conciliator between Israel and the Palestinians rests on the assumption that this group of Palestinians can disconnect themselves from their Palestinian nationhood and come to terms with the *Nakba** for the sake of their Israeli citizenship. From this strategic position, it is hoped they can bestride the gap between the two parties to the conflict. Those espousing this view inevitably draw a sharp distinction between the Occupied Palestinian Territory (OPT) and Israel, which, they assume, are ruled by two different legal systems. The former is perceived as exceptional and temporary in nature; an area in which Palestinians are not governed by the laws of an electoral democracy, but ruled by a military regime that is bound by the provisions of International Humanitarian Law (IHL). The latter is the realm of Israeli constitutionalism, which centers on the doctrine of the "Jewish and democratic" state. Israel is understood as a site of normality, in which the rule of law and the principle of legal equality of citizens hold sway—except, as

Suhad Bishara is Director of the Land and Planning Rights Unit, Adalah—The Legal Center for Arab Minority Rights in Israel. This contribution is written in a personal capacity and does not necessarily represent the view of Adalah.

* *Editor's note:* See Glossary.

Justice Barak noted in the *Qa'adan*[1] case, on matters of immigration, where Jews are privileged through the Law of Return.

In my view, this conceptual distinction fails to grasp the inherent connection between Israel's geopolitical practices and settler colonial formations in the West Bank, on the one hand, and those same practices as pursued within Israel against Palestinian citizens of the state on the other. It therefore distorts the political and legal dynamics that continue to shape colonial power-relations between Israel and all segments of the Palestinian people, fragmented though they are by multiple legal frameworks and across political borders.

I will focus here on Israel's land and displacement policies towards Palestinians who are citizens of Israel, aiming to demonstrate that the same conceptual framework applies both to the occupied West Bank and to Israel itself. To that end, I will analyze rulings delivered by the Israeli Supreme Court* in cases in which it was asked to deal with the property rights and displacement of Palestinians in both areas: Israel and the OPT.

Israel's dispossession and settlement policies in Area C of the West Bank are well documented.[2] They are exemplified by the displacement of hundreds of members of the Bedouin Jahalin tribe by the Civil Administration[§] in the 1980s and 1990s to make way for the establishment and subsequent expansion of the settlement of Ma'ale Adumim. In 1994, the Civil Administration issued eviction orders against dozens of families from land that had been allocated for

---

* *Editor's note:* Israel's Supreme Court sits as the High Court of Justice or the High Court of Appeals. The designations are in this contribution used interchangeably.

§ *Editor's note:* See Glossary.

1 High Court of Justice 6698/95, *Adel Qa'adan v. The Israel Lands Administration*, 54(1) P.D. 258 (2000) [Hebrew].

2 See B'Tselem, *Expel and Exploit: The Israeli Practice of Taking Over Rural Palestinian Land* (December 2016); B'Tselem, *Acting the Landlord: Israel's Policy in Area C, the West Bank* (June 2013).

new neighborhoods within the settlement. A petition submitted to the High Court of Justice (HCJ) opposing the expulsion was rejected.[3]

Another example is the case of Khirbet a-Duqaiqah, a West Bank village that is home to more than 300 Palestinian residents. Although the village had been standing for decades, in 2005 the Civil Administration issued demolition orders against dozens of its structures. The Supreme Court threw out a petition, finding no ground to intervene in the decision-making process of the Civil Administration.[4] The framework of IHL is notable only by its absence from the brief court rulings delivered in these and similar cases. The rulings instead originate from the legal framework set forth by the Military Government for planning and zoning purposes, which was designed to further the interests of the settlements. This framework has been imposed on the Palestinian population, was formulated contrary to their interests, and clearly falls outside the definition of military necessity in IHL.

The signing of the 1993 and 1995 Oslo Accords and the enactment in 1992 of Israel's "Basic Law: Human Dignity and Liberty" and "Basic Law: Freedom of Occupation," in what came to be known as Israel's "constitutional revolution," raised hopes among many Palestinian citizens of the state that historical injustices related to violations of their rights to property and land would be redressed. Hopes were held out that constitutional protections would lead to solutions to such long-standing issues as the return of the internally-displaced to their villages, the restitution of land arbitrarily confiscated in the two decades after the establishment of the state, and the recognition of Bedouin villages in the Naqab (Negev) desert in southern Israel. However, the reality proved otherwise.

Israel's Supreme Court has insisted that the property rights of Palestinian citizens cannot escape the dictates of political Zionism. Its legal decisions

---

[3] HCJ 2966/95, *Muhammad Ahmad Saleh Haresh, et al. v. The Minister of Defense, et al.* (decision dated 28 May 1996) [Hebrew].

[4] HCJ 7151/05, *Al-Najadah, et al. v. Commander of IDF Forces in the West Bank, et al.* (decision dated 12 January 2010) [Hebrew].

expose the inevitable connection between the "rule of law" and the colonial system and lay bare the territorial logic constitutive of settler colonial regimes.

I begin with the case of internally-displaced citizens from the village of Iqrit, whom the state prevented from returning to their homes in contravention of a Supreme Court ruling from the early 1950s.[5] In a 2003 ruling on the matter, the Supreme Court decided to support the government's decision not to allow the displaced citizens to return on the basis of political considerations that were articulated in an affidavit submitted by then-Prime Minister Ariel Sharon.[6] When the displaced asked the Court to recognize their right to return as citizens, the Court denied them because it was unable to see them as anything other than Palestinians, who, like the Palestinian refugees, must not be granted the right of return.* Their civil status as citizens therefore failed to afford them protection of their constitutional rights.

In the *Jabareen* case, the Supreme Court was asked to adjudicate the request of internally-displaced citizens from the uprooted village of Lajoun to reclaim a portion of their land (around 200 dunams) that was confiscated by the state in 1953 for alleged "settlement purposes"[7] but never used for such purposes. In its judgment, the Supreme Court again denied the property rights of Palestinian citizens and explicitly stated that,

> The Basic Law: Human Dignity and Liberty has interpretive effect on various confiscation laws, and this is evident in the case law of this Court. However, as noted above, the Land Acquisition Law [used to authorize the confiscation] is an exceptional law, to be interpreted against the backdrop of the period in which it was passed, the only time that it was actually possible to implement it . . . It can be said that

---

* *Editor's note:* See Glossary.

[5] HCJ 64/51, *Dawoud v. The Minister of Defence* P.D. 8, 1117 [Hebrew].

[6] HCJ 840/97, *Sbeit, et al. v. The State of Israel* P.D. 57(4), 803 (2003) [Hebrew].

[7] Based on the Acquisition Law (Actions and Compensation) (1953).

> the Land Acquisition Law "froze in place" and therefore I believe that the effect of the Basic Law: Human Dignity and Liberty on it, if any, is minimal.[8]

The Court's commitment to a Zionist ideology of land-use was evident in its decision, particularly in Justice Elyakim Rubinstein's opinion that, "the theme of forestation in the wilderness or in previously abandoned places has been a central part of the ethos that gave rise to the state of Israel, like the development of the country or making the desert bloom."[9]

The Court has remained faithful to this logic of conquest in response to present-day policies of displacement against Palestinian citizens. Perhaps the clearest illustration of the predisposition of the legal system against Palestinian citizens of Israel is the displacement of Bedouin citizens from the village of Atir–Umm Al-Hiran in the Naqab. Like Bedouin communities in Area C[10] they face being displaced to make way for Jewish settlements, and as citizens their constitutional rights are forfeited for the Zionist objective of Judaization.

Atir–Umm Al-Hiran was established in 1956 at the order of the Military Governor of the Naqab. It is currently home to around a thousand members of the Abu al-Qi'an tribe, a community that was forcibly displaced several times following the founding of Israel in 1948 before being moved to the village.[11] Pursuant to the government's plans to establish a Jewish town in the area, the

---

[8] C.A. (Civil Appeal) 4067/07, *Jabareen, et al. v. The State of Israel* (decision dated 3 January 2010), p. 14 [Hebrew].

[9] C.A. 4067/07, *Jabareen*, p. 17 [Hebrew].

[10] Despite their status as protected persons under IHL, most Bedouins in Area C face the threat of displacement by Israel for purposes of building Jewish settlements and establishing "security" zones.

[11] For many years, members of the Abu al-Qi'an tribe lived on their ancestral land in Khirbet Zubaleh in the Naqab, which is now part of the Jewish agricultural village of Kibbutz Shuval. After their request to return to their land was rejected in 1956, they were ordered by the military governor to move to Wadi Atir, where they built their village and remain until today.

state initiated legal proceedings to evict the entire village in 2004,[12] arguing that its residents were "trespassers" who were "squatting" illegally on state land. On 5 May 2015, in a two-to-one majority decision, the Israeli Supreme Court approved the eviction of the village for the express purpose of building the new Jewish town of Hiran on its ruins, alongside a grazing area for cattle.[13] In its ruling, the Court acknowledged that the state's intention was to demolish the Bedouin village in order to establish a town "with a Jewish majority." To justify its decision, the Supreme Court asserted, inter alia, that "the fact the appellants were permitted to reside in the area does not constitute permission for the construction that took place there illegally, and does not affect the right of the respondent [the state] to evacuate the land."

With this ruling, the Court effectuated displacement plans proposed during the Military Regime[14] and defended the state's "right" to dispossess

---

[12] Civil Case (CC) 3326/4, *The State of Israel v. Ibrahim Farhoud Abu al-Qi'an* (decision dated 30 July 2009) [Hebrew].

[13] C.A. 3094/11, *Ibrahim Farhood Abu al-Qi'an et al. v. The State of Israel* (decision delivered 5 May 2015).

[14] Following the large-scale expulsion and displacement operations carried out by Israeli forces during the 1948 War, the Military Regime that was imposed on large numbers of Palestinian citizens of Israel from 1948 to 1966 concentrated the Bedouin tribes that remained in the Naqab (numbering about 13,000 people at the time) in a restricted area to the north and northeast of Beer el-Sabe (Be'er Sheva). This area was named the *Siyag*, or "fence" in Arabic. Through this process, 95 percent of the land in the Naqab outside the *Siyag* was cleared of Arab residents. In the early 1960s, the Military Government drafted plans for a second phase of displacement that aimed to concentrate the Bedouin community in the Naqab in government-established townships, in order to retain "state" areas designated as land reserves for Jewish settlement in the future. The Israeli government began implementing these plans in 1969, when it initiated construction of seven official townships for the Bedouin. The government subsequently granted recognition to a further eleven villages within the jurisdiction of the Abu Basma Regional Council (established by the government in 2000). By definition, this recognition left all the Bedouin villages located outside these localities unrecognized. Today, thirty-five unrecognized villages remain

Bedouin citizens. The latter it perceived as an enemy of the "public interest," narrowly defined as the interest of Jewish citizens. In adopting this approach in its decision-making, the Supreme Court devised novel legal techniques based on absolute powers similar to those granted to the Military Government under the Military Government's legal framework. The Court was apparently unable to embrace Bedouin citizens living in Atir–Umm Al-Hiran within its definition of the "general public," for fear of compromising the Jewish homogeneity aspired to in the as-yet-unestablished town of Hiran.

In all the aforementioned rulings, the Supreme Court translated Zionist ideology, encapsulated in the concepts of making the desert bloom, segregation, and redemption of the land, into a legal reality in various ways, all of which undermined the right to property of Palestinian citizens. Its decisions furthermore served to incorporate this ideology into the constitutional, normative system. The result is a blurring of the Green Line: Palestinian citizens of Israel from Atir–Umm Al-Hiran and Palestinian members of the Jahalin tribe living under occupation approach the Israeli Supreme Court to seek remedy against forced displacement, and the requests of both groups are denied on Zionist grounds.

From this perspective, one cannot speak of two different legal systems, one based on equality—or even troubled equality—before the law and the other bound by IHL. The cases discussed herein point to strong convergence between Israel's legal policies toward Palestinians on both sides of the Green Line. In the OPT the Supreme Court violated provisions of IHL, while in Israel it violated constitutional rights and the principle of equality before the law. On both sides, the interest of one ethnic group (Israeli Jews) was privileged. On both sides, I argue, settler colonial formations dominate. Thus, the de-colonization of the Israeli regime, including its legal system, must take place vis-à-vis the entirety of

in the Naqab and are home to about 80,000 Bedouin citizens of Israel. The state denies these villages access to basic infrastructure such as water, sanitation, and electricity, as well as to education and health services.

the Palestinian people, and Palestinian citizens of Israel cannot act as a "bridge" to peace while they themselves remain colonized. Rather, they should play a central, integral role in a common struggle against common injustices committed against the entirety of the Palestinian people.

ꕥ

Nadim Rouhana

Since Israel's establishment, it has been clear to the native population of Palestine and many others that a Jewish state cannot be democratic. As a settler colonial state, Israel applied against its Arab citizens—those Palestinians who survived the 1948 ethnic cleaning of Palestine and were granted citizenship in the new state of Israel—the full repertoire of settler colonial policies, from land expropriation and demographic control (i.e., preventing Palestinians expelled during the 1948 War from returning to their homes) to political marginalization and attempted cultural erasure.[1] But the settler colonial state of Israel is also a Jewish democracy; that is, it is a democracy for Jews, but not for its Palestinian citizens, to which it nevertheless grants various civil and social

---

Nadim Rouhana is Professor of International Negotiation and Conflict Studies and Director of the International Affairs and Conflict Resolution Program at The Fletcher School, Tufts University. He is the Founding Director of Mada al-Carmel—Arab Center for Applied Social Research in Haifa, Israel.

[1] On Arabs' citizenship as settler colonial citizenship, see Nadim N. Rouhana & Areej Sabbagh-Khoury, "Settler Colonial Citizenship: Conceptualizing the Relationship between Israel and its Palestinian Citizens," *Settler Colonial Studies* 5.3 (2015; published online October 2014), pp. 205–25. See also Nadim N. Rouhana, "The Psychopolitical Foundations of Ethnic Privileges in the Jewish State," in Nadim N. Rouhana ed., *Israel and Its Palestinian Citizens: Ethnic Privileges in the Jewish State* (Cambridge: Cambridge University Press, 2017).

rights. Zionism, in all its major tendencies, sees Israel (in whatever borders) as the exclusive property of the Jewish people, rather than a state for all Israeli citizens; more fundamentally, it sees the homeland itself as the exclusive homeland of the Jewish people. A state and homeland are thus denied in Zionist thought and practice to Arab citizens, even though they are the indigenous people of the land.

For reasons related to geopolitical calculation and the cultural and intellectual legacies of Europe's crimes against European Jews, rather than a sober assessment of Israel's policies and institutions, Israel's self-perception as a "Jewish and democratic" state is widely accepted internationally.

But for Israel's Arab citizens—those who have experienced Israel's official settler colonial policies first-hand—the classification as "democratic" of a state which considers them by definition inferior and outsiders in their own homeland manifests a disregard for fundamental principles of democracy as well as their human dignity. In the 1990s, an Arab party advanced a simple democratic formula to transform Israel into a state for all its citizens, rather than a state for the Jewish people only as stipulated by Israeli constitutional law.[2] This was rejected by the Zionist political establishment in Israel as undermining the essence of the Jewish state, which was most revealing of the contradictions inherent in this essence.[3] Israel's Palestinian citizens, however, accepted the democratic program by consensus,[4] as demonstrated by the three "Future Vision" documents that were independently produced

---

[2] See Nadim N. Rouhana ed., *Palestinian Citizens in an Ethnic Jewish State: Identities in Conflict* (New Haven, CT: Yale University Press, 1997).

[3] The "state for all its citizens" political program was advanced by an Arab party—The National Democratic Assembly—and most powerfully articulated by its leader Azmi Bishara. Various attempts by various Israeli legislators to legally challenge the right of this party to run for the Knesset elections, on the grounds that it undermined Israel's identity as the state of the Jewish people, were struck down by Israel's Supreme Court.

[4] Except for the Islamic Movement, which doesn't run for Israeli elections.

by their civil society in 2006–7[5] and in the programs and discourse of their political parties.

This vision of Israel as a democratic state for all its citizens emerged immediately after the Oslo Accords, when a two-state solution was defined as the main objective of the Palestinian national movement. But in the post-Oslo context, the two-state framework came to seem ever more detached from political reality. Over the past two decades, Israeli politics and society have been hurtling to the right, with right-wing extremism and religious nationalism dominating Israel's policies towards the Palestinians on both sides of the Green Line. Many laws, government policies, statements from politicians and other opinion leaders, and public practices in this period reflected a trajectory that has led Israel to the point where some prominent Israelis feel moved to draw comparisons to 1930s Germany.[6]

In the midst of these political transformations, Palestinians in Israel developed a branch of nationalism that I have called "homeland nationalism."[7] It is characterized by a focus on reclaiming the homeland, defined for Palestinians as the entirety of historical Palestine. In this period, therefore, the Palestinian demand to democratize the Israeli state became coupled with a desire to reclaim as a homeland the whole of Palestine. These twin ambitions are still searching for a new political articulation and political program.

Such an articulation is becoming possible as a result of parallel developments in Palestinian politics both in Israel and in the territories occupied since 1967. Escalations in Israel's settler colonial activities in the West Bank and inside Israel proper, together with growing conviction among West Bank elites

---

[5] See Khalil Nakhleh ed., *The Future of the Palestinian Minority in Israel* (Ramallah, Palestine: Madar, 2008) [Arabic].

[6] "IDF General in Bombshell Speech: Israel Today Shows Signs of 1930s Germany," *Jerusalem Post* (4 May 2016); Daniel Blatman, "Israel Increasingly Reminds Us of 1933 Germany," *Ha'aretz* (5 January 2017) [Hebrew].

[7] Nadim N. Rouhana, "Homeland Nationalism and Guarding Dignity in a Settler Colonial Context: The Palestinian Citizens of Israel Reclaim Their Homeland," *Borderlands* 14.1 (2015).

that no amount of concessions will induce Israel to withdraw or permit the establishment of a Palestinian state, have led to a paradigm shift: increasingly, the conflict between the Palestinians and the Zionist movement is being redefined as a struggle against settler colonialism. This is effectively a return to the conceptualization of the conflict that prevailed among Palestinians until the mid-1970s.[8] The "national conflict" paradigm peaked in the mid-1990s with the Oslo Accords, and has been fading with those agreements' demise.

Many Palestinians in Israel and in the West Bank (including East Jerusalem) now share the new-old realization that Zionism is a settler colonial project that is not only making it impossible for them to have a state, but which, in its dominant ideological manifestations, denies that the Palestinians have any authentic relationship to Palestine whatsoever. While Palestinians in Israel have long recognized that the Jewish state is by definition not their own, they are increasingly aware that the homeland itself—as their motherland and place of national origin, with its landscape and cultural geography—is being denied them.

This recognition of homeland denial is spreading among civil society activists, youth organizations, cultural and intellectual elites, and political leaders. This is also true of the millions of Palestinians in exile and in Gaza. Thus, the new Palestinian struggle is being increasingly defined not in relation to statehood, but around reclaiming the homeland and living in it with the human dignity that only equal citizenship can deliver. Politically, this entails a struggle for liberation from Israel's settler colonial regime across Palestine and an attempt to establish in its place a new, de-Zionized order, in which both colonized and colonizer are liberated from their relations as occupier and occupied, oppressor and oppressed, privileged and underprivileged, and superior and inferior (in the eyes of the settler colonial order).

Palestinians in Israel were among the first to realize that partition of Palestine into two states, even if it were possible, would not solve their problems

[8] See Nadim N. Rouhana, "Decolonization as Reconciliation: Rethinking the National Conflict Paradigm in the Israeli-Palestinian Conflict," *Ethnic and Racial Studies* (in press).

as settler colonial citizens of a Zionist state, not least because a state in the West Bank and Gaza would not allow for the return of Palestinian refugees and would perpetuate a settler colonial regime within Israel that institutionalizes Jewish supremacy. Even the staunchest proponents of partition among the Palestinians in Israel—i.e., supporters of the Democratic Front for Peace and Equality, with the Israeli Communist Party at its core—have discarded the slogan of "two states for two peoples" on which they educated generations of Arab citizens. This slogan, for them, too, denotes a Palestinian state in the West Bank and Gaza for Palestinians, alongside the State of Israel for the Jewish people. Palestinians who find themselves in the latter will have no state and no homeland. Because of these implications, the Democratic Front modified its slogan to simply "two states," in which Israel is the state of all its citizens (as originally advanced by the National Democratic Assembly).

The new vision is best articulated in the Haifa Declaration (2007), a manifesto drafted by tens of Palestinian citizens in Israel—academics, intellectuals, and political and civil society leaders—and endorsed by hundreds more from all political parties. The Declaration, whose point of departure is a conceptualization of Israel as a settler colonial project, states:

> Our vision for the future relations between Palestinian Arabs and Israeli Jews in this country is to create a democratic state founded on equality between the two national groups. This solution would guarantee the rights of the two groups in a just and equitable manner. This would require a change in the constitutional structure and a change in the definition of the State of Israel from a Jewish state to a democratic state established on national and civil equality between the two national groups, and enshrining the principles of banning discrimination and of equality between all of its citizens and residents. In practice, this means annulling all laws that discriminate directly or indirectly on the basis of nationality, ethnicity, or religion—first and foremost the laws of immigration and citizenship—and enacting laws rooted in the principles of justice and equality.[9]

[9] The Haifa Declaration (15 May 2007).

The Declaration also gives central place to ending the occupation of the West Bank and Gaza and implementing the right of return of Palestinian refugees.

Many believe that the Palestinians in Israel will spearhead the new Palestinian struggle for decolonization and liberation from a settler colonial regime. Whatever one's views are about the capabilities of this segment of the Palestinian people, it cannot be doubted that they are the most familiar of all Palestinians with the settler colonial regime's practices and politics, culture, and values. If the struggle is defined in terms not of partition but of liberation in a new de-Zionized order, in which Arabs and Jews live in equality in a democratic state of all its citizens, then the Palestinians in Israel are in a position to lead the way.

Sammy Smooha

It is a common belief that Israel's Palestinian-Arab minority (1,450,000 people, 17.5 percent of Israel's citizens) constitutes a potential "bridge for peace" between Israel and the Palestinians and wider Arab world. This belief rests on two premises. First, that Israel's Palestinian-Arab citizens can effectively broker a two-state solution because they know both sides well and can perform the role of a persuasive reconciler. They are Arabs in language, culture, religion, nationality, identity, and family ties; but at the same time they are bilingual, bicultural, and Israelized in many other ways. They also stand to derive political and material benefits from the termination of the Arab-Israeli and Palestinian-Israeli conflicts. Peace would end the painful conflict between loyalty to their state and loyalty to their people, while liberating them from Jews' resentment and discrimination as a suspected fifth column. In addition, they would be well

---

Sammy Smooha is Professor Emeritus of Sociology at the University of Haifa. He served as Dean of the Faculty of Social Sciences and President of the Israeli Sociological Society and won the 2008 Israel Prize for Sociology. He is a specialist on the comparative study of ethnic relations and is the author of *Israel: Pluralism and Conflict* (1978) and *Arabs and Jews in Israel,* two vols. (1989, 1992). In 2003, he launched the annual Index of Arab-Jewish Relations in Israel. He served as Israel Institute Visiting Professor at the Department of Near and Middle East Studies at SOAS, University of London, during the 2016–2017 academic year.

placed to mediate and reap rewards from increased exchange between Israeli Jews and the Arab world.

The second premise is that a comprehensive resolution of the conflict will require that Israel address the grievances of its own Palestinians. If these are ignored, the resulting opposition and unrest will make it harder for Israel to reach an agreement with the Palestinians and might well destabilize Palestine-Israel relations in the post-conflict era. To pacify its Arab citizens, so the argument goes, Israel should let its internal refugees (over 20 percent of the Arab population in Israel) return to or rebuild their villages and towns destroyed by the state in 1948, compensate Arabs in land or money for any confiscated property, officially recognize them as an indigenous people entitled to cultural autonomy and power-sharing, and transform into a binational polity to enable Arab citizens to reconcile equality and national autonomy with loyalty to the state.[1]

A simultaneous resolution of the issues at the heart of the conflict with both the "outside" and "inside" Palestinians will stabilize peace and normalize Israel in the region. Who could object to that?

Unfortunately, this rosy scenario collides with reality at several points. Palestinian Arabs in Israel in fact cannot mediate because they are committed to and identified with the Arab side, and lack social and economic leverage. If they were to insist on tying their struggle for civic and national equality to the Palestinian struggle for independence, they would overburden peace negotiations with an additional and difficult-to-resolve issue, one which has no presence on any existing agenda and about which there is no international consensus. This would make reaching an agreement nearly impossible, not least because requiring Israel to satisfy Palestinian-Israeli claims would undermine Israeli Jews' motivations for agreeing to a two-state solution, i.e., separation from the Palestinians to secure a Jewish majority and an end of both the conflict and claims.

---

[1] Elie Rekhess, "The Arab Minority in Israel: Reconsidering the '1948 Paradigm'," *Israel Studies* 19.2 (Summer 2014), pp. 187–217.

Inserting the demands of Israel's Arab minority into the Middle East peace process would play into Israelis' fear—and Israeli government claims—that the anti-occupation campaign is really aimed at Israel's demise. It would also open the door to Israeli counter-demands. After all, why should only one side be permitted to re-open the package of "core issues"? The Jewish right-wing would demand to cede the Arab-populated Triangle to a future Palestinian state, disenfranchise potentially disloyal Arab individuals and groups, and condition full citizenship on acceptance of Israel as a Jewish and Zionist state. As a countermeasure against the Arab minority's striving for binationalism, Israel would condition a treaty with the Palestinians on their official recognition of Israel as the homeland of the entire Jewish people and a Jewish state.

A peace spoiler

These considerations raise the possibility that, rather than serving as a bridge for peace, the Arabs in Israel might instead play the role of a "peace spoiler," preventing a two-state solution by abstaining from or voting against, in a national referendum, a peace agreement that ignores their interests; by actively resisting such an agreement; or by conditioning any treaty on their radical demands. The chances of peace would also be significantly reduced if Arab citizens were to join a new Palestinian intifada or wage an intifada of their own.* Such subversive acts would reinforce Jewish fears that in the post-peace agreement era Israeli Arabs might coalesce with Palestinian spoiler groups or support a hostile Palestinian state and undermine Israel's national security and political stability.

The view that the Israeli-Palestinian dispute should fully include the Israeli segment of the Palestinian people is, not coincidentally, popular among protagonists of a one-state solution. As many of them see it, uniting the two struggles would help prevent an unjust and unrealistic partition of Palestine (i.e., the establishment of a mini-Bantustan). The BDS Movement, for instance, joins opposition to Israel's occupation with two further demands: a right of return for the Palestinian refugees and full equality for Israel's Arab minority. All told,

---

* *Editor's note:* See Glossary ("First intifada," "Second intifada").

this platform clearly intends to destroy Israel as a Jewish and Zionist state and to replace it with a binational state that would soon become a Palestinian-majority state from the river to the sea. Many Israeli Arab radicals and Western intellectuals who oppose the existence of a Jewish state share this vision.[2]

A disengaged party

It may seem that the "spoiler" scenario is more probable than the popular "bridge" one. But in truth, Israel's Palestinians cannot be a bridge for peace and are not ready to pay the price for being a peace spoiler. They in practice opt for a third alternative—*disengagement.* This position avoids the risks of the other two while enabling the Arab community to make the best of bad situation.[3]

There is a broad consensus in Israel and internationally that Arabs in Israel are not part of the "question of Palestine." All Israeli governments, right and left, have sharply distinguished between Palestinians with citizenship rights and Palestinian subjects under occupation. They define the demands of Israel's Arab citizens as domestic. The Palestine Liberation Organization and the Palestinian Authority have likewise disconnected Israel's Palestinian Arabs from the Palestinian resistance movement, urged them to vote in elections to the Knesset, and expected them to fulfill the role of a political lobby for the Palestinian cause. The international community has followed suit, focusing on the occupation and peace efforts while largely overlooking issues relating to the Arabs inside Israel. Western governments and NGOs fund activities of Arab civil society in Israel to protect human rights and Israeli democracy, not to promote binationalism.

---

[2] For views questioning or opposing the two-state solution, see John Ehrenberg and Yoav Peled eds., *Israel and Palestine: Alternative Perspectives on Statehood* (Landham, MD: Rowman and Littlefield, 2016) and Nadim Rouhana ed., *Israel and its Palestinian Citizens: Ethnic Privileges in the Jewish State* (Cambridge: Cambridge University Press, 2017).

[3] For an elaboration of this view and its support in Arab and Jewish public opinion, see Sammy Smooha, *Still Playing by the Rules: Index of Arab-Jewish Relations in Israel 2015* (Haifa: Pardes Publishing House, 2017) [Hebrew]. A summary version in English may be viewed at *pardesbooks.com*.

As a collective, Arab citizens realize that they have a duty of allegiance to Israel. They strive for a two-state solution and equality. They regard partition as feasible and the future independent Palestine as a viable state with which they would identify and fulfill their national aspirations. Their leaders increasingly make use of protest abroad, in the form of testimonies to international human rights organizations and briefings to foreign embassies in Israel, but do not explicitly link the struggle of Israeli Arabs with that of the Palestinians under occupation and in exile. Palestinians in Israel did not participate in the two intifadas and their involvement in terrorism is slim. In the Future Vision documents (2006–7), Arab public figures demanded the establishment of a Palestinian state alongside Israel and the transformation of Israel into a binational state. However, they did not condition the one upon the other. When right-wing Jewish politicians raise the irredentist goal of transferring the Triangle to a Palestinian state, Israeli Arabs feel insulted and object vehemently.[4]

How can we account for the fact that Palestinians inside Israel still play by the rules while Palestinians outside use active and even violent resistance? In short, they do not share the same status, fate, or future. Israeli Palestinians have citizenship rights. They avail themselves of democracy to better their lot. Largely free of state repression, they employ a variety of parliamentary and extra-parliamentary means to fight for change. These include appeals to the Supreme Court, demonstrations, and general strikes, as well as the formal electoral system: in 2015, fully 63.5 percent of the Arab electorate turned out to elect the Joint List, the third largest party in the Knesset (seating twelve Arabs and one Jew).

Notwithstanding significant legal and de facto discrimination, Palestinian Israelis for the most part enjoy the rule of law, benefit from welfare state services, lead a relatively modern way of life, and receive protection from Islamic

---

[4] The mainstream Arab position is presented here, disregarding the internal differences. For discussion of the various Israeli Arab political camps, see As'ad Ghanem, "Israel's Second-Class Citizens: Arabs in Israel and the Struggle for Equal Rights," *Foreign Affairs* (8 June 2016).

fundamentalism. Their growing Israelization, as they appreciate the standard of living and quality of life prevalent in Israel, moderates and balances their Palestinization. All these advantages are denied to the Palestinians across the Green Line, who fight to disengage from Israel and to form a sovereign state of their own.

Moreover, Arabs and Jews in Israel have developed over the years a minimal unifying consensus. They agree on a two-state solution, though not on its terms of implementation. They also endorse together the extension to Arabs of religious and cultural collective rights and state-funded separate schools in Arabic. It is hard to believe, but true, that the Arabs are gradually and steadily reconciling themselves to Israel as a state with a Jewish majority, a Hebrew calendar, the Hebrew language, and an Israeli-Hebrew culture. To be sure, this is reconciliation to the inevitable rather than a warm-hearted embrace. Israeli Arabs neither prefer a Jewish state nor embrace Zionism. They continue to reject the Law of Return* and the legitimacy of a Zionism that is designed to make Israel a Jewish state indefinitely.

What is to be done?

It is in the interest of all parties to the Israeli-Palestinian conflict that endeavors to resolve the conflict be separated from the domestic claims of Israel's Palestinian minority. As citizens of the Jewish state, the Arabs should negotiate their status within Israel and join the Israeli peace camp to fight for a two-state agreement with the Palestinians.[5]

While a peace agreement between the Palestinians and Israel can be achieved without the constructive involvement of Arabs in Israel, their potential destructive engagement lurks in the background. To minimize this risk, an

---

* *Editor's note:* See Glossary.

[5] For detailed analysis demonstrating the feasibility of the two-state solution, see Gershon Shafir, *A Half Century of Occupation: Israel, Palestine, and the World's Most Intractable Conflict* (Oakland, CA: University of California Press, 2017). For discussion of distrust as a critical stumbling block to reaching an agreement, see Ilai Alon and Daniel Bar-Tal eds., *The Role of Trust in Conflict Resolution: The Israeli-Palestinian Case and Beyond* (Cham, Switzerland: Springer International Publishing, 2016).

Israel genuinely interested in reaching an agreement should do what it should do anyway, namely, treat its minority population equally and fairly. Without compromising its Jewish and democratic character and without becoming a binational state, Israel should grant Arabs collective national rights in addition to the existing individual, linguistic, cultural, religious, and ethnic rights. This means recognizing them as Palestinians, granting them autonomy, assigning them resources equally, opening the power structure to them, negotiating with their leaders, and taking further steps to make them feel that Israel is their state and that they are equal citizens within it. This new dispensation would serve not only the Arab minority but also the Jewish majority, Zionism, democracy, and peace.

CHAPTER ELEVEN.

THE PALESTINIAN ECONOMY: DEVELOPMENT AND LIBERATION

Raja Khalidi

Five miserable decades have passed with Palestinians in the West Bank and Gaza Strip under the yoke of Israeli military occupation. The past twenty-five years have witnessed a peace process that has served mainly to restrain Palestinian resistance while entrenching Israeli colonialism. Just as the Palestinian national liberation project has ground to a standstill, if not recorded an historic failure

Raja Khalidi is a development economist trained at the Universities of Oxford and London (SOAS). He was a staff member with the United Nations Conference on Trade and Development (1985–2013), where he served as Coordinator of Assistance to the Palestinian People and Senior Economist in the Division on Globalization and Development Strategies. He is currently Research Coordinator at the Palestine Economic Policy Research Institute–MAS.

to unseat occupation, so have the conditions needed for Palestinian economic development receded from the horizon.[1]

Development under occupation

What role does the Palestinian economy play in Israel's political and military domination of Palestinian territory? There have traditionally been two opposed approaches to this question. The dominant academic and policy preference since before 1948 has been to pursue Palestinian economic development, modernization, and institutional reform irrespective of the prospects for statehood, or, more recently, as a step towards and demonstration of eligibility for statehood. The second approach, long prevalent at the level of public opinion, has seen national independence as a prerequisite for sustainable economic development. Anything else is dismissed as a poor substitute for justice or else a pitiful attempt to buy Palestinian consent to Israeli rule, akin to the "economic peace" advocated by the Israeli government since 2008.[2] The tension between these competing positions has today reached breaking point. The actual and potential trade-offs between political and economic peace are today more stark than ever, and demand a re-appraisal of the Palestinian people's "national" objectives and strategy. This requires sober appreciation of the cost to the national liberation struggle of diversion of popular concern to the mundane problems of having to live, work, procreate, and prosper, notwithstanding the haunting reality of dispossession and the unextinguished desire for all that has been promised yet remains unachieved.

Both approaches have their weaknesses. The problem with the first is that while Palestinians have achieved a measure of dependent and distorted

---

[1] "Development" does not refer to a static concept or absolute level of economic advancement so much as a dynamic, relative *process* that comprises many social, economic, and institutional dimensions, as distinguished from mere economic growth or incremental increases in individual social and human development indicators.

[2] Raja Khalidi and Sahar Taghdisi-Rad, "The Economic Dimensions of Prolonged Occupation: Continuity and Change in Israeli Policy towards the Palestinian Economy," *United Nations Conference on Trade and Development (UNCTAD)* (August 2009).

growth, "development" as a comprehensive and sustained socioeconomic process has proven impossible under military occupation. The economy of the Occupied Palestinian Territory (OPT) has certainly grown over the past fifty years, but it has done so along a volatile and haphazard trajectory, accompanied by de-industrialization, agricultural collapse, and social crises (poverty, youth unemployment, social marginalization). Growth spurts fueled by aid or apparent diplomatic advances have been unfailingly followed by contractions, recessions, and depressions under the shocks of wars, uprisings, and Israeli collective punishments (closures, barriers, the withholding of Palestinian trade tax revenues, sanctions). The ongoing recessionary cycle that began in 2015 is yet another case in point. Whatever the past fifty years have delivered in the way of economic and social outcomes, *development* they have not.

This should not surprise. The State of Israel's effective sovereignty over the whole territory of historic Palestine gives Israel decisive control over the key determinants of Palestinian economic life, including borders, internal movement and access restrictions, tax receipts collected by the Palestinian Authority (PA), and Palestinian natural and mineral resources. Israel is able to exploit Palestinian dependence on its economy to enforce unfair terms of exchange, in what has been termed "incorporation without integration."[3] To coordinate and oversee an effective national development plan requires a level of resource access and investment coordination that is impossible under Israeli control. The efforts of then-Palestinian Prime Minister Salam Fayyad (especially through his 2009–2011 plan, "Ending the Occupation, Building the State") to reform Palestinian institutions in order to demonstrate readiness for statehood were widely lauded by pundits and enthusiastically endorsed by donor countries as well as international organizations like the World Bank and International Monetary Fund. But whatever technical achievements Fayyad's reforms may have recorded, they could not bypass or overcome Israel's political refusal to cede sovereignty over any part

[3] Ahmad H. Sa'di, "Incorporation without Integration: Palestinian Citizens in Israel's Labour Market," *Sociology* 29.3 (1995), pp. 429–51.

of "Eretz Yisrael."* When Fayyad left office in 2013, the occupation was more entrenched than ever. The State of Palestine declared in 2012 has yet to exercise any sovereign functions, while development remains elusive.

The problem with the second approach is that political independence looks unattainable within the foreseeable future. The struggle for Palestinian national self-determination has taken many forms over the decades, from mass uprisings and armed struggle to diplomacy and state-building. These efforts have come to naught. Since 1994, Palestinians in some 40 percent of the West Bank—itself only a fraction of historic Palestine—have been "self-governed" by the "Palestinian Authority." This was established by the Oslo Accords§ as an interim administration to prepare Palestinians for the transition to statehood within five years. More than two decades later, Palestinian statehood remains elusive while the PA owes what "authority" it has primarily to international aid and its usefulness to Israeli security interests as well as to the remaining vestiges of the legitimacy earned by Fatah and the Palestine Liberation Organization when they still led a national liberation struggle.

The PA features the trappings and certain functions of a state, particularly those dealing with internal security, provision of social services, regulation of civil affairs, internal taxation, the public-sector payroll, and other non-sovereign responsibilities—akin to a regional administration in Europe or a state in the US federal system. For many in the business and political establishments, Palestinian control over these affairs is a non-trivial achievement that constitutes a necessary step towards readiness for statehood. Even so, the facts on the ground are sobering: Israeli settlers and settlements are more numerous than ever, Israeli politicians speak ever more openly of annexation, and international and Palestinian pressure to end the occupation has rarely been less effective. Most Palestinians (especially those in the West Bank) are not prepared to put at risk the limited welfare permitted to them by current arrangements for the

---

* *Editor's note:* Hebrew for the "Land of Israel."

§ *Editor's note:* See Glossary.

sake of a struggle for independence for which few believe a feasible strategy or the requisite political unity exists.

In short, a century of confrontation with settler colonialism and fifty years of military occupation have denied the Palestinian people both their national rights and the benefits of development. The latter has proven to be dependent upon the former, while the former looks unachievable. Moreover, since 1967, dependence on Israeli good will has forced Palestinians to choose between the struggle for independence and development on the one hand and ensuring immediate economic welfare on the other. Most Palestinians today opt, however reluctantly, to focus on short-term gains. Whether by design or circumstance, the basic trade-off to which Palestinians inside the OPT have been hostage since Oslo is what some call economic peace, others consider rational quality of life pursuits, and still others dismiss as collaboration. In any case, the prevailing regional reality means that, for the foreseeable future, the Palestinian governing regime is here to stay. Its concrete achievements have been to provide a degree of stability (however frayed at the edges of PA control and even as acts of individual and popular resistance are pursued daily), public sector employment, basic social services, an "enabling environment" for the development of a Palestinian corporate sector, and a liberal civic sense. But it cannot hope to resolve or mitigate the fundamental socioeconomic challenges confronting the Palestinian people.

Palestinian sovereignty is not on the horizon, yet the PA is expected to shoulder "fiscal responsibility." Indeed, as PA budget-balancing is pursued with vigor and pride, the cost of occupation may soon be covered entirely through Palestinian and donor resources, easing the colonist's burden while leaving inadequate resources for Palestinian investment in development.

Some five million Palestinians under occupation, as well as the 1.4 million Palestinians who are citizens of Israel, now confront the question of whether there is an alternative path forward that approaches the Palestinian economy neither as an alternative to, a by-product of, nor a prerequisite for national independence, but rather as a vehicle and tool for liberating the Palestinian people, whether in the context of a separate nation-state, as autonomous regions under

Israeli sovereignty, or as equal citizens of a democratic state alongside Israeli Jews. The effort to develop new thinking must begin with a clear understanding of what is meant by the "Palestinian economy."

The evolution of the "Palestinian economy"

What is called the "Palestinian economy" in actuality comprises five distinct economic regions. Four are located within the territory occupied in 1967:

1. the core West Bank economy and population in Areas A and B under PA jurisdiction;
2. a separated, if not seceded, Gaza Strip;
3. an annexed and increasingly Judaized East Jerusalem;
4. the resources and economy of the 60 percent of the West Bank under direct Israeli military rule (Area C).

The fifth component is the economy of the Palestinian Arabs in Israel, which has survived since 1948 as a distinct sector within the State of Israel and which has been partially re-connected with the rest of Palestine since 1967. While the Arab economy in Israel does not enjoy separate legal or administrative status within the State of Israel, its patterns of consumption, investment, and production, as well as its experience of confrontation with discriminatory Israeli policies, have rendered it objectively closer in content and form to the other Palestinian economies under Israeli rule than to the Israeli national economy of which it is nominally a constituent part.

The Oslo and Paris Accords defined the West Bank and Gaza Strip as a single entity, as they had been treated by Israel since 1967. But today this legal construct is belied by facts on the ground, which point to growing territorial fragmentation and increasing economic disparities between the Palestinian enclaves. Living conditions in the core (Areas A and B) are markedly better than in the peripheries of Gaza, Jerusalem, and Area C, albeit within an ever-expanding and -tightening matrix of Jewish colonization and physical control. Economically, each of these regions is heavily dependent on the dominant Israeli economy and is subject to differential regulations, all of them determined in the last instance by the Israeli sovereign. For example, Palestinians in the OPT all carry PA identity cards, but those in Areas A and B are under PA civil, legal, and security jurisdiction; those in Gaza are governed by a breakaway government with its own agenda; and those in Area C are subject to direct Israeli military rule. Meanwhile, Palestinians in annexed East Jerusalem have Israeli permission to reside in their city but must fulfill the taxation and other legal obligations of Israeli citizens without political representation at any level. PA economic policy and regulatory and social service reach is minimal in Area C, non-existent in Jerusalem, and being rolled back or replaced by the de facto government in Gaza.

The economies of the West Bank and Gaza Strip have diverged radically over the past decade owing to natural resource depletion and man-made disasters such as war and political division. The Strip is enfeebled and impoverished, the flow of goods, utilities, and persons across its borders subject to crippling Israeli restrictions, while the West Bank has scarcely broken loose of the shackles of Israeli fiscal, trade, and financial domination. The West Bank's economic dependence on Israel is reproduced through labor flows to Israel as well as Israeli control of trade routes, fiscal revenue capture, and natural resource exploitation. The economy of Jerusalem is increasingly disconnected from its natural markets in the West Bank, highly dependent on Israeli state-provided welfare and jobs, and gradually losing its claim to centrality in Palestinian life as their future capital.

In short, the notion of a "Palestinian economy" coherent with the proposed borders of a future Palestinian state may well continue to survive for reasons of politics and law. But the realities of the lingering shards of a shattered pre-1948 Arab economy of Palestine tell a different story. The "Palestinian economy" today is neither homogenous nor contiguous and its myriad components are barely inter-connected. It does not constitute a coherent entity, as does the Israeli economy. It is neither post-agrarian nor industrializing; it is not a modern service economy, nor is it an export economy. All the usual processes of economic structural transformation have been suspended in the web of interests generated by the Israeli state-building and colonization project. The prospects of a state-led development process are further undermined by the degrading impact on the PA macroeconomy of a pattern of laissez-faire capital accumulation manifested primarily in commercial and low-productivity service sector growth, intensive residential construction, and conspicuous private consumption. This trend is encouraged by a growing PA penchant for the marketization of public goods, starting with telecoms and utilities and moving increasingly to municipal and, eventually, social services.

The potential for economic development in each of these Palestinian economic regions has been thwarted by both the shocks in the peripheries from the colonial confrontation (Gaza, Jerusalem, and Area C are theaters of regular clashes and struggles over resources) and by unequal exposure to globalization (with Palestinians in Jerusalem and the West Bank enjoying notably better access and exposure to the rest of the world than those in Gaza). This has entrenched dependency on Israel at various levels and hindered efforts at intra-Palestinian economic integration.

These remnants of the indigenous Arab economy of Palestine represent the forgotten half of the solution for Palestine proposed by the United Nations in 1947. In Resolution 181 (II), the General Assembly endorsed the partition of Palestine into one Arab and one Jewish state, joined at the hip in "full economic union." In practice, Palestinians today live under economic union without political or physical partition. The Palestinian economies are completely enveloped by and dependent on their links with the Jewish economy of the State of Israel; all are subject to its fiscal, trade, monetary, and financial regime. But in the absence of partition, and with Palestinian political sovereignty unrealized, the effective terms of that economic union are unequal and preclude Palestinian development.

Recognizing this reality points the way to an alternative path forward for Palestinians living under one or another form of Israeli rule. Since 1967 (and before 1948), the Gaza and West Bank economies traded, invested, and worked together, though these links have been weakened if not severed over time. These adverse trends are not necessarily irreversible, however, as the experience of Palestinians in Israel shows. While they continue to be incorporated into Israeli labor, services, and goods markets, in recent years unrecorded commercial and service purchases in the West Bank by Palestinians from Israel are estimated by the PA to have reached at least $600 million in 2016 (equivalent to around one-half of total registered West Bank exports).[4] The northern West Bank, West Bank urban centers, and Jerusalem are increasingly favored sites for local tourism by their compatriots with greater spending power visiting from the Galilee, Triangle, and Naqab Arab majority regions of Israel.

The differential levels and forms of subservience to Israeli interests which characterize the various components of the "Palestinian economy" render the prospect of collective or individual separation from the Israeli metropole daunting. In the absence of a Palestinian readiness and a common, coordinated agenda to break free of Israeli economic domination, reintegrating these regional economies along one "national" development trajectory will be impossible. Rather than repeat failed approaches, Palestinians should seek to build on the de facto economic union and growing potential for intra-Arab economic exchange across historic Palestine to prevent further socioeconomic attrition and to recalibrate the potential Arab weight in the overall balance of economic power and relations within the union. This will require a broader range of strategies than has hitherto been pursued.

An equal economic union

Younger Palestinian scholars are exploring the idea of a "resistance economy" that empowers the Palestinian people to challenge Israeli domination. Other forms of nonviolent Palestinian mobilization advocated include "smart" popular resistance to colonization and military repression,[5] international "lawfare" to impose boycotts and sanctions upon Israel, and, most recently, a revived

---

[4] Palestinian Monetary Authority, *Developments and Transformations in the Amount of Cash for Purchases and Services by Palestinians of the Territory of 1948* (Ramallah: Palestinian Monetary Authority, 2017).

[5] See Palestine Strategy Group, *Regaining the Initiative: Palestinian Strategic Options to End Israeli Occupation* (August 2008); Sufian Abu Zaida et al., "Peaceful Popular Resistance: Is It An Option?" *Palestinian Center for Policy and Survey Research* (May 2016).

version of the concept of "resilience" (*sumud*) to enable communities to cope with prolonged occupation. However, these are defensive postures that seek at most to keep people on the land or chalk up moral victories in the court of international public opinion. They do not amount to a strategy for liberation. What, then, is to be done? The search for strategic alternatives could do worse than begin with the raw facts of Palestinian demographics, considered by some Israeli strategists to be a critical threat to the State of Israel.

The emerging demographic parity between Palestinian Arabs and Israeli Jews within the area of Palestine/Israel (with an expected Arab majority by 2020) will not necessarily translate into one person, one vote, as perhaps it should. Apartheid South Africa sustained white minority rule for decades. Israel will seek to maintain its matrix of control over Palestinians within Israel and the OPT, and any explicit Palestinian abandonment of the two-state paradigm will be met by stiff Israeli resistance and new legal and other mechanisms to thwart Palestinian irredentism. Even so, the demographic trajectories do point a way forward for a renewed Palestinian strategy of liberation and development that pursues Arab economic integration and structural transformation as a lever to augment Palestinians' political weight in the struggle with Israel.

This alternative would have to be grounded in the assets of Palestinian demographic dispersion throughout the country and population concentrations in the West Bank, Gaza, Jerusalem, and the Southern and Northern Districts of Israel; capital accumulation in the core Arab regions; and the emerging network of capital, trade, and social interaction between them. This could be pursued in such a way that these regions might together reduce the economic asymmetry of their relationships with Israel. A practical and pragmatic concept of what constitutes economic resistance is needed, encompassing civil society, private, and public actors.

If integration with the Israeli economy is the only choice that Palestinians have, and if it is ever to deliver "development" to Palestinians, it will require that the full weight of Palestinian economic potential is brought into play, so that a full and equal economic union might be forged—even if this entails another generation of struggle. Developing a minimum of Palestinian political unity and institutional coherence is no less important, even as different jurisdictions under Israeli rule may continue to exist.

In addition to tools such as popular resistance, "lawfare" to challenge the legitimacy of occupation and hold Israel accountable for violations of international humanitarian law, and resilience, a multi-level and pro-active strategy for Palestinian economic reformation throughout the territory of Palestine/Israel might involve:

- boycott measures that target settlement industries and agriculture, Israeli commercial monopolies active in Palestinian markets, and violations of Palestinian labor rights;
- import substitution and diversion from Israel as well as market diversification, flexing autonomous economic and trade policy-making functions and institutions (even without needing to renounce existing accords with Israel);
- vigorous and systematic productive sector investment programs in energy, industry, agriculture, trade, transport, and tourism;
- an active role for PA investment in leading and "crowding in" private investment in high-risk environments (Gaza, Area C, Jerusalem) that would encourage more productive forms of capital accumulation;
- promotion of Palestinian cross-border partnerships and increased trade, services, and tourism exchanges between Palestinians in Israel and in both Jerusalem and the West Bank;
- contesting the legitimacy of Israeli colonial economic measures in global trade and human rights forums and on the ground.

De-colonization of Palestine must start with empowering those most disadvantaged in the peripheries of Area C, the ghettos of Jerusalem, and the urban slums of Gaza, and should not stop at Green Lines, Barriers or provisional or recognized borders. To the extent that state-building and PA economic policy-making lose sight of the original PLO goals of "liberating the land and the people," this will serve only to validate the claims of those who have asserted since Oslo that its terms—and the "national authority" it created—were designed to subvert and destroy the Palestinian national movement.

The alternative to such a bleak outcome of the past century of Palestinian nationalism will most likely call for yet more blood, sweat, and tears. But voluntary or imposed sacrifice is already a feature of daily life in Palestine in all areas and for all classes. Harnessing this spirit to an effective strategy requires a smart and dedicated leadership armed with a renewed commitment to liberating Palestinians from the confines set by a settler colonial regime, a better appreciation of the utility in the Palestinian context of heterodox economic doctrine, and less blind dedication to the obsolete nineteenth century ideology of nationalism. Palestinian strategies must engage the entirety of Israel/Palestine, not just the PA archipelago in the West Bank. Without resort to violent force, and without the independent nation-state as the only end-game in view, such a vision could yet inspire efforts to tilt the balance of forces in a way that better reflects demographic parities and equally assertive, if conflicting, claims to land, resources, and freedoms. In its absence, neither a virtual state that nurtures a false sense of "citizenship" and pursues "development" under colonialism nor an open-ended, steeply-costed, and failing national liberation struggle for a partition whose time may have passed can reasonably be expected to secure any Palestinian rights.

RESPONSE:

THE PALESTINIAN STRUGGLE NEEDS (AND HAS) AN END-GAME

Sam Bahour

Raja Khalidi does an excellent job expressing the deep, collective frustration that has infected the entirety of the Palestinian people—from those living under Israeli military occupation for five decades to those in Israel, as well as the majority of our people living abroad as refugees or in the diaspora. However, I walked away from the analysis contemplating exactly who his case was being made to.

Khalidi makes two key arguments: that Palestinian economic development is not achievable by current strategies, and that a two-state solution is now impossible. I will address these in turn below. Given these two premises, Khalidi offers "Arab economic integration and structural transformation as a

---

Sam Bahour is a Palestinian-American business development consultant living in Ramallah. He is a Policy Advisor for Al-Shabaka, the Palestinian Policy Network, and Chairman of Americans for a Vibrant Palestinian Economy.

lever to augment Palestinians' political weight in the struggle with Israel" as a way forward, but fails to place this strategy in the context of a desired political end-game. Without a clear political trajectory, one is left wondering whether the goal is to turn back the clock to "the indigenous Arab economy of [pre-1948] Palestine" or to tactically engage across the Green Line to realize the (new) State of Palestine on the ground.

Economic development. I agree with Khalidi that genuine economic development is impossible under occupation. Actually, I've not heard any stakeholder make a case otherwise. And I agree that, nevertheless, and even under occupation, Palestinians must find a way to live. Khalidi urges "sober appreciation of the cost to the national liberation struggle of diversion of popular concern to the mundane problems of having to live, work, procreate, and prosper." But efforts to address these "mundane problems," rather than distracting from the national struggle, are a prerequisite for it; economic development should be viewed not in the context of sustainable growth or even necessarily "state-building," but as part and parcel of the struggle for national liberation.

The description of Israel's economic strategy as "incorporation without integration" is spot on. That noted, the Palestinian private sector, and to the extent possible the Palestinian government, is pushing back against Israeli efforts to hollow out Palestinian economic life. For example, the government's Palestine Investment Fund (PIF), of whose General Assembly I am a member, is introducing competition in the telecommunications sector, developing new residential zones like Al-Reehan Neighborhood, and seeking to make strategic interventions in the energy (natural gas, electricity, petroleum) sector. In the private sector, the new city of Rawabi introduced a state-building scale project that forced an increase in market capacities, while countless small and medium enterprises churn away, day in and day out, giving Palestinians livelihood and hope for a better future. The point here is that we must stop jumping between two extremes—from delusional pursuit of genuine economic development to resigned acquiescence in no economic development under military occupation. Reality and necessity sit somewhere in between.

Israel does everything in its power to suffocate our economy and induce us to voluntarily leave or lose hope and turn to violence—the only game Israel knows how to win. Every job we can create while under Israeli military occupation keeps a Palestinian in Palestine and provides a livelihood, which in turn significantly increases the chance that this Palestinian will have the means and mindset to resist the occupation and to do so nonviolently (i.e., effectively). This is the purpose of economic activity under occupation.

Political solution. The Palestinian national liberation movement was launched not to end the military occupation of the West Bank and Gaza Strip, which did not yet exist, but to safeguard the national identity of a dispossessed and displaced people. After seventy years of dispossession and fifty years of occupation, it is a miracle that Palestinians are still in Palestine, working, farming, studying, loving, marrying, and most importantly, still engaged in a national struggle for statehood and refugee return. No dotted line has been signed to close this struggle; Khalidi's claim that this movement has "ground to a standstill" and may have "recorded an historic failure to unseat occupation" is fortunately premature.

Khalidi's suggestion that "another generation of struggle" may be needed to reach a "full and equal economic union" with Israel is misguided in several respects. First, it ignores the real structural damage being done to Palestinian people and land and assumes this damage will not have lasting effect on our capacity to struggle. Second, it assumes that an "economic union" with Israel is possible without the other side, Israel, desiring true integration. Third, it assumes that the Palestinian struggle exists in a bubble, abstracted from the broader contexts of an Arab world in turmoil and a leaderless international community failing to uphold its own commitments (not least the Charter of the United Nations). Imaginative leaps forward may offer escape from painful realities. But calling for models of coexistence that have long been dismissed as infeasible by all relevant stakeholders does not provide the necessary impetus for a new generation of Palestinians to engage in a struggle for freedom and independence in ways that might achieve tangible results in their lifetimes.

Khalidi is absolutely correct to focus on Palestinian rights, but without a defined political end-game we become merely an entity trying to hold Israel accountable where the international community has consistently failed.

In my view, a *rights-based approach*, as championed by the Boycott, Divestment, and Sanctions (BDS) Movement,* is the most conducive to the current Palestinian national agenda.[1] Today, this approach focuses its demands on respect for individual human, civil, and political rights, without specifying a desired political framework. A rights-based approach should be viewed as complementary to rather than a substitute for a political solution; the *political end-game cannot be open-ended*. The struggle for national self-determination cannot be waged at the expense of the struggle for rights; nor, however, should the national cause be subordinated to campaigns for the rights of individuals.

For better or worse, Palestinian national rights have been defined in the international arena and accepted by the Palestinian leadership. The two-state solution was collectively adopted by the Palestinian leadership in 1988 at the sixteenth session of the Palestinian National Congress in Algiers and codified in the Palestinian Declaration of Independence issued that same year. The authority of this solution was further underlined when the PLO accepted UN Security Council Resolutions 242 and 338 as the basis for negotiations, thereby implicitly recognizing Israel. The Oslo peace process was launched with the PLO's explicit and written recognition of Israel, which was reaffirmed in 2002 when the PLO accepted the Arab Peace Initiative. Furthermore, UN Security Council Resolution 1397 (12 March 2002), which demanded an end to the violence that had taken place between Israelis and Palestinians since September 2000 (the second intifada), was the first Security Council resolution to call for a two-state solution to the conflict. Ten years later, the UN General Assembly passed Resolution 67/19 (29 November 2012), which acknowledged

---

* *Editor's note:* See Glossary.

[1] See Sam Bahour, "Changing the Status Quo: What Directions for Palestinians?—Asynchronous and Inseparable Struggles for Rights and a Political End-Game," *Palestinian Center for Policy and Survey Research* (May 2016).

Palestinian statehood within the framework of two-states. The choice of two-states cannot now be reversed without an international political fallout for which Palestinians are neither politically nor practically prepared.

The renowned Palestinian historian Walid Khalidi, in a 1978 essay entitled "Thinking the Unthinkable: A Sovereign Palestinian State," wrote: "the juridical status of . . . Palestine . . . [is] the concept of Palestinian sovereignty. Not half-sovereignty, or quasi-sovereignty or ersatz sovereignty. But a sovereign, independent Palestinian state." He continued:

> Only such a state would win the endorsement of the PLO. Only such a state is likely to effect a psychological breakthrough with the Palestinians under occupation and in the Diaspora. It would lead them out of the political limbo in which they have lingered since 1948. It would end their anonymous ghost-like existence as a non-people. It would terminate their dependence on the mercy, charity or tolerance of other parties, whether Arab, Israeli, or international. It would be a point of reference, a national anchorage, a center of hope and achievement.[2]

"Terminat[ing] our dependence" entails, in the first order, doing everything we can to break the chains of dependence Israel constructed to yoke the Palestinian economy to theirs since the occupation began. In reality, this is exactly what all Palestinian economic stakeholders claim to be doing. So, again, I am left unsure who Khalidi is arguing against. That noted, we must all do better to hold Palestinian economic stakeholders accountable to ensure that declarations in favor of economic independence are reflected in economic practice.

The wake-up call has arrived. State or no state, this Israeli military occupation is illegal and must end now. Our economic resources are being extorted and exploited even as donor-funded cappuccinos keep the doors of our cafés open. For real change to happen, a price must be levied on the occupier; the form that price takes is a question that must be answered by each responsible stakeholder. Palestinians have delivered their answer by aligning with

[2] Walid Khalidi, "Thinking the Unthinkable: A Sovereign Palestinian State," *Foreign Affairs* 56.4 (July 1978), p. 701.

international law and utilizing all international venues—economic ones at the forefront—to hold Israel accountable. Thus, when Israel occupies our electromagnetic spectrum, seriously disrupting the ability of our telecommunication sector to develop, we take the issue to the International Telecommunication Union to claim our rights. But international appeals cannot be effective in a vacuum. In parallel, we must be ready to deploy the fruits of our struggle. Palestinian capital must be mobilized, Palestinian know-how trained and ready, and Palestinian customers employed to ensure the wheels of the economy keep spinning.

The struggle for freedom and national liberation is by no means a linear process, but it surely requires a clear end-goal in sight. Ours is a free State of Palestine.

RESPONSE:

NO SUBSTITUTE FOR POLITICS

Arie Arnon

Since 1967, the dominant preference in Israeli policy circles regarding the OPT has been the status quo—i.e., Israeli control over its new external borders, ultimate Israeli authority over security and civil affairs within the OPT, and the exclusion of the Palestinian population of the OPT from the Israeli polity (through denial of voting rights). This approach was challenged by two alternative strategies. The doves called for partition in the context of a land-for-peace agreement (i.e., the two-state solution). "Greater Israel" hawks, meanwhile, urged formal annexation of the OPT. Israeli policy, implemented by the status quo advocates, did not annex the OPT but instead created "facts on the ground" in the form of the settlements.

Arie Arnon is Professor Emeritus of Economics at Ben Gurion University of the Negev and Israeli coordinator of the Aix Group, a joint Israeli-Palestinian think-tank. The views in this commentary do not necessarily represent those of the Aix Group.

These three perspectives—the status quo position, and its dovish and hawkish challengers—continue to vie for influence in Israeli politics. When the right-wing Menachem Begin came to power in 1977, he did not change the basic structures of the status quo, though his government intensified colonization in the OPT. In 1992, Yitzhak Rabin's Labor Party came to power, and to the surprise of many threatened the status quo with a dovish challenge. Most observers now admit, however, that this challenge was frail and short-lived.

The debate between the three Israeli political approaches also had an economic dimension. Proponents of the status quo and Greater Israel advocated an "integrated economy" across the whole of historic Palestine, in the form of a Customs Union with no labor borders between the Jordan River and the Mediterranean Sea. Dovish advocates of the two-state solution tended to defend soft borders between the two economies.[1]

In his essay, Raja Khalidi discusses the complicated links between development and sovereignty and revisits a question that once bothered many observers: Is political sovereignty a precondition for economic development, or can economic development pave the way for political sovereignty?[2] Khalidi concludes that the failure to achieve development in the OPT is the result of Israel's refusal "to cede sovereignty over any part of 'Eretz Yisrael'," but he finds that the other path is not working either:

> In short, a century of confrontation with settler colonialism and fifty years of military occupation have denied the Palestinian people both their

---

[1] For a full discussion on integration and borders between the economies from the 1960s to the 1990s, see Arie Arnon et al., *The Palestinian Economy: Between Imposed Integration and Voluntary Separation* (Leiden: E.J. Brill, 1997).

[2] See Arie Arnon and Jimmy Weinblatt, "Sovereignty and Economic Development: The Case of Israel and Palestine," *The Economic Journal* 111.472 (2001), pp. 291–308; and Arie Arnon, Yitzhak Gal, Saad Khatib, and Saeb Bamya, "Twenty Years after Oslo and The Paris Protocol—The Protocol on Economic Relations between Israel and the PLO: Analysis of its Weakness and Proposed Modifications," in Arie Arnon and Saeb Bamya eds., *Economics and Politics in the Israeli Palestinian Conflict* (Aix Group, February 2015).

> national rights and the benefits of development. The latter has proven to be dependent upon the former, while the former looks unachievable.

Khalidi thus criticizes the strategy of the PLO as an economic and political failure. He endeavors to contribute to a new discussion about alternative strategies that might prove more successful.

Khalidi conducts this discussion in economic terms, paying almost no attention to the political debates concerning "one state" or "two-states" for Palestinians and Israelis, as if these were redundant issues. He briefly mentions the alternative political options for Palestinians—"a separate nation-state," "autonomous regions under Israeli sovereignty," "equal citizens of a democratic state alongside Israeli Jews"—but then moves on, as if deciding between them were unnecessary. I find this the weakest part in his discussion. Politics, certainly in the Israeli-Palestinian conflict, but also more generally, is not secondary, and should not be treated as such.

Khalidi outlines the dismal state of the Palestinian economy in all its regions, including those within Israel's pre-1967 borders, noticing their varying levels of decline and decay. After sharply disputing the relevance of traditional ideas concerning economic development as well as efforts to advance through continued war for national liberation—both of which he thinks are doomed to fail—Khalidi asks, what is to be done? He suggests a strategy which he terms a "resistance economy": a network based on the premise that all the Arab population centers could amplify their economic and social ties, augmenting their combined economic strength through integration so as to "reduce the economic asymmetry of their relationships with Israel." Thus, Khalidi accepts the de facto economic union and seeks within it measures that could transform the balance of economic power to make Palestinian and Israeli-Jewish economic strength more equal.

The idea is intriguing, though it raises many questions. Perhaps an Israeli—even one who thinks of himself as a sympathizer with the Palestinian cause, and who has sought for many years to promote a historic compromise that would bring self-determination and prosperity to both peoples living in Palestine-Eretz Yisrael—should remain silent. Though, in my defense, I was invited to comment, and more importantly, I still believe that the deep pessimism surrounding us fifty years after 1967 does not change the reality that Jews and Arabs, Palestinians and Israelis, live, and will continue to live, side by side. Sooner or later, each national community will have to accept the reality that there are two peoples living between the river and the sea, and will have to find a political arrangement that will satisfy their legitimate needs and desires. Changing the balance of power, including the balance of economic power, is important, but failing to outline a political framework is, in my view, a non-starter.

Khalidi, declining to specify the shape of a future historic compromise, focuses exclusively on changing the balance of economic power within the de facto economic union, which these days is controlled by the Greater Israel wing of Israeli politics. This faction has agitated for fifty years against the status quo, calling openly for an economic union under full Jewish-Israeli sovereignty. As a result, the proactive Palestinian strategy proposed by Khalidi—including boycotts of settlement industries and Israeli monopolies active in Palestinian markets, encouraging import substitution and trade diversification, and promoting private and public investment programs—will be sure to provoke reactive counter-measures, especially if it proves effective.

One should not forget an important economic fact characterizing the last fifty years: throughout this period, the Palestinian economy in the OPT constituted around 5 percent of the Israeli economy, as measured by GNP. Will those who control the economic union passively acquiesce in a radical shift in this balance of economic power? Given the likelihood of Israeli resistance, implementing the "resistance economy" Khalidi has in mind will require a *political* change: the Palestinians will need more sovereignty. As the Aix Group concluded in 2015, "Economics and politics are interwoven and future arrangements . . . [will] have to relate to both."[3] In the context of today's despair, Khalidi's desire to ignore or bypass politics is understandable—but the politics is decisive.

---

[3] Arnon and Bamya eds., *Economics and Politics in the Israeli Palestinian Conflict*, p. iii.

RESPONSE:

TOWARDS A STRATEGY OF ECONOMIC RESISTANCE

Nur Arafeh

Raja Khalidi offers an excellent overview and cogent critique of the traditional approaches to the relationship between political liberation and economic development in Palestine. His conceptualization of the "Palestinian economy" as five Arab economic fragments or "economic regions" that each and collectively occupy subordinate positions in a "de facto" unequal economic union is also compelling.

Nur Arafeh is a Rhodes Scholar doing her PhD at the University of Oxford. She previously worked as the Policy Fellow of Al-Shabaka, the Palestinian Policy Network, and was an Associate Researcher at the Palestine Economic Policy Research Institute–MAS, a Visiting Lecturer of Economics at Al-Quds Bard College, and a Teaching Assistant at Columbia University. She has a dual BA degree in Political Science and Economics from the Paris Institute of Political Studies-Sciences Po and Columbia University and holds an MPhil in Development Studies from the University of Cambridge.

Despairing of prospects for statehood, Khalidi proposes instead a struggle to alter the terms of this de facto union by leveraging the developing demographic parity between Arab Palestinians and Israeli Jews and by enhancing economic integration between the Arab regions. The goal, according to Khalidi, would be to "recalibrate the potential Arab weight in the overall balance of economic power and relations within the union" so that "a full and equal economic union might be forged."

Khalidi's proposal leaves the reader with many questions. To begin with, what does it mean to have a "full" and "equal" economic union? How will trade, fiscal, monetary, and labor relations between Palestinians and Israelis be governed? Within which economic framework would "a more equal" union be forged?

Since 1994, economic relations between Israelis and Palestinians have been governed by the Paris Economic Protocol. While it was supposed to apply for an interim period of five years as the Palestinian Authority transitioned to statehood, the Paris Protocol still constitutes the basis of economic relations between the PA and Israel and the principal framework for the PA's economic, monetary, and fiscal policies, despite the expiration of the interim period more than seventeen years ago.

Khalidi suggests that Palestinians pursue import substitution and market diversification "even without needing to renounce the existing accords with Israel." However, it will be very difficult, if not impossible, to reduce the vast asymmetry between the Palestinian economies and the Israeli Jewish economy if the Paris Protocol were to remain the governing framework of economic relations inside the de facto union. In fact, the Paris Protocol has severely entrenched the dependency of Palestinians on the Israeli economy and has restricted the policy space available to Palestinians.

For example, in the area of trade, the Paris Protocol formalized a one-sided customs union in which the trade policy (customs rates and other regulations) of Israel was imposed upon the West Bank and the Gaza Strip (Article III.5),[1]

---

[1] With the exception of specific goods itemized in the so-called lists A1, A2, and B.

whose per capita Gross National Income (GNI) was a mere 9 percent of Israel's in 2015.[2] Such disregard of the gap between the two economies is very problematic, since the tariff structure that suits a strong and industrialized economy like Israel is very different from the sort of tariff structure required to rebuild an atrophied "Palestinian economy."

Furthermore, in violation of the Protocol, which stipulated free access and movement of agricultural and industrial products between the two sides (Articles VIII and IX), Israel has only allowed for the free flow of goods from Israel to the Palestinian market. Meanwhile, Israel has imposed severe restrictions on the movement of goods from the OPT to Israel as well as within the OPT. Such constraints have led to a rise in the transportation costs and in the final price of Palestinian goods, thus eroding the competitiveness of Palestinian products.[3] As a result, Palestinians have become deeply dependent on the Israeli market and developed a trade deficit that has increased their reliance on foreign aid.[4] The UN Conference on Trade and Development (UNCTAD) reported in 2016:

> The one-sided customs union, enshrined in the Paris Protocol, and obstacles to trade and productive activities effectively render the Occupied Palestinian Territory a captive market for exports from Israel. In recent years, Israel accounted for more than 70 per cent of Palestinian imports and absorbed about 85 per cent of Palestinian exports.[5]

---

[2] World Bank database.

[3] Palestinian Shippers Council, *Capacity Development for Facilitating Palestinian Trade: A Study on the Proposed Gantry Scanner at King Hussein Bridge* (July 2012).

[4] According to the UN Conference on Trade and Development, the Palestinian trade deficit represented 41 percent of GDP (Gross Domestic Product) in 2015, or $5.2 billion, reflecting a very weak Palestinian trade sector. See UNCTAD, *Report on UNCTAD Assistance to the Palestinian People: Developments in the Economy of the Occupied Palestinian Territory*, UNCTAD/APP/2016/1* (1 September 2016), p. 6.

[5] UNCTAD, *Report on UNCTAD Assistance.*

Similarly, with respect to fiscal arrangements, the Paris Protocol provides that Israel collect on behalf of the PA import taxes on goods destined for the Palestinian market from abroad, indirect taxes (Value Added Taxes and others) on Israeli products sold to the Palestinian market, and income taxes and social transfers from Palestinians employed in Israel or in the Israeli settlements. Israel is obliged to transfer these revenues—known as clearance revenues—to the PA on a monthly basis, subject to a 3 percent administration fee.[6]

These clearance revenues, collected by Israel, represented almost 75 percent of the PA's total net revenues in 2015.[7] In other words, the Paris Protocol stripped the PA of sovereignty over a large proportion of its fiscal revenues while granting Israel enormous control over tax collection and hence the PA's survival. Israel has not hesitated to exploit this leverage, repeatedly withholding Palestinian tax revenues as a punitive measure or to exert political pressure.[8]

For these reasons, among others, increasing the Arab weight in the economic union seems an unlikely prospect if the Palestinians do not break free of the Paris Protocol and Israel's stranglehold on the PA's trade, monetary, financial, and fiscal policies. It is imperative that we do not regard the rules governing economic relations between Palestinians and Israelis as fixed. It is possible and absolutely necessary to rewrite them.

It is also important to acknowledge that the prevailing economic arrangements reflect Israel's strategic political interests. Israel opted for a customs union with the OPT because this allowed Israel to defer the question of borders: a customs union requires neither the delineation of internal borders—and thus

---

[6] "Supplement to the Protocol on Economic Relations," Article 4.

[7] PA Ministry of Finance; in International Monetary Fund, *West Bank and Gaza: Report to the Ad Hoc Liaison Committee* (26 August 2016), p. 22, Table 2.

[8] It did so in 2006, November 2011, December 2012–January 2013, and December 2014–April 2015.

the establishment of a sovereign Palestinian economic and political entity—nor the total elimination of borders and complete integration. The customs union arrangement therefore aligns perfectly with Israel's "no-state solution" strategy.[9] As long as Israel wants to maintain the status quo and contain the OPT, it would be difficult to think of alternative economic arrangements that would not meet with Israeli resistance that would in turn require a political struggle to overcome.

The unaddressed issues with Khalidi's proposal notwithstanding, he is correct that our understanding of the role of economic development under occupation requires a rethink. Economic development must be understood within the framework that the Palestinian struggle is directed first and foremost against a Zionist settler colonial project. It is also a struggle for rights—freedom, justice, dignity, and equality—rather than a struggle to build a state.

Therefore, a strategy of resistance to Israel's settler colonial project and its power structures should be conceptualized and implemented in the short-run. A short-term strategy should also defy the PA's neoliberal development model and its limited focus on the archipelago of the West Bank. Khalidi makes a very important point when he emphasizes that, "Palestinian strategies must engage the entirety of Israel/Palestine, not just the PA archipelago in the West Bank."

The following suggestions build on Khalidi's proposal for a future economic strategy of resistance. They can be pursued immediately, even prior to a change in the political balance of power.

1. *Building the productive capacity of the Palestinian economies* to ensure Palestinian self-sufficiency and *strengthening Arab economic integration* so as to reduce dependency on the Israeli economy and international aid. There is an urgent need to develop a national political and economic

---

[9] Amal Ahmad, "The Customs Union & Israel's No-State Solution," *Al-Shabaka* (26 November 2014).

vision that would guide a national strategy of resistance along with local strategies that take into account the specificities of each economic region.

Further research needs to be conducted to explore *how* the agricultural and industrial sectors can be promoted, as part of the struggle against Israeli land expropriation and to build a productive economy and reduce dependency on Israel.

2. *Boycotting Israeli goods* so far as is possible, to increase the cost of the occupation while protecting Palestinian products in order to increase their competitiveness. Boycotting must therefore go hand in hand with encouraging local production and ensuring the high quality of local products. Specific committees could be established to develop boycott legislation and perform periodic evaluations and refinement of boycott strategy.
3. Internationally, more *pressure should be exerted on Israel to end the siege of Gaza*. More generally, the *international community should be reminded of its legal obligations and its responsibility to match rhetoric with action* in holding Israel accountable for rights violations. For example, European Union (EU) guidelines on the labeling of settlement products, which have yet to be enforced by member states, should be extended to an enforcement of a complete ban on all direct and indirect economic, financial, business, and investment activities with the Israeli settlements, which are illegal under international law. The EU should also consider a ban on all Israeli goods, since Israel bears primary responsibility for the occupation and the illegal settlement enterprise. These measures by the EU would address the root cause of the occupation (the Israeli government) rather than merely its symptom (the settlements).

   The EU could also establish better trading relations with the Palestinians. The EU is Israel's largest trading partner,[10] with trade totaling around 30 billion euros (US$32 billion) in 2014, representing

[10] European Commission.

some 33 percent of total Israeli exports of goods and services that year.[11] Meanwhile, the EU's trade with the OPT was just 195 million euros (US$207 million) in the same period. The EU should also halt financial relations with Israeli banks, which are heavily involved in financing the occupation and in the construction of illegal Israeli settlements.[12]

[11] Based on data from the Israeli Ministry of Economy and Industry.

[12] Who Profits, *Financing Land Grab: The Direct Involvement of Israeli Banks in the Israeli Settlement Enterprise* (February 2017).

CHAPTER TWELVE.

ARE HUMAN RIGHTS AN EFFECTIVE WEAPON IN THE STRUGGLE FOR JUSTICE IN PALESTINE?

Jessica Montell

Over the past three decades, the human rights community in Israel-Palestine has grown enormously. There are now dozens of organizations, Israeli and Palestinian, addressing a wide range of human rights issues through various strategies. These organizations are extremely professional and have accumulated a wealth of knowledge and expertise. Their work has led to policy changes that have concretely benefited hundreds of thousands of people, from stopping punitive home demolitions and rerouting the Separation Barrier to ending

Jessica Montell is Executive Director of Save Israel, Stop the Occupation. She was Executive Director (2001–2014) of B'Tselem, The Israeli Information Center for Human Rights in the Occupied Territories.

systematic torture and preventing mass displacements and deportations.[1] Yet notwithstanding these achievements—and as human rights workers are the first to acknowledge—the occupation has only grown more entrenched over this same period.

Why is this surprising? Is ending the occupation the job of human rights organizations? What tools do they have to promote the political and diplomatic developments required to end Israel's military rule over the Palestinian territories?

Human rights organizations are rooted in the discourse of international law—specifically, human rights law and international humanitarian law. This is the source of their authority, the language they must speak, and the only yardstick by which they can measure whether to support or oppose a policy or practice. International law is also the source of the human rights community's distinctive tools and levers of influence: ensuring that states uphold their legal obligations in the form of treaties and customary law that concern human rights. This is not to say that human rights are apolitical. But there is a distinction between groups that are committed to the clearly defined and circumscribed remit of human rights and groups that consider a broader range of interests and agendas in order to formulate their positions and build their strategies.

There is no doubt that ending the occupation is necessary from a human rights perspective. Human rights violations are inherent to the prolonged occupation. Yet the way to end the occupation is through a diplomatic agreement that specifies a political framework for future relations between Israel and the Palestinians and the modalities by which it is to be implemented. These necessarily transcend the scope and mandate of human rights organizations. Moreover, in negotiating a diplomatic agreement, Israeli and Palestinian leaderships will have to weigh many different factors, including but not limited to their respective human rights obligations.

---

[1] Jessica Montell, "Learning From What Works: Strategic Analysis of the Achievements of the Israel-Palestine Human Rights Community," *Human Rights Quarterly* 38.4 (November 2016), pp. 928–68.

Tensions will almost inevitably arise between diplomatic imperatives, geared toward the give-and-take necessary to bridge disagreements, and the human rights mandate, which insists that no compromise is possible on rights. In practice, a primary interface between the diplomatic process and human rights organizations has been the latter's role as naysayer, rejecting specific policies and proposals that violate human rights. The Israel Security Agency (ISA) argued that torture of opponents of the Oslo process* was necessary to thwart the bloody attacks intended to derail it. Israeli peace activists invoked a similar argument when they said B'Tselem should not criticize human rights abuses by the fledgling Palestinian security forces, themselves a product of Oslo. Of course, human rights organizations remained firm in their view that torture is never justified.

Human rights organizations have also spoken out against specific components of diplomatic negotiations. Organizations criticized many aspects of the Oslo Accords, such as the perpetuation of the settlements and the discriminatory allocation of water between Israelis and Palestinians. Amnesty International issued a position paper in 2001 calling for respect for the rights of Palestinian refugees and their descendants to return,[2] a position that could clash with political attempts to reach a compromise that would not include the return of millions of refugees and their descendants to Israel. Perhaps the most far-reaching position regarding the very basis for diplomatic negotiations was taken in 2011 by the Palestinian organization Al-Haq, which argued that "land swaps"§ which enable Israel to retain parts of the West Bank in the context of a diplomatic agreement constitute a violation of the law of occupation.[3] Regardless of the validity of any specific argument, a human rights critique of the diplomatic process is valuable and ideally serves to ensure a more just and viable diplomatic outcome. However,

---

* *Editor's note:* See Glossary

§ *Editor's note:* See Glossary.

[2] Amnesty International, "The Right to Return: The Case of the Palestinians," MDE 15/013/2001 (29 March 2001).

[3] Al-Haq, *Exploring the Illegality of "Land Swap" Agreements under Occupation* (2011).

this still leaves open the question of whether the human rights community can play a pro-active role in ending the occupation.

The most effective tools to end the occupation are not those of human rights organizations, but rather of political organizing. The first step for a political movement is to define its goal: are we advocating a two-state solution* or some other outcome? On this question, human rights organizations are agnostic: human rights could be respected under different political frameworks, and so human rights groups do not take a position. Promoting a diplomatic agreement also requires constituency-building, and here too human rights organizations are at a loss. Human rights groups can speak powerfully about the illegality and immorality of Israeli practices vis-á-vis the Palestinians. But in order to, for example, build an Israeli constituency to end the occupation, advocates must also engage with Israeli security concerns, address the social and economic implications of our control over the territories, and tap into the fears of parents sending their teenage boys (and now girls) into combat and to police a civilian population. We need to highlight how Israel's democratic institutions have been eroded as a result of legal gymnastics wrought by occupation, and to analyze the specter of Israel's growing diplomatic isolation. Human rights organizations do not speak these languages.

Could they learn them? Shouldn't human rights organizations broaden their remit to address these issues and engage in these forms of discourse, if doing so would advance the cause of human rights?

However tempting, such a course of action would likely prove damaging both to human rights and to political organizing. The moral authority of human rights organizations—and thus their political usefulness—derives from their confinement to the stipulations and idiom of law rather than politics. To blur that distinction would in the long-run be self-defeating. This does not mean that human rights organizations should restrict themselves to litigation and legal reporting. Many tools are valid to advance respect for human rights. But the only criterion by which human rights organizations should evaluate policies and

---

* *Editor's note:* See Glossary.

practices and the strategies to address them is human rights law. A policy might be problematic for any number of reasons without it being a human rights violation. In such a case, human rights organizations would have no grounds to oppose it.

The human rights community's engagement with Israel's High Court of Justice reveals some of the dilemmas involved in political as against human rights strategies. My research has shown that appeals to the High Court constitute the single most effective strategy to promote Palestinians' human rights.[4] This finding surprised many because in the aggregate the Court has an awful record when it comes to the Occupied Territories. It has consistently either refused to rule against or ruled in favor of all the fundamental components of the occupation, from settlements and home demolitions to the exploitation of Palestinian resources for Israeli benefit.

However, the Court has also played a role in virtually every achievement of the human rights community. This includes rulings that stopped systematic torture by the ISA, rerouted the Separation Barrier, and ended the practice (at least in the West Bank) of using Palestinians as human shields. It also includes the political pressure generated by dozens of individual petitions to the Court that, while not resulting in a favorable ruling, cumulatively led Israeli officials to make important policy changes, such as halting punitive home demolitions for a decade and granting family unification to thousands of foreign-born spouses living in the West Bank with no legal status.

The positive role of the Court in these cases does not negate the broader critique. Many experts have argued that when it comes to undermining occupation, the High Court is worse than useless: it is positively harmful.[5] In its role as a pressure valve in individual cases and in the mantle of legality this internationally respected institution affords to immoral and unjust policies, the

---

[4] Montell, "Learning From What Works."

[5] David Kretzmer, *The Occupation of Justice: The Supreme Court of Israel and the Occupied Territories* (Albany, NY: State University of New York Press, 2002); Michael Sfard, "The Human Rights Lawyer's Existential Dilemma," *Israel Law Review* 38.3 (Fall 2005), pp. 154–69.

High Court may well serve as one of the central mechanisms that enable the occupation to continue in its current form.

And therein lies the dilemma. It seems to me that an organization advancing a strategy to end the occupation would be wise to refrain from engagement with the Court. Yet a human rights organization that advocates on behalf of individual cases would betray its core mission if it didn't make strategic use of the High Court. This illustrates the importance of maintaining a clear distinction between human rights groups and political groups, each of which must pursue its distinct agenda.

Mission creep by human rights organizations is also liable to undermine political activism. If the human rights sector expands into politics, we risk sapping resources and further shrinking the space for the political organizing most necessary to end the occupation. In fact, this may already be happening. Some have argued that the professionalism of the human rights movement in Palestine replaced the mass, volunteer spirit of popular organizing prevalent in the first intifada.[6] It also seems that donors prefer funding human rights organizations to political groups: while the Israeli human rights sector boasts a dozen organizations all with large staffs, the overtly political groups working to end the occupation operate with small budgets and few paid workers. It is ironic that, while European funders are under attack from the Israeli government and its surrogates for political interference, in fact very little European funding goes to groups advocating systemic political change.

All of this is not to suggest that human rights organizations have no role in mobilizing political forces against the occupation. On the contrary, they have played a crucial part in putting the occupation on the public and diplomatic agenda. The research, documentation, and analysis of human rights organizations feed into political and diplomatic efforts and are relied upon by the diplomatic community, foreign ministries, parliaments, and UN bodies.

---

[6] Lori Allen, *The Rise and Fall of Human Rights: Cynicism and Politics in Occupied Palestine* (Stanford, CA: Stanford University Press, 2013).

Thirty years ago, Israelis used the phrase "enlightened occupation" to convey the idea that Palestinians were not harmed by Israeli military control. As a result of decades of human rights documentation, no one now makes this argument. Human rights organizations are, moreover, increasingly outspoken about the link between human rights and the occupation. Central to efforts to promote systemic change is the framing of specific violations in the context of the broader structures—the exploitation of natural resources, the separate and discriminatory legal systems for Palestinians and settlers in the West Bank, the fragmentation of Palestinian territory—that constitute the building blocks of the occupation.

The advocacy against the Separation Barrier illustrates the interplay between human rights and political tools. Human rights organizations were the first to identify the construction of the Barrier as a problem. Political actors then used the human rights documentation to bring the issue to the UN General Assembly, which referred the case to the International Court of Justice (ICJ). The ICJ's advisory opinion pressured the Israeli High Court to issue a ruling that led to a rerouting of the Barrier to significantly reduce harm to Palestinians. The levers of influence also worked in the opposite direction: weekly demonstrations against the Barrier by the people of Bil'in village strengthened High Court advocacy, leading to a ruling that succeeded in moving the Barrier off a portion of the village's land.

The political situation is complicated. The schism between the Palestinian Authority in the West Bank and the Hamas authorities in the Gaza Strip, the lack of a viable alternative to a right-wing government in Israel, the preoccupation of the United States and Europe with their own concerns—all these obstacles make it hard to see when or how the occupation will end. This makes the work of human rights organizations more important than ever. In the words of the Talmud, the commentary on Jewish law: "to save a single life is to save a whole world." And human rights organizations are saving lives.

But human rights is not the tool to advance political change. It may serve as a catalyst. It can certainly serve as a yardstick. Human rights organizations can criticize diplomatic proposals that violate human rights. But they cannot be the engine driving a strategy to end the occupation. The latter is the work of political movements and we should not blur the distinction between these movements and campaigns for human rights.

Neither the politicization of human rights nor the excessive legalization of political campaigning (i.e., overreliance on legal mechanisms to do the work of politics) is helpful. We should aim instead for a productive division of labor between human rights organizations and political movements. The former provide the latter with intellectual ammunition, while the latter generate the political will to turn human rights recommendations into policy. That is to say, the human rights movement must be a partner to—not a substitute for—grassroots political movements that generate the political will to bring about real change.

RESPONSE:

OCCUPATION IS A HUMAN RIGHTS VIOLATION

Raja Shehadeh

When my colleagues and I started Al-Haq in 1979, some Palestinian critics thought it would deflect from political activism to liberate Palestine. It took us many years before the struggle for human rights was recognized as a legitimate form of resistance to occupation. There remains little doubt now regarding the important role that this form of activism can play in the struggle. And yet the line between political work and human rights activism has always been thin, though necessary to preserve.

Raja Shehadeh is a lawyer and founder of the pioneering Palestinian human rights organization Al-Haq. He is the author of several acclaimed books, including *A Rift in Time* (2010), *Occupation Diaries* (2012), and *Palestinian Walks* (2007), which won the 2008 Orwell Prize. His latest book is *Where the Line is Drawn: Crossing Boundaries in Occupied Palestine* (2017). He lives in Ramallah, Palestine.

Some things are clear: it is wrong for a human rights organization to be factional and aligned with one political party or another. But a human rights organization working to bring an end to occupation does not cross the line into politics, because occupation is the greatest violator of human rights. This is why I find myself disagreeing with Jessica Montell when she writes that working to end the occupation transcends the scope and mandate of human rights organizations.

Montell is doubtless correct that "the most effective tools to end the occupation are not those of human rights organizations, but rather of political organizing." Human rights organizations never make redundant the work of political organizations. Even so, they must not shy from declaring the end of occupation as their goal for fear of appearing too political. Montell suggests that, "the moral authority of human rights organizations . . . derives from their confinement to the stipulations and idiom of law rather than politics." But should these organizations remain silent when, for example, the nature of the occupation shifts from being a temporary condition to one of colonial control over the territory of another nation? Would such a designation be dubbed "political" and therefore beyond the human rights remit?

The distinction between political work and human rights work doesn't always hold up, even when it concerns an action that has long been accepted as falling within the jurisdiction of human rights organizations. It was blurred, for example, in the question of whether or not to petition Israel's High Court to overturn the law to expropriate private Palestinian land that was passed by the Israeli Knesset on 6 February 2017. Some believed that the success of such a case would help save Israel from the international isolation to which the policies of the right-wing government are leading the country.[1]

The most fundamental consideration to the question that Montell poses at the outset of her piece—"whether the human rights community can play a pro-active role in ending the occupation"—rests on whether the occupation should be considered a domestic Israeli concern or an international one. There

[1] See Editorial, "The Court's Duty," *Ha'aretz* (8 February 2017).

is no doubt that during her tenure as director of B'Tselem, Montell worked assiduously to publicize human rights violations Israel was committing in the Occupied Territories. But it was the present director, Hagai El-Ad, who took the unprecedented step on 14 October 2016 of addressing the UN Security Council in a special discussion about Jewish settlements. In defense of his decision, he explained that he and his colleagues at B'Tselem have reached the conclusion that "the reality will not change if the world does not intervene." He said he was well aware that asking the world to intervene is a political action. But, he argued, "[i]ntervention by the world against the occupation is just as legitimate as any human-rights issue. It's all the more so when it involves an issue like our ruling over another people."[2]

In an interview on Israeli radio, El-Ad added: "The occupation isn't an internal Israeli issue, but a major international issue. There's no such thing as a democratic occupation. This can't be an internal matter."[3]

By addressing the UN, B'Tselem contributed to the Security Council's passing of Resolution 2334, which reaffirmed "that the establishment by Israel of settlements in the Palestinian territory occupied since 1967, including East Jerusalem, has no legal validity and constitutes a flagrant violation under international law and a major obstacle to the achievement of the two-State solution and a just, lasting and comprehensive peace."[4] The resolution also called "upon all States . . . to distinguish, in their relevant dealings, between the territory of the State of Israel and the territories occupied since 1967."[5] These provisions of the resolution gave a boost to the call for states to be more vigilant in their respect for Article 1 of the Fourth Geneva Convention of 1949, which requires

---

[2] Hagai El-Ad, "B'Tselem Head: Why I Spoke Against the Occupation at the UN," *Ha'aretz* (16 October 2016).

[3] Quoted in Raoul Wootliff, "B'Tselem Head: I Spoke Out Against the Occupation, Not Israel, at UN," *Times of Israel* (16 October 2016).

[4] UN Security Council Resolution 2334 (23 December 2016), para. 1.

[5] Ibid., para. 5.

states to not only respect the convention but also to undertake "to ensure respect . . . in all circumstances."[6] This in turn gives support and encouragement to the call for the international boycott of settlement products—decidedly a political action—which more than any other available tool has the potential to advance the struggle to end the Israeli occupation of the Palestinian territories.

[6] Convention (IV) relative to the Protection of Civilian Persons in Time of War (Geneva, 12 August 1949), Article 1.

RESPONSE:

SELF-DETERMINATION AS MASTER HUMAN RIGHTS NORM

Richard A. Falk

I deeply appreciate the informed lucidity and policy composure with which Jessica Montell approaches the complex topic of how to connect the protection of Palestinian human rights with the struggle to end the occupation of Palestine. She persuasively takes account of the particular context of the Israel/Palestine conflict to urge a separation of the law-driven work of human rights NGOs from a political movement against the occupation, and to clarify how the occupation is nevertheless delegitimized by way of its inherent incompatibility with respect for human rights norms.

Richard A. Falk is Albert G. Milbank Emeritus Professor of International Law and Practice and Professor Emeritus of Politics and International Affairs at Princeton University. He served as UN Special Rapporteur for Human Rights in the Occupied Palestinian Territory (2008–2014). His most recent book is *Palestine Horizon: Toward a Just Peace* (2017).

Despite my overall appreciation of Montell's essay, I have several serious reservations about her analysis. Above all, in her assessment of the context she makes no direct reference to the relevance of expansionism as a predominant component of Israel's occupation policy. Although recognizing Israel's "right-wing government" she does not explicitly connect this reality with the dead-end failures of Oslo diplomacy from start to finish. Even more pertinently for her argument, Montell fails to note the readiness of Israel to accept its poor international reputation with respect to human rights and international humanitarian law as a price worth paying to complete its overriding agenda of extending its borders. As long as this expansionist ethos dominates Israeli politics, placing any confidence in inter-governmental diplomacy and "the two-state consensus" as a path to ending the occupation seems to me misguided.[1] There is no reason think that Montell does not share this overall assessment of Israeli priorities, but her failure to say so openly invites the view that with enough *political* effort the job of peacekeeping will get done, which overlooks this abiding feature of the Zionist project that stretches back over a period of more than one hundred years.

I am also troubled by the following key sentences in the essay: "There is no doubt that ending the occupation is necessary from a human rights perspective. Human rights violations are inherent to the prolonged occupation." First of all, such a formulation seems to assume that the Palestinian right of self-determination is not to be treated as a human right despite being affirmed in common Article 1 of the two Covenants that have provided the essential international law frame for human rights discourse for more than fifty years.

[1] For a meticulously researched argument along these lines see Thomas Suárez, *State of Terror: How Terrorism Created Modern Israel* (Northampton, MA: Olive Branch Press, 2017). Despite the inflammatory title, this important contribution to the scholarly literature sheds needed light on the continuity of Israel's territorial ambitions, and the related manipulation of international diplomacy to facilitate the underlying Zionist ambition to gain sovereign control over the whole of historic Palestine. For more general treatment along the same lines, see also Victor Kattan, *From Coexistence to Conquest: International Law of the Arab-Israeli Conflict, 1891–1949* (London: Pluto, 2009).

In this regard, self-determination is not only a human right, it is the master human rights norm, informing by its special authority all the others.[2]

Secondly, if self-determination is indeed acknowledged as a human right, then the separation of human rights from the movement to end the occupation seems rather arbitrary without a second-order set of distinctions among categories of human rights. If she wanted to pursue this line of argument, Montell could quite plausibly maintain that the effectiveness of human rights organizations is connected with their focus on *specific* policies and practices rather than *structures*. Torture is such a practice; the occupation is neither policy nor practice, but a structure.

Thirdly, in the context of Israel and Palestine, this self-limitation by human rights NGOs may nevertheless be justified as a pragmatic move designed to avoid even greater suppressive pressure by the Israeli state. Israel's governing authorities are apparently themselves wrestling with the tensions between further curtailing the operations of human rights NGOs and maintaining the country's increasingly tarnished reputation as a constitutional democracy.

I believe that *conceptual* concerns are intertwined here with *tactical* issues. The conceptual concern involves identifying the scope of human rights in international law. In this regard, I believe Montell is wrong to regard ending the occupation as a "political" challenge beyond the provenance of human rights organizations, as distinct from, for example, challenging torture, which all agree is a suitable legal target. As contended here, it is deceptive to ignore self-determination for the Palestinian people as either unrelated to ending the

[2] It is notable to observe that the Universal Declaration of Human Rights (1948) fails even to mention "self-determination," even though it was intended to provide a comprehensive (albeit non-binding) formulation of an international human rights framework. In contrast, just under two decades later, the International Covenant on Civil and Political Rights (1966) and the International Covenant on Economic, Social and Cultural Rights (1966) are treaty instruments that elevate the norm of self-determination to a position of primacy in international law—the human right that gives authoritative direction to all other human rights. In common Article 1(1) of the Covenants, self-determination is described in this encompassing language: "All peoples have the right of self-determination. By virtue of that right they freely determine their political status and freely pursue their economic, social and cultural development."

occupation or as not properly considered a human right. Montell could logically argue—although it is not evident from this essay that she would want to—that ending the occupation is a distinct endeavor that may or may not involve the fulfillment of the Palestinian right of self-determination.

What is certainly true is that ending the occupation does not exhaust the content of self-determination, given fundamental additional Palestinian *legal* claims relating to refugees, Jerusalem, water, and sovereignty. It is also the case, as Montell suggests, that many of these concerns, called "final status issues" in the diplomatic jargon, have been treated as "political" issues, which in this context implies that they should not necessarily be resolved by reference to rights under international law. Such issues were deliberately never treated as "legal" issues in the so-called peace process, but rather as questions to be resolved by negotiation, bargaining, and compromise.[3] This politics/law dichotomy was itself political: international law aligned with and endorsed Palestinian demands with respect to the principal contentious issues, and so excluding it from negotiations undercut the Palestinian position.

The tactical issue concerns how to maximize the efficacy of human rights advocacy within the existing status quo, which raises questions of engagement with courts and the justiciability of human rights grievances. Montell is persuasive in claiming that the most effective venue for protecting the human rights of Palestinians has been the Israeli High Court, despite its record of consistently rejecting challenges to the occupation itself. In my terms, human rights violations narrowly conceived as Israeli policies and practices have been quite often effectively challenged by human rights NGOs, but human rights more broadly conceived to include the right of self-determination, which pertain

[3] In my view, the exclusion of international law from the dynamics of Oslo diplomacy was detrimental to Palestinian prospects and expressive of Israeli control of the process as a result of power disparities. In effect, within a diplomatic setting it tends to handicap the politically weaker party to exclude international law from negotiations. For elaboration of this position see Richard Falk, "Why International Law Matters in the Palestinian Struggle," in Richard Falk, *Humanitarian Intervention and Legitimacy Wars: Seeking Peace and Justice in the 21st Century* (London: Routledge, 2015), pp. 113–29.

to structure, can rarely be protected within the existing constitutional law framework of a sovereign state. Structural challenges are primarily mounted by political movements, although the legitimacy of such political goals can be supported by critiques developed by mainstream human rights organizations with ties to civil society activism.[4]

In one respect, our disagreement may be reflective of the divergent jurisprudential traditions of the United Kingdom and the United States. British (as well as continental) jurisprudence is intentionally constructed around a sharp separation between law and politics, as exemplified by the work of Hans Kelsen or H. L. A. Hart, while the American approach, with which I identify, rejects this separation, insisting that law cannot be properly understood apart from its sociological and political underpinnings and context. In this regard, I agree *substantively* with Montell that the work and contributions of Israeli and Palestinian human rights organizations has tangibly improved the daily lives of Palestinians living under occupation without being able to bring the occupation to an end, that any effort by human rights organizations to attempt this broader undertaking would be futile and likely weaken their domain of effective operations, and hence that this should be neither expected nor attempted. Where we disagree concerns how to contextualize the occupation and the movement that is challenging its persistence, which I regard as being informed at every stage by international law.

Although my comments have highlighted criticism, I want to restate my appreciation for this essay that encourages readers to think clearly about the fundamental connections between law and politics with respect to Israel/Palestine. It may be that a longer essay by Montell would address some of these concerns in a manner that would mute the critical tone of these remarks of mine.

---

[4] A useful analogue to the Israel/Palestine conflict is the American struggle to end slavery. Civil society organizations, especially churches and media, were effective in mounting a critique of the barbarous practices associated with slavery, generating a moral and political climate conducive to its abolition, but it required the long and bloody Civil War to challenge and end the institution itself.

RESPONSE:

THE POLITICS OF HUMAN RIGHTS

Neve Gordon and Nicola Perugini

Jessica Montell's essay begins with an uncomfortable observation: since the establishment of a plethora of human rights NGOs in Israel/Palestine in the late 1980s and early 1990s, "the occupation has only grown more entrenched." For Montell, this fact cannot be blamed on human rights organizations, since she does not believe that the role of rights groups is to end Israeli military rule over the Palestinian territories. Indeed, for her, human rights are "not the tool to advance political change."

In our view, this understanding of the role of human rights advocacy epitomizes much of what has gone afoul with human rights work. Indeed, the

---

Neve Gordon is Professor of Politics and Government at Ben-Gurion University of the Negev. He is the author of *Israel's Occupation* (2008) and *The Human Right to Dominate* (2015, with Nicola Perugini).

Nicola Perugini is Lecturer in International Relations at the University of Edinburgh. He is the author of *The Human Right to Dominate* (2015, with Neve Gordon).

assumptions underpinning Montell's essay reveal how and why a once potent weapon for resistance, emancipation, and social justice has been transformed into a band-aid, used either for treating the symptoms of structural abuse or as a vehicle that enhances domination.[1] The human rights to which Montell subscribes have been subordinated to a legal and methodological framework that alienates the very people whose rights are being violated while abandoning any demand for structural change.[2]

Montell is aware that human rights organizations' reports and press releases have political implications, but she maintains that their position is ostensibly neutral and determined by universal—i.e., non-political—legal norms. Notwithstanding the prevalence of this belief among NGO workers, human rights are actually political through and through: in their deployment, in their consequences, and in their substantive content, which is determined by a struggle among different forces within a given society.[3] In the case of Israel-Palestine, Montell appears to have forgotten that human rights entered the political scene in Israel-Palestine during the first intifada,* as a powerful popular discourse adopted by hundreds of thousands of Palestinians to unveil the oppressive character of Israeli rule and articulate their struggle for national self-determination. Alas, this discourse was quickly institutionalized, as human rights NGOs were established and international donor money flooded in.[4]

---

* *Editor's note:* See Glossary.

[1] Nicola Perugini and Neve Gordon, *The Human Right to Dominate* (New York, NY: Oxford University Press, 2015).

[2] Kenneth Roth, "Defending Economic, Social and Cultural Rights: Practical Issues Faced by an International Human Rights Organization," *Human Rights Quarterly* 26.1 (2004), pp. 63–73.

[3] See Mark Goodale, "Toward a Critical Anthropology of Human Rights," *Current Anthropology* 47.3 (2006), pp. 485–511.

[4] Neve Gordon and Nitza Berkovitch, "Human Rights Discourse in Domestic Settings: How Does it Emerge?" *Political Studies* 55.1 (2007), pp. 243–66; Sari Hanafi and Linda Tabar, *The Emergence of a Palestinian Globalized Elite: Donors, International Organizations, and Local NGOs* (Washington, DC: Institute of Jerusalem Studies, 2005).

This professionalization of human rights led to the creation of a social class authorized to define the legitimate boundaries of human rights interpretation and activism, increasingly in terms set by international donors and developing professional norms rather than local popular movements.[5] One of the requirements for entry into this privileged class was the assumption of an "appearance of neutrality."[6] Thus, as human rights organizations in Israel-Palestine became further removed from popular movements, and more tightly integrated into international financial and professional networks, the liberatory content of the human rights they espoused was diluted. Notably, whereas Palestinians in the first intifada had targeted the occupation itself as a rights violation, the professionalized NGOs largely restricted their focus to localized abuses.

The conversion of human rights into a professional legalistic discourse informed by a top-down approach in which those who are violated and abused very often have no hand or say in their own emancipation has detrimental implications. The institutionalization of human rights in the wake of the first intifada ultimately undermined efforts by the Palestinian people to continue using them as part of their own popular mobilization. From a tool of the masses, human rights were transformed into a tool of the experts.

Some of the consequences of this trend can be seen in B'Tselem's report on Israel's November 2012 attack on Gaza (dubbed "Operation Pillar of Defense"). All told, 174 Palestinians were killed in the assault, of whom 101 were civilians, including thirty-three children and thirteen women. Six Israelis,

---

[5] Benoît Challand, *Palestinian Civil Society: Foreign Donors and the Power to Promote and Exclude* (London: Routledge, 2008); Nitza Berkovitch and Neve Gordon, "The Political Economy of Transnational Regimes: The Case of Human Rights," *International Studies Quarterly* 52.4 (2008), pp. 881–904. See also Lori Allen, *The Rise and Fall of Human Rights: Cynicism and Politics in Occupied Palestine* (Stanford, CA: Stanford University Press, 2013).

[6] Pierre Bourdieu and Loic Wacquant, *An Invitation to Reflexive Sociology* (Cambridge, UK: Polity, 1992); Pierre Bourdieu, "Identity and Representation," in *Language and Symbolic Power* (Cambridge, UK: Polity Press, 1991), pp. 220–28.

including four civilians, were killed.[7] Despite the wide disparities in deaths and destruction, B'Tselem's most explicit condemnation was directed against Hamas. Hamas and other groups operating in the Gaza Strip, the rights group concluded, carried out war crimes, whereas "deciding whether the Israeli military has violated IHL [i.e., international humanitarian law] provisions is not as simple."[8] Similarly, following the 2014 Gaza War during which 1,500 Palestinian civilians and six Israeli civilians were killed, Amnesty International accused Palestinian armed factions of violating human rights because they used "inherently indiscriminate weapons," which the rights group contrasted with Israel's "surgical" capabilities.[9] The legal interpretation of these rights organizations commences only after they introduce an imaginary symmetry into an asymmetric situation. This amounts to the suspension of history, a well-known colonial mechanism of validation and justification of domination.

Another effect of the professionalization of human rights has been the creation of a social class authorized to define the legitimate boundaries of human rights interpretation and activism: the "correct" language that should be used when struggling for human rights, which techniques are effective, which fora and courts are appropriate, and who has the legitimacy to invoke human rights in public. This class of experts ultimately shapes the political field of human rights by determining the fundamental conditions that grant access to the debate, while conferring the right to speak human rights only to a select few.

The legal fundamentalism, "neutral" posturing, and disinterest in popular mobilization characteristic of most human rights NGOs are all political positions and part of the same process spurred by the professionalization of human

[7] Human Rights Council, *Report of the United Nations High Commissioner for Human Rights on the Implementation of Human Rights Council Resolutions S-9/1 and S-12/1* (Geneva: Human Rights Council, 2013).

[8] Yael Stein, *Human Rights Violations during Operation Pillar of Defense 14–21 November 2012* (Jerusalem: B'Tselem, 2013), pp. 3–4.

[9] Nicola Perugini and Neve Gordon, "Indiscriminate Attacks," *London Review of Books Blog* (6 April 2015).

rights in Israel-Palestine. The commitment to "neutral" protection of human rights in situations of extreme power asymmetry has led many NGOs to align themselves if not collude with existing power structures, as the reports on the Gaza Wars suggest.[10] The result of this non-threatening deployment of human rights is Montell's opening paradox: human rights organizations proliferated, local victories were won, and Israel's occupation became "more entrenched." Consequently, the question we need to ask is, how do we revive the threat of human rights? How do we re-politicize human rights after they have been hijacked by professionals?

By way of conclusion, we would like to offer three suggestions on how to counter existing trends. First, we believe that it is vital to adopt and disseminate a popular human rights discourse. This does not mean that human rights should be mobilized in a way that ignores the law. On the contrary, activists should appropriate the language of human rights to target the law where and when the law enhances domination. If use of the law confers legitimacy on existing repressive structures, then a short-circuit has to be created, combining human rights with other political discourses and practices of emancipation in order to undo the law-legitimacy nexus. From this perspective, Montell's claim that NGO appeals to Israel's High Court of Justice have been "the most effective strategy to promote Palestinians' human rights" does not take into account the damage these appeals have done, ignoring the fact that the very recognition of a colonial court as a legitimate arbitrator has ultimately upheld the law-legitimacy nexus underpinning the occupation.

Second, if the professionalization of human rights NGOs has profoundly impoverished human rights, we need to begin thinking seriously about ways of de-professionalizing human rights.[11] This entails broadening human rights beyond legalistic interpretations and the accompanying professional culture and dissolving the boundaries in which the contemporary political field of

---

[10] See Perugini and Gordon, *The Human Right to Dominate.*

[11] This, we think, is similar to the conclusion reached by Stephen Hopgood, *The Endtimes of Human Rights* (Ithaca, NY: Cornell University Press, 2013), pp. 162–82.

human rights has crystallized. Insofar as the politics of human rights is currently shaped by privileged classes of practitioners and intellectuals, who are granted more authority and legitimacy to speak human rights than others—and particularly those who suffer most from violations—then these class differences should be abolished. This can be effected through institutional change, either by reshaping NGOs in order to make them accountable to the people they claim to represent—i.e., democratizing them—or by establishing different institutions that are more aligned with grassroots movements.

This leads us to a final consideration. When existing forms of human rights mobilization do not challenge or help to undo domination in a given context, human rights activists need to re-conceptualize and re-frame the struggle. This is what happened in Palestine with the birth of the Boycott, Divestment, and Sanctions (BDS) Movement in 2005.* The movement has adopted a human rights framework. Yet, instead of deploying human rights to solve isolated legal cases in colonial courts, the BDS Movement mobilizes human rights in order to challenge the overarching structures of domination. In sharp contrast to professional human rights NGOs, the BDS Movement is homegrown, the product of Palestinian society. Its aim is to develop international solidarity and to mobilize international popular support. It deploys human rights alongside anti-racist, anti-colonial, and anti-apartheid discourses. Thus, while the movement uses human rights in a way that many professionals would reject, it has managed to reframe the debate on Israel-Palestine and to establish a growing alliance among Palestinian, Israeli, and international political forces. If re-conceptualized in these ways, human rights can, we believe, still be mobilized for emancipatory purposes. Indeed, they can help to create new political communities based on justice and egalitarianism, rather than propping up and oiling various apparatuses of injustice.

---

* *Editor's note:* See Glossary.

RESPONSE:

BETRAYING THE HUMAN RIGHTS MANDATE

Michael Sfard

The Knesset's adoption of the Regulation Law,[1] which legalizes the expropriation of privately-owned Palestinian land, sparked fierce strategic debate among anti-occupation activists: should the Israeli legal system, which is deeply complicit in the occupation, be engaged with in order to fight the occupation?

Michael Sfard is an Israeli human rights lawyer specializing in international human rights law and the laws of war with a special emphasis on the law of belligerent occupation. He is the legal adviser to several Israeli human rights organizations and peace groups, and he represents Palestinian communities and Israeli and Palestinian activists. Born in Jerusalem, Sfard is a graduate of the Law Faculty of the Hebrew University and has an MA in International Human Rights Law from the University College of London. He is the author of *The Wall and the Gate: Israel, Palestine, and the Legal Battle for Human Rights* (2018).

[1] Jonathan Lis and Barak Ravid, "Israel Passes Contentious Palestinian Land-Grab Bill in Late Night Vote," *Ha'aretz* (7 February 2017).

Left-wing activists, politicians, and columnists expressed opposition to efforts by human rights organizations to petition the High Court of Justice (HCJ) to strike down the law. If the petition was successful, they argued, it would just rescue Prime Minister Netanyahu from deserved international isolation and even provide Israel with cover to evade referral to the International Criminal Court.[2]

In the terms of Jessica Montell's analysis, the dilemma of whether to challenge the Regulation Law in the Israeli courts rests on the distinction between the *political* campaign to end the occupation, which advocates in this case refraining from what is likely to be a successful litigation to invalidate the law, and the *human rights* approach, which focuses on stopping abuses, even at the expense of lessening international pressure on the Government of Israel.

In an unrelated move (but clearly part of the same trend), the Israeli human rights organization B'Tselem has decided to stop filing complaints with the Military Police concerning alleged offences by Israeli soldiers against Palestinians.[3] Its director, Hagai El-Ad, explained in an interview that "collaboration" with state institutions for the purpose of challenging harmful policies or struggling for accountability is not only useless but harmful, since the rare victories won through these institutions give the state and the occupation an enabling veneer of credibility.[4]

Assessing B'Tselem's decision and the calls to refrain from litigating against the Regulation Law requires a precise definition of the human rights approach to the occupation. Jessica Montell suggests the occupation is a *source* of human rights abuses, especially when it is prolonged. I hold a firmer view. It seems to me obvious that an occupation, which by definition entails

---

[2] The ICC tends to intervene only when it assesses that internal legal mechanisms cannot ensure accountability.

[3] B'Tselem, "B'Tselem to Stop Referring Complaints to the Military Law Enforcement System," *btselem.org* (25 May 2016).

[4] "Israeli Anti-Occupation Group Refuses to be the Army's 'Useful Idiot'," *Ha'aretz* (11 February 2017).

suspension of civil rights from millions of people, is *in and of itself* a human rights violation. It is no different in this respect than administrative detention or collective punishment. An occupation *is* a human rights violation even if international law permits it (and it does, under certain conditions and temporarily).

Montell would not agree because she purports that human rights organizations are "rooted in the discourse of international law," and that "this is the source of their authority, and the only yardstick by which they can measure whether to support or oppose a policy." But human rights is not a legal concept. It is a moral and philosophical concept that is advanced by and enshrined in international law.

Historically, rights have been born and developed by human rights activists outside the realm of the law, and imported into law books only once they garnered enough public support. Each letter in the acronym LGBTQI represents a class of people whose rights were not acknowledged by human rights law for many years, and it took a tremendous effort by human rights activists who did not accept the existing law as their only yardstick to have it evolve to encompass and protect them. Aside from the creation of new rights and the reformulation of the scope of existing ones, the human rights community may also oppose a "legal violation" of a right and fight for its abolition if the balance of interests embodied in international law strikes it as unacceptable. A good example is the practice of administrative detention—a human rights violation that is nevertheless permissible under international humanitarian law (IHL). Hence, gaps can and do open up between positions taken by the human rights community and norms set in international human rights law or IHL.

Back to the occupation. The human rights violations that are inherent in any occupation regime grow and become more severe with the passage of time. Hence, ending the occupation is a human rights goal that becomes more acute as time goes by. In that respect, the human rights approach to the occupation converges with the ambitions of the political anti-occupation camp.

However, even with this shared objective, I agree with Montell that political and human rights strategies may, and sometimes do, collide. The reason for this is the special emphasis the human rights approach (and ethics) places on the individual as the subject of its struggles. This does not negate the status of ending the occupation as a human rights goal, but it does complicate the matrix of interests it promotes and impose restrictions on the methods of realizing it. While the political anti-occupation activist has one goal to advance, the human rights activist is tasked with two.

Some further explanation is required here. Human rights advocacy and litigations may operate in three different "purpose planes": *individual redress*, *policy change*, and—in cases involving an inherently and gravely abusive regime, like military occupation—*regime change*. Pursuing these simultaneously runs the risk of conflict between them. To avoid strategic missteps, the human rights lawyer, activist, or NGO must establish clear priorities vis-à-vis these different purposes. Since human rights morality dictates focusing on the individual and her well-being, as a rule of thumb it does not permit sacrificing her rights in the name of promoting some general good. This means that the first purpose plane—individual redress—has a default priority over the other two. It would require an extreme set of circumstances to justify deviating from it. The relevant variables in the priority equation are: the likelihood of a particular human rights campaign or litigation securing a significant advance towards a desired policy or regime change, the severity of the abuse to the individual, and the prospects for ending that abuse. Given the complex nature of the underlying causes of major political change, it is hard to imagine cases in which the interest of the individual victim will not take precedence.

The idea of boycotting Israeli enforcement institutions in order to deny them legitimacy is, I think, a good example of how complex the human rights approach can be. If one accepts that the boycott may contribute to ending the occupation while engagement might secure remedy for at least some victims, we are confronted with a conflict of interests that is inherent in the human rights discourse.

I take issue with the boycott thesis,[5] at least in its radical (and simplistic) form. Let's take the Regulation Law as an example. For those who define their actions as a struggle against human rights violations, challenging it in the Israeli courts should not be a difficult call. According to data provided by the oldest and biggest Israeli peace group, Peace Now, the law will lead to the theft of more than 11,000 dunams of private Palestinian land on which Israelis have built illegally and the expropriation of at least 25,000 dunams more of Palestinian agricultural land that Israelis have taken over. This would amount to a transfer of land from probably tens of thousands of Palestinians to the Israeli settlers who have illegally invaded it. If those opposed to the filing of the petition are right, and there is a high likelihood that the HCJ will strike down the law, then the petition will probably succeed in preventing a grave and extensive violation of human rights. Given a colossal abuse and a good chance of preventing it, the human rights approach demands petitioning the court.

As Montell puts it, under such circumstances, refraining from engagement with the court would amount to a betrayal of the human rights organization's core mission: defending the rights of individuals.

But if one accepts the notion that ending the occupation is also a human rights endeavor, one must appreciate that there might be extreme cases in which the balance between the chance of securing a remedy for the individual and the danger of causing damage to the struggle to end the occupation would yield a different conclusion.

Hence, the question of participation in the legal mechanisms afforded by an unjust regime is not susceptible to answer by formula, but requires careful judgement in each case. It demands a complex assessment of the costs and benefits of the use of legal means in the struggle for individual rights and for a regime change, such as that directed against the occupation. There may be cases where the desire to avoid legitimizing the legal façade and thus contributing to

---

[5] I am one of the attorneys who did bring a petition challenging the constitutionality of the Regulation Law on behalf of Palestinian communities and land owners and a group of Israeli human rights NGOs. At the time of writing, this challenge is ongoing.

the stability of the occupation wins out. For this to happen, the case must be one in which there is small chance of obtaining redress for the individual, in petitioning a high-prestige government body (controversial decisions by low-prestige bodies do not create legitimacy), where effective alternative means of struggle are available.

The choice of which battles to fight, and where, can and should factor into considerations relating to ending the occupation. But these considerations may not trump the primacy of defending the human rights of individual victims. When the fate of individuals and their rights are at stake, the human rights lawyer and organization must not invoke the fight to change a policy or to end the occupation as a justification for failure to act. In a direct collision, the defense of a specific individual almost always wins over the other two human rights purpose planes.

A debate comparable to this one took place in early 1980s South Africa. Law professor Raymond Wacks caused a sensation when he argued that a decent judge who opposed apartheid must resign.[6] This debate spilled over to the question of what human rights lawyers should do amid concerns that their work might grant legitimacy to an evil regime. The person who responded to Wacks was Professor John Dugard, who later became the UN special rapporteur on human rights in the Occupied Palestinian Territory. This legitimization is a price worth paying, he wrote, so as not to forsake the campaign for justice.[7] Resignation in these circumstances would be a dereliction, one all the more grave in view of the fact that the victims of injustice were asking for legal representation, petitioning for protection, and praying the courts would rule in their favor.

---

[6] Raymond Wacks, "Judges and Injustice," *South African Law Journal* 101 (1984), pp. 266–85.

[7] John Dugard, "Should Judges Resign? A Reply to Professor Wacks," *South African Law Journal* (1984), pp. 286–94.

REJOINDER

Jessica Montell

I am very glad to be part of this important and overdue discussion about the distinction between human rights and political advocacy to end the occupation. I take Sfard's point that the human rights movement is under constant evolution and not well served when activists bind themselves to an overly literal reading of existing human rights treaties. In any case, as Falk rightly points out, self-determination is an internationally recognized human right, making prolonged occupation itself (and not just its repressive manifestations) a human rights concern. So, to respond to Shehadeh's (rhetorical) question: yes, human rights organizations must speak out against the occupation itself. It is the case that in the 1980s and 1990s, Israeli organizations did not target the occupation per se; even settlements were initially viewed solely as a political issue. Today, however, that is not the case, and most if not all human rights organizations make clear that only by ending the occupation can we ensure human rights are respected. This declarative function, affecting the public conversation, is an important part of the work of human rights organizations.

These groups, however, are not able to formulate a strategy to end the occupation. It is not a question of whether the occupation is an international concern—it clearly is, and Israeli human rights organizations have appealed to international bodies for over a decade, including UN agencies and the foreign ministries and parliaments of Israel's closest allies. It is a question, rather, of scope: the steps required to end the occupation take us well beyond the remit of human rights organizations. Deciding whether the preferred resolution is two-states, one state, or some other arrangement requires that we "go beyond the human rights data." So too does developing an effective strategy to advance this arrangement.

Gordon and Perugini are correct that our respective attitudes towards human rights as a discourse and a movement are quite different. Much of what they identify as weakness, I see as strength: the emphasis on the individual, the adherence to universal standards even at the expense of utilitarian considerations. Much of what they advocate as the future direction for human rights, I see as the sole purview of political movements, with clear dangers in their recommendation to integrate the two.

Gordon and Perugini bemoan the approach in which those whose rights are violated have no say in their own emancipation. Yet ensuring better participation of "the Palestinians" in formulating human rights strategy is complicated. Take the dilemma almost all of the respondents addressed of whether to petition Israel's High Court against the Israeli law legalizing land confiscation. Palestinian spokespeople and Israeli activists have argued against such a petition, given the Court's role in sustaining Israel's regime in the OPT. That the Court has played such a role is clear. Yet as Sfard has pointed out elsewhere, the Palestinian landowners themselves are interested in petitioning the Court to get their lands back. Who then gets to decide? The human rights logic would say the individual victims. The political logic would say the *collective* victims. Political movements have a tendency to sacrifice individuals for the greater good. Human rights provides a counterweight to this tendency.

As I argued in my initial essay, a clear understanding of the distinction between human rights and political advocacy will increase the effectiveness of efforts to end the occupation. As I am arguing here, such a distinction also ensures that human rights remains true to its formative DNA of protecting individual rights.

There is broad agreement that human rights is an important *part* of the strategy for ending the Israeli occupation. The question is how important and what the interface ought to be between human rights and other aspects of this strategy. These are vital topics that warrant further debate.

CHAPTER THIRTEEN.

APARTHEID IN SOUTH AFRICA AND THE OCCUPIED PALESTINIAN TERRITORY: A USEFUL COMPARISON?

John Dugard

Today comparisons are frequently drawn between apartheid as applied in South Africa and Israel's occupation of Palestine. Although the apartheid analogy receives considerable attention, little attention is paid to the real similarities between the two regimes and the different responses of the United Nations (UN) and the international community to apartheid as practiced in South Africa and occupied Palestine. This contribution examines the apartheid analogy in this broader

---

John Dugard is Professor Emeritus of International Law at the Universities of Leiden and the Witwatersrand. He was UN Special Rapporteur on Human Rights in the Occupied Palestinian Territory, and chaired international fact-finding missions into the second intifada and Israel's 2008–2009 assault on Gaza. He was a member of the UN International Law Commission and is the author of many books on international law and apartheid in South Africa. This paper is based in part on the Edward Said Memorial Lecture delivered by the author in Adelaide, South Australia, on 15 October 2016.

context and addresses the question whether it serves a useful purpose in ending the occupation of Palestine.

At the outset it must be made clear that the present article is concerned with this analogy in the context of the Occupied Palestinian Territory (OPT), comprising the West Bank, East Jerusalem, and Gaza. Although some have likened discrimination against Palestinians in Israel itself to apartheid,[1] there are significant differences between these two discriminatory regimes in respect of matters such as political rights, legal regimes, repression, and the gravity of the discrimination. These differences make it difficult to argue that discrimination in Israel itself reaches the threshold for apartheid set by international law. Another caveat: although it remains occupied territory,[2] Gaza differs from the West Bank and East Jerusalem in that since 2005 it has had no settlement enterprise in its midst.* It may be seen as a Bantustan-like entity controlled by Israel, making the apartheid analogy apt. However, this article focuses on apartheid and the settlement enterprise in the West Bank, including East Jerusalem.

The apartheid analogy

The similarities between the regimes of apartheid in South Africa and occupied Palestine have been examined in detail elsewhere.[3] These examinations divide into two kinds: empirical and legal.

---

* *Editor's note:* See Glossary ("Disengagement").

[1] See, for example, Uri Davis, *Israel: An Apartheid State* (London: Zed Books, 1987). In March 2017, the Economic and Social Commission for Western Asia (ESCWA) published a report authored by Richard Falk and Virginia Tilley (E/ESCWA/ECRI/2017/1) which declared that apartheid was practiced in Israel itself, in addition to the Occupied Palestinian Territory. The report was shortly afterwards removed from the website of the ESCWA on the instruction of the Secretary-General of the United Nations.

[2] See Yoram Dinstein, *The International Law of Belligerent Occupation* (Cambridge: Cambridge University Press, 2009), pp. 276–80.

[3] Virginia Tilley ed., *Beyond Occupation: Apartheid, Colonialism and International Law in the Occupied Palestinian Territories* (London: Pluto Press, 2012); John Dugard & John Reynolds,

Empirically, apartheid in South Africa was characterized by discrimination, repression, and territorial fragmentation.[4] Law and practice broadly divided the population of South Africa into two racial groups: the white minority and the black majority, the latter comprising Africans, persons of mixed descent (termed "coloureds"), and Asians. The legal system provided for advantaged treatment of whites in respect of ownership of land, residence, freedom of movement, access to public amenities, education, healthcare, and most other aspects of individual and collective life. The security laws restricted freedom of speech, association, and assembly; authorized detention without trial; and provided for the prosecution and punishment of those who opposed the system of apartheid. The detention of political detainees inevitably led to torture. The territory of South Africa was fragmented along racial lines. Certain parts of the country, known as Bantustans, were set aside for black Africans, within which they had considerable autonomy. Cities were divided into white group areas and black group areas, and rigid territorial separation was enforced throughout the country.

Discrimination, repression, and territorial fragmentation are also the main empirical features of the occupation of Palestine. There are two racial groups in the West Bank and East Jerusalem: the Jewish settler minority, numbering more than 600,000, and the Palestinian majority of approximately three million. Law and practice provide for special facilities for Jews and the unequal treatment of the Palestinian majority. Jewish settlers live in affluent settlements set aside for exclusive occupation by Jews; for Palestinians, there are severe constraints on the building of houses and legal provision for the destruction of homes built without permits which does not apply to settlers. The free movement of Jews is facilitated by separate roads superior in quality to those used by Palestinians; serious restraints are placed on the movement of Palestinians by

---

"Apartheid, International Law, and the Occupied Palestinian Territory," *European Journal of International Law* 24.3 (2013), pp. 867–913.

[4] For a detailed account of the law and practice of apartheid, see John Dugard, *Human Rights and the South African Legal Order* (Princeton, NJ: Princeton University Press, 1978).

checkpoints which do not apply to Jews. Settler schools, clinics, and hospitals are better resourced than those of Palestinians, and settlers consume a disproportionate amount of the water resources of the OPT. Jewish settlers are protected by the Israeli legal system while Palestinians are subject to military law and tried before special military courts that fail to comply with international standards of criminal justice.

The occupation is founded on repression. Extra-judicial assassinations and executions, military attacks on civilians, torture, detention without trial, the demolition of family homes, and massive imprisonment of Palestinians are regular features of the occupation.

The West Bank has been fragmented into enclaves and separate areas for Jews and Palestinians by the construction of settlements, the building of a Wall to incorporate settlements into Israel, the construction of settler roads, and the zoning of land for military exercises.[5] South Africa's Bantustan policy failed to achieve such a comprehensive territorial fragmentation.

Israel argues that the occupation is a typical temporary regime following a military operation and that like other occupations it will end when a peace treaty is signed between the parties. Consequently, it cannot be compared to a regime of apartheid practiced by one people in a single state over another people in the same state.[6] But this is nonsense. Unlike the short occupations of Western European states in World War II, the occupation of Palestine has persisted for fully fifty years—the bulk of Israel's existence as a state—and shows no sign of ending. Only the fear of international sanctions prevents Israel from formally annexing the West Bank. De facto there is little distinction between Israel's occupation of the West Bank and South Africa's sovereignty over South Africa. Of course, as far as East Jerusalem is concerned, Israel cannot raise the

---

[5] See further on this subject Eyal Weizman, *Hollow Land: Israel's Architecture of Occupation* (London: Verso, 2007).

[6] See generally on this theme Benjamin Pogrund, *Drawing Fire: Investigating the Accusations of Apartheid in Israel* (Lanham, MD: Rowman & Littlefield, 2014).

argument that it is merely occupied: in 1980 Israel purported to annex East Jerusalem and treats it as part of Israel.[7]

Perhaps the most important difference between apartheid in South Africa and apartheid in the OPT is that the former was more honest in its discriminatory intent. The law prescribed discrimination in clear and unambiguous terms. Notices provided for segregated facilities for black and white. By contrast, Israeli law seeks to conceal its discriminatory intent in a body of inaccessible military orders. How Israeli law operates is well illustrated by Shulamit Aloni, a former Israeli Minister of Education from a more enlightened cabinet. One day she confronted an Israeli soldier confiscating a Palestinian's car for driving on separate road reserved for settlers. She asked him how the Palestinian driver was to know that the road was for the exclusive use of settlers. The soldier replied:

> "It is his responsibility to know that this road is for settlers only. Besides, what do you want us to do? Put up a sign here and let some anti-Semitic journalist take a photo so that he can show the world that apartheid exists here?"[8]

An analysis of the law and practice of Israel in occupied Palestine in the context of international law also substantiates the charge of apartheid.

The 1973 Convention on the Suppression and Punishment of the Crime of Apartheid and the Rome Statute of the International Criminal Court[9] together define apartheid as the commission of certain inhumane acts in the context of an institutionalized regime of systematic oppression and domination by one racial group over another. Both instruments make clear that the crime is not confined to apartheid in South Africa. The transfer of more than 600,000 Jewish settlers into

---

[7] "Basic Law: Jerusalem, Capital of Israel, 5740-1980." The Security Council has, however, declared this act of annexation to be null and void. See UN Security Council Resolution 480 (1980).

[8] Shulamit Aloni, "Indeed there is Apartheid in Israel," *Middle East News Service* (10 January 2007; translated from Hebrew, originally published in *Yediot Aharonot*, 31 December 2006).

[9] Article 7(1)(j), 7(2)(h).

the West Bank and East Jerusalem, living in some 200 settlements and outposts,* has given rise to policies and practices that fall squarely within this definition. One racial group—Jewish settlers together with Israel's occupying forces—systematically commits inhumane acts, such as extra-judicial assassinations and executions, torture, house demolitions, punitive constraints on freedom of movement, and the indiscriminate use of violence against civilians. These acts oppress the population of occupied Palestine by means of an institutionalized regime that results in the domination of one racial group over another.

The inescapable conclusion is that Israel is guilty of applying a policy of discrimination, repression, and territorial fragmentation in the West Bank and East Jerusalem that bears the hallmarks of apartheid as applied in South Africa between 1948 and 1994 and as defined by the 1973 Convention on the Suppression and Punishment of the Crime of Apartheid and the Rome Statute of the International Criminal Court. In 2002, Israel's leading human rights organization, B'Tselem, reached a similar conclusion. In a major report on Israel's "land grab" in the OPT, it found that the settlement enterprise had created a regime of separation based on discrimination, with two systems of law in the same area such that the rights of individuals were based on nationality. This regime, it concluded, "is reminiscent of distasteful regimes from the past, such as the apartheid regime in South Africa."[10]

The legal basis for the concern of the international community: South Africa and Israel compared

In comparing and contrasting the response of the international community to apartheid in South Africa and occupied Palestine, it is necessary to consider the legal rules that provided the basis for international action against South Africa and the legal rules that Israel is accused of violating. The question that arises from this consideration is whether the international community has a sounder legal basis for action against Israel than it did in the case of South Africa.

---

* *Editor's note:* See Glossary ("Settlement," "Outpost").

[10] B'Tselem, *Land Grab: Israel's Settlement Policy in the West Bank* (May 2002), p. 133.

South Africa. The apartheid regime was careful to ensure that it did not undertake any legal obligation requiring it to prohibit racial discrimination or political repression. The Charter of the United Nations, adopted before the advent of apartheid in 1948, requires member states to promote human rights without discrimination[11] and is committed to the principle of self-determination of peoples.[12] However, Article 2(7) of the Charter provides that "nothing contained in the present Charter shall authorize the United Nations to intervene in matters which are essentially within the domestic jurisdiction of any state," and this was generally accepted until the early 1960s as preventing any interference by the United Nations in a state's internal affairs. In 1948, the General Assembly of the United Nations adopted the Universal Declaration of Human Rights, but South Africa was one of eight states that abstained from voting for this non-binding resolution. This Declaration inspired a host of multilateral human rights conventions binding on states, including the International Convention on the Elimination of All Forms of Racial Discrimination (1965), the International Covenant on Civil and Political Rights (1966), and the Convention against Torture (1984), but South Africa refused to become a party to any of these conventions. It continued to insist that its racial policies were a domestic affair protected from scrutiny by Article 2(7) of the UN Charter, and argued that it was not bound by General Assembly resolutions which it had not supported or by international treaties to which it was not a party. Although South Africa's legal arguments reflected a conservative interpretation of international law, they were undoubtedly tenable interpretations. This was probably the reason why the United Nations preferred to confront apartheid through its political organs and not to have recourse to the International Court of Justice (ICJ) for an advisory opinion on the lawfulness of apartheid. Opposition to apartheid in South Africa was inspired by moral outrage, not law.

---

[11] Article 55.

[12] Articles 1 and 55.

Israel. Most of the charges leveled at Israel today are based on international law. These include the denial of self-determination to the Palestinian people, the seizure of Palestinian land, the construction of the Wall in Palestinian territory, the establishment of a settlement enterprise, racial discrimination, repression, and the violation of rules of international humanitarian law. Whereas South Africa carefully avoided subjecting itself to the rules of international law, Israel is a party to many treaties on human rights and international humanitarian law. To make matters worse for Israel, the obligations contained in these agreements have been confirmed by the International Court of Justice.[13]

The right of self-determination is affirmed by the Charter of the United Nations and proclaimed by the International Covenant on Civil and Political Rights, to both of which treaties Israel is a party. It was held to be applicable to the Palestinian people by the International Court of Justice in the *Wall Opinion,* which found that Israel had unlawfully denied this right to the Palestinian people.[14] The prohibition on the annexation and seizure of land following an armed conflict is a foundational principle of the international order contained in Article 2(4) of the UN Charter.[15] Israel's annexation of East Jerusalem in 1980 violates this prohibition and for this reason has not been recognized by any state, including the United States. The construction of the Wall* has resulted in the seizure of Palestinian land and has been held to be unlawful by the International Court of Justice.[16] The establishment of settlements in the OPT has been found by

---

[13] International Court of Justice, *Legal Consequences of the Construction of a Wall in the Occupied Palestinian Territory* (advisory opinion of 9 July 2004).

[14] ICJ, *Legal Consequences,* para. 149.

[15] The 1970 Declaration on Principles of International Law Concerning Friendly Relations and Co-operation Among States in Accordance with the Charter of the United Nations, Resolution 2625 (XXV), makes it clear that, "No territorial acquisitions resulting from the threat or use of force shall be recognized as legal."

* *Editor's note:* See Glossary.

[16] ICJ, *Legal Consequences,* paras. 121, 163.

the International Court of Justice to violate Article 49(6) of the Fourth Geneva Convention, which prohibits an occupying power from transferring part of its own civilian population into the territory it occupies. (Israel became a party to the Geneva Conventions in 1951.) In December 2016, the Security Council reaffirmed that the establishment of settlements by Israel in the OPT "has no legal validity and constitutes a flagrant violation under international law."[17]

Israel is a party to the International Convention on the Elimination of All Forms of Racial Discrimination. The body responsible for monitoring compliance with the Convention, the UN Committee on the Elimination of Racial Discrimination, has held that the Convention is applicable to the OPT and has censured Israel for practicing racial discrimination and apartheid in the OPT.[18] Israel is also a party to the International Covenant on Civil and Political Rights, which prohibits torture; inhuman treatment; and restrictions on freedom of movement, speech, and assembly, which the International Court of Justice has held to be applicable in the OPT.[19] There is abundant evidence contained in the reports of the monitoring body of this convention, NGOs, and UN special rapporteurs of the violation of these prohibitions by Israel.

The rules governing the treatment of persons in occupied territory and the conduct of the occupying power in armed conflict are mainly to be found in customary international law and the Geneva Conventions of 1949, which the International Court of Justice has found to be binding on Israel in the OPT.[20] Among the rules which are clearly binding on Israel under the Fourth Geneva Convention are the prohibition of collective punishment, intimidation, and terrorism; the destruction of private property unless absolutely necessary for military operations; attacks on hospitals; and the failure to treat the occupied

---

[17] UN Security Council Resolution 2334 (23 December 2016).

[18] UN Committee on the Elimination of Racial Discrimination, "Concluding Observations: Israel," UN Doc CERD/C/ISR/CO/14-16 (9 March 2012), para. 24.

[19] ICJ, *Legal Consequences*, paras. 102–13.

[20] Ibid., para. 101.

people humanely. Two cardinal principles govern the customary law of armed conflict: the principle of proportionality, which requires parties to an armed conflict to avoid or minimize collateral or excessive damage to civilians; and the principle of distinction, which requires parties to an armed conflict to distinguish between military objectives and the civilian population, to refrain from indiscriminate attacks which fail to make such a distinction, and to avoid targeting civilians. There is evidence of the violation of these prohibitions and principles in Israel's occupation of the OPT contained in the reports of fact-finding missions, human rights NGOs, and UN special rapporteurs. Israel's failure to respect the principles of proportionality and distinction in its bombing of Gaza in 2008–9, 2012, and 2014 was vividly displayed on television screens throughout the world.

The binding force of the rules of international law and the transgression of these rules is undoubtedly clearer in the case of Israel than it was in the case of South Africa. The rules of international law are clearer because Israel is a party to human rights treaties that South Africa was not. And the transgressions are clearer because the past twenty years has witnessed an explosion of official and non-official fact-finding missions and media coverage. The world is a much smaller place than it was twenty years ago and it is impossible today to conceal or cover up the violations of international humanitarian law and human rights law.

The different responses of the international community

The response of the international community to apartheid in South Africa took different forms. The Security Council imposed a mandatory arms embargo on South Africa in 1977[21] and in a 1985 non-binding resolution urged states to suspend all new investments and guaranteed export loans in and to South Africa, prohibit the sale of computer equipment that might be used by the army and police, and restrict cultural and sporting relations.[22] Starting in

[21] UN Security Council Resolution 418 (1977).

[22] UN Security Council Resolution 569 (1985).

1962,[23] the General Assembly called on states to break off diplomatic ties with South Africa; boycott all South African goods; impose an arms embargo on South Africa; refuse landing and passage facilities to South African aircraft; and suspend all cultural, educational and sporting exchanges with South Africa. The Organization of African Unity, the Commonwealth, and the European Community imposed different sanctions on South Africa, while individual states enacted legislation to prohibit trade. Many withdrew or refrained from entering into diplomatic relations with South Africa. In 1986, the US Congress passed the Comprehensive Anti-Apartheid Act, which imposed limited economic sanctions on South Africa and suspended the landing rights of South African Airways on US territory. Cultural and sporting associations and foreign universities ended all contacts with South Africa. South Africa was forced to withdraw from the Commonwealth and several UN specialized agencies[24] and was expelled from others.[25] South Africa's credentials were rejected by the General Assembly and it was prohibited from participating in the work of that body.

Israel's violations of international law are clearer and more serious than those of South Africa. But the international response has been minimal. The UN Security Council, in a non-binding resolution, has declared the annexation of East Jerusalem to be illegal,[26] but sanctions of the kind imposed on Russia for its annexation of the Crimea have not followed. The Security Council has likewise declared settlements to be illegal[27] but taken no action to sanction this illegality. The General Assembly and Human Rights Council have repeatedly condemned Israel for violating human rights in many fields, but these resolutions have had little impact as they have not been endorsed by the Security

[23] UN General Assembly Resolutions 1761 (XVII) (6 November 1962), 39/72 (13 December 1984).

[24] Such as the FAO, UNESCO, ILO, WHO, ITU, WIPO, and ICAO.

[25] Universal Postal Union (UPU).

[26] UN Security Council Resolution 478 (1980).

[27] UN Security Council Resolutions 446 (1979), 452 (1979), 465 (1980), 2334 (2016).

Council. Israel is secure in the knowledge that the United States will prevent any such endorsement.

For most states it is business as usual. Israel maintains trade, financial, diplomatic, sporting, cultural, and academic relations with most countries. The campaign for boycott, divestment, and sanctions (BDS)* against Israel, which is modeled on the South African Anti-Apartheid Movement, is, unlike its South African predecessor, subject to threats of criminalization in the United States, France, the UK, and Canada.

Why is it that Israel's illegal actions have met with so little response? What explains the silence and indifference of states, particularly of the West, that claim to be concerned about human rights and the rule of law? What induces such states to acquiesce in Israeli crimes, permitting Israel to violate international law with impunity while insisting that other states respect international law?

The value of the apartheid analogy

Israel and its apologists are determined to present a picture of occupied Palestine that betrays no hint of deliberate systematic oppression. The occupation is portrayed as a normal and legal consequence of armed conflict. The argument that Israel has established an institutionalized policy of racism in which Jews systematically oppress Palestinians, akin to apartheid as applied in South Africa, is condemned as heresy because it debunks the notion of Israel as a moral exemplar: the "only democracy in the Middle East." To accept Israel's occupation as apartheid is to accept that Israel's democracy is premised on the exclusion and brutal domination of the Palestinian people within the borders it controls with permanent intent. This explains the vehemence of the opposition to the apartheid analogy and its depiction as an extreme display of antisemitism.

Whereas Israel portrays its rule in the OPT as a temporary military regime aimed at maintaining order in anticipation of a settlement, the apartheid analogy reveals the occupation as a carefully calculated, permanent policy of racist

* *Editor's note:* See Glossary.

oppression. And whereas even Israel's most devoted publicists will concede that Israel has committed occasional legal violations in the course of maintaining security, the apartheid analogy focuses attention on the moral repugnance of the regime itself, as an exercise in discrimination and repression. To portray the regime in the OPT as apartheid is to draw attention to features of the regime that conjure up memories of apartheid in South Africa, and to remind the international community of the opprobrium that it attached to this infamous policy.

Opinion polls in many Western countries reveal a growing awareness of the true nature of Israel's regime in the OPT on the part of the general public and of opposition to this regime. The governments of most Western states, however, remain committed to support for Israel and to a firm rejection of the apartheid analogy.

Israel succeeds in securing such continued support by means of a combination of factors that weigh more heavily with politicians and legislators than with ordinary citizens. The principal instruments employed to maintain this support are pro-Israel lobbies, Holocaust guilt, and the labeling of those who oppose Israel as antisemites. If, however, Israel's regime in the OPT is seen to be a form of apartheid, all these pillars of support for Israel will be threatened. Powerful lobbies in the United States, such as AIPAC, will find difficulty in promoting a system of racist oppression that evokes memories of America's own racist past, and which contradicts the proud history of the Civil Rights Movement in which so many Jewish Americans participated. Holocaust guilt will likewise lose its currency with European decision-makers when balanced against more recent memories of racism in South Africa. The label of antisemitism is a powerful weapon in the hands of Israel and its apologists. Public figures can be—and have been—destroyed by it. But the label of racism is also powerful. It alone can hope to neutralize that of antisemitism.

The time has come to see Israel's policies and practices in the OPT as apartheid, and for the international community to invoke measures to eradicate this scourge along the lines employed against apartheid in South Africa. A common offense demands a common response.

RESPONSE:

"KIBBUSH" IS BAD ENOUGH

Alon Liel

I am not a legal expert nor a human rights activist. If I have a profession, it is that of "diplomat"—although many would question whether diplomacy is really a profession. However, this task of mine brought me many times to South Africa during and after the era of apartheid, and enabled me to see and hear a lot about its conduct and wrongdoings.

It also happens that I was born in Israel shortly after the state was established. I studied here at school and university, fought as a soldier and officer, was badly wounded in battle, and, at a later stage, fought Israel's diplomatic battles for three decades.

I am probably one of the few Israelis who worked with all four leaders—Nelson Mandela, F. W. De Klerk, Benjamin Netanyahu, and

---

Alon Liel, a peace activist, served as Israel's Ambassador to South Africa (1992–1994) and Director General of Israel's Ministry of Foreign Affairs (2000–2001).

Mahmoud Abbas—spending hours in conversation with them at different periods of time.

I come to the topic in question against the backdrop of this first-hand experience. My personal conclusion is quite well known. Israel within its legitimate 1967 borders is not an apartheid state. The occupation of the West Bank, however, with the realities it created on the ground and its two separate legal systems—one for Israelis and one for Palestinians—merits the apartheid designation. Responsibility for this apartheid regime in the West Bank rests with the State of Israel. For expressing this conclusion, I have paid a heavy price here in Israel, where many people revile me for speaking out at home and, especially, abroad. I am proud and willing to pay this price for my own truth and, hopefully, for the future benefit of the country I love so much.

My personal position, however, is of no importance. It is a fact that the international community, generally speaking, refrains from accusing Israel of being an apartheid regime, or even of overseeing an apartheid system in the West Bank. The reasons are myriad, starting with Israel's strength and international influence, its special relationship with the United States, and the overall deterioration in the Middle East, with its regional and especially European implications. The upshot is, Israel has won the public relations battle regarding its identification as a new apartheid.

All the above does not detract from the magnitude of Israel's wrongdoing. Israel is operating a cruel and devious West Bank occupation, called in Hebrew "*Kibbush*" (a term that most Israelis avoid like the plague). This *Kibbush* is no less abusive or punitive than South Africa's apartheid, although it is different in its character and motives. The exact label—whether Hebrew, English, or Afrikaans—is less important than what it amounts to and involves in practice. Whether defined as "apartheid" or not, the Israeli occupation is bad enough, and must be fought against on the diplomatic battlefield.

UN Security Council Resolution 2334 (December 2016) shows how to go about confronting the West Bank occupation. The resolution is clear, detailed, and scathing, and comes down unambiguously against Israel's occupation. It has massive global support, with fourteen of the fifteen UN Security Council members having voted in favor and the United States, while abstaining, having expressed its unequivocal support for the content. The pressing task now is to implement it. A coherent, determined implementation of UNSC 2334 can gradually bring the occupation—*Kibbush*—to its end.

Prime Minister Netanyahu claims that Israel's international standing is improving. He is correct with respect to bilateral relations only. Governments pursue their own perceived interests, and these often lead them to a close association with Israel. Netanyahu is wrong, however, when it comes to large international organizations. Individual countries behave (and vote) differently in an organization with 200 members than during private tête-à-têtes with Israel.

This is an important distinction. One should bear in mind that it was the United Nations that paved the way, during the 1970s and 1980s, for toppling South African apartheid. The end of the apartheid regime was finally brought about by governments—especially through the European sanctions of summer 1986—but this would not have happened without the anti-apartheid consensus built up over decades in the UN.

These are dark times for those who would like to see a negotiated resolution of the Israel-Palestine conflict. Supporters of the two-state solution must unite behind and demand the implementation of UNSC Resolution 2334, which opposes the occupation (*Kibbush*) and Israeli settlements and calls for action to these ends. International action is what we need at this stage.

RESPONSE:

POLITICAL RESOLVE IS IN SHORT SUPPLY, NOT DEFINITIONS

Hagai El-Ad

John Dugard writes that, "Whereas Israel portrays its rule in the OPT as a temporary military regime trying to maintain order in anticipation of a settlement, the apartheid analogy reveals the occupation as a carefully calculated, permanent policy of racist oppression." I believe that Israel's representation of its policies as temporary, lawful, or both has already been thoroughly debunked and can be authoritatively refuted with or without resorting to the apartheid analogy. Unfortunately, the main obstacle to ending the occupation is not one of semantics or finding the appropriate historical analogy.

In February 2017, a front-page headline reported a seemingly startling warning from Israeli President Reuven Rivlin. A law just passed by Israel's

---

Hagai El-Ad is Executive Director of B'Tselem, The Israeli Information Center for Human Rights in the Occupied Territories.

parliament would, he said, "make us look like an apartheid state."[1] Rivlin was referring to the Regulation Law, the gist of which is easy to summarize: the theft of duly registered, privately-owned Palestinian land was made legal, provided the thieves are Israeli.

One cannot but agree with the president's sentiments: organized theft by one class of people of land owned by another class of people—that would certainly affect what reality "looks like." And this may be a problem for Israel in a world primarily concerned with appearances.

But what of the good old days, before the Orwellian-named law was passed? What did reality "look like" in those bygone days—say, January 2017—before land theft became enshrined in law?

Well, it appears that land theft was already the law of the land. Indeed, for the forty-nine and a half years before the new legislation was passed, Israel systematically, in broad daylight, and with the High Court's tacit or explicit approval grabbed Palestinian land for the exclusive benefit of its citizens. Did that not make Israel "look like" something? Who knew that the difference between business-as-usual and apartheid, between the acceptable and the repugnant, between silence and a front-page headline, consisted simply in adding a dash of private Palestinian property to the ocean of so-called "state land" already seized?

The reality of Israel's rule over Palestinians is appalling, and has been for quite some time. Since 1967, its key elements have been oppression, dispossession, and organized state violence. Use of the apartheid analogy to describe or arouse opposition to this regime is far from new. As far back as 2002, a B'Tselem report (in fact quoted by Dugard) stated that Israel's rule in the OPT "is reminiscent of distasteful regimes from the past, such as the apartheid regime in South Africa."[2]

---

[1] Yossi Verter, "Israel's President on Land-Grab Law: We Will Look Like an Apartheid State," *Haaretz* (12 February 2017).

[2] B'Tselem, *Land Grab: Israel's Settlement Policy in the West Bank* (May 2002).

The fact that this reality was masked for decades by a paper-thin veneer of legality did not fool those who looked honestly—or who had the misfortune to live at its sharp end. Israel's policies were as unmistakable as the "facts on the ground" established day in and day out by Israeli governments of the left, right, and center. These policies and their implications have long been thoroughly documented, analyzed, and exposed in the work of human rights groups and other stakeholders.

In short, the fight against the occupation does not lack for legal analysis, historical memory, factual accuracy, or even an unflinching depiction of reality in all its ugliness, bureaucratic minutiae, cynicism, violence, and whitewash. We have all had plenty of that.

What is missing is something else. What is missing, in Israel and internationally, is *resolve*: the determination to take decisive political action. As long as the world persists in accepting—and in fact supporting—the continuation of this well-known and well-defined reality, there is little hope for a nonviolent way out. Israelis have grown used to living quite complacently with what things "look like," and even with how things "are," but they are not the only ones; the world has also grown accustomed to this ever-so-slightly changing status quo, where today and tomorrow are basically no different than yesterday, with just a bit more of more of the same.

Consequently, the urgency confronting us is not semantic. It is about demanding action instead of mere lip service—and about enabling the resolve for political action to finally materialize. This urgency is what has led B'Tselem to make a paradigm shift toward fostering a human rights-based demand to end a regime that is in itself the problem. One does not need new terminology to reach this conclusion: all that is needed is a grasp on reality and a basic sense of decency. Reaching this conclusion, after half a century of occupation, is grounded in the very commitment—moral and professional—to the realization of human rights.

The practical implications of this paradigm shift are expressed in B'Tselem's advocacy of a redefinition of the fight for human rights in the OPT. It is both practically impossible as well as morally self-defeating to try and rectify a system that is so evidently structured to successfully sustain and whitewash endless human rights violations. Therefore, if one is to credibly hope for a different outcome, the human rights struggle must strive to end the occupation. B'Tselem has adopted this route by disengaging from self-serving Israeli mechanisms such as the military law enforcement system. B'Tselem has also come to a realization as to the means that may help bring about an end to the occupation. After half a century of living with this reality, Israelis are unlikely to be shamed out of it. But they may be moved to reconsider their choices if the world were to stop letting Israel have it both ways: to be treated as a first-world democracy, while persisting in treating Palestinians as third-class (non-) citizens.

How likely are we to see such political resolve finally emerge? Even in the uncertain times we live in, it seems safe to bet that the theme of this book will still need to be revisited. But facts do still matter, and they cannot be disregarded forever. For the thirteen million people living under one form or another of Israeli control on the small bit of land between the Jordan River and the Mediterranean Sea, there are many possible political futures. But only a future based on freedom, equality, and human rights can achieve justice, stability, and healing. That is a future worth fighting for.

RESPONSE:

THE APARTHEID ANALOGY AND POLITICAL STRATEGY

Ran Greenstein

John Dugard makes a convincing case that Israeli policies of discrimination, repression, and territorial fragmentation in the OPT meet the legal definition of apartheid. He goes on to argue that the apartheid analogy "reveals the occupation as a carefully calculated, permanent policy of racist oppression," and that it "focuses attention on the moral repugnance of the regime." Conjuring up memories of apartheid in South Africa should help undermine support for Israel and enhance solidarity with the Palestinian cause, based on moral considerations.

Ran Greenstein is Associate Professor of Sociology at the University of the Witwatersrand, South Africa. He is the author of, inter alia, *Genealogies of Conflict: Class, Identity and State in Palestine/Israel and South Africa* (1995) and *Zionism and its Discontents: A Century of Radical Dissent in Israel/Palestine* (2014).

Dugard is right, in my view. And yet, there are gaps in his analysis on which I wish to focus. These concern the sociological and political implications of the apartheid analogy and their consequences for activism and solidarity.

Sociologically, the apartheid analogy obscures a crucial dimension of the South African apartheid system: the role of labor. The apartheid regime and its predecessors relied heavily on exploiting black labor for the prosperity of white companies and households. Without black labor, the white-dominated economy would have collapsed. This gave black workers leverage to extract political concessions. The regime resorted to repression to prevent black workers organizing, but repression led to lower productivity, rising costs, and a bloated and inefficient state that ultimately harmed white welfare.[1] The road to negotiations and change was thus opened, leading ultimately to the demise of the apartheid system, which had become an economic burden rather than an asset (for whites).

This is not the case in Israel-Palestine, where the economic imperative of creating jobs for Jewish immigrants has made the employment of Arab workers an obstacle to the realization of Zionist goals. Although Palestinian labor was used by Israeli employers after 1967 (mostly in agriculture and construction), it was always marginal to Jewish prosperity. With the first intifada of the late 1980s, Russian Jewish immigration, and the globalization of Israel's labor supply it declined even further in importance for the Israeli economy.

This means Palestinian workers are dispensable and do not have the leverage that their black South African counterparts deployed successfully from the 1970s onwards to undermine the system from within. The apartheid analogy, with its focus on political mechanisms of domination, is unable to identify this key social difference between the two situations.[2]

Politically, this difference explains why organized workers and trade unions played a leading role in the anti-apartheid struggle inside the country,

---

[1] Stanley Greenberg, *Legitimating the Illegitimate: State, Markets and Resistance in South Africa* (Berkeley, CA: University of California Press, 1987).

[2] Ran Greenstein, "Israel, the Apartheid Analogy, and the Labor Question," in Jon Soske and Sean Jacobs eds., *Apartheid Israel: The Politics of an Analogy* (Chicago, IL: Haymarket Books, 2015), pp. 27–42.

while they have been marginal to the Palestinian struggle, which is waged from a position external to the system it seeks to undo. The Anti-Apartheid Movement operated in factories, streets, townships, schools, and communities located in South Africa itself, making the country ungovernable. Palestinians face much greater difficulties due to their exclusion from Israeli political, social, and economic institutions.

The result is a deflection of Palestinian resistance efforts to solidarity campaigns overseas, particularly the BDS Movement. In South Africa, such efforts were supplementary to the struggle by South African activists and masses within the country and in exile. In the Palestinian case, solidarity has replaced internal mass action to become the central feature of the campaign. This is an anomaly, and the apartheid analogy does not help us correct it.

By no means does the above challenge Dugard's legal analysis and moral call for global solidarity. Both are necessary but insufficient components of the struggle against the occupation. The question facing Palestinians and solidarity activists is, how can we build on these useful aspects of the apartheid analogy to develop an effective political strategy?[3]

A good place to start is with the anti-apartheid resistance movement inside South Africa. It was based on three principles: forging unity by creating broad fronts and alliances; putting pressure on the regime internally to expose its weaknesses and mobilize the masses against it; and combining different modes of action, including marches, strikes, boycotts, defiance campaigns, overseas solidarity, diplomacy, and armed struggle.[4] Making effective use of the apartheid analogy means borrowing elements of this strategy in the struggle against the occupation and for Palestinian rights:

- To counter the Israeli strategy of fragmentation, unity requires placing the struggle against the occupation above factional squabbles between Fatah

[3] Discussions of various aspects of the analogy can be found in Ilan Pappé ed., *Israel and South Africa: The Many Faces of Apartheid* (London: Zed Books, 2015).

[4] A useful overview of the internal mass movement is Jeremy Seekings, *The UDF: A History of the United Democratic Front in South Africa, 1983–1991* (Cape Town: David Philip, 2000).

and Hamas, developing a plan to mobilize popular forces on the basis of a shared platform of resistance, and coordinating efforts with Palestinians in the diaspora and inside the Green Line.* All these constituencies face similar challenges but operate under different circumstances; unity of purpose in diversity of conditions is the key. Alliances with Israeli forces—not just the usual liberal-left opposition but also marginalized Jews (Mizrahim in particular)—is another component of this approach, though more difficult to achieve.

- To undermine the occupation regime, its weak spots must be targeted. The coordination between the Palestinian Authority and Israeli security forces is crucial to the regime's survival and therefore a prime target for a non-collaboration campaign. The sale of Israeli products to a captive market, which helps make the occupation profitable, is a promising target for a boycott. Identifying more such vulnerabilities will enhance an anti-occupation movement from within.
- Utilizing diplomacy and solidarity in the service of the internal movement, in line with its priorities rather than goals determined from without, would enable better coordination and prospects for progress. The current situation, in which official and civil society forces operate in a disparate manner, frequently at cross purposes, undermines chances for success.

Of course, to become sustainable this anti-apartheid strategy will require dedication, discipline, and willingness to sacrifice. Outsiders may provide advice, but the burden—and therefore the responsibility for choosing the course of action—will be carried by local people and organizations. The apartheid analogy will be useful insofar as it provides them with a set of viable options for analysis, reflection, and action.

---

* *Editor's note:* The "Green Line" refers to the pre-June 1967 armistice boundary established in 1949, now recognized by the International Court of Justice as the legal border of the State of Israel.

RESPONSE:

ISRAEL HAS NOTHING IN COMMON WITH APARTHEID

Robbie Sabel

The word "apartheid" is, rightfully, regarded as synonymous with racism and malevolence. As part of a campaign to delegitimize Israel, there is a clear attempt to smear it with this moral taint.[1] Under apartheid, black South Africans were denied the vote. They were required by law to live, work, study, travel, enjoy leisure activities, receive medical treatment, and even go to the

---

Robbie Sabel is Professor of International Law at the Hebrew University of Jerusalem. He is a member of the Permanent Court of International Arbitration at The Hague and the former Legal Advisor to Israel's Ministry of Foreign Affairs. Among his publications is *Procedure at International Conferences* (2006–second edition; third edition forthcoming, 2018).

[1] See, for instance, Daryl J. Glaser, "Zionism and Apartheid: A Moral Comparison," *Ethnic and Racial Studies* 26.3 (May 2003), pp. 403–21; "US Professor on How Zionism and Apartheid are Alike," *ArabicNews.com* (9 June 2006).

lavatory separately from those with a different color of skin. Interracial relationships and marriages were illegal.[2]

One has only to walk the streets of Israel to perceive the multi-racial and multi-colored nature of its population. Incitement to racism is a criminal offense in Israel.[3] Israel has an Arab minority of some 20 percent. They undoubtedly have the problems of being a minority, yet Arabic is an official language of Israel; Arabs can vote; and there are Arab political parties, Arab members of parliament, Arab judges (including an Arab Supreme Court judge), senior Arab police officers, Arab diplomats representing Israel abroad, Arab political leaders (including an Arab Cabinet member), and Arab academics (including the Dean of the Law Faculty of the Hebrew University of Jerusalem).[4] Although Arabs are not subject to military conscription, they may volunteer for military service, some reaching the rank of general.[5] Apartheid, this is not.

Most of Israel's critics are aware that the stain of apartheid clearly does not apply to Israel, but try and apply it to Israel's policies in the Administered Territory of the West Bank.

There is undoubtedly very little, if any, international support for Israel's position as to the status of the West Bank and Gaza. Nevertheless, Israel's

---

[2] Prohibition of Mixed Marriages Act, Act No 55 (1949); South African Immorality Amendment Act, Act No 21 (1950; amended in 1957 (Act 23)); South African Group Areas Act, Act No 41 (1950); South African Bantu Building Workers Act, Act No 27 (1951); South African Separate Representation of Voters Act, Act No 46 (1951; as amended in 1956); South African Natives (Abolition of Passes and Co-ordination of Documents) Act, Act No 67 (1952); South African Native Labour (Settlement of Disputes) Act (1953); South African Bantu Education Act, Act No 47 (1953); South African Extension of University Education Act, Act No 45 (1959); South African Reservation of Separate Amenities Act, Act No 49 (1953).

[3] Section 144B of the Penal Law provides for a penalty of up to five years' imprisonment for "a person who publishes material with the intent to incite racism, even if ineffectual in result."

[4] The present author teaches at the faculty.

[5] Except for the Arab Druze population, Arabs are exempt from compulsory army service. They can and some do volunteer to serve in the army, notably the Bedouin Arabs.

legal argumentation is not specious and deserves greater attention than it has received. The gist of the Israeli argument is that it is doubtful whether the West Bank and Gaza are occupied territories of other states. The argument is based on the fact that, although the Hashemite Kingdom of Jordan occupied the West Bank from 1949 until 1967, there were doubts even then as to the legal sovereignty of Jordan over the area. These doubts were settled in 1988 when Jordan officially relinquished claims to the West Bank.[6] Likewise, Gaza was occupied by Egypt from 1949 to 1967 but Egypt never claimed sovereignty there. Gaza and the West Bank may well form part of an independent Palestinian State in the future, but it is highly debatable whether Palestine today fulfils the criterion of the Montevideo definition of a state[7] while nobody knows what the boundaries of Palestine are or will be. Meanwhile, Israel and the Palestine Liberation Organization are parties to the Oslo Accord,[8] which prohibits the Palestinian Authority from conducting foreign relations, prohibits unilateral changes to the status of the territories, and stipulates that future status issues, explicitly including settlements and borders, are to be determined by Israeli-Palestinian negotiations.

Despite doubts as to the status of the West Bank, Israel grants the local population all the rights and privileges of protected persons in occupied territory, within the definition of the 1907 Hague Regulations Respecting the Law and Customs of War and the Fourth Geneva Convention of 1949.[9] The Israeli Supreme Court, sitting as a High Court of Justice (HCJ), enforces these

---

[6] Speech of King Hussein of Jordan (31 July 1988).

[7] See Malcolm N. Shaw, *International Law*, seventh edition (Cambridge: Cambridge University Press, 2014), p. 144.

[8] "Declaration of Principles on Interim Self-Government Arrangements" (1993).

[9] Hague Regulations Respecting the Law and Customs of War (18 October 1907); Convention (IV) relative to the Protection of Civilian Persons in Time of War (Geneva, 12 August 1949).

rights.[10] The rights of "protected persons" include the rule that existing laws must remain in force and that the occupier is not permitted to apply its own laws or to impose new taxes.[11] This Israeli commitment to treat the local population as "protected persons" in a situation where sovereignty is disputed could serve as a useful international precedent, although little international attention has been paid to this legal aspect.

The accusation of apartheid in the territories appears to be based on two claims. The first is that Israel applies different laws to the Israeli settlers and to the local population. The second is that there are roads that the local population cannot use. As to the first accusation, Israel is damned if it does and damned if it doesn't. If Israel were to apply Israeli law to the local population it would be considered annexation and, no doubt, Israel would be castigated for such an act. If Israel were to apply local laws to Israeli citizens in the West Bank, it would lead to an absurd situation whereby these Israeli citizens would be exempt from paying Israeli income tax, exempt from Israeli army service, and subject to Jordanian law regarding their family and personal status. There are two legal systems but, again, this is not apartheid.

As to the road situation. Palestinians in the West Bank undoubtedly experience hardships as a result of Israeli actions to combat terrorism. These actions include restrictions on road use, the security barrier, checkpoints, and control of access into Israel. However, these procedures and structures are in place to thwart potential terrorist actions against Israeli vehicles, not to segregate. Ninety percent of the Palestinians in the West Bank are under the jurisdiction of the Palestinian Authority, in which there is a road system without any restrictions. In Israeli-controlled sections of the West Bank, Palestinian traffic on roads that lead to crossings into Israel or to Israeli settlements may be restricted

---

[10] See, for example, HCJ 337/71, *Christian Society for the Holy Places v. Minister of Defense* (1971) [Hebrew]; HCJ 256/72, *Electricity Company for Jerusalem District v. Minister of Defense et al.* (1972) [Hebrew]; HCJ 3239/02, *Iad Ashak Mahmoud Marab et al. v. The Commander of the IDF Forces in the West Bank* (2003) [Hebrew].

[11] Hague Regulations (1907), Articles 48–51.

because of potential terrorist attacks from Palestinian cars on Israeli civilian vehicles. The UN regards an act as terrorist if directed "against civilians"[12] for political ends "committed… for whatever purposes."[13] There were no restrictions on Palestinian use of roads until the wave of terrorist attacks began. The restrictions are a temporary security measure and not a policy decision. For the same security reasons, the passage of Israeli motor vehicles on some roads that lead to Arab villages is restricted, and, on those roads, there are no restrictions on Palestinian vehicles.

Professor Dugard claims that Gaza is under Israeli occupation. Israel maintains a naval blockade in an attempt to prevent arms shipments from entering Gaza; this, however, does not constitute "occupation." Occupation requires effective control by the occupier including "boots on the ground." The classic definition of occupation requires that the occupier "actually establish an administration over a territory."[14] The International Court of Justice ruled that "territory is considered occupied when it is actually placed under the authority of the hostile army, and the occupation extends only to the territory where such authority has been established and can be exercised."[15] There are no Israeli troops or Israeli civilians in Gaza. Hamas runs Gaza with its own heavily armed militias; applies Hamas law (*Sharia*); has its own taxation, court system, police, and jails; and even applies the death penalty (Israel has no death penalty). Hamas has a border with Egypt along which there is no Israeli presence whatsoever. Dugard claims that Gaza "may be seen as a Bantustan-like entity controlled by Israel." I think it strange to claim that Israel appointed and controls the Muslim Brotherhood regime of Hamas in Gaza.

---

[12] International Convention for the Suppression of the Financing of Terrorism, Article 2 (1)(b), adopted in UN General Assembly Resolution 54/109 (9 December 1999).

[13] UN General Assembly Resolution A/RES/66/282 (12 July 2012).

[14] Lassa Oppenheim, *International Law: A Treatise*, ed. H. Lauterpacht, Vol. II—Disputes, War and Neutrality, seventh edition (London: Longmans, 1952), p. 435.

[15] ICJ, *Armed Activities on the Territory of the Congo (Democratic Republic of the Congo v. Uganda)* (decision of 19 December 2005), para. 173.

In conclusion, describing Israel's policy as apartheid is, I believe, an attempt to render Israel a pariah state, with all that such a definition entails. As every Israeli will tell anyone willing to listen, Israel society is often fractious and cacophonic. Israelis argue among themselves continually and are often abrasive, brash, and sometimes downright rude. However, with all its faults, Israel is a pluralistic, democratic, and open society, with an extremely active and vocal civil community. It has nothing in common with apartheid.

❧

John Dugard

Professor Sabel is right in saying that there is an open and fractious debate in Israel about the real issues facing Israel, as there was among whites in apartheid South Africa. In this respect it is unlike most Western States, in which a frank discussion of the Israel-Palestine conflict is a taboo that might lead to accusations of antisemitism. So it is in this spirit that I welcome our exchange.

A major part of Professor Sabel's response is devoted to two issues that I stated clearly in my introduction I did not intend to examine: discrimination against Palestinians in Israel itself and the status of Gaza. On the first of these issues I made it clear that my article was confined to apartheid in the OPT as I had doubts whether "discrimination in Israel itself reaches the threshold for apartheid set by international law." As to the occupation of Gaza, the international community views Gaza as occupied because Israel effectively controls its land boundaries, sea space, and airspace. In support of my assertion that Gaza remains occupied I cited *The International Law of Belligerent Occupation* by Israel's leading humanitarian lawyer, Professor Yoram Dinstein. I suggest that Professor Sabel study this treatise carefully.

Professor Sabel contests the assertion that the West Bank (including East Jerusalem) is occupied territory within the meaning of the Fourth Geneva Convention of 1949. This matter was considered by the International Court of Justice in its 2004 advisory opinion on the *Legal Consequences for States of the Construction of a Wall in the Occupied Palestinian Territory*, in which the Court held *unanimously*[16] that the OPT has the status of occupied territory in international law.[17] Significantly, Israel failed to present legal arguments on this subject—or indeed any subject—before the International Court of Justice. The fact that South Africa appeared before the International Court of Justice on the six occasions that the Court considered the legal status of South West Africa/Namibia suggests that South Africa was more confident in the correctness of its legal arguments than was Israel.

My principal thesis is that Israel's settlement enterprise in the West Bank and East Jerusalem is contrary to international law and has resulted in an apartheid state in which the Israeli government, in order to protect and promote the interests of more than 600,000 Jewish settlers, discriminates against and represses the local Palestinian population.

That the settlement enterprise is illegal is clear. This illegality was affirmed by the Security Council of the United Nations in Resolution 2334 of December 2016. The International Court of Justice has likewise *unanimously* affirmed this.[18] That the law and practice of the Israeli occupation constitutes discrimination and repression is likewise clear.

Israel discriminates against Palestinians in respect of freedom of movement. Separate roads are only part of these restrictions. In 2015, there were eighty-five checkpoints in the OPT of which only nine were on the Green Line.[19] Palestinians are humiliated and intimidated at checkpoints in the same manner that blacks in South Africa were humiliated by the notorious

[16] Dissenting Judge Buergenthal agreed with the Court on this subject. See "Declaration by Judge Buergenthal," para. 2.

[17] ICJ, *Legal Consequences*, para. 101.

[18] Ibid., para. 120 (Judge Buergenthal concurring on this subject).

[19] UN Human Rights Council, "Human Rights Situation in the Occupied Palestinian Territory, including East Jerusalem—Report of the Secretary-General," A/HRC/31/44 (20 January 2016), para. 33.

"pass laws." Only Israelis and tourists may enter the "seam zone" between the illegal Wall and the Green Line without permits, which has led to great suffering by residents in the seam zone and farmers whose lands lie in the seam zone. (Professor Sabel's claim that the Wall is a security wall is difficult to reconcile with the fact that only 70 per cent of the Wall has been completed after thirteen years. Rather, it is a wall designed to protect settlements and seize land.) There is discrimination in the destruction of houses, in the administration of justice, and the allocation of water. (400,000 settlers in the West Bank consume approximately six times the amount of water used by 2.6 million Palestinians.)

Israel likewise represses the Palestinian people by means of frequent military incursions, administrative detention, torture, targeted killings, and assassinations.

Professor Sabel portrays the fact that different laws apply to settlers and to Palestinians as practical and harmless. The trouble is that Israeli law, which applies to settlers, confers privileges and advantages on Jewish settlers that are denied to Palestinians. It results in a separate but unequal system. Settlers are free to travel through the West Bank. They are not subject to checkpoints; they are not required to obtain and present a permit to enter the "seam zone"; they are free to drive on the good roads. Settlers are not denied building permits and their houses are not demolished; they are not tried by unfair military courts but are instead tried by fair Israeli courts; they are not denied a reasonable allocation of water. Only Palestinians are subjected to these discriminatory measures in terms of military decrees applicable to Palestinians. It is this dual legal system that provides evidence of institutionalized racism and shows that Israel is determined to secure the domination of settlers—Israeli Jews—over Palestinians.

Israel's discriminatory and repressive policies and practices not only resemble those of apartheid in South Africa, but meet the definition of apartheid in the 1973 Convention on the Suppression and Punishment of the Crime of Apartheid and the Rome Statute in that they constitute "inhumane acts" committed "for the purpose of establishing and maintaining domination by one racial group over any other group of persons and systematically oppressing them."[20]

ᘓᘏ

Robbie Sabel

In a historically tragic move the Arab population of the West Bank and Gaza, unlike the Jewish population, refrained in 1948 from declaring independence and at the instigation of the Arab states refused to recognize any right to self-determination of the Jewish population. Unhappily, certain Palestinian elements still refuse to recognize the Jewish right of self-determination and we continue to see such declarations as: "Jerusalem and all of Palestine—from the [Jordan] River to the Sea—are the land of the Palestinian people, and their history is its history . . . Jerusalem is Palestinian Arab. It belongs only to the followers of Islam and Christianity, and not Judaism";[21] "Palestine is an Islamic *Waqf* land consecrated for Moslem generations until Judgement Day"; "There is no solution for the Palestinian question except through *Jihad*. Israel will exist and will continue to exist until Islam will obliterate it."[22] This is the core of the dispute. It is vastly different from the South African situation.

In the area of Israel, Jews constitute 80 percent of the population. In the West Bank, Arabs are 90 percent of the population. The issue both people have to decide is what will be the border between them. Once a border is agreed it will solve the settlement issue. It is a political problem that can only be resolved through the difficult process of negotiations. Israel grants full Israeli citizenship to its Arab minority and prohibits by law any racial discrimination. I can only hope that a future Palestinian state will extend to Jews the same terms.

In the limited space available, I would like to respond to some of the allegations in the response of Professor Dugard. Israelis in Israel and in settlements do

---

[20] Convention on the Suppression and Punishment of the Crime of Apartheid (1973), Article 2.

[21] Official Palestinian Authority daily *Al-Hayat Al-Jadida* (30 January 2017).

[22] The Covenant of the Islamic Resistance Movement [Hamas] (18 August 1988).

indeed use more water than the Arabs in the West Bank. The water for settlements comes from Israeli sources and not from local wells or springs, and is paid for by the settlers. Most of Israel's drinking water is supplied by desalination. The restrictions on drilling new wells are to ensure the sustainability of the water table; these restrictions apply indiscriminately. Torture is illegal and there are no targeted killings or assassinations. I addressed in my initial response the application of different legal systems. As to the claim that Gaza is under Israel occupation, Dugard maintains that Israel controls Gaza's land borders and quotes in support a 2009 book by Yoram Dinstein. Dugard fails, however, to make any reference to the fact that Gaza has a border with Egypt with no Israeli control or presence, or to conflicting academic views such as that of Professor Nicholas Rostow, who writes, in a volume edited by the same Professor Dinstein, that "it is difficult to conclude that Israel remains a belligerent occupant in the Gaza Strip."[23]

Dugard states that frank discussion of the Israel-Palestine conflict might lead to accusations of antisemitism. Undoubtedly Dugard himself is not antisemitic but many antisemites do disguise their hatred of Judaism by cloaking it in anti-Israeli language. The definition of antisemitism adopted by the European Parliament Working Group on Antisemitism is instructive in this regard:

> Examples of the ways in which anti-Semitism manifests itself with regard to the state of Israel taking into account the overall context could include: Denying the Jewish people their right to self-determination, e.g., by claiming that the existence of a State of Israel is a racist endeavor.[24]

In regard to the separation barrier. The barrier is of the same design as the fences on Israel's borders with Jordan and Egypt. Most of it is a fence, not "a Wall," and it has proven to be highly effective in preventing suicide

[23] Nicholas Rostow, "Gaza, Iraq, Lebanon: Three Occupations under International Law," in Fania Domb and Yoram Dinstein eds., *Progression of International Law: Four Decades of the Israel Yearbook on Human Rights: An Anniversary Volume* (Leiden: Brill, 2011), p. 409.

[24] European Parliament Working Group on Antisemitism, "EUMC Working Definition of Antisemitism," *antisem.eu* (n.d.).

bomber vehicles. In the present circumstances, it is not reasonable to demand that Israel have open borders. I think it remiss that Professor Dugard in his article and in his response made no mention whatsoever of the terrorist and security threats facing Israel. During the decades preceding the waves of terrorist activities there was no security fence or restrictions on travel. Dugard places great emphasis on the ICJ advisory opinion on this issue. The Court indeed criticized the route of the barrier but not even by implication did it compare it to the South African situation or use the word apartheid.

As to the claim that the territories are occupied territory of an enemy state, Dugard does not attempt to refute the legal quandary of such a statement. For example, the Jewish population of East Jerusalem had lived there for hundreds of years and were the majority population. They were expelled during the twenty years (1948–1967) of Jordanian control. Returning to their homes is not a racist war crime. Trying to smear Israel with the malicious stain of apartheid is propaganda, but it has no basis in fact or in law. Israel faces real security threats and the steps it has taken are temporary security measures not based on color of people's skin. It bears no resemblance to apartheid.

SECTION III.

INTERNATIONAL

CHAPTER 14.

PALESTINE AND THE ARAB UPHEAVAL: CAN PALESTINE STILL INSPIRE THE ARAB WORLD?

Gilbert Achcar

The year 1988 saw two major events in the Arab world that could be regarded in retrospect as precursors of the Arab upheaval of 2011: the Palestinian intifada, which erupted in December 1987,* and the October 1988 riots that shook Algeria and led to radical political reform. Of the two, the Palestinian intifada had by far the greater regional impact, because of Palestine's centrality to Arab politics and the fact that the intifada lasted much longer than the brief Algerian episode.

Gilbert Achcar is Professor and Chair of the Center for Palestine Studies at SOAS, University of London. His books include *The Arabs and the Holocaust: The Arab-Israeli War of Narratives* (2010), *The People Want: A Radical Exploration of the Arab Uprising* (2013), and, most recently, *Morbid Symptoms: Relapse in the Arab Uprising* (2016).

* *Editor's note:* See Glossary.

In truth, however, neither of these events had any direct influence on the shockwave that spread throughout the Arab-speaking region in 2011, triggered by a desperate young man setting himself on fire in central Tunisia on 17 December 2010. The generation that went into revolt in 2011 was in early childhood or not yet born in 1988. By 2011, the 1988 intifada had been displaced in most memories by the second (or Al-Aqsa) intifada, which began in September 2000 and signaled the collapse of the Oslo peace process (itself an indirect result of the pressure brought by the first intifada).

The transition from the essentially nonviolent uprising of 1988 to the four years of militarized confrontation and brutal Israeli onslaught that started in 2000 and ended in a crushing defeat of Palestinian aspirations foreshadowed the trajectory of the 2011 Arab upheaval. It, too, transformed from a peaceful uprising, dubbed the "Arab Spring," into civil war and ultimate defeat for the aspirations of those who had started the movement. The common factor responsible for these parallel trajectories was the intractability of the incumbent regime: both the Zionist state structure and the Arab regional state system proved immune to alteration by means of nonviolent popular struggle, thus leading to conflagration.

When the "Arab Spring" was at the peak of its euphoric phase in 2011, it was widely noted that the issue of Palestine was barely mentioned by the millions who demonstrated from one end of the Arab-speaking region to the other. Their focus was on democracy and social justice in the Arab countries, not on justice for the Palestinians. The Arab regimes were their immediate enemies, not Israel and not even the United States. Many observers welcomed this as a refreshing departure from the long-established tradition of Arab governments using the Israel-Palestine conflict to divert and diffuse popular discontent. Yet, the near-absence of the Palestinian issue from the 2011 regional uprising—bar one episode of clashes around the Israeli embassy in Cairo—did not signal popular disaffection with Palestine. It was simply a matter of prioritizing the immediate struggle: Palestine had lost its urgency.

The Palestinian struggle against Israeli occupation had reached a nadir in 2011. Hopes for a "two-state solution"* had given way to a deplorable three-state reality as a result of the June 2007 split between the Palestinian Authority (PA) in the West Bank and the Hamas government in Gaza, each presenting a sorry picture. The Palestinians, drained of hope, lacking trust in their leaderships, and stifled by factional divisions, were demoralized. The only foreseeable change to the status quo was a "one-state solution," in the form of an official annexation of the West Bank by Israel after decades of creeping de facto annexation through the construction of settlements. With Palestinian resistance at a low ebb, Palestine remained a source of anger and bitterness in the region, but it was no longer a source of inspiration.

The first post-1967 wave of Palestinian struggle in the form then widely designated the "Palestinian Resistance"—i.e., the armed struggle led by the Palestine Liberation Organization (PLO)—had been an important inspiration for the youth radicalization of the late 1960s and the 1970s, not only in the Arab world but at the global level as well. The 1987 intifada was likewise a major inspiration for regional and global revolt, to the point that the Arabic term "intifada" entered the vocabulary of many languages. Even the Al-Aqsa intifada managed to inspire solidarity movements, incensed by the violence of Israel's repression. Notably, the Kifaya movement in Egypt was born as an outgrowth of Palestine solidarity activism. Given Kifaya's role in preparing the ground for the 2011 uprising against Egyptian President Hosni Mubarak, its pedigree establishes a connection, albeit a tenuous one, between Palestine and the regional upheaval.

In 2011, however, the traditional relationship was reversed: instead of Palestine inspiring the Arab world, many looked for the Arab Spring to inspire the Palestinians—alas, in vain. Even if a broad section of the Palestinians in the West Bank and Gaza resented the PA and Hamas governments, and even if most Palestinians identified with at least the initial phase of the regional uprising, their profound demoralization and fear that Israel might exploit the opportunity of a mass rebellion against Hamas and/or the PA in order to

* *Editor's note:* See Glossary.

further its de facto annexation of the Occupied Territories was enough to dissuade most young Palestinians from joining the regional wave. A few attempts in this direction quickly fizzled out. Thus, Palestine was absent from the Arab Spring two times over: as a mobilizing demand and as a participant.

But this is not to say that the regional upheaval did not affect Palestine. It had a major impact, primarily through its implications for Israel-US relations. The conjunction of the turmoil engulfing almost all Arab countries with the completion of the withdrawal of US forces from Iraq—the outcome of the biggest disaster of US imperial policy since Vietnam, if not the biggest ever, given the strategic stakes—greatly enhanced Israel's strategic value to Washington.

As a rule, Israel's value to the US waxes and wanes inversely to the US's strategic status in the region. It increased tremendously after the US's setback in 1962, when Washington was compelled to evacuate its Dhahran air base in the Saudi kingdom under pressure from Nasser's Egypt, and peaked when the US's capacity to intervene abroad militarily was severely constrained by "Vietnam Syndrome" between 1973 and 1990. Conversely, when the US seized the opportunity afforded by the eclipse of the Soviet Union and Iraq's invasion of Kuwait to stage a massive comeback in the Gulf, Israel's strategic value declined. This provoked intense anxiety in Israel, stirred up by the US demand that Israel refrain from retaliating to the Scud missiles fired on it by Saddam Hussein in an attempt to provoke it into joining the fray. The 1990s were years of "peace process," with Israel under constant pressure to accommodate Washington's efforts to broker a comprehensive Arab-Israeli settlement.

The pendulum swung back again after the United States was hit by the 9/11 attacks. Seizing this opportunity for a massive expansion of US presence and domination in the "Greater Middle East," the George W. Bush administration needed all the force it could mobilize regionally. Israel under Ariel Sharon was given free rein to deploy its full might against the Palestinians. Waging the Afghan war as a prelude to invading Iraq under the banner of the "War on Terror," the Bush administration, ridden with neoconservative friends of the Israeli Likud, granted Israel extensive freedom of action. This only increased when the Iraq adventure turned into a quagmire, considerably weakening the US posture in the Middle East. In summer 2006, the US expected Israel to avenge its loss of ground to Iran in Iraq by dealing a heavy blow to the Iranian-sponsored Hezbollah in Lebanon. Israel failed miserably, but even so, Tehran's growing regional clout emphasized Israel's strategic importance.

By further undermining US regional dominance and destabilizing one of its central pillars (Egypt), the Arab upheaval enhanced Israel's strategic value to Washington still further. This accounted for the unprecedented arrogance displayed by Israeli Prime Minister Benjamin Netanyahu toward President Barack Obama and his administration, and the latter's perhaps unprecedented cowardice in return. Paradoxically enough, this cowardice reached its high-water mark when the Obama administration permitted the UN Security Council to condemn Israel's action over the settlements.[1] Obama held off on this until the very last minute, when the administration had become a "lame duck" and just a few weeks before the inauguration of a new president who promised to outbid all his predecessors in "friendship" with Israel.

These internal, regional, and global trends do not augur well for Palestine. Even so, never write out the Palestinian people! In the hundred years since the Balfour Declaration of 1917, it has shown extraordinary resilience and resistance—what the Palestinians call *sumud*. The people of the West Bank and Gaza have displayed exceptional heroism since coming under occupation fifty years ago. And the popular intifada that they launched thirty years ago, in December 1987, remains to this day one of the most glorious episodes of grassroots mobilization and democratic organization in the history of struggles in the Arab world and globally. Eventually, and probably sooner rather than later, as US-backed Israeli oppression together with oppression by Arab states and their own sclerotic leaderships become ever more intolerable, the Palestinians will take their turn in the long-term revolutionary process that was unleashed in the Arab region in 2011 and which will surely persist with successive upsurges and backlashes for years and decades to come.

[1] UN Security Council Resolution 2334 (23 December 2016).

When Palestine does join the regional revolt, it will certainly recover its role as a beacon of regional and international popular struggle, as it has so often been over the past half-century. Far from abating, Zionist oppression of the Palestinian people has only escalated since the *Nakba*.* For as long as it continues, Palestine's symbolic status as the last unresolved case of direct European colonialism will remain central to the worldwide cause of popular emancipation.

☙❧

* *Editor's note:* See Glossary.

Rami G. Khouri

With the Arab world in chaos and its lynchpin states prioritizing internal affairs and the contest for regional leadership with Iran, Palestine has faded into obscurity. Even at the grassroots, offenses against Palestinians no longer have the mobilizing capacity they once did. For the Palestinians, one of their few lifelines—Arab state support sustained by Arab public opinion—appears to have been severed. In my assessment, however, the muting of the Palestine issue in Arab politics is temporary, reflecting, not lack of concern for Palestine, but the overwhelming scale and urgency of other regional crises. An examination of the historical connections between the Palestine-Israel struggle and today's regional tumult suggests that Palestine will remain pivotal to people across our region, even as it is overshadowed by more immediate threats.

Arab political agendas are today dominated by the region's myriad civil and international conflicts and the state fragmentation and mass refugee flows these have generated. But Arab citizens in many countries are also concerned with the long-standing structural problems that precipitated the regional destabilization in 2010–11. Prominent among these

---

Rami G. Khouri is Senior Public Policy Fellow and Adjunct Professor of Journalism at the American University of Beirut, as well as a Non-Resident Senior Fellow at the Harvard Kennedy School. He is a syndicated columnist with Agence Global Syndicate, USA.

are the legacy of foreign political and military intervention in internal Arab affairs and the legacy of military men seizing power and overseeing developmental catastrophes. The issue of Palestine has been implicated in both.

Military men. The Palestinian cause was exploited by Arab military officers in the late 1940s and early 1950s to establish and sustain perhaps the single greatest scourge of the modern Arab world: military officials who become presidents for life, ruling entire countries with their families and business partners as well as the active support of foreign powers. The Egyptian colonels led by Gamal Abdel Nasser, as well as their counterparts in Syria, Iraq, Libya, and elsewhere, seized power in part by arguing that only their military rule could promote domestic development, create a regional Arab power sphere, and thereby protect Arab states from the threat posed by Israel.

The Cold War and subsequent oil-boom decades disguised the incompetence of the military men who took power. It became clear by the mid-1990s, however, that a direct line could be traced from prolonged Arab military rule to destabilizing socioeconomic imbalances and deficiencies, extremely low levels of popular political participation, and the hollowing out of states now suffering terrible internal and regional wars. Decades of military governance produced the underlying phenomena that triggered the 2010–11 uprisings, from institutionalized corruption and lack of citizen rights to wasteful militarization and reliance on foreign powers that have served the military's incumbency more than national development and citizen well-being.

The 1948, 1956, and 1967 military debacles against Israel demonstrated that Arab leaders and militaries were unable to protect the Arab countries against Zionism (or for that matter to promote sustained and equitable national development). Failure to check Israeli expansion and domination in the decades since has contributed greatly to tens of millions of Arab citizens losing faith in the integrity, capabilities, and even ultimately the legitimacy of their governments. Polling evidence[1] from the period 1995 to 2010 charts a long-term decline in two important political attitudes among Arab citizens: belief that their well-being will improve in the years ahead, and trust in the critical organs of government (i.e., parliament, executive, judiciary, internal security forces, media, political parties).[2]

Foreign intervention. Many Arabs view Israel as the vanguard and symbol of Western imperial and colonial manipulation in our region. The Israel-Palestine conflict is a constant, painful reminder of our long and difficult history with foreign powers. Indeed, the ongoing Zionist colonization of Palestine, combined with Israel's influence over US policy towards Arab states, reminds most Arabs that the colonial period of the late nineteenth century never truly ended. Foreign powers near and far still seem to dictate events in the region and determine the fate of hundreds of millions of Arabs—be it the US, Great Britain, France, Russia, Iran, or Turkey, all of which intervene directly and militarily in Arab countries.

The diplomatic and material support for Israel that defines American policy in the region is a principal driver of anti-American government sentiment among Arab publics, which in turn exacerbates tensions between Arab citizens and their (pro-American) governments. Arab weakness and subservience has repeatedly led to humiliating situations in which Arab rights or aspirations were negated by the US to satisfy Israel. Examples include a refusal to sell advanced American weapons systems to certain Arab states and the American-Israeli maneuver in December 2016 to prevent Egypt from presenting a UN Security Council resolution critical of Israeli settlements (in the event, other,

---

[1] See, for example, the trends in Egypt and Tunisia: "Egypt: The Arithmetic of Revolution. An Empirical Analysis of Social and Economic Conditions in the Months Before the January 25 Uprising," *Abu Dhabi Gallup Center* (March 2011); "Tunisia: Analyzing the Dawn of the Arab Spring," *Gallup* (n.d.). See also the many Arab country survey reports conducted by the Arab Barometer between 2006 and 2014: "Waves I–III," *ArabBarometer.org*.

[2] The exceptions were the oil-rich emirates and kingdoms, which used the proceeds of natural resource wealth to fund generous transfers to citizens.

non-Arab states stepped in to the breach).[3] For ordinary Arab men and women, such humiliations sting. They are left to conclude that the US-Israeli veto has stripped their governments of the power to safeguard Arab interests. Many Arabs see their own governments as less than sovereign and understand this to be an indirect consequence of the Palestine-Israel struggle.

The Palestine-Israel conflict has also played a major role in stoking Iranian-Israeli and Iranian-Arab tensions. Had the conflict been resolved amicably and equitably before 1979, it is possible that post-1979 Iran would not have been able to exploit the Palestine issue to appeal to the Arab masses or to develop military ties with Hezbollah and Hamas. Similarly, one reason for the growth across the region of nonviolent Islamist opposition movements, above all the Muslim Brotherhood, has been their opposition to Israeli policies in Palestine and adjacent Arab lands.

Public opinion surveys conducted across the Arab world over the past decade, such as those by the Doha-based Arab Center for Research and Policy Studies, consistently find that the question of Palestine matters deeply to Arabs.[4] Polls also show that Palestine is a litmus test for Arab views of external actors. Shibley Telhami of the University of Maryland, who has been polling Arab public opinion for the past twenty-five years, observes from his cumulative results that "[t]he Palestinian-Israeli conflict is paramount" in determining

---

[3] UN Security Council Resolution 2334 (23 December 2016). See Barak Ravid, "A Tweet From Trump and Pressure on Egyptians: How Israel Blocked UN Vote on Settlements," *Ha'aretz* (23 December 2016); "Egypt: Trump Convinced Sisi to Withdraw UN Resolution," *Al Jazeera* (23 December 2016).

[4] The Arab Opinion Index survey has been conducted annually since 2011. The 2012–13 survey found that: "The overwhelming majority of the Arab opinion was able to name countries that constitute threats to the Arab national security, 73% of respondents stated that Israel (52%) and the United States (21%) presented the largest threats to Arab national security . . . When asked about which state posed the largest threat to the security of their specific home country, 36% of respondents held that this was Israel, while 11% believed it was the United States." See "The ACRPS Announces the Results of the 2012/2013 Arab Opinion Index," *Arab Center for Research & Policy Studies* (13 June 2013).

Arab attitudes towards the US. He also finds consistent testimony that the best way to achieve positive relations with the US would be for Washington to promote a just and lasting resolution of the Palestinian-Israeli conflict.[5] To be sure, public opinion on Palestine is not uniform across the region. Some groups resent how their countries have been impacted by the Palestine-Israel conflict—many Lebanese, for example, due to the presence of several hundred thousand Palestinian refugees in the country and Israel's repeated destruction of parts of Lebanon in recurring wars. Others, rightly or wrongly, blame Palestinians for hostility toward them (e.g., many Kuwaitis are still aggrieved at Palestinian support for Iraq's invasion of Kuwait in 1990). But these are exceptions to the rule.

In general, the Palestine-Israel conflict has for a century been, and remains today, directly and indirectly the single most destructive, radicalizing, and destabilizing force in the Middle East. It touches the lives and hearts of hundreds of millions of ordinary Arab men and women. It will remain a central concern across the region, not just for its historical and symbolic significance, but because it has become implicated in the core grievances driving Arab politics.

The continued resonance of Palestine in the Arab world was vividly demonstrated in July 2017, almost fifty years to the month since Israel's occupation began. After Israel installed new security measures at the entrance to the Al-Aqsa Mosque, Palestinians protested to have them removed.* For two weeks, Palestinian residents of East Jerusalem enacted an inspiring display of communal solidarity and nonviolent resistance. By boycotting the Mosque and holding prayers on the streets outside, demonstrators succeeded not merely in removing Israel's security measures—a rare feat—but in directing and coordinating their communal capabilities (for perhaps the first time in the past half-century) and, crucially, in recalling wider Arab attention to Palestine.

---

* *Editor's note:* See Glossary ("Temple Mount/Al-Haram Al-Sharif," "East Jerusalem").

[5] Shibley Telhami, *The World Through Arab Eyes: Arab Public Opinion and the Reshaping of the Middle East* (New York, NY: Basic Books, 2013), chapter 7, especially pp. 109, 123.

East Jerusalemites are one of the most vulnerable Palestinian communities, being neither full Israeli citizens nor fully within the jurisdiction of the Palestinian Authority. The Al-Aqsa resistance prayers shattered almost overnight decades of perceived weakness, not least because of the public support that the Palestinian demonstrators were able to generate across the Arab and Muslim worlds. Most significant in this respect was the participation in the protest prayers of Palestinian citizens of Israel, who travelled to Jerusalem by the busload to demonstrate solidarity. The power of Al-Aqsa is that, as a site of immense religious as well as national importance, it resonates well beyond the Palestinians themselves. The Palestinians must hope that new forms of activism by civic and religious leaders in Jerusalem can keep the pressure on Israel and Arab regimes, and eventually force them to move.

Glen Rangwala

Political movements in the Arab Middle East have long mobilized around the issue of Palestine and the Palestinian cause. While Arab governments have often talked up the issue of Palestine in an attempt to channel hostility away from unrepresentative and unaccountable systems of rule and towards an external enemy, popular movements have drawn attention to the disjuncture between these governments' rhetoric of enmity to Israel and the ambiguity or absence of their practical actions. Palestine has been a key pole around which progressive movements have developed across the Arab world, politicizing the young, encouraging the theorization of relationships of international hierarchy and oppression, and providing a space within which the spirit of critique can be fostered.[1]

Drawing upon the critical literature about the impulses around international aid,[2] the valorization of Palestinian solidarity in Arab countries might be termed "Palestine as autobiography." That is, adherence to the Palestinian cause becomes important principally for the generative effect it has in organizing

---

Glen Rangwala is a University Lecturer and Fellow of Trinity College, University of Cambridge. He is the author of *Iraq in Fragments: The Occupation and its Legacy* (2006, with Eric Herring).

[1] See, for example, John Chalcraft, *Popular Politics in the Making of the Modern Middle East* (Cambridge: Cambridge University Press, 2016), pp. 377–78, 420, 451, 507–8, and passim.

[2] David Williams, "Aid as autobiography," *Africa* 72.1 (2002), pp. 150–63.

and reordering politics in other contexts. The success of movements that speak for Palestine around the rest of the Arab Middle East is measured and judged in terms of those movements' own activities: how many people come out on protest marches, whether the diverse opposition movements coalesce around a single platform, what popular confrontations develop with state security forces. Palestine has in this way served as the leading symbol for structures and relations of repression that are in some sense generalizable across worldwide political struggles.

While there is, rightly, debate about whether the Palestinian cause retains its symbolic value for movements that seek justice across the Middle East in the aftermath of the Arab uprisings, there is a different question to be asked about what effect the transposition of Palestine into an iconic role has upon the Palestinians themselves. Palestine, of course, is not just a symbol: it is a lived experience of subjugation, with daily brutality and the arbitrary exercise of control, which is more entrenched today than at any point since 1948. And the plight of its people is not the universal experience of oppression: it is colored with multiple forms of distinctiveness that prevent it being plausibly viewed as an extreme version of a global political condition.

The juxtaposition of the long history of Palestine acting as an inspiration for others with the equally long history of unjustified Israeli domination over the Palestinians should make us question more urgently than ever what purpose solidarity movements have for the Palestinians. If there were to be no purpose, or if wider solidarity across the Arab world were even found to be counterproductive for Palestinian rights and Palestinians' well-being, then the fading of those movements within the Arab uprisings would hardly be cause for regret, at least in respect of the Palestinians themselves.

The idea that wider Arab support for the Palestinians has inspired the Palestinians' own struggle—enhancing their resilience and self-belief—in particular deserves challenge. The Palestinian "Revolution" of 1965, as it used to be called,* was born specifically out of a rejection of the manner in which wider Arab political movements gave their own reading to the Palestinian cause,

* *Editor's note:* See Chronology.

drowning out Palestinian voice and agency.[3] The intifada began in December 1987 while the attention of the Arab world was focused on revolutionary Iran within the context of the war with Iraq, an issue which preoccupied discussions around the preceding month's Arab summit in Amman.[4] Palestine may have inspired others, but it is far from clear that Palestinians have ever been inspired by those who use their cause as a rallying call elsewhere.

Can we go further with this critical line of analysis? Is it plausible to think that the extensive, enduring movement of support for Palestine across the Arab Middle East, not to mention around the world, has perversely created the conditions for the deepening of their oppression? There are three possible arguments that one could make for this position.

First, one could point to how, as support for Palestine has become a symbol of the left, so support for Israel—and hence, explicitly or not, for the oppression of the Palestinians—has increasingly become a symbol for the authoritarian right. From Sisi's Egypt to Trump's America, the new ascendance of the right is linked into relations of support for Israel's continued strategy of dispossession and arbitrary violence.[5] If the Palestinian cause is turned into a metonym for justice in the Arab Middle East, then powerholders, acting to thwart the articulation of popular grievances, will find a natural ally in the Israeli state.

Secondly, one could posit that the wider cause of Palestine feeds into the sort of paranoia with which successive Israeli governments have won their own majority population's support for deepening structures of repression. A mid-2016 poll showed that 40 percent of Israeli Jews believed that the Palestinians wanted to commit genocide against the Jews, and a further 19 percent believed

---

[3] Yezid Sayigh, *Armed Struggle and the Search for State: the Palestinian National Movement, 1949-1993* (Oxford: Clarendon Press, 1997), pp. 84–85, 89–90, 105–6.

[4] Edward Said, "Intifada and Independence," *Social Text* 22 (1989), pp. 23–39.

[5] Asher Schechter, "'We've won': How Trump Empowers Israel's Far Right," *World Policy Journal* 34.1 (2017), pp. 33-41; Steven A. Cook, "Egypt's Nightmare: Sisi's Dangerous War on Terror," *Foreign Affairs* 95 (2016), pp. 114–15.

the Palestinians wanted to destroy the State of Israel.[6] The perception of regional enmity readily translates into the sense that a highly militarized stance is justified, or indeed, required. Within a rampant moral panic, however unjustified and unrealistic, extreme violence against the native finds its place.

Finally, one could argue that the multiple platforms accorded to advocates of the Palestinians across the Arab Middle East, from the rally stage to the academic roundtable, in which speakers perform the expression of victimization and the presentation of Palestine as an exemplar of global justice, act to deter or limit the sorts of pragmatic compromises that can over time wear away the motivation for brutalization. Adhering to the cause comes to take on its own value, associated with international status and the perceptions of heroism. And from the official Palestinian side, there is a plausible argument to be made that a consistent overestimation of regional and global support, derived through taking solidarity as a more meaningful concept than it really is, has led to an unrealistic sense of bargaining power in relations with the US and Israel.[7]

Those would, I think, be the strongest challenges to the idea of Palestine's "inspirational" role. This article is not an attempt to prove that these potential criticisms are correct. One can very well argue back that without regional and global attention on the situation in the occupied territories, Israeli violence against the Palestinians would be even harsher than it has been. But it is intended to remind—as yet another boycott slogan is aired, yet another statement of solidarity released—that Palestine is not just a symbol in someone else's autobiography.

---

[6] "The Palestinian-Israeli Pulse: A Joint Poll—Tables of Findings," *Palestinian Center for Policy and Survey Research* (June 2016), p. 5.

[7] Nathan Thrall, *The Only Language They Understand: Forcing Compromise in Israel and Palestine* (New York, NY: Metropolitan Books, 2017), p. 66. Note, though, that Thrall draws a different conclusion out of this point from the one indicated here.

CHAPTER FIFTEEN.

HOW TO GET ISRAEL TO WITHDRAW: LESSONS FROM PRESIDENT JIMMY CARTER'S MIDDLE EAST DIPLOMACY

Norman G. Finkelstein

Since Israel's founding in 1948, it has withdrawn, or appeared to withdraw, from Arab territory it had occupied on five occasions:

- 1957—Israel withdrew from the Egyptian Sinai after an ultimatum by President Dwight D. Eisenhower;

Norman G. Finkelstein is a leading scholar of the Israel-Palestine conflict. His books include *The Holocaust Industry: Reflections on the Exploitation of Jewish Suffering* (2000), *Beyond Chutzpah: On the Misuse of Anti-Semitism and the Abuse of History* (2005), and *Knowing Too Much: Why the American Jewish Romance with Israel is Coming to An End* (2012). His most recent book is *Gaza: An Inquest into Its Martyrdom*, forthcoming from the University of California Press.

- 1979–81—Israel withdrew from the Egyptian Sinai in accordance with the 1978 Camp David Accords and 1979 Egyptian-Israeli Peace Treaty;
- 1993–2000—Israel withdrew from densely populated areas in the West Bank and Gaza in accordance with the 1993 and 1995 Oslo Accords;*
- 2000—Israel withdrew from south Lebanon after protracted Lebanese armed resistance;
- 2005—Israel withdrew its army and settlers from inside Gaza in a political ploy to retain the West Bank.

Most of these instances do not provide guideposts for Palestinians struggling to end Israel's occupation and achieve self-determination.

When Eisenhower ordered Israel to withdraw, the domestic Israel lobby was still in its infancy while Eisenhower wasn't dependent on the Jewish vote, and the Israeli occupation was not entrenched. The Israeli withdrawal after the Oslo Accords in actuality amounted to a redeployment of its troops and rationalization of its occupation, as an indigenous Palestinian security force freed Israel from the burdens of quelling internal resistance. The 2005 Israeli withdrawal from Gaza was designed to mitigate international pressure on Israel to leave the West Bank; it was also effectively a redeployment, as the occupation persisted by remote control and has been punctuated by periodic large-scale Israeli massacres in Gaza. The 2000 Israeli withdrawal from south Lebanon came after Hezbollah's guerrilla army cumulatively exacted a too high toll on the occupiers; but, however much Hamas might protest otherwise, Palestinians in the Occupied Territories do not have such a military option. Even as they have the moral and legal right to use armed force against an occupying power denying them the right to self-determination, it is, as a practical matter, not a viable strategy.

The one Israeli withdrawal that provides instructive lessons harks back to Jimmy Carter's presidency—namely, the sequence of negotiations over

---

* *Editor's note:* See Glossary.

which he presided and that culminated in Israel's full withdrawal from the Egyptian Sinai. The critical backdrop for Carter's diplomacy was the 1973 war. Until Egypt (and Syria) attacked, Israel and the US proceeded on the premise that the Arabs did not have a war option and Israel could, if it were so inclined, maintain in perpetuity its occupation of the Arab lands it had conquered in 1967. After the 1973 war and, in particular, as Egypt demanded a full Israeli withdrawal beyond the interim disengagement agreements negotiated by Henry Kissinger, the incoming Carter administration resolved to find a solution to the Israel-Arab conflict in its multiple facets.[1] Carter attached top priority to resolving the conflict as its persistence jeopardized "American national interests."[2] Israel's occupation of Arab lands and concomitant denial of Palestinian national rights had been conspicuously backed by Washington. "Radical" forces in the region appeared to gain ground as they denounced the Israeli occupation and US complicity in it, putting the status quo "moderate" Arab regimes aligned with the US (in particular, oil-rich Saudi Arabia) on the political defensive and enabling Soviet inroads in the region.[3] (To be sure, this last factor was inflated, especially by Egyptian President Anwar Sadat as he manipulated Washington with the prospect that Egypt's army would guard Western regional interests against alleged Soviet proxies.[4]) It was also feared

[1] The ensuing remarks are largely based on the two hefty volumes in the Foreign Relations of the United States series, running to some 3,000 pages, entitled *Arab-Israeli Dispute, January 1977–August 1978* (Volume VIII) and *Arab-Israeli Dispute, August 1978–December 1980* (Volume IX). These fascinating fly-on-the-wall verbatim records of the negotiations are indispensable reading for every student of the conflict.

[2] Volume VIII: Document 107, "Memorandum of Conversation" (21 September 1977), p. 553.

[3] Volume IX: Document 170, "Letter from President Carter to Secretary of Defense Brown" (9 February 1979), p. 593.

[4] "The most serious threat to security" in the Arab world, Carter's Secretary of Defense advised him, "is likely to be internal security," not Soviet aggression. Volume IX: Document 172, "Memorandum from Secretary of Defense Brown to President Carter" (19 February 1979), p. 604.

that Egypt might provoke another military confrontation with Israel in order to trigger a crisis that in turn would force Washington's hand.[5]

If the US and Egypt had powerful incentives to effect an Israeli withdrawal, the same could not be said of Israel. Although Israel suffered significant combatant casualties in the 1973 war and was initially gripped by panic as Egyptian forces crossed the Suez Canal and Syrian troops ascended the Golan Heights, by the time Carter launched his diplomatic initiative, Israel's overwhelming military preponderance had been restored. It felt no special urgency to end the occupation of the Sinai, let alone the Golan Heights and Palestinian territories.[6] However, a separate peace with Egypt did present a distinct, if not pressing, advantage: it would preclude any future Arab attack on Israel. "If you take one wheel off a car," Foreign Minister Moshe Dayan pithily observed, "it won't drive. If Egypt is out of the conflict, there will be no war."[7] From the outset of Carter's diplomatic foray, Israel was resolved that, if a treaty was to be brokered, it would only be a separate peace with Egypt.

The rounds of diplomacy culminating in Israel's withdrawal from the Sinai, and then extending into talks on the self-governing authority to be established in the Occupied Palestinian Territory, divided into more or less discrete phases. Carter originally hoped to resolve the conflict in the framework of a Geneva conference under the aegis of the US and Soviet Union. The principal stumbling block was Palestinian representation, as the US, acting at Israel's behest, but also because it itself opposed an independent Palestinian state (Carter favored a Palestinian confederation with the Kingdom of Jordan),[8]

---

[5] Volume IX: Document 24, "Minutes of a National Security Council Meeting" (1 September 1978), p. 72.

[6] Volume IX: Document 21, "Memorandum from the President's Assistant for National Security Affairs (Brzezinski) to President Carter" (31 August 1978), p. 60.

[7] Volume VIII: Document 124, "Memorandum of Conversation" (4 October 1977), p. 671.

[8] Volume VIII: Document 32, "Memorandum of Conversation" (9 May 1977), p. 255; Document 49, "Memorandum for the Files of a Meeting with President Carter" (7 July 1977), p. 332; Document 52, "Memorandum of Conversation" (19 July 1977), p. 338; Document 113,

objected to a separate Palestine Liberation Organization (PLO) delegation at Geneva unless PLO Chairman Yasser Arafat officially and unilaterally recognized Israel.[9] It's possible that this hurdle could have been cleared. But, acting apparently on his own initiative, Sadat journeyed to Jerusalem in November 1977 and in the same stroke aborted the Geneva conference.

Exactly what propelled Sadat on this course is a matter of speculation. After food riots in January 1977 threatened his political survival, he was desperate to end the Israeli occupation (the military burden of which was a severe drain on Egypt's economy) and simultaneously to recast Egypt as Washington's key regional asset, so as to obtain material subsidies commensurate with its upgraded status.[10] In addition, Israeli emissaries had already promised Sadat in secret talks before his journey to Jerusalem a full Israeli withdrawal in exchange for a peace treaty. Sadat was also a none-too-bright megalomaniac—Carter gently put it that Sadat "sees himself as the inheritor

---

"Memorandum of Conversation" (26 September 1977), p. 592; Document 124, "Memorandum of Conversation" (4 October 1977), p. 658; Document 234, "Memorandum of Conversation" (22 March 1978), p. 1083. Volume IX: Document 351, "Memorandum of Conversation" (15 April 1980), pp. 1155, 1160, 1163; Document 353, "Memorandum of Conversation" (16 April 1980), p. 1199; Document 378, "Memorandum of Conversation" (17 June 1980), p. 1267; Document 379, "Memorandum of Conversation" (18 June 1980), p. 1282. The consensus was that an independent Palestinian state would become a proxy of "radical" Arab states or the Soviets. Volume VIII: Document 36, "Memorandum of Conversation" (24 May 1977), p. 271; Document 183, "Memorandum of Conversation" (3 January 1978), p. 910.

[9] There were many indications from the outset of Carter's diplomacy that Arafat *would* recognize Israel if it (or the US) reciprocally recognized a Palestinian state in the West Bank and Gaza. Volume VIII: Document 3, "Minutes of a Policy Review Committee Meeting" (4 February 1977), p. 19; Document 10, "Memorandum of Conversation" (17 February 1977), p. 76; Document 51, "Memorandum from the President's Assistant for National Security Affairs (Brzezinski) to President Carter" (undated), p. 335; Document 84, "Telegram from the Embassy in Lebanon to Secretary of State Vance in Jerusalem" (10 August 1977), p. 459; Document 103, "Memorandum from William Quandt of the National Security Council Staff to the President's Assistant for National Security Affairs (Brzezinski)" (19 September 1977), Tab B, p. 506.

[10] Volume VIII: Document 21, "Memorandum of Conversation" (9 March 1977), p. 161.

of the Pharaonic crown"[11]—who had convinced himself that the Arab world would eventually "come around" and bow to his inspired leadership.[12]

After Sadat's trip, Carter gradually lowered his sights. Instead of a comprehensive peace, he focused, at any rate, in the immediate term, on a separate agreement between Egypt and Israel. He (and Sadat) proclaimed that such an accord would be but the prelude to a comprehensive peace that would at some point include Israeli withdrawal from Syria's Golan Heights. Whether he actually believed this is hard to say. But the Palestinian struggle, which deeply resonated in the Arab world, could not be even temporarily shunted aside. Although negligible if measured in its material dimensions, the symbolic significance of this cause endowed it with outsized veto power. If he was perceived to be betraying Palestine, Sadat would suffer vilification and ostracism by the Arab world, leaving him dangerously exposed[13] (which, indeed, is what came to pass), while, in a reversal of Carter's original intent, it would inflame the entire region against Washington as the principal architect of Sadat's treachery.[14] Carter thus labored hard to wrest face-saving concessions from Israel on the Palestinian front.

---

[11] Volume IX: Document 346, "Memorandum of Conversation" (20 March 1980), p. 1119.

[12] Volume VIII: Document 25, "Memorandum of Conversation" (4 April 1977), p. 172 ("I am the only leader in the Arab world who can take real steps toward peace"); Document 155, "Telegram from the Embassy in Egypt to the Department of State" (23 November 1977), p. 770. Volume IX: Document 214, "Memorandum of Conversation" (18 March 1979), p. 762 (referring to his Arab critics as "all those scarecrows"), p. 763 ("These 40 million people (in Egypt) are the dream of the Arab world. The others are bedouins"). He didn't hesitate to make huge concessions to Israel regarding the West Bank and Gaza on behalf of the Palestinians. Volume VIII: Document 240, "Memorandum of Conversation" (26 April 1978), pp. 1120–21.

[13] Volume VIII: Document 158, "Memorandum from Secretary of State Vance to President Carter" (24 November 1977), p. 781. After the Egyptian-Israeli Peace Treaty was signed, the US ambassador in Egypt warned that "the threat of Sadat's assassination has been heightened." Volume IX: Document 241, "Telegram from the Embassy in Egypt to the Department of State" (27 April 1979), p. 814.

[14] Volume IX: Document 207, "Intelligence Memorandum Prepared in the Central Intelligence Agency" (15 March 1979), pp. 733–35.

A US briefing paper in advance of the 1978 Camp David summit captured the conflicting aims of Egypt and Israel:

> The pivotal issue at Camp David will be the relationship that exists in the minds of both [Israeli Prime Minister Menachem] Begin and Sadat between the resumption of Sinai negotiations and progress on the West Bank/Gaza/Palestinian complex of questions. . . . Stated very briefly, the two fronts are linked in each man's mind in the following manner: Israel has placed top priority since last November on reaching a separate agreement with Egypt on the Sinai. Having now realized that that is not in the cards, Begin will be trying to acquire Sadat's commitment to conclude a final Sinai agreement, or failing that a "partial" Sinai agreement, in return for the minimum change in the present Israeli position on the West Bank/Gaza. Sadat also seeks a Sinai agreement that will bring about Israeli withdrawal from Egyptian territory, but cannot *politically* afford to pursue such an agreement in the absence of a clear change in the Israeli position regarding military withdrawal from the West Bank and Gaza, the settlement of Israeli citizens there, and Palestinian involvement in the ultimate disposition of the territory. (emphasis added)[15]

In the event, the Camp David Accords divided into two parts: one adumbrating an Egyptian-Israeli peace treaty, and the other an interim self-governing authority in the Occupied Palestinian Territory. In private meetings, Carter professed that, derisory as the self-governing powers might appear, if Palestinians on the ground jumped in and persevered, they would set in motion a political dynamic that, ultimately, yielded genuine Palestinian self-determination (if less than a full-fledged independent state).[16] After the Camp David Accords

[15] Volume IX: Document 7, "Briefing Paper Prepared in the Department of State and the National Security Council" (undated), pp. 16–17.

[16] Volume VIII: Document 238, "Memorandum of Conversation" (22 April 1978), p. 1112. Volume IX: Document 58, "Memorandum of Conversation" (20 September 1978), p. 214; Document 59, "Memorandum of Conversation" (21 September 1978), pp. 228, 232; Document 212, "Memorandum of Conversation" (17 March 1979), pp. 744–46; Document 213, "Memorandum of Conversation" (18 March 1979), p. 752; Document 330, "Memorandum of

were ratified, Egypt and Israel entered into negotiations to formalize a separate treaty. These were quite bitter, filled with mutual recrimination, seemed on the verge of collapse until the last minute, and required intensive US mediation.[17] Carter next turned his attention to the self-governing Palestinian authority. But it was agonizingly clear from the get-go that Begin was not about to cede any ground. The "autonomy" he envisaged for Palestinians would leave them bereft of substantive power. These negotiations left off without agreement when Carter's term of office expired.

From the inception of negotiations, Sadat put forth a simple, straightforward formula: full withdrawal from the Sinai in exchange for full peace. He was open to any security arrangements so long as Israeli troops didn't encroach on Egyptian territory. But Israel held out on dismantling the settlements it had built in the Sinai. "No one in Israel can agree to dismantle settlements" in the Sinai, Begin informed the US. "Israel will never destroy the homes of its settlers."[18] (On a lesser note, Israel did not want to give up the airfields it built and the oilfields it drilled there.[19]) Sadat essentially passed the diplomatic

---

Conversation" (5 February 1980), p. 1077; Document 350, "Memorandum of Conversation" (9 April 1980), pp. 1148, 1150; Document 378, "Memorandum of Conversation" (17 June 1980), p. 1270; Document 379, "Memorandum of Conversation" (18 June 1980), pp. 1281–86.

[17] In particular, Israel sought to delink the peace treaty with Egypt from the overarching Camp David Accords that bound Israel to also negotiate on the Palestinian front. For a testy exchange between Carter and Israeli representatives on this point, see Volume IX: Document 90, "Memorandum of Conversation" (20 October 1978), pp. 328–32.

[18] Volume VIII: Document 194, "Memorandum of Conversation" (16 January 1978), pp. 936, 940. Begin told Carter's Assistant for National Security Affairs (Zbigniew Brzezinski) that "his hand would fall off, his eyes would fall out, before giving up a single Israeli settlement." Volume IX: Document 330, "Memorandum of Conversation" (5 February 1980), p. 1075; Document 379, "Memorandum of Conversation" (18 June 1980), p. 1284.

[19] Initially Israel also insisted on maintaining a "presence and control" in Sharm al-Shaikh, but it eventually dropped this demand. Volume VIII: Document 18, "Memorandum of Conversation" (7 March 1977), p. 138; Document 177, "Memorandum of Conversation" (16 December 1977), p. 864.

baton to Carter. In so many words, he instructed Carter to get him the best deal he could, keeping in mind his red lines. The two leaders effectively plotted to trap Begin and break his will.[20] Carter could be warm and fuzzy, even dewy-eyed,[21] and he was a master at massaging egos (both Sadat and Begin were alarmingly insecure). However, although formally avowing that "no outside imposition of a settlement is advisable or feasible," and that "I am not a high pressure kind of person. I prefer to talk and discuss,"[22] Carter could also be ruthless with Israel. True, he promised not to "withhold essential equipment or economic assistance as a way of putting pressure on Israel,"[23] and by and large kept his word. But ultimately Carter didn't need to resort to these weapons. The mere threat of isolating Israel diplomatically in the domestic and international arenas was sufficient to frighten it into submission. "We don't want to use any pressure," Carter reassured Israel, but then inserted the caveat, "except for public opinion."[24] (He intuited that Israel was "most vulnerable to pressure from American Jews, from Congress" when it came to the settlements.[25])

---

[20] Volume VIII: Document 211, "Memorandum of Conversation" (4 February 1978), pp. 1000–1; Document 267, "Memorandum of Conversation" (17 July 1978), pp. 1198–1201.

[21] "Many Americans who share my religious background," he told Israeli Prime Minister Yitzhak Rabin, "feel in a very personal way that the establishment of Israel is the fulfillment of religious prophecy." Volume VIII: Document 20, "Memorandum of Conversation" (8 March 1977), p. 156.

[22] Volume VIII: Document 18, "Memorandum of Conversation" (7 March 1977), p. 133; Document 124, "Memorandum of Conversation" (4 October 1977), pp. 654, 658, 660.

[23] Volume VIII: Document 124, "Memorandum of Conversation" (4 October 1977), pp. 662, 666.

[24] Volume VIII: Document 124, "Memorandum of Conversation" (4 October 1977), pp. 658, 674. Volume IX: Document 21, "Memorandum from the President's Assistant for National Security Affairs (Brzezinski) to President Carter" (31 August 1978), pp. 61–62.

[25] Volume VIII: Document 211, "Memorandum of Conversation" (4 February 1978), pp. 994–95.

In a memorable showdown with Begin (one of several), Carter brutally depicted Israeli intransigence:

> The Israeli position, as I understand, is that even if there were a clear statement by us, and if it were accepted by Egypt, against total withdrawal in the West Bank and against a Palestinian state, Israel would not stop new settlements, or the expansion of settlements; Israel would not give up the settlements in Sinai; Israel would not permit an Egyptian or UN protection over the Israeli settlements in Sinai; even with military outposts, Israel would not withdraw political authority from the West Bank and Gaza; Israel will not recognize that Resolution 242 applies on all fronts, including the principle of withdrawal; Israel will not give the Palestinian Arabs, at the end of the interim period, the right to choose whether they want to be affiliated with Israel, with Jordan, or to live under the interim arrangement. This is my understanding of the present situation. If I am correct, the likelihood that the talks can be resumed with Egypt is very remote. There are no immediate prospects of substantial movement toward a peace agreement. I would like to have your comment. I would like you to correct any mistaken impressions that I may have.

"Your definitions are all negative," Begin desperately pleaded in reply.[26] In the end, however, he (and his Cabinet) folded on the Sinai settlements, agreeing to dismantle them. Carter later engaged in a bit of historical revisionism, as he alleged that, although "it was torture for Begin to have the settlers come out of the Sinai, . . . he did it" because "the Israeli people want a permanent peace that would make them secure." But the fact is, Begin did it because Carter twisted his arm and left him no choice.[27]

---

[26] Volume VIII: Document 234, "Memorandum of Conversation" (22 March 1978), p. 1084.

[27] Volume IX: Document 378, "Memorandum of Conversation" (17 June 1980), p. 1267; Document 379, "Memorandum of Conversation" (18 June 1980), p. 1280 (the formulation in this memorandum is slightly more accurate, as Carter says "*world* and Israeli opinion was with Sadat. Begin yielded"—emphasis added).

Carter used much less political muscle and consequently had much less to show on the Palestinian front. To be sure, none of the "moderate" Arab states (Jordan, Saudi Arabia, Egypt) were at heart committed to an independent Palestinian state. (The "radical" Arab regimes were probably no less cynical in exploiting the Palestinian cause.) If he had been reelected to a second term, Carter would probably have exerted a mite more pressure on Israel,[28] calibrating it to extract sufficient concessions so as to provide Sadat (and the US) with political cover,[29] but also to preserve his own personal credibility, which was on the line. "My word of honor is at stake," Carter told Begin. "We agreed to recognize the legitimate rights of the Palestinians."[30] But, as a key member of Carter's National Security Council Staff (William Quandt) presciently observed, "On the basis of my understanding of the Israeli position, I doubt if we will ever get far with the West Bank/Gaza negotiations."[31]

What political lessons can be extrapolated from Carter's diplomacy? I would suggest two:

- It's inconceivable that Israel would have withdrawn from the Sinai had it not been for Carter's steady, firm hand. Only the president had the power and authority to break Israel's will. Carter was a consummate, infinitely patient negotiator (although Begin's parochialism, pettifoggery,

---

[28] Volume IX: Document 357, "Memorandum of Conversation" (26 April 1980), p. 1208.

[29] Volume IX: Document 318, "Telegram from the Embassy in Egypt to the Department of State" (24 December 1979), pp. 1040–41, 1047.

[30] Volume IX: Document 198, "Memorandum of Conversation" (11 March 1979), p. 699.

[31] Volume IX: Document 114, "Memorandum from William B. Quandt of the National Security Council Staff to the President's Assistant for National Security Affairs (Brzezinski)" (31 October 1978), p. 398; Document 257, "Memorandum from William B. Quandt of the National Security Council Staff to the President's Assistant for National Security Affairs (Brzezinski)" (15 June 1979), p. 856.

pedantry, and sheer pigheadedness clearly drove him bananas,[32] Carter handled it with ironic grace[33]); was fully engaged (he reportedly mused that not since his submarine duty had he so immersed himself in an assignment[34]); and was preternatural in his mastery of detail. However, when the occasion required it, he could also be brutal in the face of Israeli recalcitrance. (He was almost never at loggerheads with the ever ingratiating, obsequious Egyptian president.)

- Although he entered office pretending to a unique human rights agenda, Carter's diplomacy did not spring from humanitarian impulses. He made no bones about the fact that vital US interests were at stake and, accordingly, that he was prepared to muster the resources and, if need be,

---

[32] At any given moment, Begin could be weirdly expatiating on the Bolshevik seizure of power or insufferably quoting Montesquieu and Martin Luther. He said of the Irgun, the terrorist army he once commanded, that "as far as I studied, . . . there were never cleaner fighters"; of returning Sinai to Egyptian sovereignty, that it was "the greatest sacrifice ever made for peace"; of his non-starter "autonomy" proposal, that it was "one of the best ideas of Judaism and Zionism." At one point in the Camp David summit, Carter noted in his diary, "It's becoming clearer that the rationality of Begin is in doubt." Volume IX: Document 111, "Letter from the Israeli Ambassador to the United States (Dinitz) to President Carter (29 October 1978), p. 388; Document 184, "Memorandum of Conversation" (2 March 1979), pp. 631, 642; Document 198, "Memorandum of Conversation" (11 March 1979), pp. 697, 701; Document 351, "Memorandum of Conversation" (15 April 1980), p. 1161; Document 353, "Memorandum of Conversation" (16 April 1980), p. 1200; Volume IX: p. 92n31.

[33] Carter occasionally ribbed Begin that the latter "should not destroy his reputation for flexibility, which he (the President) and Prime Minister Begin worked hard to protect!" He wasn't always able, however, to contain himself. When Begin presumed to instruct him in the fine points of English grammar, Carter exploded that he "reads English!" Carter told King Hussein of Jordan, "He has spent as much time with Begin as with his (the President's) wife—since each hour with Begin is magnified a hundred fold." Volume IX: Document 352, "Memorandum of Conversation" (15 April 1980), p. 1180; Document 353, "Memorandum of Conversation" (16 April 1980), p. 1200; Document 379, "Memorandum of Conversation" (18 June 1980), p. 1280.

[34] Volume IX: Document 347, "Memorandum for the Files by the President's Special Representative for Middle East Peace Negotiations (Linowitz)" (29 March 1980), p. 1126.

deliver the mailed fist in order to secure them. The Israel lobby and its "friends" in Congress did put checks on how much Carter was prepared to turn the screws.[35] To gainsay the efficacy of the lobby is to gainsay a potent reality. But it was not omnipotent. Carter would not hold back if the lobby tried denying him even the attenuated achievement of, if not a comprehensive peace, then plucking Egypt from the Arab fold and turning it into a US client state.[36] "I don't object to pressure, and I'm not afraid of a confrontation or a showdown when the right time comes," he confided in his Egyptian co-conspirators. "But it should be clear to the world that the breakdown of progress is not due to Washington, but to Begin. . . . [Israel] will respond to pressure if we don't get in a position of being seen as the obstacle to peace, and if we don't threaten the security

[35] Volume VIII: Document 28, "Minutes of a Policy Review Committee Meeting" (19 April 1977), p. 196; Document 36, "Minutes of Conversation" (24 May 1977), p. 275; Document 38, "Memorandum from the President's Assistant (Jordan) to President Carter" (June 1977), pp. 279–95; Document 40, "Minutes of a Policy Review Committee Meeting" (10 June 1977), pp. 300, 307; Document 107, "Memorandum of Conversation" (21 September 1977), p. 554; Document 124, "Memorandum of Conversation" (4 October 1977), p. 673; Document 182, "Memorandum of Conversation" (1 January 1978), p. 906; Document 211, "Memorandum of Conversation" (4 February 1978), p. 996. Volume IX: Document 249, "Summary of Conclusions of a Presidential Review Committee Meeting" (17 May 1979), pp. 834–35; Document 295, "Memorandum of Conversation" (11 October 1979), pp. 967, 969–70; Document 314, "Memorandum from Secretary of State Vance to President Carter" (undated), p. 1031.

[36] Carter thusly assessed his diplomatic achievement:

> If the Soviet Union moved into Pakistan; if the Iranians tried to unsettle the ruling family in Saudi Arabia; if there is Iranian-Iraqi violence . . .—then the importance to them of having a strong and stable Israel and Egypt would greatly increase. We see the strategic importance of a friendly and strong combination of Egypt and Israel. This can be a stable rock, about which the waves of region swirl.

Volume IX: Document 319, "Memorandum of Conversation" (28 December 1979), p. 1048; Document 331, "Memorandum from the President's Assistant for National Security Affairs (Brzezinski) to President Carter" (7 February 1980), p. 1081.

> of Israel."[37] If Carter did not squeeze Israel more on the Palestinian question, it was because he himself did not support an independent Palestinian state; the "moderate" Arab states either opposed or would acquiesce in less than full Palestinian sovereignty; and he had not yet despaired of salvaging something in negotiations with Israel, such that Egypt and other US client states would not appear to have sold Palestine down the river. Alas, his term of office ended before the autonomy talks concluded, so it's impossible to know how far he would have gone in risking the lobby's wrath as he nudged Israel.

In general, the amount of force a US administration will bring to bear on Israel is the resultant of two vectors: (1) How vital is the US interest at stake, and (2) How legitimate is Israel's demurral, for that will determine how effective a public campaign the administration can mount in the face of the lobby's opposition. In the case at hand, the Carter administration resolved that, in order to stabilize the Middle East, at bare minimum Israel would have to withdraw from the Sinai, while, insofar as Sadat acquiesced in any security protocol that didn't violate Egyptian sovereignty, and the US denied the legality of Jewish settlements, Israel's obduracy on the Sinai front was wholly indefensible in the court of public opinion. But Carter attached no importance to Palestinian rights except insofar as some realization of them provided a fig leaf for "moderate" Arab states,[38] while he joined Israel in its leeriness of an independent Palestinian state—although he recoiled at Begin's autonomy plan, which reduced Palestinians to a helot population. The principal point of contention in the waning years of Carter's diplomacy was Israel's brazen settlement push in the Occupied Palestinian Territory; it openly put the lie to Carter's

[37] Volume VIII: Document 211, "Memorandum of Conversation" (4 February 1978), pp. 997, 999; Document 270, "Memorandum of Conversation" (18 July 1978), p. 1223.

[38] Volume IX: Document 344, "Briefing Memorandum from the Assistant Secretary of State for Near Eastern and South Asian Affairs (Saunders) to Secretary of State Vance and the President's Special Representative for Middle East Negotiations (Linowitz)" (19 March 1980), pp. 1107–8.

pretension that, if Palestinians joined the self-governing authority, they would willy-nilly achieve self-determination.[39]

It can be distilled from Carter's diplomacy that Washington will only force Israel to withdraw from the Occupied Palestinian Territory if and when a vital US interest is at stake. The challenge is much more daunting now than in the past. The Palestinian cause no longer reverberates in the Arab world as other regional crises (Syria, Iraq, Libya, Yemen, Bahrain) have overshadowed it, and "moderate" Arab states have, de facto, entered into a strategic alliance with Israel.[40] When Carter appeared to embrace the Palestinian cause as his own, it was only in order to burnish the bona fides of these Arab client regimes. But their legitimacy no longer hinges on championing the Palestinians. It's true that, until a resolution of the conflict is achieved, the Saudis will probably refrain from an overt alliance with Israel. But otherwise, Palestine no longer commands veto power in the Arab world. Moreover, whereas Israel had a "material interest" in withdrawing from the Sinai, as it disabled the Arab war machine, it

[39] In a meeting with Israeli officials, Carter lamented:

> The most serious aggravation in the entire world is the settlements. He [i.e., Carter] understands the Israelis need to do something, but for us in dealing with the French, the Japanese, and the Moslem world, they are no help. They are a constant aggravation to us. It is hard to say to the French that Israel works for peace if it builds settlements. He knows that the number of settlers is small. The settlements have symbolic importance for Israel; but on the contrary, they have extreme symbolic importance as well. He has had a long-standing argument with Begin and others about this. Begin has seen public opinion polls for the US, that indicate that the support and esteem for Israel have gone down, because of a few dozen settlers. This (reduction in esteem) is of great concern to him (the President) . . . [F]or him, for the Europeans, and for the moderate Arabs it would be easier to reach the ultimate objective of peace if this obstacle were overcome.

Volume IX: Document 319, "Memorandum of Conversation" (28 December 1979), pp. 1048–49.

[40] Already during Carter's diplomacy, Israel was proposing to "cooperate with the Saudis against radical movements anywhere in the Middle East . . . to be done quietly, directly or through [Carter]." Volume VIII: Document 8, "Telegram from Secretary of State Vance to the Department of State" (17 February 1977), p. 55.

has no comparable interest in withdrawing from the West Bank and Gaza. The occupation is effectively cost-free: Palestinian security forces police the occupation, Europeans pick up the financial tab, and Washington shields Israel from political retribution. Still, the justice of the Palestinian cause resonates globally at a popular level. If Palestinians can organize mass nonviolent resistance, and mobilize their reserves of support abroad, around a platform firmly anchored in international law and indefeasible principles of justice, it can capture the imagination of public opinion and galvanize it into action, make life unbearable for the illegal Jewish settlers, and compel the US—shamed in its isolation, outed in its hypocrisy—to either lay down the law with Israel or abstain from sabotaging international action to budge it.

RESPONSE:

REFLECTIONS ON CARTER'S DIPLOMACY

William B. Quandt

Norman Finkelstein has carefully read the recently released records of the Carter administration's Middle East diplomacy and has drawn conclusions that are solidly anchored in the archival evidence. His main point, with which I agree, is that Carter (and the team that worked with him on Middle East issues) was primarily motivated by a sense of national interest, not so much a concern for human rights or international law. This is somewhat surprising only because President Carter himself was such a strong proponent of human rights and in his post-presidency has continued to pursue humanitarian and rights-related issues.

William B. Quandt is Professor Emeritus of Politics at the University of Virginia. He served on the National Security Council with responsibility for the Middle East (1977–1979).

The obvious national interest concern for Carter as he looked at the Middle East in 1977 was to build on the gains of Henry Kissinger's step-by-step diplomacy which had begun a process of negotiation between Israel and the neighboring Arab states. No one wanted this process to end or for the regional situation to return to armed hostilities. Memories of the oil crisis of 1973–74 were still vivid; the Cold War was a reality; and the possibility of moving Egypt away from its dependence on Moscow seemed very real and important.

This is not to say that Carter began his presidency with a laser-like focus on achieving an Egyptian-Israeli peace and nothing more. In fact, his initial view was that a more comprehensive set of negotiations should be pursued, including Syria and Jordan, and it was Carter who came up with the phrase that a "Palestinian homeland" should be part of the eventual outcome of negotiations. (Finkelstein says that Carter opposed a Palestinian state, but I think it is fairer to say that he saw the need for the Palestinian issue to be addressed as a political issue, not just a matter of refugees, and that he might well have come to the point of accepting a Palestinian state, as he did in his post-presidency). Carter began with an interests-based strategy, but one that was also colored with an optimistic hope that a comprehensive peace, including something substantial for the Palestinians, perhaps a Palestinian-Jordanian confederation, might be possible.

Carter's retreat from his initial grand design came in response to several developments. First was the election of Menachem Begin as prime minister of Israel in mid-1977. Second was PLO leader Yasser Arafat's unwillingness in fall 1977 to accept UN Security Council Resolution 242. Third was the sharp domestic reaction to Carter's attempt to coordinate policy with the Soviet Union in early October 1977. Next was Egyptian president Anwar Sadat's surprise trip to Jerusalem in November 1977, which made it clear that the Egyptian-Israeli track was moving much more rapidly than any other and should not be sacrificed in the name of a comprehensive agreement as the preferred approach. Finally, the Iranian revolution in late 1978–79 convinced Carter that closing the Egyptian-Israeli deal as soon as possible in early 1979 was a high priority.

I have just a few specific points to note on Finkelstein's thorough account of this period. First, although the two massive volumes of the *Foreign Relations of the United States* (FRUS) devoted to Carter's Middle East policy are essential reading, they are not a complete record of what happened. The records of conversations with Sadat and Begin and other leaders are not, in fact, verbatim transcriptions, contrary to what Finkelstein says in his first footnote. Carter did not have a taping system and no stenographer was present for these meetings. I was usually the note-taker and would try to reconstruct the notes as if they were natural conversation, a convention used at the National Security Council dating back to at least the Johnson presidency. The records are as accurate as can be expected, but they are not quite "fly-on-the-wall" quality. Moreover, during the crucial Camp David negotiations, there were many important meetings where no notes were taken. We were simply too busy to adhere to normal procedures. As a result, we only have memoir accounts that provide a partial insight into what happened at important moments in the negotiations.

On points of substance in Finkelstein's account, I would note that the secret meeting between Israeli Foreign Minister Moshe Dayan and Egyptian envoy Hassan al-Touhami in Morocco in September 1977 did not, as far as I know, reach any explicit understandings. Egypt wanted to be assured that Israel would withdraw from all of Sinai, but Dayan did not make such a commitment at that meeting. Dayan wanted to know if Egypt was ready for a separate peace with Israel, in essence dropping its commitment to a comprehensive settlement. Egypt at this point was not ready to make such a concession. So, the meeting was interesting, but inconclusive, and Touhami was such a strange character that one could never put much credence in what he said in any case.

One of Finkelstein's main points is that Begin only agreed to full withdrawal from Sinai because of sustained pressure from Carter. That is largely true, but it is worth noting that Carter had allies within Begin's own cabinet. Both the Israeli Foreign Minister and Defense Minister, at crucial moments, joined Carter in pressing Begin to make concessions, on one occasion going so far as to threaten to resign if Begin did not show flexibility.

Finkelstein also refers to Carter and Sadat "plotting" to put pressure on Begin. This was briefly the case, from early February 1978 to about June or July of that year. But by the time of the Camp David talks in September, Carter was no longer on the same page with Sadat in this regard. Once again, I think that domestic US politics had something to do with it. Carter had fought a hard battle with Congress to get through an arms package that included equipment for Israel, Saudi Arabia, and Egypt. He encountered a lot of resistance, including from Democrats. The idea of continuing to "plot" with Sadat behind Begin's back faded away in the face of Carter's awareness of the fragile support that he would have in any overt confrontation with Begin.

At one point in his text, Finkelstein refers to "frightening" Israel into submission, but I think this is an exaggeration. At Camp David, Begin held out in the face of a great deal of pressure until he got assurances that any "linkage" of the Egyptian-Israeli agreement to the Palestinian issue would be minimal, and that he would not be obliged to freeze settlement activity in the West Bank for a prolonged period. This last point, not mentioned by Finkelstein, was the most obvious mistake on the American side at Camp David. Carter to this day believes that he had a commitment from Begin for such a settlement freeze, but he did not get it in writing, and Begin seems to have given him something more ambiguous than a clear commitment—along the lines of, "you will have my answer in writing tomorrow." When the promised letter arrived on the last day of the summit it was not what Carter had expected and he sent it back, asking for a stronger commitment. No such revised letter arrived during the remainder of the day, but Carter decided to go ahead with the signing of the Camp David Accords without it. So, in my view, Begin was pretty happy with what he had managed to get at Camp David, even if the price was full withdrawal from Sinai. He was not frightened into agreement.

Finally, Finkelstein says that Carter never had to put much pressure on Sadat. But at Camp David, when Sadat threatened to leave on about the tenth day, Carter was brutal in telling him that he could not do so. In brief, he said that if Sadat left, the US-Egyptian relationship would be over, as would their personal relationship. Sadat protested that he was being given no choice.

Carter replied, "That's right." At which point Sadat said, "You know what I need. Do the best you can." I cannot imagine an American president putting this kind of pressure on any Israeli prime minister. Nor would it be credible, since the US-Israeli relationship goes well beyond the personal relationship of the two leaders.

The main point that Finkelstein wants to make is that Israel will only withdraw from occupied Arab territories if it confronts sustained pressure from a determined American president. His example is Carter and Israel's full withdrawal from Sinai. And he makes the case that it is unlikely that any future president will follow Carter's example. Based on the experience of all US presidents since Carter, and the very slim prospects today for a resumption of serious Arab-Israeli peace diplomacy, he is doubtless correct.

RESPONSE:

A BLEAK PRECEDENT

John J. Mearsheimer

Norman Finkelstein has written a fascinating account of President Jimmy Carter's Middle East diplomacy. He makes clear that the former president was not principally motivated by human rights concerns, but rather by his belief that a comprehensive Middle East peace was in America's national interest. Carter comes across as a shrewd negotiator, who was effective at manipulating both Egypt's Sadat and Israel's Begin.

Finkelstein focuses on this particular case because he believes the crowning achievement of these negotiations—Israel's agreement in 1979 to withdraw from the Sinai—provides "guideposts for Palestinians struggling to end occupation and achieve self-determination."

John J. Mearsheimer is the R. Wendell Harrison Distinguished Service Professor of Political Science at the University of Chicago. He is the author of, among other books, *The Tragedy of Great Power Politics* (2001, 2014) and *The Israel Lobby and US Foreign Policy* (with Stephen M. Walt, 2007).

The story Finkelstein tells is terribly depressing from the Palestinians' perspective—both then and now. Carter had two main objectives: 1) get Israel to return the Sinai to Egypt and obtain a peace agreement between those two countries; and 2) persuade Israel to end its occupation of the West Bank and Gaza and put in place "a self-governing authority" for the Palestinians, which would fall short of being a sovereign state. Finkelstein focuses primarily on the first goal, because it was achieved, and he is searching for a past success that might illuminate possibilities going forward. But the second objective, which is obviously more relevant for thinking about Israel and the Palestinians today, was an utter failure. Carter never came close to getting Begin to agree to end the occupation.

Even the deal on the Sinai was a close call. As Finkelstein shows, Begin was deeply reluctant to return that territory, even though doing so made good strategic sense for Israel. After all, a separate peace with Egypt promised to effectively eliminate the possibility of the Arab armies joining together to launch a conventional war against Israel. Moreover, unlike the West Bank, the Sinai is not sacred territory for Israel. Nonetheless, it took a Herculean effort by Carter to get Begin to agree to pull Israeli military forces and settlers out of the Sinai.

There was never any hope of getting a deal on the Occupied Territories, especially the West Bank. As Finkelstein notes, "[i]t was agonizingly clear from the get-go that Begin was not about to cede any ground. The 'autonomy' he envisaged for Palestinians would leave them bereft of substantive power." It is unsurprising that Carter left office in 1981 with no agreement on the Palestinian issue. Even if he had been reelected, Finkelstein believes Carter would have only "exerted a mite more pressure on Israel."

Finkelstein maintains that Carter's success with Sinai shows that American presidents will put pressure on Israel and force it to change its policy only when doing so is clearly in the American national interest. At the same time, he maintains that Carter "attached top priority" to resolving the Palestinian problem, among others, because "its persistence jeopardized 'American national interests'." Yet Carter put hardly any pressure on Israel to leave the West Bank and reach an agreement with the Palestinians.

I would ascribe Carter's reticence to fear of antagonizing the Israel lobby, which surely would have played hardball with him had he pushed Israel to make concessions to the Palestinians. Finkelstein downplays the influence of the lobby, but this leaves him without a convincing explanation for why Carter failed to get tough with Begin over the occupation, which the United States had a deep-seated interest in ending.

Finkelstein emphasizes that the likelihood of Israel making peace with the Palestinians is even slimmer today. Not only has the Palestinian cause been "overshadowed" by the many other crises in the Arab world, but "the occupation is effectively cost-free: Palestinian security forces police the occupation, Europeans pick up the financial tab, and Washington shields Israel from political retribution." One might add: the number of settlers in the Occupied Territories is far greater today than in the late 1970s; the political center of gravity in Israel has moved further to the right, and there is no sign that movement is slowing down; and the Israel lobby is more powerful than ever. Moreover, the end game is now a viable Palestinian state on Israel's border, which is sure to generate fear among many Israelis.

In short, there is virtually no prospect of a deal between Israel and the Palestinians in the near future. Nevertheless, Finkelstein believes there is a sliver of hope. One important lesson from Carter's experience is that Israel is deeply fearful of diplomatic isolation. Israelis crave legitimacy for their state, and they recognize that there are major problems on that front, because their never-ending occupation has led to a Greater Israel that is an apartheid state. Although Israelis and their defenders in the West go to prodigious lengths to hide and deny this reality, it is increasingly difficult in the age of the Internet to disguise what is happening to the Palestinians in the Occupied Territories. This development is doing significant damage to Israel's reputation and ultimately threatens its legitimacy.

Finkelstein believes the Palestinians can take advantage of this situation and do more to win over world opinion and increase the pressure on Israel. He advocates that they "organize mass nonviolent resistance" and plead their case to the wider world on the basis of "international law and indefeasible principles of justice." This strategy will leave Israel and the United States isolated, which will compel Washington to put the necessary pressure on Israel to abandon the occupation and allow the Palestinians to have a sovereign state.

This strategy is the best option available today, and there is a reasonable chance it will work. After all, apartheid is such an abhorrent system that it is difficult to see how Greater Israel can avoid international condemnation as it becomes increasingly apparent what it is doing to the Palestinians. Indeed, it is hard to see how Greater Israel's supporters in the West will be able to defend this profoundly unjust system for another fifty years.

Still, one does not want to underestimate Israel's ability to undermine Palestinian efforts to adopt a Gandhi-like strategy. The Israelis have much experience sowing division among the Palestinians and portraying them as violent extremists who are principally responsible for their own fate. Nor should one underestimate the continued influence of the Israel lobby, which will go to enormous lengths to keep the United States—and other Western countries—from pressuring Israel to end its brutal and racist occupation.

Let us hope, however, that Finkelstein's optimism is warranted, and that the Palestinians eventually get either a viable state of their own or are afforded equal rights within Greater Israel. If not, this long and painful struggle will continue unabated.

RESPONSE:

NOT ALL ROADS TO WITHDRAWAL RUN THROUGH WASHINGTON

Mark Tessler

Two inter-connected themes run through Norman Finkelstein's well-researched and insightful essay. First, that only pressure from the United States, and presumably intense pressure, will force Israel to withdraw from the Arab and Palestinian territory that it occupied in the course of the June 1967 War. And, furthermore, that the US will exert this pressure only when vital American national interests are at stake. Second, that Jimmy Carter, despite his reputation for a deep commitment to the protection of human rights, was actually guided during the Camp David summit of September 1978 by strategic considerations pertaining to his perception of the US national interest. This, as Finkelstein reports, led Carter to

---

Mark Tessler is the Samuel J. Eldersveld Professor of Political Science at the University of Michigan. He is the author of, among other books, *Islam and Politics in the Middle East: Explaining the Views of Ordinary Citizens* (2015), *Public Opinion in the Middle East: Survey Research and the Political Orientations of Ordinary Citizens* (2011), and *A History of the Israeli-Palestinian Conflict* (2009, second edition).

pressure Israel to accept a complete withdrawal from the Sinai Peninsula, and to pressure Anwar Sadat to accept a separate peace with Israel and abandon his pursuit of a deal that included the Palestinian dimension of the conflict.

Finkelstein's discussion of the first theme—that Israeli withdrawal from occupied territory occurs only in response to intense American pressure—is instructive and persuasive in the context of his essay, but it is also incomplete, presumably because Finkelstein's primary interest is in Carter and the 1978 summit. A clear exception is the 2005 Israeli withdrawal from Gaza,* which Finkelstein discusses briefly and attributes to Ariel Sharon's goal of tightening Israel's grip on the West Bank. In this connection, Sharon told his countrymen, particularly his right-wing critics, that removing 1.5 million Palestinians from Israeli control would lessen whatever demographic challenge might come with permanent retention of the West Bank. But Sharon acknowledged that Palestinian resistance and its increasing toll on the Israeli army also influenced his decision, a factor for which Hamas took credit and which contributed, albeit secondarily, to the party's victory in the Palestinian elections of January 2006.

Other Israeli withdrawals, most of which Finkelstein lists at the beginning of his essay, are diverse with respect to the relevance of American pressure. Finkelstein does not discuss the 1974–75 disengagement agreements negotiated by Henry Kissinger, which obviously did involve American leadership. However, these are usually attributed to Kissinger's deal-making skill, in which he managed to convince both the Israelis and the Egyptians and Syrians that they had more to gain than to lose by reaching an agreement, rather than to the application of intense US pressure in the service of a vital American interest. The Israeli withdrawals that followed the signing by Yitzhak Rabin and Yasser Arafat of the 1993 Declaration of Principles (DOP) also involved the US, beginning with George H. W. Bush's "New World Order" speech after the Gulf War, followed by the Madrid Conference that the US co-convened, and then with Bill Clinton's hosting of the DOP signing on the south lawn of the White House. But the path to these withdrawals, admittedly neither extensive nor permanent, owes much to critical developments, including the first intifada, in which Israelis and

---

* *Editor's note:* See Glossary ("Disengagement").

Palestinians were themselves critical actors and in which the US did not play a determinative role.

Finkelstein might respond that these examples go beyond what he intends to be the lessons of Carter's actions at the Camp David summit. And to an extent such a response would be justified. But I read Finkelstein's essay as suggesting, even if he does not explicitly say so, that the key to any Israeli withdrawal from occupied Arab (and especially Palestinian) territory lies in America's readiness to conclude that its national interest is served by pressuring Israel to relinquish territory. Thus, he writes, "the one Israeli withdrawal that provides instructive lessons harks back to Jimmy Carter's presidency." And in this connection, the lessons Finkelstein draws from the 1978 Camp David summit are indeed worth learning. But even if the road to what little prospect there is for territorial concessions by Israel most likely does run through Washington, Israeli withdrawals from occupied territory have not always been in response to American pressure. This, too, is worth remembering, especially at a time when there is little hope that the administration in Washington will see a serious peace process, one seeking meaningful territorial compromise, as something that is in America's national interest.

Most of Finkelstein's essay is devoted to Carter's actions at Camp David, and here, drawing upon newly available documents, he offers a valuable and instructive portrait that contrasts with the frequently-held view that the American president was motivated primarily by a sincere desire for peace and that his understanding of what was needed included an appreciation of the legitimate rights of the Palestinians. Carter has an admirable record of working on behalf of justice and human rights, reflected not only following his presidency in the work of the Carter Foundation but also during his time in office. His efforts in Latin America during this period are particularly notable. Also, some of his statements before the Camp David summit appeared to indicate the view, for which he was severely criticized by some supporters of Israel, that the Palestinians would have to be part of any durable peace agreement.

But while these perceptions about Carter's priorities and intentions brought praise from some and condemnation from others, with the latter not only complaining about the substance of his priorities but also labeling him weak and naïve, Finkelstein offers a very different portrait of the thirty-ninth US president. Carter, Finkelstein tells us, was clearly focused on American national interests, and believed that the persistence of the Arab-Israeli conflict jeopardized those interests. Accordingly, Carter was "ruthless" in extracting from both Sadat and Begin concessions that neither wanted to make. And he was equally prepared, in pursuit of an agreement between Egypt and Israel, to relegate the Palestinian question to a separate framework agreement and "autonomy" talks, which he probably knew, or at least should have known, had little chance of producing an agreement.

Israel's withdrawal from the Sinai Peninsula and the Israel-Egypt peace treaty are by no means trivial accomplishments. Indeed, the opposite is the case. And Jimmy Carter deserves a significant share of the credit for this. But the outcome of the Camp David summit and the negotiations it spawned left the Palestinians no closer to statehood; and Carter, who until very recently was urging Barack Obama to recognize Palestine before he left office,[1] did not hesitate in 1978 and 1979 to abandon whatever had initially been his hope for a comprehensive peace. As Finkelstein states when summarizing the lessons to be extrapolated from Carter's diplomacy, his actions were not, or not only, guided by humanitarian impulses. Rather, when he judged vital US interests to be at stake, Carter "was prepared to muster the resources and, if need be, deliver the mailed fist." This portrait is a valuable addition to our understanding of Carter's record, placing both the achievements and the inadequacies of the Camp David summit in context and making clear how both of these reflect Carter's hard-nosed pursuit of an agreement that he deemed to be in America's national interest.

[1] Jimmy Carter, "Jimmy Carter: America Must Recognize Palestine," *New York Times* (28 November 2016).

FURTHER READING

Overview.

- Shlomo Ben-Ami, *Scars of War, Wounds of Peace: The Israeli-Arab Tragedy* (London: Weidenfeld & Nicolson, 2005)
- Noam Chomsky, *Fateful Triangle: The United States, Israel & The Palestinians*, updated edition (London: Pluto Press, 1999)
- Robert Fisk, *Pity the Nation: Lebanon at War*, third edition (Oxford: Oxford University Press, 2001)
- Zeev Maoz, *Defending the Holy Land: A Critical Analysis of Israel's Security Foreign Policy* (Ann Arbor, MI: University of Michigan, 2009)
- Benny Morris, *Israel's Border Wars: Arab Infiltration, Israeli Retaliation, and the Countdown to the Suez War*, revised edition (Oxford: Clarendon Press, 1996)
- Benny Morris, *Righteous Victims: A History of the Zionist-Arab Conflict, 1881–2001*, updated edition (New York, NY: Vintage, 2001)
- Edward Said, *The Politics of Dispossession: The Struggle for Palestinian Self-Determination, 1969–1994* (London: Vintage, 1995)
- Avi Shlaim, *The Iron Wall: Israel and the Arab World*, second edition (London: Penguin, 2014)
- Charles D. Smith, *Palestine and the Arab-Israeli Conflict: A History with Documents*, ninth edition (Boston, MA: Bedford/St. Martin's, 2016)

Chapter One. Can the Current Palestinian Leadership and Its Institutions End the Occupation?

- Palestinian Authority, "Palestine: Ending the Occupation, Establishing the State—Program of the 13th Government" (Ramallah, 25 August 2009), in *Journal of Palestine Studies* 39.1 (Autumn 2009), pp. 173–78
- Nathan J. Brown, *Palestinian Politics After the Oslo Accords: Resuming Arab Palestine* (Berkeley, CA: University of California Press, 2003)

- Nathan J. Brown, "Requiem for Palestinian Reform: Clear Lessons from a Troubled Record," *Carnegie Papers* 81 (Carnegie Endowment for International Peace, February 2007)
- Anne Le More, *International Assistance to the Palestinians After Oslo: Political Guilt, Wasted Money* (Oxon: Routledge, 2008)
- Asem Khalil, "Constitution-Making and State-Building: Redefining the Palestinian Nation," in Rainer Grote and Tilmann Röder eds., *Constitutionalism in Islamic Countries: Between Upheaval and Continuity* (Oxford: Oxford University Press, 2012)
- Mouin Rabbani, "Palestinian Authority, Israeli Rule: From Transitional to Permanent Arrangement," *Middle East Report* 201 (October-December 1996), pp. 2–6, 22
- Glenn E. Robinson, *Building a Palestinian State: The Incomplete Revolution* (Bloomington and Indianapolis: Indiana University Press, 1997)
- Yezid Sayigh, "Policing the People, Building the State: Authoritarian Transformation in the West Bank and Gaza," *Carnegie Papers* (February 2011)

Chapter Two. Is Israel's Annexation of East Jerusalem Irreversible?

- Meron Benvenisti, *City of Stone: The Hidden History of Jerusalem* (Berkeley and Los Angeles, CA: University of California Press, 1996)
- Amir Cheshin, Bill Hutman, and Avi Melamed, *Separate and Unequal: The Inside Story of Israeli Rule in East Jerusalem* (Cambridge, MA: Harvard University Press, 1999)
- Michael Dumper, *The Politics of Jerusalem Since 1967* (New York, NY: Columbia University Press, 1997)
- Michael Dumper, *Jerusalem Unbound: Geography, History and the Future of the Holy City* (New York, NY: Columbia University Press, 2014)
- Jan de Jong, "'To Save What Can Be Saved': Reading Between the Lines of Palestinian Strategy on Jerusalem," *News From Within* 7.5 (May 1996)
- Lior Lehrs, "Jerusalem on the Negotiating Table: Analyzing the Israeli-Palestinian Peace Talks on Jerusalem, 1993–2015," *Israel Studies* 21.3 (2016), pp. 179–205
- Rami Nasrallah and Rassem Khamaisi, *The Jerusalem Urban Fabric: Demography, Infrastructure, and Institutions* (Jerusalem: International Peace and Cooperation Center, 2003)
- Nadav Shragai, *Jerusalem: Delusions of Division* (Jerusalem: Jerusalem Center for Public Affairs, 2015)

Chapter Three. Have the Settlements Made a Two-State Solution Impossible?

- Al Jazeera, *Palestine Papers*, searchable at: http://tinyurl.com/nbdjtsa.
- Geoffrey Aronson and Jan de Jong, "Israeli Settlements and the Palestinian Refugee Question: Evaluating the Prospects and Implications of Settlement Evacuation in the West Bank and Gaza—A Preliminary Analysis," in Rex Brynen and Roula El-Rifai eds., *Palestinian Refugees: Challenges of Repatriation and Development* (London: I.B. Tauris, 2007)
- Geneva Initiative (2003), http://www.geneva-accord.org/.
- Gershom Gorenberg, *The Accidental Empire: Israel and the Birth of the Settlements, 1967–1977* (New York, NY: Times Books, 2006)
- Jan de Jong, "The Geography of Politics: Israel's Settlement Drive After Oslo," in George Giacaman and Dag Jørund Lønning eds., *After Oslo: New Realities, Old Problems* (London: Pluto Press, 1998)
- Idith Zertal and Akiva Eldar, *The Lords of the Land: The War Over Israel's Settlements in the Occupied Territories, 1967–2007* (New York, NY: Nation Books, 2007)

Chapter Four. Can Gaza Survive?

- Sara Roy, *The Gaza Strip: The Political Economy of De-development*, third edition (Washington, DC: Institute for Palestine Studies, 2016)
- "Ten Years Later," *Gisha—Legal Center for Freedom of Movement* (September 2015).
- "Report on UNCTAD Assistance to the Palestinian People: Developments in the Economy of the Occupied Palestinian Territory," *United Nations Conference on Trade and Development* (July 2015)
- "Gaza in 2020: A Liveable Place?" *United Nations Country Team in the OPT* (August 2012)

Chapter Five. Can Armed Struggle End the Siege of Gaza?

- Joel Beinin and Rebecca L. Stein eds., *The Struggle for Sovereignty: Palestine and Israel, 1993–2005* (Stanford, CA: Stanford University Press, 2006), part 5.
- Roane Carey ed., *The New Intifada: Resisting Israel's Apartheid* (London: Verso, 2001)
- Anis Kassim et al., "Debating Forms of Resistance," *al-shabaka.org* (11 April 2011)
- Rashid Khalidi, *The Iron Cage: The Story of the Palestinian Struggle for Statehood* (Boston, MA: Beacon Press, 2006)

- Augustus Richard Norton, *Hezbollah: A Short History*, second paperback edition (Princeton, NJ: Princeton University Press, 2014)
- Wendy Pearlman, *Violence, Nonviolence, and the Palestinian National Movement* (Cambridge: Cambridge University Press, 2011)
- Yezid Sayigh, *Armed Struggle and the Search for a State: The Palestinian National Movement, 1949–1993* (Oxford and Washington, DC: Clarendon Press and Institute for Palestine Studies, 1997)

Chapter Six. Can Hamas Be Part of the Solution?

- Tareq Baconi, *Hamas Contained: The Rise and Pacification of Palestinian Resistance* (Stanford, CA: Stanford University Press, 2018)
- Khaled Hroub, *Hamas: Political Thought and Practice* (Washington, DC: Institute for Palestine Studies, 2000)
- Khaled Hroub, "A 'New Hamas' Through Its New Documents," *Journal of Palestine Studies* 35.4 (2006), pp. 6–27
- Beverley Milton-Edwards and Stephen Farrell, *Hamas: The Islamic Resistance Movement* (Cambridge: Polity, 2010)
- Shaul Mishal and Avraham Sela, *The Palestinian Hamas: Vision, Violence, and Coexistence*, second edition (New York, NY: Columbia University Press, 2006)
- Avraham Sela and Moshe Ma'oz eds., *The PLO and Israel: From Armed Conflict to Political Solution, 1964–1994* (Basingstoke: Macmillan, 1997)
- Alvaro de Soto (UN Special Coordinator for the Middle East Peace Process), *End of Mission Report* (May 2007)
- Matti Steinberg, *In Search of Modern Palestinian Nationhood* (Tel Aviv: Moshe Dayan Center for Middle Eastern and African Studies, 2016)
- Azzam Tamimi, *Hamas: A History from Within* (Northampton, MA: Olive Branch Press, 2007)

Chapter Seven. Floating in an Inch of Water: A Letter from Gaza

- Jean-Pierre Filiu, *Gaza: A History* (London: C. Hurst & Co., 2014 [2012])
- Norman G. Finkelstein, *Gaza: An Inquest Into Its Martyrdom* (Berkeley, CA: University of California Press, 2018)
- Amira Hass, *Drinking the Sea at Gaza: Days and Nights in a Land Under Siege* (New York, NY: Henry Holt, 1999 [1996])
- Donald Macintyre, *Gaza: Preparing for Dawn* (London: Oneworld, 2017)
- Sara Roy, *The Gaza Strip: The Political Economy of De-development*, third edition (Washington, DC: Institute for Palestine Studies, 2016)

Chapter Eight. Lessons from the Intifadas

- Ghassan Andoni, "A Comparative Study of Intifada 1987 and Intifada 2000," in Roane Carey ed., *The New Intifada: Resisting Israel's Apartheid* (London: Verso, 2001)
- Joost R. Hiltermann, *Behind the Intifada: Labor and Women's Movements in the Occupied Territories* (Princeton, New Jersey: Princeton University Press, 1991)
- Zachary Lockman and Joel Beinin eds., *Intifada: The Palestinian Uprising Against Israeli Occupation* (Boston, MA: South End Press, 1994)
- Wendy Pearlman, *Violence, Nonviolence, and the Palestinian National Movement* (Cambridge: Cambridge University Press, 2011)
- Graham Usher, "Facing Defeat: The Intifada Two Years On," *Journal of Palestine Studies* 32.2 (2003), pp. 21–40

Chapter Nine. Is a Third Intifada Possible?

- Marwan Darweish and Andrew Rigby, *Popular Protest in Palestine: The Uncertain Future of Unarmed Resistance* (London: Pluto Press, 2015)
- Norman G. Finkelstein, Mouin Rabbani, and Jamie Stern-Weiner, "Is This the 3rd Palestinian Intifada?" *The Nation* (21 October 2015)
- Wendy Pearlman, *Violence, Nonviolence, and the Palestinian National Movement* (Cambridge: Cambridge University Press, 2011)
- Mazin B. Qumsiyeh, *Popular Resistance in Palestine: A History of Hope and Empowerment* (London: Pluto Press, 2010)

Chapter Ten. Can There Be a Resolution of the Conflict If Palestinian Citizens of Israel Are Not Involved?

- "The Future Vision of the Palestinian Arabs in Israel," *The National Committee for the Heads of the Arab Local Authorities in Israel* (2006)
- "The Haifa Declaration," *Mada al-Carmel* (May 2007)
- Amal Jamal, *Arab Minority Nationalism in Israel: The Politics of Indigeneity* (Oxon: Routledge, 2011)
- Nadim Rouhana ed., *Israel and its Palestinian Citizens: Ethnic Privileges in the Jewish State* (Cambridge: Cambridge University Press, 2017)
- Sammy Smooha, *Still Playing by the Rules: Index of Arab-Jewish Relations in Israel 2015* (Haifa: Pardes Publishing, 2017); summary version in English available from *pardesbooks.com.*
- Oren Yiftachel, *Ethnocracy: Land and Identity Politics in Israel/Palestine* (Philadelphia, PN: University of Pennsylvania Press, 2006)

Chapter Eleven. The Palestinian Economy: Development and Liberation

- Arie Arnon et al., *The Palestinian Economy: Between Imposed Integration and Voluntary Separation* (Leiden: E.J. Brill, 1997)
- Arie Arnon and Saeb Bamya eds., "Economics and Politics in the Israeli Palestinian Conflict," *Aix Group* (October 2015)
- Raja Khalidi, "The Economics of Palestinian Liberation," *Jacobin* (15 October 2014)
- Mark LeVine and Mathias Mossberg eds., *One Land, Two States: Israel and Palestine as Parallel States* (Berkeley and Los Angeles, CA: University of California Press, 2014)
- Mushtaq Husain Khan et al. eds., *State Formation in Palestine: Viability and Governance during a Social Transformation* (Oxon: Routledge, 2004)

Chapter Twelve. Are Human Rights an Effective Weapon in the Struggle for Justice in Palestine?

- Lori Allen, *The Rise and Fall of Human Rights: Cynicism and Politics in Occupied Palestine* (Stanford, CA: Stanford University Press, 2013)
- Norman G. Finkelstein, *Gaza: An Inquest Into its Martyrdom* (Berkeley, CA: University of California Press, 2018)
- Lisa Hajjar, *Courting Conflict: The Israeli Military Court System in the West Bank and Gaza* (London: University of California Press, 2005)
- David Kretzmer, *The Occupation of Justice: The Supreme Court of Israel and the Occupied Territories* (Albany, NY: State University of New York Press, 2002)
- Samuel Moyn, *Human Rights and the Uses of History*, second edition (London: Verso, 2017)
- Samuel Moyn, *Not Enough: Human Rights in an Unequal World* (Cambridge, MA: Belknap Press, 2018)
- Nicola Perugini and Neve Gordon, *The Human Right to Dominate* (Oxford: Oxford University Press, 2015)
- Mouin Rabbani, "Palestinian Human Rights Activism Under Israeli Occupation: The Case of Al-Haq," *Arab Studies Quarterly* 16.2 (Spring 1994), pp. 27–52
- Michael Sfard, *The Wall and the Gate: Israel, Palestine, and the Legal Battle for Human Rights* (New York, NY: Metropolitan, 2018)
- Gordon Silverstein, *Law's Allure: How Law Shapes, Constrains, Saves, and Kills Politics* (Cambridge: Cambridge University Press, 2009)

Chapter Thirteen. Apartheid in South Africa and the Occupied Palestinian Territory: A Useful Comparison?

- Robert P. Barnidge, Jr., *Self-Determination, Statehood, and the Law of Negotiation: The Case of Palestine* (Oxford and Portland, OR: Hart Publishing, 2016)
- John Dugard, "The Role of International Law in the Struggle for Liberation in South Africa," *Social Justice* 18.1-2 (1991), pp. 83–94
- John Dugard and John Reynolds, "Apartheid, International Law, and the Occupied Palestinian Territory," *European Journal of International Law* 24.3 (2013), pp. 867–913
- Ilan Pappé ed., *Israel and South Africa: The Many Faces of Apartheid* (London: Zed Books, 2015)
- Benjamin Pogrund, *Drawing Fire: Investigating the Accusations of Apartheid in Israel* (Lanham: Rowman & Littlefield, 2014)
- Jon Soske and Sean Jacobs eds., *Apartheid Israel: The Politics of an Analogy* (Chicago, IL: Haymarket, 2015)
- Virginia Tilley ed., *Occupation, Colonialism, Apartheid? A re-assessment of Israel's practices in the occupied Palestinian territories under international law* (Cape Town: Human Sciences Research Council of South Africa, May 2009)

Chapter Fourteen. Palestine and the Arab Upheaval: Can Palestine Still Inspire the Arab World?

- John Chalcraft, *Popular Politics in the Making of the Modern Middle East* (Cambridge: Cambridge University Press, 2016)
- Paul Thomas Chamberlin, *The Global Offensive: The United States, the Palestine Liberation Organization, and the Making of the Post-Cold War Order* (Oxford: Oxford University Press, 2012)
- Norman G. Finkelstein, Mouin Rabbani, and Jamie Stern-Weiner, "Palestine After the Arab Spring," *Insight Turkey* 17.3 (2015), pp. 23–32
- Michael Hudson, "The Palestinian Arab Resistance Movement: Its Significance in the Middle East Crisis," *Middle East Journal* 23.3 (1969), pp. 291–307
- Michael C. Hudson, *Arab Politics: The Search for Legitimacy* (New Haven and London: Yale University Press, 1977)

- Aaron David Miller, *The Arab States and the Palestine Question: Between Ideology and Self-Interest* (New York, NY: Praeger and the Center for Strategic and International Studies, 1986)
- Moshe Shemesh, *The Palestinian Entity, 1959–1974: Arab Politics and the PLO,* second edition (London and Portland, OR: Frank Cass, 1996)

Chapter Fifteen. How to Get Israel to Withdraw: Lessons from President Jimmy Carter's Middle East Diplomacy

- Foreign Relations of the United States (FRUS), *Arab-Israeli Dispute, January 1977–August 1978*, volume VIII (Washington, DC: United States Government Printing Office, 2013); FRUS, *Arab-Israeli Dispute, August 1978–December 1980*, volume IX (Washington, DC: United States Government Printing Office, 2014)
- Ann Mosley Lesch and Mark Tessler, *Israel, Egypt, and the Palestinians: From Camp David to Intifada* (Bloomington, IN: Indiana University Press, 1989)
- John J. Mearsheimer and Steven M. Walt, *The Israel Lobby and U.S. Foreign Policy* (New York, NY: Farrar, Straus and Giroux, 2008)
- William B. Quandt, *Camp David: Peacemaking and Politics* (Washington, DC: Brookings, 2016 [1986])

GLOSSARY

Al-Aqsa Intifada *See* Second intifada.

Arab League ("League of Arab States") A regional organization of Arab states, established in 1945. The Arab League comprises twenty-two member-states, including Palestine. In 1974, the Arab League formally recognized the Palestine Liberation Organization as the "sole legitimate representative of the Palestinian people."

Arab-Israelis *See* Palestinian citizens of Israel.

Blockade of Gaza *See* Siege of Gaza.

Boycott, Divestment, and Sanctions (BDS) A campaign by Palestinian and international solidarity activists for consumer boycotts, institutional divestment, and state sanctions against Israel. The BDS manifesto, launched by Palestinian civil society groups in July 2005, demands an end to Israel's occupation, equality for Arab-Palestinian citizens of Israel, and the right of return for Palestinian refugees.

Civil Administration An Israeli body established in 1981 under the Ministry of Defense to administer the Occupied Palestinian Territory (OPT). In 1994, responsibility for most civil matters in Areas A and B of the West Bank (i.e., the 40 percent of the West Bank in which most Palestinians are concentrated) as well as internal security matters in Area A was transferred to the Palestinian Authority.

Disengagement (from Gaza) In 2005, the Israeli government under Prime Minister Ariel Sharon (Kadima) unilaterally dismantled Israel's civilian settlements in the Gaza Strip and redeployed Israeli forces to the territory's perimeter. The preponderance of the international community still regards Israel as the occupying power in Gaza. Four settlements in the northern West Bank were also evacuated.

East Jerusalem That part of Jerusalem that was militarily occupied by Israel in the course of the June 1967 War. Immediately after the 1967 War, Israel unilaterally expanded the municipal borders of East Jerusalem and de facto annexed this expanded territory. The annexation is not recognized under international law or by the international community.

Palestinians living in East Jerusalem hold permanent residency status in Israel. This entitles them to live and work in Israel and East Jerusalem, receive state benefits, and vote in municipal (but not national) elections. East Jerusalem encompasses within it the Temple Mount/Al-Haram Al-Sharif and the Old City.

Eretz Yisrael Hebrew for the "Land of Israel."

Fatah A Palestinian nationalist organization founded in 1958–1959 by, among others, Yasser Arafat. It is the largest faction in the Palestine Liberation Organization.

Fedayeen Palestinian guerrillas.

First intifada A mass civil revolt against Israel's occupation that erupted in December 1987. Tactics deployed by Palestinians included general strikes, demonstrations, economic self-sufficiency, tax boycotts, and stone-throwing. The uprising was led by grassroots organizations based in the Occupied Palestinian Territory, which wrested the initiative from the external Palestine Liberation Organization (PLO) leadership based in Tunis. As a result of the intifada, Jordan disengaged from the West Bank and the PLO formally endorsed the two-state solution. The end of the intifada is conventionally dated 1993, but popular participation began to decline already in 1990.

Green Line The Armistice Demarcation Line of 1949 which has been accepted by the International Court of Justice and the international community as the border between Israel and occupied Palestine.

Hamas The Islamic Resistance Movement. Established during the first intifada, Hamas is one of the two largest Palestinian factions (alongside Fatah). Hamas won a majority of seats in the 2006 Palestinian Authority legislative election. As a result of escalating inter-factional conflict, Hamas consolidated its control of Gaza in June 2007, while Fatah consolidated its control of the West Bank.

The Jewish Home A far-right, religious-nationalist political party in Israel. Established in 2008, it opposes the creation of a Palestinian state and supports Israel's settlement project. The Jewish Home Party has participated in Israel's government since 2009 as a member of ruling coalitions led by the Likud.

Judea and Samaria The official Israeli government designation for what is internationally termed the West Bank, excluding East Jerusalem.

Kadima A centrist Israeli political party established in 2005 by Ariel Sharon to support the unilateral disengagement from Gaza. The 2006 election resulted in a Kadima-led coalition government under the premiership of Ehud Olmert, who represented Israel at the 2007 Annapolis Conference. The party declined thereafter and did not contest the 2015 election.

Labor Historically Israel's largest center-left party. Prior to 1977, all Israeli prime ministers emerged from the Labor Party and its precursors. In the 1990s, Labor-led governments under Yitzhak Rabin and Ehud Barak pursued negotiations with the Palestine Liberation Organization within the framework of the Oslo Accords.

Land swap A proposed territorial exchange between the State of Israel and the prospective State of Palestine in the context of a permanent status agreement. Intended to enable Israel to annex the major Israeli settlement blocs in the West Bank without drastically reducing the total area of land to be allotted to a future Palestinian state.

Likud Israel's largest right-wing party. Established in 1973 through a merger of smaller groups, Likud's 1977 electoral victory led to Israel's first right-wing government, under the premiership of Menachem Begin. The 2015 general election in Israel produced a Likud-led coalition government and a third term as prime minister for Likud chairman Benjamin Netanyahu.

Law of Return Israeli legislation, enacted in 1950, giving every Jewish person the right to immigrate to Israel and claim Israeli citizenship.

Mandatory Palestine ("Historical Palestine") The area now comprising the State of Israel and the Occupied Palestinian Territory, which was administered by the United Kingdom as a League of Nations mandate between 1922 and 1948.

Nakba Arabic for "catastrophe." Refers to the 1947–48 expulsion and displacement of some 700–750,000 Palestinians from what is now the State of Israel.

Occupation The status under international law of a territory that is under the effective control of foreign armed forces. The International Court of Justice has determined that the West Bank, including East Jerusalem, and Gaza constitute Occupied Palestinian Territory.

Occupied Palestinian Territory (OPT) The West Bank, including East Jerusalem, and Gaza Strip. These areas came under Israeli military occupation in the course of the June 1967 War.

Occupied Territories *See* Occupied Palestinian Territory (OPT)

One-state solution The proposal to resolve the Israel-Palestine conflict by establishing a single state on the entire territory of Mandatory Palestine.

Oslo Accords Two agreements—the Oslo I Accord (1993) and Oslo II Accord (1995)—reached between Israel and the Palestine Liberation Organization (PLO) which together established the framework for the Oslo peace process. These provided inter alia for the establishment of an interim Palestinian self-government authority in the Occupied

Palestinian Territory (the Palestinian Authority); the sub-division of the West Bank into three areas—A, B, and C—with different levels of Palestinian autonomy; and the commencement of negotiations between Israel and the PLO toward a conflict-ending agreement within five years. The permanent status agreement was never concluded. The Oslo Accords did not commit Israel to dismantling settlements, freezing settlement construction, or recognizing a Palestinian right to independent statehood.

Outpost An Israeli settlement constructed without formal Israeli government authorization. Whereas all Israeli settlements are illegal under international law, outposts are illegal under Israeli law as well.

Palestine Liberation Organization (PLO) An organization established in 1964 at the initiative of the Arab League to represent Palestinians. In 1969, the PLO came under the control of Palestinian forces led by Yasser Arafat. It eventually incorporated the major Palestinian factions (excluding Hamas) and was recognized regionally and internationally as the "sole legitimate representative of the Palestinian people." The PLO was led by Arafat from 1969 until his death in 2004, when he was succeeded by Mahmoud Abbas.

Palestinian Authority (PA) A Palestinian interim self-government body established in 1994 as part of the Oslo peace process. The PA was invested with limited authority over the Gaza Strip and the 40 percent of the West Bank not under direct Israeli rule. In June 2007, the PA lost de facto control in Gaza through factional violence with Hamas. Mahmoud Abbas was elected president of the PA in 2005.

Palestinian citizens of Israel Most Palestinians living in what became the State of Israel were expelled in 1947–48. The remnant became Israeli citizens. Israel's Palestinian minority lived under formal military rule until 1996. It remains subject to various forms of legal and de facto discrimination.

Palestinian Legislative Council (PLC) The legislature of the Palestinian Authority.

Palestinian National Council (PNC) The legislature of the Palestine Liberation Organization.

Qassam Brigades The military arm of Hamas.

Quartet on the Middle East ("Middle East Quartet") The Quartet comprises the European Union, Russia, United Nations, and United States. It was established in 2002 to oversee diplomacy on the Israel-Palestine conflict.

Refugees (Palestinian) Palestinians who were forced into exile in the run-up to and during the 1948 War and 1967 War, and their descendants.

Right of return The right under international law of the Palestinian refugees to return to their homes. Amnesty International upholds the right of return for "Palestinians who fled or were expelled from Israel, the West Bank or Gaza Strip, along with those of their descendants who have maintained genuine links with the area." *See also* UN General Assembly Resolution 194.

Roadmap A "performance-based," multi-phased diplomatic process launched by the Middle East Quartet in April 2003, intended to achieve a two-state solution to the Israel-Palestine conflict by 2005.

Salafism A fundamentalist strand of Sunni Islam.

Second intifada A Palestinian uprising against Israel's occupation that erupted in September 2000 after the failure of the Camp David peace talks and following a provocative visit to the Temple Mount/Al-Haram Al-Sharif by the right-wing Israeli politician Ariel Sharon. Between September 2000 and February 2005, approximately 1,000 Israelis and 3,000 Palestinians were killed in the violence.

Settlement An Israeli Jewish colony established in occupied territory in violation of international law.

Settlement blocs Clusters of settlements in which the large majority of Israeli settlers live. The blocs have not been precisely defined but their location and extent are approximately marked out by the route of the Wall.

Security barrier/fence *See* Wall.

Separation barrier/fence *See* Wall.

Siege of Gaza Also known as the Gaza "blockade" or "closure." When Hamas took control of Gaza in June 2007, Israel closed Gaza's border crossings and sharply reduced the passage of goods and people across its borders. This caused sharp increases in poverty, unemployment, and aid dependence. The international community has deemed the siege a form of collective punishment and consequently a flagrant violation of international law.

Temple Mount/Al-Haram Al-Sharif A Muslim and Jewish sacred site located in Jerusalem's Old City. Jewish tradition holds it to be the location of the destroyed First and Second Jewish Temples, while the Al-Aqsa Mosque, built within the compound, is considered the third holiest site in Islam. The Temple Mount/Al-Haram Al-Sharif came under Israeli military occupation in June 1967, but Israel left the Jordanian *Waqf* to administer the compound and prohibited Jews from worshipping in it, directing them instead to pray at the site's retaining wall (the "Western Wall" or "Kotel"). This arrangement is known as the "status quo." The 1994 Israel-Jordan peace treaty recognized Jordan's "special role" in administering the "Muslim Holy shrines in Jerusalem."

Two-state solution The proposal to resolve the Israel-Palestine conflict by establishing an independent State of Palestine alongside the State of Israel. The two-state solution has been near-unanimously endorsed by the General Assembly of the United Nations.

UN General Assembly Resolution 181 (II) In November 1947, the General Assembly voted thirty-three to thirteen (with ten abstentions) to endorse the partition of Palestine into a Jewish and an Arab state.

UN General Assembly Resolution 194 In December 1948, the General Assembly resolved, by a vote of thirty-five to fifteen (with eight abstentions), that "the [Palestinian] refugees wishing to return to their homes and live at peace with their neighbours should be permitted to do so at the earliest practicable date."

UN Security Council Resolution 242 In November 1967, following the June 1967 War, the Security Council affirmed the "inadmissibility of the acquisition of territory by war"; called for a "just and lasting peace in the Middle East" based on the "[w]ithdrawal of Israeli armed forces from territories occupied in the recent conflict"; and simultaneously called for the "[t]ermination of all claims or states of belligerence and respect for and acknowledgement of the sovereignty, territorial integrity and political independence of every State in the area and their right to live in peace within secure and recognized boundaries free from threats of acts of force." Security Council Resolution 242 remains a key reference point for international efforts to resolve the conflict. It is commonly referred to as the "land for peace" formula for resolving the conflict.

Wall A structure separating Palestinians from Israelis, under construction since 2002. The bulk of the Wall is located within the occupied West Bank, along a route designed to encompass most of Israel's settlers. In July 2004, an advisory opinion of the International Court of Justice determined that those sections of the Wall built on Occupied Palestinian Territory are illegal under international law.

Waqf An Arabic term referring either to an Islamic endowment for charitable or religious purposes, or to a Muslim charitable or religious foundation. The Islamic holy sites in Jerusalem's Old City are managed by the Jerusalem Islamic Waqf.

Zionism The movement for a Jewish national home or state in Eretz Yisrael/Palestine, originating in nineteenth-century Europe.

LIST OF CONTRIBUTORS

Musa Abuhashhash is Hebron Field Researcher for B'Tselem, The Israeli Information Center for Human Rights in the Occupied Territories. He grew up in Fawwar refugee camp.

As'ad Abukhalil is Professor of Political Science at California State University, Stanislaus. He writes a weekly column in *Al-Akhbar* and is the author of, among other books, *Historical Dictionary of Lebanon* (1998) and *The Battle for Saudi Arabia* (2004).

Mkhaimar Abusada is Associate Professor of Political Science at Al-Azhar University in Gaza.

Gilbert Achcar is Professor and Chair of the Center for Palestine Studies at SOAS, University of London. His books include *The Arabs and the Holocaust: The Arab-Israeli War of Narratives* (2010), *The People Want: A Radical Exploration of the Arab Uprising* (2013), and, most recently, *Morbid Symptoms: Relapse in the Arab Uprising* (2016).

Ghaith Al-Omari, a Senior Fellow at The Washington Institute for Near East Policy with extensive experience in the Palestinian-Israeli peace process, is a former Executive Director of the American Task Force on Palestine. He has also served in various positions within the Palestinian Authority, including Advisor to former Prime Minister Mahmoud Abbas and Advisor to the negotiating team during the 1999–2001 permanent status talks.

Ghassan Andoni is Professor of Physics at Birzeit University. He is co-Founder of the International Solidarity Movement (ISM) and Founder of the International Middle East Media Center (IMEMC).

Usama Antar received his PhD in Political Science & Economic Policy in Germany in 2004. He has worked as a university lecturer in Gaza and served in several Gaza-based international organizations.

Nur Arafeh is a Rhodes Scholar doing her PhD at the University of Oxford. She previously worked as the Policy Fellow of Al-Shabaka, the Palestinian Policy Network, and was an Associate Researcher at the Palestine Economic Policy Research Institute–MAS, a Visiting Lecturer of Economics at Al-Quds Bard College, and a Teaching Assistant at Columbia University. She has a dual BA degree in Political Science and Economics from the Paris Institute of Political Studies-Sciences Po and Columbia University and holds an MPhil in Development Studies from the University of Cambridge.

Shaul Arieli was the Commander of the Israel Defense Forces Northern Brigade of the Gaza Strip; Head of the Interim Agreement Administration in the governments of Yitzhak Rabin, Shimon Peres, and Benjamin Netanyahu; and Head of the Peace Administration in the government of Ehud Barak. Col. (ret) Dr. Arieli has published five books about the Israeli-Palestinian conflict as well as four collections of articles. He teaches courses on the conflict at the Academic College of Tel Aviv-Yaffo, the Hebrew University of Jerusalem, and the IDC Herzliya.

Arie Arnon is Professor Emeritus of Economics at Ben Gurion University of the Negev and Israeli coordinator of the Aix Group, a joint Israeli-Palestinian think-tank.

Tareq Baconi is the author of *Hamas Contained: The Rise and Pacification of Palestinian Resistance* (2018). He is a Visiting Scholar at Columbia University's Middle East Institute.

Sam Bahour is a Palestinian-American business development consultant living in Ramallah. He is a Policy Advisor for Al-Shabaka, the Palestinian Policy Network, and Chairman of Americans for a Vibrant Palestinian Economy.

Sari Bashi is co-Founder and former Executive Director (2005–2014) of the Israeli human rights organization Gisha—Legal Center for Freedom of Movement.

Shlomo Ben-Ami was Israel's Minister for Internal Security (1999–2000) and Foreign Minister (2000–2001). He is a historian of Spain and the Middle East and the author of *Scars of War, Wounds of Peace: The Israeli-Arab Tragedy* (2006).

Suhad Bishara is Director of the Land and Planning Rights Unit, Adalah—The Legal Center for Arab Minority Rights in Israel.

Nathan J. Brown is Professor of Political Science and International Affairs at George Washington University where he directs the Institute for Middle East Studies. He also serves as a Non-Resident Senior Fellow at the Carnegie Endowment for International Peace. His current work focuses on religion, law, and politics in the Arab world. Author of seven books, Brown's most recent work, *Arguing Islam after the Revival of Arab Politics,* was published by Oxford University Press in 2017. He is a past recipient of Fulbright, Guggenheim, Woodrow Wilson Center and Carnegie fellowships.

Diana Buttu served as Legal Advisor to the Palestine Liberation Organization (2000–2004) and Advisor to Palestinian President Mahmoud Abbas (2004–2005). A Palestinian-Canadian lawyer, she has held fellowships at the Harvard Kennedy School of Government, Harvard Law School, and the Stanford Center for Conflict Resolution and Negotiation.

Jan de Jong is a Strategic Development Planner who was a chief consultant of the Arab Jerusalem Rehabilitation Project (Passia, Jerusalem–2000), the PLO Negotiations Affairs Department (2000–2006), and the Office of the Quartet Representative in Jerusalem (2013). He was also a team leader commissioned to evaluate European land development programs in the Palestinian Territories (2012–2014).

John Dugard is Professor Emeritus of International Law at the Universities of Leiden and the Witwatersrand. He was UN Special Rapporteur on Human Rights in the Occupied Palestinian Territory, and chaired international fact-finding missions into the second intifada and Israel's 2008–2009 assault on Gaza. He was a member of the UN International Law Commission and is the author of many books on international law and apartheid in South Africa.

Michael Dumper is Professor of Middle East Politics at the University of Exeter. His research focuses on refugees and Jerusalem as permanent status issues in the Middle East Peace Process, as well as archaeology, conservation, and politics in Jerusalem and other divided cities. He is the author of *Jerusalem Unbound: Geography, History, and the Future of the Holy City* (2014).

Hagai El-Ad is Executive Director of B'Tselem, The Israeli Information Center for Human Rights in the Occupied Territories.

Richard A. Falk is Albert G. Milbank Emeritus Professor of International Law and Practice and Professor Emeritus of Politics and International Affairs at Princeton University. He served as UN Special Rapporteur for Human Rights in the Occupied Palestinian Territory (2008–2014). His most recent book is *Palestine Horizon: Toward a Just Peace* (2017).

Norman G. Finkelstein is a leading scholar of the Israel-Palestine conflict. His books include *The Holocaust Industry: Reflections on the Exploitation of Jewish Suffering* (2000), *Beyond Chutzpah: On the Misuse of Anti-Semitism and the Abuse of History* (2005), and *Knowing Too Much: Why the American Jewish Romance with Israel is Coming to An End* (2012). His most recent book is *Gaza: An Inquest into Its Martyrdom*, forthcoming from the University of California Press.

Neve Gordon is Professor of Politics and Government at Ben-Gurion University of the Negev. He is the author of *Israel's Occupation* (2008) and *The Human Right to Dominate* (2015, with Nicola Perugini).

Ran Greenstein is Associate Professor of Sociology at the University of the Witwatersrand, South Africa. He is the author of, inter alia, *Genealogies of Conflict: Class, Identity and State in Palestine/Israel and South Africa* (1995) and *Zionism and its Discontents: A Century of Radical Dissent in Israel/Palestine* (2014).

Yoaz Hendel is Chair of the Institute for Zionist Strategies and former Director of Communications for Israeli Prime Minister Benjamin Netanyahu. He is a journalist and military historian, and has a PhD from Tel Aviv University.

Jamil Hilal is an independent sociologist affiliated to Birzeit University and a Senior Research Fellow at Muwatin—The Palestinian Institute for the Study of Democracy and the Institute of Palestine Studies. He is based in Ramallah and has authored many books and articles. He has been a member of the Palestinian National Council since 1983.

Khaled Hroub is Professor in Residence of the Faculty of Liberal Arts at Northwestern University in Qatar. He is also a Senior Research Fellow at the Center of Islamic Studies at the University of Cambridge, where he was Director of the Cambridge Arab Media Project. Between 2000 and 2007, he hosted a weekly review of books on Al Jazeera. His own works include *Hamas: Political Thought and Practice* (2000) and *Hamas: A Beginner's Guide* (2006, 2010).

Amal Jamal is Professor of Political Science at the School of Political Science, Government, and International Affairs at Tel Aviv University. He was Chair of the Political Science Department (2006–2009) and is co-Editor-in-Chief of the political science journal *The Public Sphere*. His books include *Arab Civil Society in Israel* (2017), *The Nakba in Israel's National Memory* (2015), and *Arab Minority Nationalism in Israel: The Politics of Indigeneity* (2011).

Leila Khaled is a member of the Palestinian National Council and the politburo of the Popular Front for the Liberation of Palestine (PFLP). In 1969 she became the first woman to hijack an aircraft, following which she became a global icon of Palestinian and anti-colonial struggle.

Raja Khalidi is a development economist trained at the Universities of Oxford and London (SOAS). He was a staff member with the United Nations Conference on Trade and Development (1985–2013), where he served as Coordinator of Assistance to the Palestinian People and Senior Economist in the Division on Globalization and Development Strategies. He is currently Research Coordinator at the Palestine Economic Policy Research Institute–MAS.

Rami G. Khouri is Senior Public Policy Fellow and Adjunct Professor of Journalism at the American University of Beirut, as well as a Non-Resident Senior Fellow at the Harvard Kennedy School. He is a syndicated columnist with Agence Global Syndicate, USA.

Lior Lehrs is an Israel Institute Postdoctoral Fellow at the Taub Center for Israel Studies at New York University. He wrote his doctoral dissertation in the Department of International Relations at the Hebrew University of Jerusalem and served as a researcher at the Jerusalem Institute for Policy Research, where he focused on the topic of Jerusalem within Israeli-Palestinian peace negotiations.

Gideon Levy is a journalist for the Israeli newspaper *Ha'aretz*. His regular column, "Twilight Zone," has covered Israel's occupation since 1988. Between 1978 and 1982 he was an aide to Shimon Peres, then-leader of the Israeli Labor Party.

Alon Liel, a peace activist, served as Israel's Ambassador to South Africa (1992–1994) and Director General of Israel's Ministry of Foreign Affairs (2000–2001).

John J. Mearsheimer is the R. Wendell Harrison Distinguished Service Professor of Political Science at the University of Chicago. He is the author of, among other books, *The Tragedy of Great Power Politics* (2001, 2014) and *The Israel Lobby and US Foreign Policy* (with Stephen M. Walt, 2007).

Jessica Montell is Executive Director of Save Israel, Stop the Occupation. She was Executive Director (2001–2014) of B'Tselem, The Israeli Information Center for Human Rights in the Occupied Territories.

Rami Nasrallah is Founder and Chairman of the International Peace and Cooperation Center in Jerusalem. He was General Director of the Jerusalem Affairs Department of the Prime Minister's Office, Palestinian Authority (2003–2006) and Director of the Special Projects Unit in the Orient House (1996–1998), where he formulated policy and position papers for future negotiations over Jerusalem. He was a Research Associate of the "Conflict in Cities" project at the University of Cambridge (2007–2012).

Wendy Pearlman is the Martin and Patricia Koldyke Outstanding Teaching Associate Professor of Political Science at Northwestern University. She is the author of *Occupied Voices: Stories of Everyday Life from the second intifada* (2003), *Violence, Nonviolence, and the Palestinian National Movement* (2011), and, most recently, *We Crossed a Bridge and it Trembled: Voices from Syria* (2017).

Nicola Perugini is Lecturer in International Relations at the University of Edinburgh. He is the author of *The Human Right to Dominate* (2015, with Neve Gordon).

William B. Quandt is Professor Emeritus of Politics at the University of Virginia. He served on the National Security Council with responsibility for the Middle East (1977–1979).

Mazin B. Qumsiyeh is Professor and Director of the Palestine Museum of Natural History and Palestine Institute for Biodiversity and Sustainability. He is the author of *Sharing the Land of Canaan: Human Rights and the Israeli/Palestine Struggle* (2004) and *Popular Resistance in Palestine: A History of Hope and Empowerment* (2010).

Glen Rangwala is a University Lecturer and Fellow of Trinity College, University of Cambridge. He is the author of *Iraq in Fragments: The Occupation and its Legacy* (2006, with Eric Herring).

Glenn E. Robinson is Associate Professor at the Naval Postgraduate School and Research Associate at the Center for Middle Eastern Studies, University of California, Berkeley. He is the author of *Building a Palestinian State: The Incomplete Revolution* (1997).

Nadim Rouhana is Professor of International Negotiation and Conflict Studies and Director of the International Affairs and Conflict Resolution Program at The Fletcher School, Tufts University. He is the Founding Director of Mada al-Carmel—Arab Center for Applied Social Research in Haifa, Israel.

Sara Roy is Senior Research Scholar at the Center for Middle Eastern Studies at Harvard University. Her most recent book is an expanded third edition of *The Gaza Strip: The Political Economy of De-development* (2016; previous editions 1995, 2001).

Bashir Saade is Lecturer in Religion & Politics at the University of Stirling. He is the author of *Hizbullah and the Politics of Remembrance: Writing the Lebanese Nation* (Cambridge: Cambridge University Press, 2016).

Robbie Sabel is Professor of International Law at the Hebrew University of Jerusalem. He is a member of the Permanent Court of International Arbitration at The Hague and the former Legal Advisor to Israel's Ministry of Foreign Affairs. Among his publications is *Procedure at International Conferences* (2006–second edition; third edition forthcoming, 2018).

LIST OF CONTRIBUTORS

Dahlia Scheindlin is a public opinion researcher and political advisor for electoral campaigns, governments, and civil society in Israel and more than a dozen other countries. She has expertise in public dynamics around conflict, negotiations, and post-conflict and transitional societies, and holds a PhD in Political Science from Tel Aviv University.

Daniel Seidemann is an Israeli attorney specializing in the geopolitics of Jerusalem. He is Founder of the Israeli NGO, Terrestrial Jerusalem.

Michael Sfard is an Israeli human rights lawyer specializing in international human rights law and the laws of war with a special emphasis on the law of belligerent occupation. He is the Legal Advisor to several Israeli human rights organizations and peace groups, and he represents Palestinian communities and Israeli and Palestinian activists. Born in Jerusalem, Sfard is a graduate of the Law Faculty of the Hebrew University and has an MA in International Human Rights Law from the University College of London. He is the author of *The Wall and the Gate: Israel, Palestine, and the Legal Battle for Human Rights* (2018).

Muhammad Shehada is a writer and civil society activist from the Gaza Strip. He is a student of Development Studies at Lund University, Sweden, and was a Field Researcher and Public Relations Officer for the Gaza office of the Euro-Med Monitor for Human Rights.

Raja Shehadeh is a lawyer and Founder of the pioneering Palestinian human rights organization Al-Haq. He is the author of several acclaimed books, including *A Rift in Time* (2010), *Occupation Diaries* (2012), and *Palestinian Walks* (2007), which won the 2008 Orwell Prize. His latest book is *Where the Line is Drawn: Crossing Boundaries in Occupied Palestine* (2017). He lives in Ramallah, Palestine.

Sammy Smooha is Professor Emeritus of Sociology at the University of Haifa. He served as Dean of the Faculty of Social Sciences and President of the Israeli Sociological Society and won the 2008 Israel Prize for Sociology. He is a specialist on the comparative study of ethnic relations and is the author of *Israel: Pluralism and Conflict* (1978) and *Arabs and Jews in Israel*, two vols. (1989, 1992). In 2003, he launched the annual Index of Arab-Jewish Relations in Israel. He served as Israel Institute Visiting Professor at the Department of Near and Middle East Studies at SOAS, University of London, during the 2016–2017 academic year.

Mark Tessler is the Samuel J. Eldersveld Professor of Political Science at the University of Michigan. He is the author of, among other books, *Islam and Politics in the Middle East: Explaining the Views of Ordinary Citizens* (2015), *Public Opinion in the Middle East: Survey Research and the Political Orientations of Ordinary Citizens* (2011), and *A History of the Israeli-Palestinian Conflict* (2009, second edition).

Nathan Thrall is the author of *The Only Language They Understand: Forcing Compromise in Israel and Palestine* (2017). He is a regular contributor to *The New York Review of Books* and the *London Review of Books* and is Senior Analyst for Israel/Palestine at the International Crisis Group.

Ahmed Yousef is Senior Political Adviser to former Palestinian Prime Minister Ismail Haniyeh. He was previously Deputy Minister of Foreign Affairs.

Ido Zelkovitz is Head of Middle East Studies at the Max Stern Yezreel Valley College, Israel. He is a Research Fellow at the Ezri Center for Iran and Persian Gulf Studies at the University of Haifa and a Policy Fellow at Mitvim—The Israeli Institute for Regional Foreign Policies.